CONTEMPORARY

Heroes and Heroines
Book II

CONTEMPORARY

Heroes and Heroines
Book II

DEBORAH GILLAN STRAUB

introduction by **Ray B. Browne**
Head of the Popular Culture Department
at Bowling Green University and
Secretary-Treasurer of the
Popular Culture Association

Gale Research Inc. · DETROIT · LONDON

Deborah Gillan Straub, *Editor*

Gale Research Inc. Staff

Lawrence W. Baker, Christine B. Hammes, *Senior Developmental Editors*
Leslie Joseph, *Developmental Editor*

Mary Beth Trimper, *Production Director*
Evi Seoud, *Assistant Production Manager*
Mary Winterhalter, *Production Assistant*
Arthur Chartow, *Art Director*
C.J. Jonik, *Keyliner*
Kathleen A. Hourdakis, *Cover Designer*

Library of Congress Cataloging-in-Publication Data
(Revised for vol. 2)

Contemporary heroes and heroines.

   Bk. II by Deborah Gillan Straub.
   Includes bibliographical references and indexes.
   Brief profiles of more than 100 contemporary men and women from all walks of life whose activitie
reflect heroic traits.
   1. Heroes—Biography—Juvenile literature. 2. Heroines—Biography—Juvenile literature.
Biography—20th century—Juvenile literature. 4. Biography. I. Browne, Ray Broadus. II. Browne, Glen
J. III. Browne, Kevin O. IV. Straub, Deborah Gillan.
CT120.C662   1990   920'.009'04 [B]   90-13261

ISBN 0-8103-4860-8 (bk. 1)
ISBN 0-8103-8336-5 (bk. 2)

While every effort has been made to ensure the reliability of the information presented in th
publication, Gale Research Inc. does not guarantee the accuracy of the data contained herein. Gal
accepts no payment for listing; and inclusion in the publication of any organization, agency, institution
publication, service, or individual does not imply endorsement of the editors or publisher. Error
brought to the attention of the publisher and verified to the satisfaction of the publisher will be correcte
in future editions.

    ∞™ This book is printed on acid-free paper that meets the minimum
requirements of American National Standard for Information Sciences
Permanence Paper for Printed Library Materials, ANSI Z39.48-1984.

ISBN 0-8103-8336-5
Printed in the United States of America
Published simultaneously in the United Kingdom
by Gale Research International Limited
(An affiliated company of Gale Research Inc.)

Contents

Heroes and Heroines
listed by area of endeavor

ART AND ARCHITECTURE
Ansel Adams
Mary Cassatt
Maya Lin
Grandma Moses
Gordon Parks

CONSERVATION
Ansel Adams
Jacques Cousteau
Richard Leakey
Chico Mendes
Pete Seeger

EDUCATION
Mary McLeod Bethune
Leonard Bernstein
George Washington Carver
Marie Curie
W. E. B. Du Bois
Albert Einstein
Anne Sullivan Macy
J. Robert Oppenheimer
Booker T. Washington

ENTERTAINMENT AND PERFORMING ARTS
Marian Anderson
Louis Armstrong
Joan Baez
Leonard Bernstein
Chris Burke
Jacques Cousteau
Duke Ellington
Jose Feliciano
Jim Henson
Marlee Matlin
Gordon Parks
Paul Robeson

Albert Schweitzer
Pete Seeger
Oprah Winfrey
Stevie Wonder

JOURNALISM
W. E. B. Du Bois
Gordon Parks

LAW
Clarence Darrow
Thurgood Marshall

MEDICINE
Christiaan Barnard
Clara Barton
Ben Carson
Tom Dooley
Anthony S. Fauci
Alexander Fleming
Karl Menninger
Margaret Sanger
Albert Schweitzer

MILITARY
Colin Powell
H. Norman Schwarzkopf

NOBEL PEACE PRIZE RECIPIENTS
Jane Addams
Dalai Lama
Albert Einstein
Mikhail Gorbachev
Albert Schweitzer
Aung San Suu Kyi

Jacques Cousteau

WRITERS

Ansel Adams
Jane Addams
Arthur Ashe
Joan Baez
Robert D. Ballard
Christiaan Barnard
Christy Brown
Pearl Buck
Ben Carson
Jimmy Carter
Rosalynn Carter
Winston Churchill
Jacques Cousteau
Tom Dooley

W. E. B. Du Bois
Elizabeth Glaser
Alex Haley
Vaclav Havel
Stephen W. Hawking
Thor Heyerdahl
Langston Hughes
Ron Kovic
Maggie Kuhn
Malcolm X
Karl Menninger
Toni Morrison
J. Robert Oppenheimer
Gordon Parks
Albert Schweitzer
Corrie ten Boom

Individuals profiled in
Contemporary Heroes and Heroines

These profiles appear in the first *Contemporary Heroes and Heroines*, by Ray B. Browne, and published by Gale Research Inc. in 1990.

Hank Aaron
Ralph Abernathy
Joy Adamson
Maya Angelou
Corazon Aquino
Oscar Arias Sanchez
Neil Armstrong
Daniel and Philip Berrigan
Diettrich Bonhoeffer
Margaret Bourke-White
Bill Bradley
Ralph Bunche
Helen Caldicott
Ernesto Cardenal
Rachel Carson
Challenger crew
Wilt Chamberlain
Cesar Chavez
Shirley Chisholm
Roberto Clemente
Marva Collins
Mairead Corrigan and Betty Williams
Bill Cosby
Norman Cousins
Francis Crick
Walter Cronkite
Vine Deloria, Jr.
Walt Disney
Amelia Earhart
Jaime Escalante
Medgar Wiley Evers
Betty Ford
Dian Fossey
Terry Fox
Anne Frank
Betty Friedan
Indira Gandhi
Mohandas K. Gandhi
Bob Geldof

John Glenn
Jane Goodall
Billy Graham
Dick Gregory
Florence Griffith Joyner
Dag Hammarskjold
Katharine Hepburn
Edmund Hillary and Tenzing Norgay
Bob Hope
Lee Iacocca
Jesse Jackson
Ann Jillian
Steven Jobs
Pope John Paul II
Barbara Jordan
Jackie Joyner-Kersee
Helen Keller
John F. Kennedy
Martin Luther King, Jr.
Henry Kissinger
C. Everett Koop
Candy Lightner
Charles A. Lindbergh
Greg Louganis
Sean MacBride
Nelson and Winnie Mandela
Mickey Mantle
Margaret Mead
Golda Meir
James Howard Meredith
Mother Teresa
Ralph Nader
Patricia Neal
Sandra Day O'Connor
Georgia O'Keeffe
Rosa Parks
Linus Pauling
Itzhak Perlman
Sally Ride

Jackie Robinson
Oscar Romero
Eleanor Roosevelt
Bill Russell
Anwar Sadat
Carl Sagan
Andrei Sakharov
Jonas Salk
Jan C. Scruggs
Alan Shepard
Karen Silkwood
Mitch Snyder
Aleksandr Solzhenitsyn

Steven Spielberg
Benjamin Spock
Gloria Steinem
Margaret Thatcher
Desmond Tutu
Lech Walesa
Alice Walker
Elie Wiesel
Roy Wilkins
Frank Lloyd Wright
Chuck Yeager
Jeanna Yeager and Dick Rutan

Preface

Aguide to twentieth century figures and their achievements, *Contemporary Heroes and Heroines, Book II*, carries on in the tradition established by its predecessor, *Contemporary Heroes and Heroines*, by furnishing biographical portraits of people whose activities reflect a variety of heroic traits. Included are inspiring profiles of prominent figures in many fields of endeavor, from art to technology, from conservation to social activism, all in one volume. It's the only reference source that brings together in one place lively sketches of contemporary figures collected around the theme of heroism.

Variety of Figures Profiled Helps Define Contemporary Heroism

The heroes and heroines profiled in this volume were chosen after nearly two hundred public and school librarians were surveyed for their help in identifying heroic figures of the twentieth century. The survey yielded a wide range of individuals for inclusion. From pioneering physicist **Marie Curie** to Nazi-hunter **Simon Wiesenthal,** this collection represents many fields of endeavor. International in scope, *Contemporary Heroes and Heroines, Book II,* includes essays on Czech president **Vaclav Havel,** Brazilian ecologist and union organizer **Chico Mendes,** and Myanmarese dissident **Aung San Suu Kyi.** The survey's results also demonstrate the spectrum of qualities that are considered heroic. Of course, no individual embodies every heroic ideal, but each listee was selected on the basis of a heroic aspect evident in her or his accomplishments.

Like undersea explorer **Jacques Cousteau,** some listees face an element of risk in contributing to modern life, while others, such as folksinger **Pete Seeger,** combine talent and charitable work to garner both prominence and wide admiration. Some listees, like humanitarian **Albert Schweitzer,** illustrate an altruistic type of heroism, joining those—like gun-control activists **Jim and Sarah Brady,** for example—who make a significant contribution to contemporary society. American Red Cross founder **Clara Barton** is among the heroines and heroes profiled in this volume who were selected for the lasting nature of their accomplishments, and like the

Dalai Lama others were chosen for the example they provide of achieving goals without violating another's rights to freedom, life, and dignity.

Graceful determination in the face of overwhelming obstacles characterizes the activities of listees such as opera singer **Marian Anderson**, AIDS research fund-raiser **Elizabeth Glaser,** and track star **Jesse Owens,** whose gold medal-winning performance at the 1936 Olympics inspired several generations of Black-American athletes. While some twentieth-century figures profiled—like **Louis Armstrong, Pope John XXIII,** and **Margaret Sanger**—enjoy enduring status, other listees—like **Jim Abbott, Maya Lin,** and **Stevie Wonder**—are active in the 1990s.

The changing nature of heroism is reflected in the demand for entries on people who might not have been included in a book like this twenty or thirty years ago. In 1962, for example, it would have been difficult to predict how enormously influential and popular Black-American nationalist **Malcolm X** is today. And the inclusion of Generals **Colin Powell** and **H. Norman Schwarzkopf** is testimony to the ability of these much-admired men to restore an entire nation's respect for the military.

Entry Format Sets the Stage for World-Class Research

- A vivid photograph, a telling quote, and a "vital statistics" box open each entry in *Contemporary Heroes and Heroines, Book II,* giving you an immediate sense of the person whose profile you're about to read. Addresses are included in most instances so that you can contact a favorite heroine or hero directly. In the case of some deceased listees, the address of an agent, organization, or foundation points the way to alternative sources of information or assistance.

- You'll look forward to reading the appealing essays, which provide an overview of the heroines' and heroes' lives and highlight their remarkable achievements.

- Source citations at the end of each entry lead you to more information about the heroine or hero you're interested in.

Features Put the Information You Need in the Limelight

- With its unique focus, *Contemporary Heroes and Heroines, Book II,* furnishes essays compiled with heroic criteria in mind. To capture the essence of each listee as well as ensure accuracy, the editor has consulted autobiographies and biographies as well as newspaper and magazine articles of current and historical interest, thus eliminating the need to search for information scattered in a variety of sources.

- The Introduction, written by popular culture expert Ray B. Browne, discusses a variety of heroic traits and explains the concept of heroism—how it has changed over time and how it is currently viewed.

- The primary table of contents in *Contemporary Heroes and Heroines, Book II*, includes a brief descriptor that matches a listee with his or her claim to fame.

- A second table of contents grouping biographees by category is headed Heroes and Heroines listed by area of endeavor. It allows you to scan names in a desired field and learn more about who has made a lasting contribution in a given arena.

- Following this alternative table of contents is a list of people who appear in the first *Contemporary Heroes and Heroines*, demonstrating the breadth of coverage in these unique works.

- The volume's General Index lists key words, places, events, awards, institutions, and people cited in the essays, making it easy to trace a common thread through several profiles. It also contains references to biographees in the original *Contemporary Heroes and Heroines*—just look for the abbreviation "CHH" after a name to know that you'll need to consult the first book for an essay on that particular person.

Put *Contemporary Heroes and Heroines, Book II,* on Your Team

- If you're a student researching contemporary heroic figures, no other source will present you with short, readable essays collected according to a heroism theme.

- Working as a researcher in current events, history, or popular culture, you'll turn to *Contemporary Heroes and Heroines, Book II*, for the biographical material that personalizes the topic you're investigating.

- As an educator, member of the media, or interested general reader, when a "local hero" makes the news, you'll appreciate the backdrop provided by *Contemporary Heroes and Heroines, Book II*, that puts it all in perspective.

Acknowledgements

The editor wishes to thank the Periodicals Department staff of the Grand Rapids (Michigan) Public Library for their assistance with this project.

Make Your Contribution—Send Suggestions

Just as we looked for your input before compiling the original *Contemporary Heroes and Heroines* as well as *Contemporary Heroes and Heroines, Book II*, the editors welcome your comments and suggestions for future editions so that we can best meet the needs of the greatest number of users. Send comments or suggestions to:

> The Editors
> *Contemporary Heroes and Heroines, Book II*
> Gale Research Inc.
> 835 Penobscot Building
> Detroit, MI 48226-4094
>
> Or, call toll-free at 1-800-347-GALE

Introduction

"The history of the world is but the biography of [heroes]."

—Thomas Carlyle, *On Heroes, Hero-Worship, and the Heroic in History*

Heroes and heroines have always been necessary in human society because they provide strong figures and symbols of society itself. There is in society, writes Ernest Becker in *Denial of Death*, a constant hunger for heroes and heroines, because we realize our own limitations as human beings, and because we all must die with our hopes and dreams largely unfulfilled. For Becker, life has always been almost too big for the individual to bear alone, too often filled with frustrations and disappointments. So we create heroes and heroines and use them as our alter egos, the driving force for the movement and development of ourselves and for society as a whole.

Heroes Provide Models of Behavior

In earliest societies, models of behavior were usually men. In Greek civilization of three thousand years ago, for example, Homer's Odysseus, the hero of the *Odyssey*, provided an excellent example of a typical hero who was a model of warlike behavior.

Through time societies have grown larger and more complicated and so has the role of the hero and heroine. Nineteenth-century English essayist Thomas Carlyle felt that the story of a society is really only the accounts of its great people. Though developments of the last one hundred years have demonstrated that there is more to society than its heroes and heroines, there is obviously still some truth in Carlyle's feeling. Surely the opposite point of view, that held by historian and former Librarian of Congress Daniel J. Boorstin in *The Image: A Guide to Pseudo-Events in America*, that all our heroes and heroines have disappeared, cannot be true. Boorstin regrets that those heroes and heroines have all become mere celebrities. In today's swiftly moving society, heroes and heroines undergo rapid transformation. They exist in a highly technological society that is driven by the mass media, and they often change. "Here today and gone tomorrow," they may be. But while they are with us, they provide the same objects of modeling and emulation we have always needed.

According to Joseph Campbell in *The Hero with a Thousand Faces*, earlier societies were built around "monomyths"—simple stories about their creation and perpetuation. The heroic pantheon in such societies was therefore filled with only a few figures. The people in those societies did not want much information about their heroes and heroines. They accepted their "betters" on faith. Now, of course, we are not inclined to accept misty, shadowy figures as heroes and heroines. We want our people to be three dimensional. Heroes and heroines still serve a mythological purpose, clarifying the meaning of life and eternity, and helping us maintain some kind of balance and personal stability. But today's heroes and heroines serve more as role models than as spiritual leaders. Their accomplishments, however, are just as important as they used to be.

Napoleon is supposed to have said, "No one is a hero to his valet." But that was an observation by a man who wanted to remain distant and mysterious and is not very accurate. In fact, one can easily become a hero or heroine to someone who knows him or her well. Parents are often heroes and heroines to their children. Children are heroic to their siblings. Often the more one gets to know the hero or heroine, the more heroic that individual becomes. George Washington, "Father of his country," and Betsy Ross, "Creator of the U.S. Flag," for example, have become all the more heroic as we have gotten to know them better. Martin Luther King, Jr. and Mother Teresa (both profiled in the first *Contemporary Heroes and Heroines*) grow in our consciousness and admiration as we learn more about their achievements.

Today's Heroes Help Define Our World

Heroes and heroines shape and reflect society. They are created by the society they serve and serve the society that creates them. The careful observer of today's society will see that heroes and heroines serve different purposes now than they did in the past. Society has changed dramatically. Because society now reflects many different peoples and cultures, the "monomyth" has become the multimyth.

Recent surveys of New York City and Los Angeles County, for example, showed that in the former community seventy-eight languages were spoken. In Los Angeles County the number was eighty-two. Undoubtedly, there must be well over one hundred languages and dialects spoken in the United States today. Truly, America is a culture of cultures, and each culture is supported by its own heroes and heroines.

Democracy Makes Heroes Familiar To Us All

Heroes and heroines are also becoming more democratic than they used to be. Democracy makes them familiar to us all. As we did in more primitive times, we refer to heroes and heroines by their first names. We like to see them, talk with them, touch them, and make them one of us. We travel great distances and pay large sums of money to get close to our heroes and heroines, to experience them firsthand. We also live with them through the media. As we in effect make them a part of our lives, we tend to demystify our heroes and heroines, to make them more human, not superhuman.

Democracy teaches that all of us can become heroic if we try. We are primarily interested in a group of individuals who best represent a democracy worthy of the ideals we think made America great. This means that our heroes and heroines should continue to be people heroic enough to represent a heroic country, and people with heroic ideals and goals large enough to fit the hero and heroines—and perhaps us.

Heroes Can Embody Our Ideal Selves

All people rise with the tide of their heroes' and heroines' accomplishments and sink with their failings. That is the basis of the American Dream and the freedom for individual development which has always been the basis of that dream. "Be all that you can be" is the motto of the U.S. Army in its recruiting drive, and those words voice a universal ideal of people developing into something better than they are. "A mind is a terrible thing to waste," cautions the United Negro Fund, again saying that everyone is capable of upward mobility if willing to develop the mind. Heroes and heroines seem to teach, "Be like me—be all you can be. I did it. So can you." Everyday figures like sports heroes and heroines, minority figures, and those with the greatest lack of privilege and opportunity demonstrate that no matter how far the distance or steep the climb, one can become a success. When boxer Muhammad Ali bragged, "I'm the greatest!" it was not difficult for some people to think that they too could become the greatest in their particular field if they worked hard. When Martin Luther King, Jr. had "A Dream," it was easy for others to see a vision and aspire to it.

A nation is known by its heroes and heroines. Those individuals, by being flesh and blood people, demonstrate what a people love, what they respect, what they have become, and what they aspire to become. The ninety people in this volume come from all areas of society. They represent the dreams of all kinds of people.

The Democratic Appeal of Heroes

Those of us interested in politicians will find inspiring the examples of **Franklin Delano Roosevelt, Winston Churchill, Harry Truman, Jimmy and Rosalynn Carter,** and **Mikhail Gorbachev,** as well as the several others included. It was Roosevelt, thirty-second president of the United States, who, in 1933, during the darkest hour of America's deepest depression, announced in his first Inaugural Address that "the only thing we have to fear is fear itself." In the same gritty frame of mind, Winston Churchill, prime minister of Great Britain during World War II, displayed great courage when he announced that the English would resist invasion of their homeland hedgerow by hedgerow and house by house until they had thrown the Nazis back into the sea. Harry Truman, thirty-third president of the United States, demonstrated great leadership when he became president following the death of Franklin Roosevelt. Although Truman announced that having that office forced upon him was like having a ton of bricks fall on him, the heroic stature of the man was displayed in his willingness to shoulder all responsibility for the office. "The buck stops here," he announced, and he always stood up to it.

The democratic heroic appeal of President Jimmy Carter and First Lady Rosalynn Carter was revealed at his Inauguration as thirty-ninth president of the United States when they stepped out of the parade limousine that was ceremoniously driving them from the Inaugural speech on the Capitol steps to the White House, and walked up Pennsylvania Avenue. Since leaving the White House, Jimmy and Rosalynn Carter have added to their heroic stature by remaining active in all kinds of human rights causes. But perhaps no politician ever presided over such a series of momentous events as Mikhail Gorbachev did at the dissolution of the Union of Soviet Socialist Republics in 1991. Those readers who are interested in political change and the people who bring about the change will find this leader's short career in public life very revealing.

Heroic Diversity Illustrated Worldwide

Many Americans find their heroes and heroines in the international arena. Norwegian explorer **Roald Amundsen,** for example, achieved the goal of many explorers, as the first person to reach the South Pole. French undersea explorer and environmentalist **Jacques Cousteau's** heroic exploits are well-known to everybody who has ever watched documentaries on television. No one can forget the undersea discoveries of Cousteau and his many crew members and his tireless devotion to protecting the environment. No one likewise can forget the exhilarating explorations of **Thor Heyerdahl,** the Norwegian explorer/anthropologist who had the imagination to reconstruct replicas of ancient ships that sailed from the Old World to the New World, and then sailed them himself to prove that such voyages could have been made.

Heroes Found In Sports, Entertainment

Those readers of this volume who like sports heroes and heroines will find many of the greatest here in this collection. There is **Jim Abbot,** who became a professional baseball player despite a handicap that would have benched less determined people; **Arthur Ashe,** one of the world's top tennis players until sidelined by a heart attack; **Lou Gehrig,** one of baseball's greatest players until brought down by Amyotrophic Lateral Sclerosis, otherwise known as ALS or Lou Gehrig's disease; **Michael Jordan,** one of the most famous American basketball players of all time; **Jesse Owens,** a Black-American athlete who won a gold medal in the 1936 Olympics in Germany and outraged Adolph Hitler; **Wilma Rudolph,** who became a track star despite her battle with polio as a child; **Jim Thorpe,** an American athlete who excelled in football and baseball and became an Olympic gold medalist; and **Babe Didrikson Zaharias,** the great American track and field athletic champion who fought cancer at the very height of her career.

Other readers who find their heroes and heroines among entertainers will be given numerous examples in this volume such as **Marian Anderson,** Black-American opera singer whose quiet dignity won over many opponents in a race-charged society; **Louis "Satchmo" Armstrong,** Black-American jazz trumpeter and singer who suffered from the sharpest racial discrimination, but became one of America's unofficial ambassadors of goodwill; **Joan Baez,** American folksinger and social activist who sang her way into the hearts of many people around the world; **Leonard Bernstein,** surely one of the most active composers and conductors America has ever produced; **Pete Seeger,** folksinger, composer and environmentalist who has devoted his entire life to the use of music as a weapon in the war for social justice; and **Stevie Wonder,** a blind Black-American singer and composer who has thrilled millions of people with his inimitable style of singing and entertaining.

Heroes Inspire With Faith Or Action

Readers who heroize those people who are willing to go against the grain in society to fight for social and political change will find in this collection such inspiring examples as **Malcolm X,** Black Muslim activist of the 1960s who sought social reforms and pride in race and racial achievements; **Thurgood Marshall,** associate justice of the U.S. Supreme Court from 1967 to 1991, who fought for the rights of Blacks and other disadvantaged people in the United States; **J. Robert Oppenheimer,** father of the atomic bomb who, after its development, had second thoughts about the morality of the instrument of mass destruction and became a target of the anticommunist hysteria that swept the United States during the 1950s; and **Paul Robeson,** the very talented American singer and actor who was blacklisted for his unpopular political views.

For those readers who find their heroes and heroines among winners of distinguished prizes, there are many examples in this volume including **Marie Curie,** who, with her husband, Pierre Curie, discovered radium and received the 1903 Nobel Prize for physics and later, after her husband's death, received the 1911 Nobel Prize for chemistry; the **Dalai Lama,** Tibetan religious leader and winner of the 1989 Nobel Prize for Peace; **Aung San Suu Kyi,** winner of the 1991 Nobel Prize for Peace; **Albert Einstein,** American physicist and winner of the 1921 Nobel Prize for physics; **Alexander Fleming,** winner of the 1945 Nobel Prize for medicine for the discovery and development of penicillin; **Marlee Matlin,** Academy Award-winning actress and activist on behalf of the hearing impaired; **Toni Morrison,** Black-American novelist who won the 1988 Pulitzer Prize; and **Albert Schweitzer,** French missionary physician and music scholar who won the 1952 Nobel Prize for Peace.

Readers who find youthful heroes and heroines appealing will find several of the most outstanding here: **Chai Ling,** Beijing

Normal University student who was a leader in the movement for democracy against the tanks of Tiananman Square; **Maya Lin,** American architect who designed the Vietnam Veterans Memorial and the Civil Rights Memorial; and **Ryan White,** the teenager with AIDS who through words and actions pleaded for understanding and tolerance for AIDS victims.

Examination of these heroes and heroines reveals the many ways people can rise from the ordinary and become heroic. The roads to success are numerous and varied. Study of the people included in this volume who achieved this success will reveal that the way is seldom easy but satisfies a drive in people that makes them dissatisfied with anything less than the best. They have brought the best to themselves and through their efforts made some accomplishments in society.

Ray B. Browne

Jim Abbott

"If you keep harping on a disability, then you'll start believing there is one. So I don't.*"*

Born on September 19, 1967, in Flint, Michigan, Jim Abbott plays professional baseball for the California Angels.

Address: California Angels, Anaheim Stadium, 2000 State College Blvd., Anaheim, CA 92806.

In March, 1989, the California Angels surprised the baseball world when they named Jim Abbott a starting pitcher for the upcoming season. Just twenty-one years old, he was only the tenth pitcher since 1965 to join the major leagues without any minor league experience. It was a noteworthy achievement made all the more remarkable by the fact that this young athlete—Little League standout, high school and college star, and Olympic gold medalist—was born without a right hand. While some people might consider that a disability, Abbott refuses to think of it as such. "I've been blessed with a pretty good left arm and a not-so-great right arm" is how he put it in an interview with Hank Hersch of *Sports Illustrated.* "If I hadn't grown up having to do everything with my left, I don't know if it would have developed like this."

Abbott credits his parents, Mike and Kathy Abbott, with raising him to believe that there was no reason he had to live his life differently. When he was six, they let him discard the awkward and much-hated hook he had been fitted with the year before. They encouraged him to play sports and steered him toward soccer, a game in which they felt he could better compete with other children. But baseball was his real love, so his father worked with him to perfect what is now known as the "Abbott Switch"—a smooth and speedy transfer of his glove from his right wrist to his left hand that enables him to throw the ball, then prepare to field it. The boy spent hours practicing the tricky maneuver, pitching imaginary games against the wall of his family's house.

By the time he was eleven, Abbott was ready for Little League. In his very first game, he pitched a five-inning no-hitter that prompted the umpire to invoke the mercy rule. News of his skill soon spread via the local press, and with the publicity came words of encouragement. Abbott now looks back on that time as crucial to his future success, noting that "if someone had said, 'No, Jim, with that arm maybe you should sit this out and keep score,' I might have been crushed and never gone on."

During his high school years at Flint Central, Abbott continued to amaze coaches and spectators with his abilities. Not only did he excel in baseball, he also led the intramural basketball league in scoring and quarterbacked the varsity football team to the state playoffs during his senior year. As graduation neared, the Toronto Blue Jays came calling with an offer of $50,000 to play in their minor league farm system. But Abbott had always dreamed of pitching for the University of Michigan, so he declined the offer and headed to Ann Arbor in 1985 on a baseball scholarship.

Abbott's numerous college successes made him the undisputed star of amateur baseball. His freshman record was 6–2, including the win that gave Michigan the Big Ten title in 1986. His sophomore record improved to 11–3, but his biggest thrill that season was carrying the flag for Team USA during the opening ceremonies of the 1987 Pan American Games, then pitching his team to victory over world champion Cuba—the first time an American team had won in Havana in twenty-five years. (Team USA received a silver medal for its efforts.) The following year brought an even greater honor when he was named to the 1988 U.S. Olympic Team; at the summer games in Seoul, South Korea, he clinched the gold medal for Team USA with a win over defending champion Japan. By the end of his junior year at Michigan, Abbott had also received two other major tributes: the Golden Spikes Award as the outstanding amateur baseball player in the United States (the equivalent of football's Heisman Trophy) and the Sullivan Memorial Trophy as the most outstanding amateur athlete in the United States.

When the California Angels drafted him in the first round in June, 1988, Abbott felt it was time to give pro ball a try. He left Michigan after his junior year with an overall record of 26–8, a 3.03 earned-run average, and a 90-mph fastball. But after reporting to the Angels' spring training camp in March, 1989, he was somewhat discouraged to find that despite his stunning success as an amateur, he still needed to make believers out of those who had doubts about a one-handed pitcher's ability to make it in the major leagues. "There are times it hurts," Abbott told *Sport* reporter Johnette Howard. "Especially when you work as hard and do as much as anybody else has done, you feel maybe there's not much more to prove, and yet, there's still that skepticism. . . . I'm pretty much used to it. But it wouldn't be true to say I don't get sick of it. Whenever I read a scouting report about me, people always use the word 'risk' or 'liability.' I never thought of myself as a risk or liability. . . . To me, this isn't a revenge thing to prove people wrong. It's an opportunity. All I ever wanted was a shot."

His debut at the plate that spring of 1989 was covered by news media from around the world. As Bruce Anderson recounted in *Sports Illustrated:* "Japanese camera crews filmed him. So many photographers snapped his picture that [his] pitching coach . . . asked him if he would be able to pitch without a constant *click, click,*

click. Hordes of writers braved winds of as much as 35 mph at Desert Sun Stadium to watch him pitch and to ask him tasteless questions." Accustomed to such distractions, Abbott seemed oblivious to the attention and pitched an impressive three innings, striking out four batters and walking none and giving up only two singles and no runs. His subsequent outings were equally noteworthy, ensuring him an immediate spot on the Angels' roster.

By mid-summer, Abbott's 8–5 record was being hailed as the best rookie start in baseball. Early doubts about his ability to field certain kinds of hits, particularly bunts, were soon put to rest, prompting Milwaukee Brewers star Paul Molitor to comment, "If he can look past his disability the way he has, then my advice to batters who face him is that they better do the same thing." Angels manager Doug Rader paid Abbott an even greater compliment, describing him as perhaps "the most remarkable individual I've ever known in baseball. Beside it all, he's just a red-blooded kid who's one of the guys in the clubhouse. It's been wearing at times. He's had to answer some of the dumbest, most undignified questions I've ever heard, but he's handled everything with dignity and grace. And he's one helluva pitcher."

Abbott is very much aware that his success has made him a role model for handicapped children, but he is admittedly somewhat uncomfortable with the part, probably because, as he puts it, "[I] was never inspired by people like me. I didn't grow up thinking about not having a right hand. I just strove to be normal." Knowing that not everyone receives the encouragement he did has made him realize that as much as he wants to be considered just another baseball player, he has a certain responsibility to those children who want to grow up to be like Jim Abbott. He gives generously of his time off the field to organizations like the March of Dimes. He was especially moved by parents he talked to during his playing days in Cuba and Japan, where what he has done wouldn't have been allowed. "That just made me hope my playing has opened some eyes," he says. "Maybe it will—not that I'm some kind of frontiersman paving new ways across the world or anything. But you never know—maybe it will."

Abbott's future in major league baseball seems secure; he ended his first season with a promising 12–12 record, his second season with a disappointing 10–14 record, and his third season with a very respectable 18–11 record. "You do wonder," he once told *Time* magazine's Tom Callahan, "if you're going to be the guy who was billed to make it, who never did, or if you're going to look back someday and say, 'This is where it all began.' But I've always dreamed, 'What if this happens,' and it always has. I've been lucky."

Sources

➤ **Books**

White, Ellen Emerson, *Jim Abbott: Against All Odds,* Scholastic, 1990.

➤ **Periodicals**

Detroit Free Press, "The Boy Wonder," September 24, 1988, p. 7C (opening quote).

Life, "One for the Angels," June, 1989, pp. 118–120.

Newsweek, "The Complete Jim Abbott," June 12, 1989, p. 60.

People, September 30, 1985, p. 108.

Sport, "'All I Ever Wanted Was a Shot,'" March, 1989, pp. 26–29.

Sports Illustrated, "That Great Abbott Switch," May 25, 1987, pp. 28–29; "Angel on the Ascent," March 13, 1989, p. 27; "No More Doubts," July 24, 1989, pp. 64–65; "Ace of the Angels: California's Jim Abbott Has Emerged as One of the Game's Preeminent Pitchers," September 8, 1991.

Time, "Dreaming the Big Dreams," March 20, 1989, p. 78.

Ansel Adams

"Sometimes I think I do get to places just when God is ready to have somebody click the shutter."

One of the twentieth century's foremost photographers and conservationists, Ansel Adams was born on February 20, 1902, in San Francisco, California. His haunting landscapes of the American West helped legitimize photography as an art form and call attention to the importance of preserving wilderness areas. He died on April 22, 1984, near his home in Carmel, California.

In 1916, fourteen-year-old Ansel Adams accompanied his parents on a vacation to California's Yosemite National Park. The morning after their arrival, Mr. and Mrs. Adams presented their son with a simple box camera, a Kodak Brownie. He took many pictures of the places he visited that summer, compiling an assortment of ordinary snapshots that "couldn't have meant anything at all to anyone else." Yet as Hal Hinson observed nearly seventy years later in the *Atlantic,* "few artists have their lives and their subjects handed to them, but, in a sense, everything Adams was to become was determined during those first days at Yosemite."

Born and raised in the San Francisco Bay area, Ansel Easton Adams was the only child of Olive Bray and Charles Hitchcock Adams, a well-to-do life insurance agent whose family had once prospered in the local lumber trade. Young Ansel grew up in an unusual chalet-type house his father built to overlook the water and the dunes, and it was there that the boy first learned to enjoy the beauty of nature.

Because he was a restless student, Adams quit school after the eighth grade and was tutored at home by his father and several private instructors. One of his earliest passions was music; he taught himself to play the piano and then took lessons from an elderly German professor who instilled in him the idea that technical excellence requires strict discipline and attention to detail—the very qualities he later brought to his photography. "He turned me from a Sloppy Joe into a good technician," Adams said of his teacher. "If it hadn't been for that, I don't know what would have taken its place."

Adams's vacation in Yosemite sparked an intense interest in the outdoors, which complemented his interest in photography. He returned to the park every year after that first visit, and in 1919 he joined the Sierra Club and spent summers hiking through the Sierra Nevadas and Yosemite. Besides perfecting his mountaineering skills and developing into an ardent conservationist during these forays into the wilderness, Adams gained valuable experience in photographic technique as he learned to compensate for the changes in light and climatic conditions typical of the region. But taking pictures was still just another one of the young man's hobbies, "a way to record where I went and who I was with—what tree I slept under," as he later said. "It was a while before I saw anything else in those pictures, before they started to remind me of how I had *felt* at the time."

Although he continued his music studies throughout the 1920s with the goal of becoming a concert pianist, Adams found himself devoting more and more time to his second love. He published his first collection of photographs—a portfolio on the High Sierras—in 1927 and followed it up in 1930 with a series of pictures taken around Taos, New Mexico. About that same time, he reluctantly acknowledged that his small hands made it unlikely that he would ever succeed as a professional musician. Realizing that taking photographs had actually begun to give him more personal satisfaction than playing the piano, Adams made up his mind to pursue a career in photography instead. While his wife of two years, Virginia Best, supported his decision, both his mother and his aunt expressed great disappointment and begged him to reconsider, pointing out that the camera could not express the human soul. "Perhaps the camera cannot," Adams replied, "but the photographer can."

He had first entertained the possibility that photography could hold its own with other forms of art as a means of personal expression during his stay in Taos, where he met fellow photographer Paul Strand. Looking over some of Strand's work, Adams noted that he had abandoned the soft-focus, often hand-tinted "impressionistic" style common at the time in favor of sharply detailed images and rich, clear tones. "It flipped me out," Adams later recalled. "That was the first time I saw photographs that were organized, beautifully composed. . . . I came home thinking, 'Now photography exists!'"

Adams began his own experiments with so-called "straight photography" and its crisp realism. He banded together with several others who shared his views to form Group f/64, a name taken from the camera setting that produced great depth of field and overall sharpness. They aimed for strong contrasts, and they closely cropped and isolated their subjects, which were usually things in nature with "inherent shape": seashells, pieces of driftwood, rocks, and so on. Although the group disbanded in less than two years—"we didn't want to establish a cult," said Adams—their work was very influential in bringing an end to what they saw as the overly sentimental and imprecise "fuzzy-wuzzies" of pictorial photography.

As he worked at his craft throughout the 1930s, Adams earned a living by teaching, lecturing, taking pictures for industrial brochures and other advertising pieces, and writing articles on techniques and equipment for popular and technical periodicals. He held his first one-man show in 1932 in San Francisco and shortly after that opened his own gallery. In 1935 the publication of his book, *Making a Photograph,* brought him international attention. Basically a "how-to" manual that Adams illustrated with carefully printed reproductions of his own work, it caught the eye of famed photographer Alfred Stieglitz, a passionate advocate of photography's value as an art form. Stieglitz sponsored a one-man show of Adams's works in 1936 and subsequently served as his mentor.

In 1937, Adams moved to the Yosemite Valley to be closer to the mountains and wilderness country that served as his chief inspiration. During the 1930s, he had developed his concept of "visualization"—the process of deciding in advance how a photograph should look rather than just shooting one picture after another in the hope that one will turn out right. During the 1940s he turned his attention to perfecting his "zone system" of exposure calculation, a technique that divides darks and lights into ten distinct shades or zones from black to white. Learning to control these values to create different effects and moods was perhaps his greatest contribution to the art of photography.

Adams continued lecturing and writing on technique throughout the 1940s, 1950s, and 1960s. He also traveled extensively, photographing not only his favorite landscapes of the American West but also views of other national parks, still lifes, architectural studies, and even portraits. His work was the focus of many one-man shows throughout the country, and soon his pristine images of such scenes as moonrise over a cemetery in Hernandez, New Mexico, and the majestic Half Dome in Yosemite came to define the western United States for many people. Adams took issue with that "postcard" view of his photographs, saying, "I'm not interested in scenery. . . . I don't think my pictures tell you about the landscape. They aren't realistic. They are a departure from reality." Indeed, as Carole Lalli reported in the *Reader's Digest,* "In Adams's view, a perceptive photograph does not merely record a scene; it *uses* the external subject to create other feelings."

In 1965, Adams stopped taking pictures for public consumption and concentrated instead on making prints from the hundreds of negatives he had accumulated over the years. As the demand for his work increased, however, he quickly discovered that he was spending far too much of his time involved in printmaking—a process that, given his painstaking technique, might take him as long as one or two days per print to achieve the appropriate effect. In 1974, he announced that he was giving up retail printmaking completely as of 1976. Prices for his photographs immediately soared, and for the first time, the seventy-four-year-old Adams enjoyed financial rewards that matched his critical and popular acclaim.

As Adams's popularity increased, so, too, did his influence as an advocate for the environment. Ever since he was first awed by the beauty of Yosemite, he firmly believed in the power of nature to refresh the human spirit. "Some people belong to a church— everybody needs something to believe in," he told Pamela Abramson of *Newsweek*. "Conservation is my point of focus." His longtime association with the Sierra Club—he was a director of the organization for over thirty years—gave him a position from which he lobbied government officials (including a number of presidents) to preserve wilderness areas. He also felt his photographs helped the cause, even though none of them had been taken with an environmental objective in mind. Yet as Adams told an *Art News* reporter in an interview shortly before his death, he feared for the future given the "state of potential destruction" in the world. "People ask me why I am so presumptuous as to write letters to the newspapers and all that. Somebody has got to do it. . . . I wish I had gotten into the environmental work earlier because I think that's a citizen's fundamental responsibility."

Adams died of heart disease on April 22, 1984, at a hospital near Carmel, California, where he moved after leaving his beloved Yosemite Valley in 1962. His ashes were later scattered over a mountain in the park known as Mount Ansel Adams. In the estimated 13,000 prints developed by his own hands, as well as book sales exceeding one million copies, Adams left a legacy of "uncompromising craftsmanship," according to *Time* magazine's Richard Stengel. "Nature never seemed so still or so spiritual as in his photographs," observed Stengel. "In their purity and precision, their balance of epic vistas and exquisite detail, Ansel Adams' photographs celebrated an ideal vision of nature and the American West. That black-and-white vision was of a landscape unsullied by neon and Day-Glo plastic, a majestic continent that still seemed for all the world like a new-found land. . . . Adams made himself into a photographer and then made others see the world through his eyes. The result of his work was not an instant captured in time but timelessness captured forever in an instant."

Sources

➤ **Books**

Adams, Ansel, *Ansel Adams: Images 1923–1974*, New York Graphic Society, 1975.

Adams, Ansel, and Mary Street Alinder, *Ansel Adams: An Autobiography*, Little, Brown, 1985.

Newhall, Nancy Wynne, *Ansel Adams: The Eloquent Light*, Harper, 1980 (opening quote).

➤ **Periodicals**

Art News, "Ansel Adams: The Last Interview," Summer, 1984, pp. 76–89.

Atlantic, "Nature Made Perfect," October, 1985, pp. 99–101.

Esquire, "Portrait of the Photographer as a Grand Old Man," September, 1979.

Maclean's, "A Folk Hero of the Art," May 7, 1984, p. 73.

Newsweek, "Two Faces of Ansel Adams," September 24, 1979, pp. 90–94; "A Vision as Majestic as Yosemite," May 7, 1984, pp. 106–107.

New York Times, April 24, 1984, p. B6; April 25, 1984, p. C15.

Reader's Digest, "The Master Eye of Ansel Adams," March, 1980, pp. 139–145.

Time, "Master of the Yosemite," September 3, 1979, pp. 36–44; "The Old Master of Majesty," May 7, 1984, p. 124.

Jane Addams

*"**I** gradually became convinced that it would be a good thing to rent a house in a part of the city where many primitive and actual needs are found, in which young women who had been given over too exclusively to study might . . . learn of life from life itself."*

Born on September 6, 1860, in Cedarville, Illinois, Jane Addams was best known as the founder of Hull House, a community center located in one of Chicago's poorest neighborhoods. Addams died in Chicago on May 21, 1935.

In late 1887, twenty-seven-year-old Jane Addams accompanied a few friends on a trip to Europe. During a stay in Madrid, she attended a bullfight that thrilled her with its magnificent pageantry. Reflecting on the experience later that same evening, she was horrified and ashamed at her lack of compassion for the bulls and horses that had met such a bloody end at the spectacle. The young woman's thoughts then turned to the aimlessness of her life, the idle days devoid of goals or purpose. She pledged then and there to take on some responsibilities and exercise her considerable intelligence and creativity on behalf of the urban poor. Less than two years later, Addams opened Hull House, a Chicago community center that focused on providing hope, self-respect, and better lives to impoverished residents of the surrounding neighborhood. While not the first "settlement house" in the country, Hull House quickly became the most famous, and its founder enjoyed the respect and admiration of people around the world as "America's most useful citizen," to quote President Theodore Roosevelt.

Jane Addams grew up in the small Illinois village of Cedarville, where her father, John Huy Addams, was a prominent, self-made businessman who served sixteen years in the state senate. An ardent abolitionist and reformer, he had a profound influence on his daughter, who adored him and made a conscious effort to pattern her own beliefs and behavior after his. She remembered virtually nothing of her mother, Sarah Weber Addams, who died when Jane was only three. Five years later, her father married a widow, Anna Haldeman, who made the Addams home a place where business and political leaders congregated to talk and be entertained.

Although her dream was to attend Smith College in Massachusetts, Addams bowed to her father's wishes and went off to nearby Rockford Seminary instead, where students prepared for married life or missionary work through a combination of domestic training and religious and cultural instruction. Addams had no desire to be either a missionary or a homemaker, so she took as many academic courses as possible with the idea that she would go on and earn her B.A. at Smith, travel in Europe, and then go to medical school.

An outstanding student, Addams graduated from Rockford at the top of her class in 1881. Her father's sudden death just a few months later sent her into a deep depression. She tried to go on with her life by enrolling in the Women's Medical College in Philadelphia, but dropped out in February, 1882, weakened by backaches and a rundown feeling. As a child, Addams had suffered from tuberculosis of the spine, which left her with a slightly curved back and caused her to walk pigeon-toed and to hold her head tilted to one side. When doctors suggested operating on her back, she consented to the surgery in April, 1882, and spent the next six months recovering flat on her back, encased in an uncomfortable brace.

While Addams's physical health slowly improved, her mental outlook did not. Her doctors advised her to go abroad for additional rest, and in August, 1883, she left for Europe in the company of her stepmother and four other women. Strenuous hiking throughout the countryside strengthened her back, but a visit to London filled her with despair as she saw for the first time the wretched conditions common in urban slums. Returning to the United States in 1885, Addams again felt depressed and restless as she contemplated what she had seen and her inability to do anything about it.

She traveled to Europe again in late 1887, this time with her best friend from college, Ellen Gates Starr, and several other women. Her experience at the bullfight in Madrid led to a period of intense self-examination, and the idea of giving her own life meaning through service to the poor began to take shape in her mind. Addams had read of some cultured and well-to-do young Londoners who established a few special residences in the city's poorest slums. These so-called "settlement houses" addressed spiritual as well as material poverty, offering people the use of a library and meeting rooms and the chance to attend workshops and classes. Convinced that she could undertake a similar project in the United States, Addams immediately cut short her trip and, after a brief visit to London to see one of the residences firsthand, left for Chicago. There she purchased a rundown mansion built in 1856 by a local businessman named Hull. Using some of her own money as well as funds she and her friend Starr solicited from wealthy Chicagoans, Addams renovated and redecorated the mansion, and on September 18, 1889, the two women opened the doors of Hull House to the thousands of immigrants crowded into the surrounding slum.

Although they were met with suspicion at first, Addams, Starr, and the other volunteers who staffed Hull House soon won over their new neighbors. In its first year of operation, Hull House served some fifty thousand people. It offered infant care, a nursery and kindergarten, youth clubs, vocational training, workers' groups, cultural programs such as plays and concerts, and a variety of classes, including ones in reading and speaking the English language and becoming a U.S. citizen. Volunteers also worked on behalf of abandoned women, widows, injured workers, and tenants to make sure that they were not being intimidated or shortchanged because of their social and economic status. Addams herself lived in Hull House (and did so for the rest of her life) and was available at any hour of the day or night to do whatever needed to be done. She delivered babies, taught classes, helped with housework, kept the books, babysat, counseled those looking for a job or those in trouble with the law, nursed the sick, and tended to the affairs of the dead.

At the same time that she was ministering to the individual needs of the poor, Addams functioned as the driving force behind the entire operation—the person who organized events and services, recruited dozens of talented and dedicated volunteers, and tirelessly raised funds by giving speeches (at which she was particularly skilled) and writing numerous articles and books. Hull House became a center of innovation as Addams opened the first successful cooperative residence for working women, established Chicago's first public playground, and spearheaded efforts to create the first juvenile court in the nation. She also launched investigations into such issues as child labor, prostitution, and even garbage collection, producing reports on her findings that often led to changes in the law or increased diligence on the part of neglectful city officials. By the end of the century, the settlement house idea had spread across the country, and Addams had become a celebrity. In 1910, the publication of her autobiography, *Twenty Years at Hull-House*, further enhanced Addams's reputation as one of the best-known and best-loved women in the United States.

By the time her autobiography appeared, however, Addams had begun to shift her attention to other issues that concerned her, including unionism, women's rights, and racial prejudice. But the subject that most occupied her thoughts was the quest for world peace. When World War I erupted in Europe, Addams vigorously opposed U.S. intervention and advocated a peacemaking role instead for America. In 1915, she co-founded the Woman's Peace Party (later the Women's International League for Peace and Freedom) and became its leader. Unlike many of her fellow activists, she remained a pacifist even after the United States entered the war. This was an extremely unpopular position that led some people to denounce her as a traitor. After the war, when she lobbied for aid to help the defeated Germany's starving children, she was again attacked in the press and in speeches as un-American. During the 1920s, her defense of those accused of being communists and anarchists made Addams the target of even more criticism and hatred, and by the middle of the decade, the woman who had once been lauded as the compassionate champion of the poor and oppressed was now being dubbed "the most dangerous woman in America."

Deeply hurt by these attacks on her character and reputation, Addams began to spend long periods of time abroad, where she still met with widespread respect and acclaim. Although she continued to manage affairs at Hull House, she devoted most of her time to issues of war and peace on behalf of the Women's International League for Peace and Freedom. In recognition of her efforts, Addams was awarded the Nobel Peace Prize in 1931, the first American woman to be so honored.

As the passions associated with World War I faded and a new threat to peace in Europe emerged in the person of Adolf Hitler, the public's opinion of Addams changed considerably. With the Nobel Peace Prize came renewed respect—even adulation—from her fellow citizens. By then, however, the seventy-one-year-old Addams's health was beginning to fail due to the combined effects of bronchitis and heart problems. She was diagnosed with intestinal cancer in 1935, and on May 21 of that year she died in Chicago. Thousands of mourners from the neighborhood came to pay their respects as her body lay in state at Hull House, and on the day of the funeral services, thousands more jammed the streets. Afterwards, her body was returned to Cedarville for burial near her father.

Today, Hull House is still in operation, "a beacon of decency in Chicago's drab West Side," as Karl Detzer describes it in a *Reader's Digest* article. "Here for nearly half a century [Jane Addams] strove against injustice and unkindness, against dirt and disease, against greed and dishonesty in public office, against intolerance, bigotry, ignorance and war." But as Mary Kittredge concludes in her biography of Addams, "perhaps her principal legacy is the lesson of her life: She demonstrated that one woman could make a difference, not only in her own community and during her own lifetime but in many cities and for many years into the future."

Sources

➤ **Books**

Addams, Jane, *The Second Twenty Years at Hull-House*, Macmillan, 1930.

Addams, Jane, *Twenty Years at Hull-House*, Macmillan, 1910 (opening quote).

Davis, Allen F., *American Heroine: The Life and Legend of Jane Addams*, Oxford University Press, 1973.

Johnson, Emily Cooper, editor, *Jane Addams: A Centennial Reader*, Macmillan, 1960.

Kittredge, Mary, *Jane Addams*, Chelsea House, 1988.

➤ **Periodicals**

American Heritage, December, 1960, pp. 12–17.

Christian Century, "Jane Addams in Retrospect," January 13, 1960, pp. 39–41.

Commentary, "Jane Addams and the Radical Impulse," July, 1961, pp. 54–59.

Reader's Digest, "What We Owe to Jane Addams of Hull House," September, 1959, pp. 175–182.

Virginia Quarterly Review, "Jane Addams and the City," Winter, 1967, pp. 53–62.

Roald Amundsen

"**I** had decided that we would all take part in the historic event; the act itself of planting the flag. . . . Five roughened, frostbitten fists it was that gripped the post, lifted the fluttering flag on high and planted it together as the very first at the Geographic South Pole."

Born on July 16, 1872, in the Borge district of Norway, Roald Amundsen was the first man to reach the South Pole. He disappeared in June, 1928, on a flight to the Arctic to rescue a fellow explorer.

As the nineteenth century drew to a close, the Arctic and the Antarctic were among the few unexplored regions remaining on earth. The race to see who would be the first to reach the poles became an international contest, one that pitted various European countries against each other and the United States. The adventurers who rose to the challenge faced conditions almost beyond human endurance; many died because they underestimated their needs in such a harsh climate. Their dramatic stories nevertheless inspired others to try, including a determined young Norwegian named Roald Amundsen.

Roald Engebreth Gravning Amundsen was born in 1872 in the Borge district of Norway, which was then part of Sweden. His father, Jens Engebreth Amundsen, was a wealthy shipowner and captain who spent much of his time at sea; he died when Roald was sixteen. Both Jens and his wife, Hanna Henrikke Gustava Sahlquist, wanted their second son to be a doctor, but Roald was a below-average student who barely graduated from high school. To please his widowed mother, he enrolled in medical school. Following his mother's death in 1893 when Roald was twenty-one, he dropped out to pursue his interest in polar exploration, a subject that had fascinated him since childhood.

As a member of a seafaring family, young Amundsen was quite knowledgeable about such things as the weather, currents, and how ships were built and repaired. He was also an avid outdoorsman, active in gymnastics, ice-skating, and especially skiing. But every time he tried to sign up for a polar expedition, he was turned down for lack of experience. He then decided to work on improving those skills he thought would be most in demand—particularly sailing and mountain skiing—and soon was hired to join the crew of a sealing ship headed for the Arctic Ocean. The slaughter he witnessed on this trip and on subsequent trips with a whaling vessel sickened him, but he did gain an appreciation of the perils of sailing in icy waters as well as a new respect for animal life. Amundsen continued his training on one of his family's merchant ships but found it much too sedate for his liking.

When the British declared their intention to reach the South Pole by the turn of the century, the rest of the world felt challenged to try to beat them to it. The Belgians were the first to respond, launching a scientific expedition in 1897, and Amundsen was one of those on board. Conditions were much more severe than anyone had expected, however, and the never-ending darkness, cold, and inadequate food supplies left the men physically and psychologically weakened. After spending thirteen months trapped in the ice, they blasted and sawed their way out to open water and sailed back to Europe, arriving in 1899. Despite the hardships and brush with death, Amundsen considered the voyage the greatest experience of his life, for it taught him much about what humans needed to survive in Antarctica.

After serving another stint on one of his family's merchant ships, Amundsen felt he was ready to lead his own expedition. He decided to revisit the site of the north magnetic pole, which scientists believed had shifted since it was first pinpointed in 1831, and from there go on to navigate the Northwest Passage. He purchased a wooden sloop and refurbished it, then selected and trained a crew, obtained supplies, and taught himself how to drive sled dogs.

Amundsen and his men left Norway on June 16, 1903. Severe weather plagued the journey at first and kept them from reaching the magnetic pole, but eventually Amundsen and another crew member managed to make their way to the pole's last known location, where they confirmed that the scientists' suspicions had been correct. With that part of the expedition complete, they continued to thread their way through the Arctic. In 1905, they at last sailed into the Bering Sea, thus becoming the first to navigate the entire Northwest Passage. More than three years after their departure, they returned to Norway as heroes.

Soon Amundsen was making preparations for his next expedition: becoming the first person to reach the northernmost point on earth, the north geographic pole. His plans were well under way when word came that explorer Robert Peary had beaten him to it in April, 1909. Amundsen then quietly changed his plans; becoming the first person to reach the *South* Pole would be his new goal. His chief rival was the Englishman Robert Scott, who launched his own Antarctic expedition in June, 1910.

Keeping his destination a secret from all but his brother Leon, Amundsen set out on August 9, 1910. It was not until his ship docked in Madeira that Amundsen revealed his true intent and gave every crew member the chance to return home. No one wanted to drop out, so Amundsen cabled Scott that the Norwegians were also on their way to Antarctica. On January 15, 1911, they arrived on the Ross Ice Shelf and established their camp. At one point, members of the Scott expedition stopped by for a visit. Relations between the two groups were cordial but marked by a certain wariness;

neither wanted to do or say anything that might help the other, especially when both were clearly so close to success.

In September, 1911, Amundsen decided to set out for the pole, but bad weather soon forced the party back to camp. They ventured out again on October 19, and with Amundsen in the lead, they finally reached the general area of the pole on December 14, a date they commemorated by planting a Norwegian flag in the snow. To make sure no one would be able to dispute their claim, they spent the next three days calculating their exact geographic position, discovering the true location of the pole on December 17. Just in case he did not make it back alive, Amundsen erected a small tent on the site in which he left a letter to the King of Norway as well as a brief note to his rival, Scott, asking him to confirm the Norwegians' success by delivering the letter to the king. He and his men then returned to their base camp, arriving on January 25, 1912. About a week later, they set sail for Tasmania, where Amundsen announced his triumph to the world and was again hailed as a hero.

But as the weeks passed with no word from Scott, fears for his safety began to overshadow Amundsen's accomplishment. In November, 1912, search parties made a grim discovery: Scott and his men had died of cold and hunger on their way back to camp from the South Pole, which they had managed to reach about a month after the Norwegians. With Scott's body were Amundsen's two letters as well as a dramatically eloquent account of his own expedition. Once the world learned of this tragedy—which was without a doubt a consequence of poor planning—Amundsen fell from public favor. The British speculated that perhaps he had just been "lucky" and even went so far as to hint that he was indirectly responsible for Scott's death. Such criticism deeply wounded Amundsen, who was also burdened with huge debts from the Antarctic trip. He soon announced that he was retiring from exploration in order to pay off his creditors. But after a fling with aviation (he earned the first civilian pilot's license issued in Norway), he was drawn to the sea once again. From 1918 to 1920, Amundsen attempted to drift across the North Pole from Asia to North America. While this proved to be impossible, he did manage to sail the Northeast Passage (the water route linking the Arctic Ocean near Norway to the Bering Sea), thus becoming the first man to navigate both the Northwest Passage and the Northeast Passage.

In 1925, Amundsen teamed up with a wealthy American named Lincoln Ellsworth, and the two men announced their intention to be the first to fly over the North Pole. They nearly died when their plane crashed on the way, but nevertheless they set a record for flying the farthest north, a feat that won them worldwide acclaim. They tried for another record in May, 1926, this time in a blimp designed and piloted by an Italian, Umberto Nobile; it became the first blimp to fly over the North Pole. Controversy erupted upon its return, however, when Nobile publicly declared that he and not Amundsen deserved credit for the successful flight. The ensuing squabble damaged the Norwegian's reputation and left him bitter. Again he retired from exploration.

In May, 1928, Amundsen learned that Nobile had disappeared on another blimp flight over the North Pole. Although the two men were far from friends, Amundsen volunteered to lead a rescue operation on behalf of the Norwegian government; Italian dictator Benito Mussolini, still angry over the earlier incident, flatly rejected the offer. Amundsen went ahead and organized a search of his own using a French seaplane and crew. The aircraft disappeared shortly after takeoff on June 18 and was not seen or heard from again until early September, when a fisherman found one of its pontoons floating off the coast of Norway. No trace was ever found of the rest of the plane or of Amundsen and the members of his crew; Nobile was eventually rescued by others.

Many regarded this as a sad but fitting end to a man whose entire life had been devoted to pursuing adventure. While still a teenager, Amundsen had made up his mind to become a polar explorer and methodically set out to learn what he needed to know to succeed. As one who took few risks and never depended on luck, his careful planning later paid off in a big way: he was the first to navigate the Northwest Passage, the first to reach the South Pole, and the only one of his peers to have visited both poles.

Sources

➤ **Books**

Amundsen, Roald, *My Life as an Explorer*, translated from Norwegian, Doubleday, 1927.

Huntford, Roland, *The Last Place on Earth*, Atheneum, 1986 (opening quote).

Sipiera, Paul P., *Roald Amundsen and Robert Scott*, Children's Press, 1990.

➤ **Periodicals**

New York Times, "Amundsen Overdue in Kings Bay Flight; Nobile Again Passed," June 20, 1928, p. 1; "Amundsen Pontoon Found off North Norway Coast; Hope for Crew Abandoned," September 2, 1928.

Marian Anderson

"I *was never a real great fighter. There are people who will fight . . . but there are some who hope that if they're doing something worthwhile, it will speak for them."*

Born on February 17, 1902, in Philadelphia, Pennsylvania, Marian Anderson was among the first singers to break the color barrier in the world of classical music.

Address: c/o ICM Artists Ltd., 40 West 57th St., New York, NY 10019.

Blessed with a deep, rich contralto voice, which conductor Arturo Toscanini declared "one hears once in a hundred years," Marian Anderson achieved greatness in an era when Black-American singers were almost as unwelcome on the stage as they were in many of America's hotels and restaurants. As Barbara Klaw of *American Heritage* notes, Anderson challenged the barriers she faced "quietly, with dignity, and without fanfare," communicating through her music a profound spirituality that rose above race and nationality and touched the very hearts of her audience. In the process, she emerged as a symbol of the struggle for racial equality, a role Klaw says the gentle and unassuming Anderson "would never have picked for herself." Yet she did more than virtually any other Black-American singer to pave the way for those who followed her.

The oldest of three girls, Marian Anderson was born and grew up in Philadelphia. Her father, John, sold ice and coal at a downtown market until his death from a brain tumor in 1912, and her mother, Anna, was a cleaning woman at a department store. Even as a teenage member of both the junior and adult choirs at her church, Anderson had an exceptional voice, with a range that enabled her to sing some tenor and baritone parts usually sung by men. Soon she was being invited to perform at benefits and church socials all around the Philadelphia area. In 1917, eager to take formal voice lessons, Anderson tried to enroll in a local music school and was abruptly told: "We don't take colored." This first encounter with overt racism "was a tremendously great shock," she told Klaw. "So you learn. I don't say you ever accept, but you learn that there are people who are like that."

Private lessons followed, first with Mary Saunders Patterson, a locally famous Black-American soprano who waived her usual fee, and then with Giuseppe Boghetti, an Italian-born vocal coach who had trained some of the most prominent concert performers of that era. Anderson's church paid Boghetti's fee for her first year of study before he offered his services free of charge. Under Boghetti's tutelage, Anderson developed proper vocal techniques and expanded her repertoire of mostly hymns and spirituals to include French and German operatic pieces performed by her idol, Black-American tenor Roland Hayes. Although Anderson also took lessons from others, Boghetti remained her primary vocal coach for the rest of his life.

After graduating from high school, Anderson devoted even more of her time to performing, not only in churches but also at colleges, schools, and private clubs in the Black-American community. In April, 1924, she decided to hold a recital before a predominantly White audience in Manhattan's Town Hall. Crushed by a low turnout and poor reviews that criticized her mechanical pronunciation of foreign words, she gave up singing in public for over a year and seriously considered abandoning her career. She made up her mind to return to the stage when her mother became ill yet went to work anyway because she could not afford to miss a paycheck. Anderson vowed then and there to earn enough money so that her mother could retire. Determined to correct the faults critics had noted at her Town Hall concert, she resumed training with Boghetti and also took lessons in German, French, and Italian.

A year later, Anderson entered a national music competition and beat three hundred other singers for first prize—the chance to perform as a soloist with the New York Philharmonic Orchestra. Unlike the Town Hall recital, this concert met with critical and commercial success. It led to a Carnegie Hall appearance with a well-known group of Black-American singers, the Hall Johnson Choir and eventually to a contract with one of the country's most prominent concert management agencies.

Heartened as she was by this turn of events, Anderson was still unhappy with her progress in mastering German pronunciation and disappointed when her career did not take off in the late 1920s as she had hoped it would. So from 1929 until 1935, she spent most of her time in Europe, studying music and languages and building her reputation as a singer. She was especially popular in the Scandinavian countries. In Paris, flamboyant American impresario Sol Hurok attended one of her recitals on a whim and was so impressed that he immediately offered her a contract to perform in the United States. Feeling ready once again to test her abilities at home, she accepted and set sail for New York.

On December 30, 1935, Anderson made her second appearance at Town Hall. Unlike her disastrous debut, this concert was a triumph that received rave reviews. She followed it up with a three-month tour of the U.S. and then a tour of Europe and the Soviet Union. Throughout the rest of the 1930s, she became increasingly popular at home and abroad as a result of her extensive touring schedule, which sometimes had her giving more than one hundred recitals a season in various American, European, and South American cities. In 1936, she became the first Black-American singer to perform at the White House as a guest of Franklin and Eleanor Roosevelt. Three years later, Eleanor Roosevelt presented her with the NAACP's Spingarn Medal for her noteworthy accomplishments as a Black American.

It was another event in 1939, however, that forever linked Marian Anderson's name with the struggle for racial equality. That spring, the Daughters of the American Revolution (DAR) barred her from singing at Constitution Hall in Washington, D.C. This blatant act of racial discrimination made headlines worldwide and prompted widespread criticism; an outraged Eleanor Roosevelt resigned from the DAR in protest. At the Roosevelts' urging, the Secretary of the Interior offered the Lincoln Memorial as an alternative site for a free public recital. Reluctant at first to participate in what she feared would become a spectacle, Anderson almost declined the invitation, then realized her presence would be symbolic of the struggles of her people and of democracy.

On a chilly Easter Sunday morning in April 1939, some seventy-five thousand people gathered to hear her deliver a highly emotional concert with the massive seated figure of Abraham Lincoln as her backdrop. "It was a tremendous thing and my heart beat like mad— it's never beat like that before—loud and strong and as though it wanted to say something," Anderson recalled in her interview with Klaw. "I don't like to use the word protesting but my reaction was, what have I done that should bring this onto my heart? I was not trying to cut anybody down. I just wanted to sing and to share." As Allen Hughes noted in *Musical America,* the concert attracted a wide variety of people, most of whom were there "because they sensed somehow that Marian Anderson stood for something good. She represented something beyond the range of mere professional achievement, some undefinable thing that had to do with them, something that was, perhaps, eternal."

Besides focusing public attention on the problems Black-American artists faced in American society, the Lincoln Memorial concert elevated Anderson to superstar status and enabled her to command higher fees for her appearances. After making sure her family was provided for, she began to donate generous sums to her favorite organizations, including the NAACP, the Urban League, the YMCA, and the International Committee on African Affairs. In 1941, she used her $10,000 prize from the Bok Award (presented annually to an outstanding Philadelphia citizen) to establish a scholarship program for young vocalists.

Throughout the 1940s and 1950s, Anderson continued to tour extensively, taking time out in 1943 to marry architect Orpheus Fisher. On January 7, 1955, she became the first Black American to sing with New York City's Metropolitan Opera, appearing in the role of the sorceress Ulrica in Verdi's *The Masked Ball*. For Anderson, it marked the fulfillment of a childhood dream, a "joyful" experience that made her wish "it had come earlier in life when I might have been able to bring more to it." She sang in only a few performances, but her debut opened the door for other Black Americans to sing with major American and European opera companies.

The late 1950s were filled with more concert tours and a flood of recognition for her efforts to promote international understanding. In 1958, following a goodwill tour of the Far East on behalf of the U.S. State Department, President Dwight Eisenhower named her to a one-year term as a U.S. delegate to the United Nations, where she served on a committee responsible for overseeing colonies in Africa and the Pacific Ocean area, which were in the process of becoming independent countries. Her concern for the third world was also reflected in her efforts to eradicate hunger, a goal she pursued through the Freedom from Hunger Foundation, which she co-founded. In recognition of this service to others and to her country, President Lyndon Johnson awarded her a Presidential Medal of Freedom in 1963.

Anderson retired from performing in public in 1965 after a fifty-city farewell tour that took her to packed concert halls around the world. She remained involved in the arts, however, donating her time and talent to a number of different activities. In 1978, she was part of the first group of Americans to receive Kennedy Center awards for lifetime achievement in the arts.

Despite the accolades that have come her way, Anderson has never felt entirely comfortable with her role as a symbol. She downplays her contributions, insisting that those who came before her—singers like Roland Hayes and Paul Robeson—actually laid the groundwork for Black Americans to be taken seriously as classical artists. She herself has always avoided talking politics and quietly yet firmly refused to be drawn into the battles that raged around her, preferring instead to let her music be her only voice. "Certainly I have my feelings about conditions that affect my people," Anderson explained to Klaw. "But it is not right for me to try to mimic somebody who writes, or who speaks. That is their forte. I think first of music and of being there where music is, and of music being where I am. What I had was singing, and if my career has been of some consequence, then that's my contribution."

Sources

➤ **Books**

Anderson, Marian, *My Lord, What a Morning,* Viking, 1956.

Tedards, Anne, *Marian Anderson,* Chelsea House, 1988.

Truman, Margaret, *Women of Courage,* Morrow, 1976.

➤ **Periodicals**

American Heritage, "An Interview with Marian Anderson," February, 1977, pp. 50–57.

Ebony, "Farewell, Marian Anderson," June, 1965, pp. 39–46; "A Tribute to Marian Anderson," November, 1989, pp. 182–186.

McCall's, April, 1976.

Musical America, "Something Eternal," February, 1959; "Marian Anderson Says Farewell," September, 1964, pp. 8–11.

National Review, "The First Lady," September 29, 1989, pp. 65–66.

Newsweek, "The Beacon," April 26, 1965, pp. 87–88.

New York Times Magazine, "Other Voice of Marian Anderson," August 10, 1958; "A Bravo for Opera's Black Voices," January 17, 1982.

USA Today, May 8, 1991, p. 3D (opening quote).

Louis Armstrong

"**W**hen I blow I think of times from outa the past that give me an image. A town, a chick somewhere back down the line, an old man with no name you once seen in a place you don't remember. What you hear coming from a man's horn, that's what he is."

Born in New Orleans, Louisiana, around July 4, 1900, trumpeter Louis Armstrong was one of the most influential figures in American jazz. He died on July 6, 1971, in New York City.

Born and raised in the slums of New Orleans, abandoned by his father and neglected by his mother, sent to a youth home at the age of thirteen—the grim facts of Louis Armstrong's childhood do not suggest the kind of background conducive to happiness and success in later life. Yet the man the world came to know as "Satchmo" triumphed over poverty and racism and almost single-handedly created and popularized a new form of music with his virtuoso trumpet playing and radiant stage presence. As jazz's first big star, he paved the way for virtually everyone who followed him to fame.

The exact date of Daniel Louis Armstrong's birth is unknown, but it was most likely 1900, perhaps a year or two earlier. His father, Willie, deserted the family when Armstrong was just an infant, and his mother, Mayann, more or less abandoned him to the care of his grandmother, Josephine. Until he was seven, home was a squalid shack in a tough area of New Orleans known as the Battlefield. Later, he lived with his mother and younger sister in the Storyville district of New Orleans, a sleazy neighborhood of dance halls, brothels, and bars. There the sound of music filled the air day and night, mesmerizing Armstrong as he stood outside the honky-tonks or tagged along after the bands while they paraded through Storyville trying to attract business.

A turning point in Armstrong's life came on New Year's Eve, 1913, when he took a pistol loaded with blanks outside to celebrate and was arrested for firing it at another boy. Sentenced to a term in the Colored Waifs' Home, a military-type school run by a Black-American man who took in youngsters headed for trouble, Armstrong enjoyed the discipline as well as unaccustomed pleasures such as regular meals and clean clothes. Best of all, the home had its own band. Armstrong started out on the tambourine and eventually worked his way up to the lead position on the cornet. By the time he was released, he was easily able to play melodies and harmonies by ear. But because the band master was not a thoroughly trained musician, he failed to recognize that his prize pupil was developing some bad habits that would later damage his lips and teeth.

Armstrong left the Colored Waifs' Home determined to become a professional musician. During the day he worked at various odd jobs to help support his family, but at night he wandered the streets of New Orleans listening to different bands. Now and then someone let him borrow an instrument and sit in on a session, and slowly he improved his technique and expanded his repertoire. His progress accelerated dramatically after a friend loaned him ten dollars to buy a used cornet. Practicing every chance he could, the teenager increased his stamina, widened his range, polished his sound, and learned more tunes. Soon a few bands began using him as a substitute, and before long he was a regular with one band. Over the next few years, Armstrong continued to hone his skills under the tutelage of such legendary performers as Joseph "King" Oliver and Kid Ory. He then signed on with a Mississippi riverboat band, where he learned how to give a piece that special touch by holding back a little on one note or jumping in early on another. He also became a master at improvisation, adding surprising twists and turns to the melody as he played.

By 1922, Armstrong was ready to try his luck up north. Over the next seven years, he played first with King Oliver's Creole Jazz Band at clubs and dance halls around the Midwest and then briefly in New York City as part of the Fletcher Henderson band, with whom he made some memorable blues recordings backing up Bessie Smith and other singers. Awed by what a writer for *Time* described as "his heaven-splitting, jubilant sound," Armstrong's fellow musicians urged him to form his own band, which he did when he returned to Chicago in late 1925. For the next four years, he played in and around that city at a variety of cabarets and Black theaters. Up to that time, jazz had usually been performed in ensemble, with no one musician taking center stage. But Armstrong's skills were such that he and his trumpet could not help but stand out. To make himself even more of a featured performer, he began adding some singing, dancing, and comedy routines to his set. Audiences loved his coarse, raspy voice and "scat" singing, which he has been credited with inventing.

During this same period, Armstrong teamed up with some fellow New Orleans musicians to make a series of records under the name of the "Hot Five" and the "Hot Seven." They were a tremendous hit, at first only with urban Black Americans, but soon White musicians were impressed by the young trumpet player's expertise and creativity. His fame quickly spread throughout the country among serious admirers of jazz, and by the end of the 1920s, Armstrong was regarded as the foremost living jazz musician.

Success followed Armstrong into the early 1930s. Just before the new decade began, he signed up with a White manager, Tommy Rockwell, a tough and unscrupulous man who nevertheless managed to broaden his client's appeal by opening doors for him in the

White-dominated entertainment industry. As head of his own band, Armstrong also toured extensively, made regular radio broadcasts, and began appearing in movies. Soon he was a bona fide "star," known and liked by the general public as well as by those familiar with him as a jazz musician.

By mid-decade, however, his career was in a shambles. Cheated and manipulated—first by Rockwell and then by his successor, an even more dishonest character named Johnny Collins—Armstrong found himself deeply in debt to the U.S. government, members of his band, and his wife, Lillian Hardin, whom he had married in 1924 and then separated from in 1931. In their eagerness to make as much money off their client as possible, his managers also scheduled far too many appearances too close together. As a result, Armstrong began to experience serious and painful problems with his lip, which often split open due to the incorrect pressure he applied when playing his trumpet.

Armstrong hated confrontations and was especially hesitant about standing up to a White man he was conditioned to think of as his "boss." Eventually, however, he fired Collins and hired a new manager, Joe Glaser, who helped the entertainer get out of debt and attain a level of fame enjoyed by no other Black-American performer before him. Focusing more on producing popular music than true jazz, he appeared in major motion pictures and became the first Black American to have his own sponsored radio show, leading jazz purists to criticize him for "going commercial." But after the troubles he had faced during the mid-1930s, he *was* more interested in being popular and making money than in producing great jazz. This attitude alienated some of his old followers, and up-and-coming musicians began to seek out new trumpeters to imitate. By the end of World War II, Armstrong was no longer a force in jazz.

In the late 1940s, however, Armstrong returned to his roots and formed a New Orleans-style Dixieland band that was a huge success. Throughout the rest of the 1940s and well into the 1950s, his star continued to rise as he returned to the recording studio, toured, and appeared regularly on television and in films. He also traveled extensively on behalf of the U.S. Department of State, meeting with wildly enthusiastic receptions wherever he went.

Throughout the 1960s, Armstrong was unquestionably one of the most famous and beloved entertainers in the world. In 1963, he had his all-time greatest hit when his version of "Hello, Dolly," bumped the Beatles' "Can't Buy Me Love" out of first place on the *Billboard* chart. By then, he had made nearly two thousand recordings, some of which dated back to the 1920s and 1930s; his best cuts from that era are considered classics today. As the decade came to a close, however, a variety of heart, liver, and kidney disorders forced Armstrong to slow down. He was so ill during the spring of 1971 that he was not expected to recover, but by June he felt well enough to announce his return to work. On July 6, however, he suffered a heart attack and died at his home in Queens.

Louis Armstrong triumphed over the dismal circumstances of his youth to become a man some consider the greatest jazz musician who ever lived. He also faced bigotry and prejudice at every turn, from unethical managers, promoters, and others who exploited his talent for their own gain to hotel clerks who would not rent rooms to him and his bandmates even if they had just performed in the very same establishment. Through it all, Armstrong remained a happy person who clearly loved what he was doing and managed to pass along a great deal of that enthusiasm to his audiences. "I think I've had a beautiful life," he remarked not long before his death. "I didn't wish for anything I couldn't get, and I got pretty near everything I wanted."

Sources

➤ Books

Armstrong, Louis, *Satchmo: My Life in New Orleans*, Prentice-Hall, 1954. Reprint. Da Capo, 1986.

Collier, James Lincoln, *Louis Armstrong: An American Genius*, Oxford University Press, 1983.

Collier, James Lincoln, *Louis Armstrong: An American Success Story*, Macmillan, 1985.

➤ Periodicals

Ebony, "Why We Must Preserve Our Jazz Heritage," November, 1990, pp. 159–164.

Newsweek, "Good-by, Louis," July 19, 1971, p. 76.

New York Times, July 7, 1971.

New York Times Magazine, "Satchmo Wears His Crown Gaily," January 29, 1950; "Africa Harks to Satch's Horn," November 20, 1960.

New Yorker, January 15, 1966.

Reader's Digest, "Ambassador with a Horn," July, 1957, pp. 93–96; "Unforgettable Satchmo," December, 1971, pp. 81–85 (opening quote).

Saturday Review, "Man Who Revolutionized Jazz," July 4, 1970; "Funeral of Louis Armstrong," July 31, 1971, p. 43.

Time, "Last Trumpet for the First Trumpeter," July 19, 1971, p. 34.

Arthur Ashe

"Success is a journey, not a destination. The doing is often more important than the out-come. Not everyone can be No. 1. What happens to the person who ends up No. 2 or No. 20?"

Arthur Ashe is the first Black American to win top honors in singles competition at the U.S. Open and Wimbledon tennis championships. He was born in Richmond, Virginia, on July 10, 1943.

Address: c/o ProServ, 1101 Wilson Blvd., Arlington, VA 22209.

Around 1950, a scrawny seven-year-old named Arthur Ashe borrowed a tennis racket and began practicing with it on a city court next to his home in Richmond, Virginia. As playground instructor Ronald Charity recalled many years later, the youngster was so skinny that "it was difficult to tell whether Arthur was dragging the racket or the racket was dragging Arthur." But it was not difficult to tell that he had talent. First under the tutelage of Dr. Walter Johnson (mentor of National Women's Champion Althea Gibson) and later University of California at Los Angeles (UCLA) tennis coach J. D. Morgan and tennis star Pancho Gonzalez, Ashe rose to become one of the top-ranked players in the world, a superstar acclaimed as much for his athletic skills as for his impeccable conduct on the court. Indeed, as Steve Flink declared in *World Tennis,* "Arthur Ashe set an example for his peers to follow. Dignified and deliberate, thoughtful and intelligent, Ashe did for tennis what Jack Nicklaus did for golf and Bill Bradley for basketball."

Arthur Robert Ashe, Jr., is the older of two sons of Mattie Cunningham and Arthur Robert Ashe, Sr., who was a caretaker for the Richmond parks and recreation department and owner of a landscaping business. Widowed when Arthur was only six, the elder Ashe refused to turn over his boys to relatives, raising them himself with help from a housekeeper until he remarried several years after his wife's death. His high standards of honor and decency made a profound impression on his namesake, who also credits him with passing along a determination to succeed and an ability to accept defeat as well as victory with ease and graciousness.

Almost as influential in Ashe's life were his coaches, for they were responsible for developing his talents and helping him become what Ron Bookman of *World Tennis* magazine calls "the all-time class act of tennis." Richmond was a segregated community that restricted Black tennis players to their own courts and thus prevented Blacks and Whites from challenging each other. Recognizing Ashe's potential despite his slight build and limited opportunities, Ronald Charity arranged for Ashe to spend the summer in Lynchburg, Virginia, at the home of Dr. Walter Johnson, a Black-American physician who had made a second career out of nurturing young Black tennis players.

Ashe trained in Lynchburg for several summers, working on his strokes and boosting his hitting power until he became unusually strong for a boy his size. From his mentor he also learned how to deal with the pressures of competition and breaking into the overwhelmingly White world of tennis. Adopting a strategy of nonconfrontation, Johnson advised his students to play shots that were bad by only an inch or two as if they were good and to accept their mistakes with a smile, never with any sign of frustration or anger. Ashe took these words to heart, exhibiting an almost "super-human calmness" that often drove his more high-strung opponents to distraction and sometimes created the mistaken impression that he didn't really care about his game.

In 1958, Ashe entered his first major competition, the junior national championships, where he made it to the semifinals. In 1960 and again in 1961, he won the National Junior Indoor singles title, victories that brought him to the attention of Richard Hudlin, a tennis official from St. Louis, Missouri, who became the teenager's next coach. By 1962, Ashe was the fifth-ranked junior player in the country, and after graduating from high school, he went off to UCLA on a tennis scholarship. There he continued to improve his game with the help of his longtime idol, tennis great Pancho Gonzalez, and UCLA coach J. D. Morgan.

Throughout the rest of the 1960s, Ashe racked up an impressive series of accomplishments and built up a loyal following of fans. In 1963, he became the first Black American to be named to America's Davis Cup team and eventually was recognized as one of its best singles players, losing only two matches in his six years on the roster. In 1965, he was the national intercollegiate singles champion and by the end of the year took over second place in the U.S. rankings. Following his graduation from UCLA in 1966 (he received a B.S. in business administration), Ashe began a stint in the United States Army, working in the data-processing office at West Point. He was allowed to continue playing tennis whenever possible, however, and in 1968 he reached the peak of the amateur ranks with a series of thirty straight singles victories, including the U.S. Amateur Championship (the first American player to win the title since 1955) and the U.S. Open Championship in Forest Hills, New York, where he became the first Black American to win top honors. That same year, he also reached the semifinals in the prestigious All-England Open at Wimbledon and led the U.S. team to victory in the Davis Cup, a performance he repeated the following year. When his army service ended in 1969, Ashe turned professional and began devoting himself full time to tennis.

Ashe's winning ways continued into the next decade. In 1970, he triumphed at the singles competition in the Australian Open and paired with Stan Smith to earn the doubles title in the U.S. Indoor match. He won the French Open doubles in 1972 and the World Championship Tennis singles competition in 1975. But by far the greatest achievement of his career came later that year at Wimbledon, when Ashe made history by defeating top-ranked Jimmy Connors for the men's singles title, making him the first Black American to claim that honor. According to Bookman, it was "a victory where Arthur's version of physical chess defused Jimmy's crashing and bashing." The outcome was especially meaningful to the thirty-two-year-old Ashe, who by then was considered to be in the autumn of his career and no longer capable of pulling off such an upset. Looking back on that moment, he says that "Wimbledon provided a very satisfying capstone to my career."

Ashe closed the 1970s with several more victories, including one at the Australian Open doubles in 1977. As he had in 1972, he also captained the U.S. Davis Cup team in 1976 and 1978. Then heel surgery and an eye infection took their toll, and the former No. 1 player saw his ranking plummet to No. 257. He fought back, however, zooming to the No. 7 position and giving John McEnroe some stiff competition at the Grand Prix Masters final in early 1979.

Then, during the night of July 30, 1979, and again throughout the next day, Ashe experienced several bouts of severe chest pain, which he attributed to indigestion. When the pain did not subside, a doctor playing at the club where Ashe was conducting a tennis clinic urged him to check into a hospital immediately. There the thirty-six-year-old athlete discovered to his astonishment that he had suffered a heart attack. Although he felt much better after a brief hospitalization, he continued to suffer chest pain whenever he tried to exert himself. Additional tests revealed that his arteries were seriously blocked, and in December, 1979, he underwent quadruple bypass surgery. Hoping to ease his way back into tennis, he worked to regain his strength by riding an exercise bicycle and lifting weights. But when the pain returned as he went for a run in the spring of 1980, Ashe knew his days of playing competitive tennis were over.

Ashe then concentrated his efforts behind the scenes and as what *World Tennis* calls "the game's ambassador-at-large." Character-ized by Bookman as "an articulate voice with a strong reputation for a professional approach to problems and obligations," he co-found-ed the Association of Tennis Professionals in 1972 and served as its president from 1974 until 1979. He also acted as co-chairman of the United States Tennis Association's player development committee and has been especially concerned with promoting the sport among inner-city youths. Despite being officially "retired" from the game, he captained the U.S. Davis Cup team from 1981–85 and even made a series of instructional videodiscs.

In addition, Ashe has tackled a variety of non-tennis jobs: sports commentator, host of his own syndicated television show, newspaper and magazine columnist, recruiter of minority applicants for industry, public relations worker, and spokesman for various equipment and clothing manufacturers. In 1981, the American Heart Association drafted him to serve as national campaïgn chairman; more recently, he has become active on behalf of other charities, particularly the Children's Defense Fund. An outspoken foe of apartheid, he was instrumental in getting South Africa banned from Davis Cup competition. He is also the author of more than a half-dozen books, including *A Hard Road to Glory*, a history of the Black athlete in America.

On April 7, 1992, however, Ashe made a startling announcement: he was infected with the AIDS virus, apparently as a result of a blood transfusion he had received during a second heart bypass operation in 1983. In order to protect his family, Ashe revealed his illness to only a few people until a *USA Today* reporter contacted him to say that the paper had received a tip about his health and wanted a statement for an upcoming story.

At an emotional press conference the next day, Ashe confirmed the AIDS rumors and quietly but firmly expressed anger at the invasion of his privacy. He has since made it clear that he intends to keep busy with his current projects. Only when he feels the time is right will he become actively involved in the fight against AIDS, probably focusing his efforts on ways to reduce public hysteria surrounding the disease. "There's no question that some of the coping and surviving mechanisms I've used all my life to deal with racism, I'll call on again to deal with medical discrimination," Ashe told *Sports Illustrated* reporter Sally Jenkins. "You make sure that your facts are right and that you haven't fallen short personally. Armed with that, you take your stand."

Sources

➤ Books

Ashe, Arthur, and Neil Amdur, *Off the Court*, New American Library, 1981.

Holloway, Charles M., *Profiles in Achievement*, College Board, 1987.

➤ Periodicals

Harper's Bazaar, February, 1990, pp. 146–147.

Newsweek, "Arthur Ashe's Secret," April 20, 1992, pp. 62–63.

People, "For Recovering Arthur Ashe, His Heart Attack May Not Be a Net Loss," September 17, 1979, pp. 86–89; "An Athlete Nearly Dying Young: A Tennis Champ Tells His History," September 21, 1981, pp. 113–114.

Senior Scholastic, "Arthur Ashe: Defeat Doesn't Scare Him," September 22, 1977, p. 7.

Sports Illustrated, "Service, But First a Smile," August 29, 1966, pp. 47–50; "It Couldn't Be a Heart Attack—But It Was," September 3, 1979, pp. 24–25, "Another Battle Joined," April 20, 1992, pp. 24–25.

Time, "Fair Game?," April 20, 1992, pp. 74–75.

USA Today, April, 9, 1992.

World Tennis, "Arthur Ashe: Still Classy After All These Years," August, 1980, pp. 26–30; "A Tale of Two Champions," May, 1981, pp. 74–78; "Shifting Gears," September, 1981, pp. 116–119 (opening quote); "Ashe Goes Ivy," May, 1983, pp. 54–55; "Wimbledon '75: The Art of Ashe," July, 1985, pp. 116–119; "Twelve Who Mattered," June, 1987, p. 46.

Joan Baez

"**M**y concern has always been for the people who are victimized, unable to speak for themselves and who need outside help."

Born on January 9, 1941, in Staten Island, New York, Joan Baez is a folk singer and human rights activist.

Address: c/o Diamonds and Rust Productions, P.O. Box 1026, Menlo Park, CA 94026.

Virtually ever since she burst upon the national folk music scene more than thirty years ago, Joan Baez has made it her goal to educate as well as entertain her audiences. She has lent her voice to a wide variety of causes, from the antiwar movement of the 1960s to the fight against AIDS in the 1990s. In between, she has spoken out on the subject of migrant workers, political repression in Chile and Argentina, Southeast Asian refugees, Poland's Solidarity organization, women's rights, nuclear power, and the death penalty, most of the time incurring the wrath of conservatives but occasionally angering those on the left as well. Through it all, she has remained strongly committed to the principles of nonviolence and an orientation she describes as "pro-human."

Joan Chandos Baez is the second of three daughters of Joan Bridge and Alberto Vinicio Baez, a former physicist, university professor, and consultant to UNESCO. Both of the elder Baezes began attending Quaker services when their children were young, and the pacifist teachings of that faith made a strong impression on Joan and her sisters. Also influential was Alberto Baez's decision in the late 1940s to refuse the potentially lucrative option of working in the defense industry and pursue an academic career instead.

Growing up mostly in California, Baez felt isolated and "different" as a result of her mixed Scottish and Mexican heritage. During junior high school, she decided to use music as a way to gain acceptance, concentrating first on developing her singing voice. She also took up the ukelele and later the guitar, performing at high school dances and even entertaining at gatherings of her parents' friends.

In 1958, shortly after graduating from high school, Baez moved with her family to Boston and enrolled in the School of Fine Arts at Boston University. One evening, her father took her to a Harvard Square coffee house where amateur musicians were encouraged to display their talents. "I was lost right on the first visit," Baez later recalled. "I was ready to join up and pick up the guitar." Bored with school, she dropped out and began spending all of her time perfecting her singing and playing technique, expanding her repertoire to include a wide variety of American and English folk songs, ballads, spirituals, and blues, and performing in various coffee houses in the Boston area, where her clear soprano voice and simple style quickly made her a local favorite.

During the summer of 1959, Baez played a two-week engagement at a Chicago nightclub that specialized in folk music. There she met folk singer Bob Gibson, who invited her to participate in the first Newport (Rhode Island) Folk Festival, to be held that August. Although her name did not even appear on the program, Baez electrified the audience of some thirteen thousand people when she sang several spirituals with Gibson. Her appearance led to offers of recording contracts and concert tours, but Baez opted to return to Boston and the coffeehouse scene. It was not until after another triumphant performance at the 1960 Newport Folk Festival that she felt ready to sign with a record company.

The 1961 debut of her first album, *Joan Baez,* brought the twenty-year-old singer immediate nationwide recognition. Following a successful tour that took her to college campuses and concert halls, Baez turned down numerous opportunities to appear on television and in movies and perform in nightclubs. Instead, she worked out a schedule that put her on tour for only about two months of the year; the rest of the time she wanted to be free to prepare material for an album or to support the political and social causes that were increasingly demanding her attention.

Baez's activism had first emerged when she was a teenager. Already a committed pacifist in the ninth grade, she was one of the few students in her school who openly expressed her fear of and opposition to armaments. In high school she refused to participate in an air-raid drill because she found it "ludicrous" to pretend that anyone could survive an atomic blast. But it was at a Quaker youth conference she attended during her junior year of high school that Baez first felt she was "going somewhere" with her pacifism. Listening to the orations of a young Black-American preacher from Alabama named Martin Luther King, Jr., she was "galvanized by the discussions, inspired in a way I had never been before. . . . King [gave] a shape and a name to my passionate but ill-articulated beliefs."

By the early 1960s, Baez had fused political action with her music; from that time on, her professional singing career took a back seat to the more compelling demands of promoting nonviolence to achieve political and social justice. Besides giving many free performances on behalf of various charities, UNESCO, and the civil rights movement, she became involved in the early student uprisings. Later in the 1960s, Baez's attention shifted to the Vietnam War. By now known as the "Queen of the Folksingers," she sang and demonstrated at numerous antiwar rallies. Her activism put her at odds with much of the American public; conservatives even went so far as to accuse her of being a Soviet agent. Her popularity among folk music fans was largely unaffected, however, and she continued to release an occasional album throughout those turbulent years and performed at the legendary Woodstock Festival in 1969.

Baez continued her antiwar activities into the 1970s, drawing the ire of still more people when she was part of a delegation that visited the North Vietnamese capital of Hanoi during the American bombing raids of December, 1972. As the war wound down, she became involved in other causes, including promoting Amnesty International and singing at rallies held to protest human rights abuses in Central and South America. But it was a stand she took in 1979 that once again put her in the limelight—this time on behalf of a cause that alienated many of her old allies and left her "awash in mainstream support," as one reporter put it.

Early that year, two Vietnamese refugees visited Baez and described in graphic detail how people who opposed the new regime were being tortured and imprisoned. Investigating further, she learned that such human rights violations were widespread and that thousands had fled the country, often making their escape in rickety, overcrowded boats. Horrified at these reports, Baez decided to tackle the issue head-on. In May, 1979, under the auspices of a group she founded and headed called Humanitas/International Human Rights Committee, she wrote an open letter to the Vietnamese government. Published in five major U.S. newspapers, the letter accused the regime of brutally disregarding human rights and asked for an end to the imprisonment and torture.

Her stand on this issue angered many of her former antiwar allies, some of whom felt it was inappropriate to criticize *any* socialist government, even one that was victimizing its own citizens. "People were not exactly eager to donate to this," she admitted to a reporter for *People* magazine. "Some felt they didn't have a right to speak out against Vietnam. Others just didn't want to think about it. But I am willing to risk my reputation with the American peace community because I am a friend of the Vietnamese people. I think I am being true to the same people I was being true to all those years in the '60s." Despite continuing harsh words from the left as she broadened her efforts to support those fleeing communist repression in Cambodia and Laos, Baez refused to back off. "If what you're saying is the truth," she explained, "you're not betraying anyone."

Because her music has so often taken a back seat to her activism and her worldwide travels, Baez has seen her singing career falter a bit in recent years. Her biggest hit was the 1972 release, "The Night They Drove Old Dixie Down," and her last major tour was with her old friend Bob Dylan in the mid-1970s. She has, of course, continued to record from time to time and do numerous benefit performances; in 1985, for example, she was selected to open the Live Aid concert with her rendition of "We Are the World." But as much as she would enjoy a revival of her earlier popularity, she is not about to devote much energy to making it happen. "It'll always be this way," Baez remarked. "I'm not interested in talking about music. If there's a choice between people picking and singing in one room and a group of mothers of disappeared Argentinians in another room, I'm gonna go and talk to the mothers."

Sources

➤ **Books**

Baez, Joan, *Daybreak*, Dial, 1968.

Baez, Joan, *And a Voice to Sing With*, Summit Books, 1987.

➤ **Periodicals**

Maclean's, "Baez Gives Voice to Cambodia's Horrors," November 26, 1979, pp. 6–8.

New York Times Book Review, "Life on Struggle Mountain," June 21, 1987, p. 30.

People, "Joan Baez Travels to Moscow and Sings to the Sakharovs That They Shall Overcome Too," July 24, 1978, p. 30; "All Her Trials Aren't Over Yet: Joan Baez Takes a New, Dark View of Vietnam and Gets the Cold Shoulder," June 18, 1979, pp. 40–41 (opening quote); "A Brave Antiwarrior Raises Her Voice for the Boat People—and Loses Some Old Allies," December 24, 1979, pp. 62–63.

Progressive, "A Passionate Survivor," February, 1983, pp. 52–53.

Rolling Stone, "Joan Baez: Old Folk at Home," April 14, 1983, pp. 17–20; November 5-December 10, 1987.

Time, November 23, 1962.

U.S. News and World Report, "Now the Times They Are a-Changin'," June 29, 1987, p. 60.

Robert D. Ballard

"I am an explorer who's a geologist. I'm an explorer who loves the ocean. And I'm an explorer who loves technology. To be an explorer I had to be a scientist. I love science. I love the pursuit of anything, and the pursuit of truth is very noble."

An undersea explorer and marine scientist, Robert D. Ballard led the expedition that located the wreckage of the steamship *Titanic*. He was born on June 30, 1942, in Wichita, Kansas.

Address: Woods Hole Oceanographic Institution, Woods Hole, MA 02543.

Around 1 A.M. on September 1, 1985, Robert D. Ballard hurried to the command center aboard the U.S. Navy research ship *Knorr*, summoned there by fellow scientists who had come across something they wanted him to check out. Staring at one of the many video screens displaying pictures of the ocean below, he saw before him what he and the others on board had hoped to find: the remains of the *Titanic*, the ill-fated steamship that struck an iceberg and sank in the North Atlantic on April 15, 1912, carrying more than fifteen hundred people to their deaths. It was the culmination of years of research in robotics and Ballard's own near-obsession with what is no doubt the most famous shipwreck in history. The discovery captured worldwide attention and made the highly respected marine geologist a celebrity.

Born in Kansas but raised in California, Robert Duane Ballard is the son of Harriet Nell May and Chester Patrick Ballard, an aerospace engineer. He became especially drawn to the sea as a teenager, when he spent hours near his San Diego home walking along the beach, swimming, scuba diving, and surfing, fascinated by what he found washed up on shore and comforted by the gentle, rhythmic lapping of the waves.

In the late 1960s, after earning a B.S. in both chemistry and geology at the University of California at Santa Barbara and pursuing postgraduate study at the University of Hawaii and the University of Southern California, Ballard headed east. There he served in the U.S. Navy's Office of Naval Research as liaison officer with the Woods Hole Oceanographic Institution, a nonprofit marine research facility headquartered on Cape Cod. After his naval assignment ended in 1969, he decided to remain at Woods Hole and pursue his research in marine geology and ocean engineering, particularly the development of deep-sea submersible vessels.

During the 1970s, Ballard made a name for himself with several underwater discoveries that rank among the most significant of the century. To complete his Ph.D. from the University of Rhode Island, he supplied geological evidence that helped prove the then-revolutionary theory of plate tectonics, which maintained that segments of the earth's outer crust are in constant motion. Next, Ballard investigated the source of mysterious variations in sea-floor water temperatures noted off the coast of Ecuador and discovered mineral-laden spouts of water known as hydrothermal vents erupting from cracks in the earth's crust. His stunning photographs of the vents and other geyser-like phenomena he called "black smokers" revealed large colonies of bizarre, never-before-seen underwater creatures feeding on the sulphur and other minerals in the water. Ballard's findings amazed marine biologists, who did not think anything could live in those sunless depths, and sparked new debates about the origin of life.

During the early 1980s Ballard switched from exploration to engineering. Committed to the idea that unmanned exploration of the ocean is less expensive and more productive than manned missions, he decided to expand on the rather primitive technology of the equipment he had designed for his early research trips. Instead of the *Alvin*, a three-man submarine with a remote-controlled mechanical arm, and the *Angus*, a survey sled on which he had mounted three 35mm cameras, Ballard envisioned a deep-sea submersible vessel loaded with technologically advanced robotic gear, which would eliminate the need for human passengers. He refers to this as "telepresence, of being able to project your spirit to the bottom, your eyes, your mind, and being able to leave your body behind."

Funded primarily by the U.S. Navy and the National Science Foundation, Ballard formed the Deep Submergence Laboratory at Woods Hole in 1981 and within a few years designed what he calls the *Argo-Jason* system. Unlike the *Angus* and its still cameras, the *Argo* boasts three video cameras that are so sensitive they can see in almost total darkness. Images from the *Argo* are immediately visible on the main ship's video screens, which scientists monitor around the clock. And unlike its predecessor, the *Argo* has an assistant— *Jason*, a smaller, self-propelled robot "eye" with mechanical arms that can be sent out from the *Argo* whenever it comes across something of special interest.

Although Ballard was convinced his system would revolutionize underwater exploration, others, including some of his colleagues at Woods Hole, were not ready to give up on manned missions. Realizing he needed to test the *Argo* and *Jason* in order to prove his critics wrong, he decided to do so in rather dramatic fashion. "The *Titanic* was in the back of my mind for a long time," Ballard explained to Edward Oxford of *American History Illustrated*. "My idea was to pursue her remains in the spirit of exploration. A kind of coming together of science and history."

Teaming up with a group of French scientists who were eager to test a new sonar search vehicle they had invented, Ballard put together Operation *Titanic* by the summer of 1985. The U.S. Navy furnished the research ship *Knorr* as well as detailed maps of the sea floor where the *Titanic* was believed to have come to rest. The French started their sonar search in late June; by early August, they had scanned about 80 percent of the target site and had found nothing. The *Knorr* arrived later in the month, and Ballard continued the search alone with the *Angus* and the *Argo* when the French research ship had to head back home. Less than a week later, on September 1, 1985, the *Argo*'s cameras captured the image of one of the *Titanic*'s distinctive boilers, which Ballard instantly recognized from his extensive research on the ship. After celebrating their good fortune—a "fluke," as the leader of the expedition put it—those aboard the *Knorr* paused for a moment of silence in memory of those who had gone down with the luxury liner.

Over the next eight days, the cameras of the *Angus* and the *Argo* took more than twenty thousand still and videotape pictures of the wreck, determining its exact position on the ocean floor and the extent of the damage that had been done to the ship. Also revealed in vivid color were poignant images of hundreds of different artifacts, among them bottles of wine, china plates, a silver serving tray, and, perhaps most moving of all, the empty lifeboat cranes. "To me that was the symbolism of the *Titanic*," Ballard later told an interviewer for *Omni* magazine. "They were what all the people who died saw as they were looking for a lifeboat. . . . And there it was in the picture. We came up over the top of that with *Argo,* saw the picture, and—*Bang!*—it was like a sock to my stomach." All in all, he told Frederic Golden of *Discover* magazine, "these were terribly moving scenes."

The members of Operation *Titanic* received a hero's welcome upon their return to Woods Hole on September 9. In a speech to the crowd assembled to greet them, Ballard recounted their experience in almost poetic terms. And as he had done from the moment the discovery was announced to the world, he came out firmly against any attempts to salvage the ship and expressed his hope that it would be declared an international maritime memorial. Reflecting on the expedition some months later, Ballard told Oxford: "To me, the finding of the *Titanic* has two meanings. It is epilogue—an ending to the unfinished maiden voyage. But it is also prologue—the beginning of a new era in exploration. The *Titanic* is the first pyramid to be found in the deep sea. There are thousands of others, waiting to tell their tales."

In July, 1986, Ballard visited the *Titanic* once again, this time going "one on one" with the wreckage in the trusty old *Alvin*. He also took along *Jason Jr.*, a "swimming eyeball" that took them inside the ship where the *Alvin* could not maneuver. There they came across still more artifacts, including the porcelain head of a child's doll and a man's shoe. Despite the wealth of souvenirs within easy reach, Ballard refused to bring back anything. Instead, he left behind two memorials—one from the Explorers Club and another from the Titanic Historical Society.

In June, 1989, Ballard and the *Argo* discovered another famous wreck, that of the *Bismarck,* the World War II German battleship. Located six hundred miles off the French coast, about fifteen thousand feet below the surface, it is "in an excellent state of preservation," according to the scientist. But he has no plans to salvage it, maintaining that, like the *Titanic,* it should remain undisturbed as a memorial to the more than two thousand men who went down with it.

Ballard uses the celebrity status his adventures have brought him to lobby extensively for additional development and use of his *Argo-Jason* system, turning to lectures, television appearances, magazine articles, and books to generate more interest in deep-sea exploration and research. He has also established the Jason Foundation for Education and its Jason Project, a program that hopes to foster students' interest in science by enabling them to work side-by-side with scientists and all kinds of underwater exploration equipment (including *Jason*) at research sites around the world.

Unusually adept at conveying the excitement and importance of his work to a lay audience—sort of a "Carl Sagan with gills," as one colleague describes him—Ballard emphasizes that the technology is not limited to the sea. "Machines would climb the mountains, or ride the rocket at blast-off," he told Oxford. Ballard expanded on this idea in his conversation with Golden, noting how a robot could one day send back images of Mars or Jupiter. "How glorious it would be to see the surface of those distant worlds on your television screen," he enthused. "With telepresence, you won't need drugs, or *Star Wars,* or Spielberg to get your jolts. You'll get them out of reality."

Sources

► **Books**

Ballard, Robert D., *Discovery of the Titanic: Exploring the Greatest of All Lost Ships,* Warner Books, 1989.

Ballard, Robert D., *Exploring Our Living Planet,* National Geographic Society, 1983.

► **Periodicals**

American History Illustrated, "Titanic: First Pyramid in the Sea," April, 1986, pp. 33–37.

Discover, "A Man with Titanic Vision," January, 1987, pp. 50–62.

Maclean's, "Exploring History," May 14, 1990, p. 60.

National Geographic, "The *Bismarck* Found," November, 1989.

New York Times, "Hulk of Titanic Reported Intact," September 4, 1985, p. A15; "Scientist Plans to Study Titanic by Submarine," September 5, 1985, p. A15; "Scientist Describes Harrowing Moment in Search for Titanic," September 7, 1985; "Airhorns Blare as Titanic Researchers Sail In," September 10, 1985; "Robert Ballard: Explorer of the Sea," September 10, 1985, p. C3; "Finder of Titanic Aims to Capitalize," September 11, 1985, p. D26; "Debris Shows Titanic Lost Her Entire Stern End," September 12, 1985, p. B11.

Omni, July, 1986 (opening quote).

Time, "A Marker on a Chilly Grave," June 26, 1989, p. 46.

U.S. News and World Report, "Robert Ballard: Undersea Explorer Who Found *Titanic,*" September 23, 1985, p. 9.

Christiaan Barnard

*"T*he realization that there was a man lying in front of me without a heart but still alive was, I think, the most awe-inspiring moment of all."*

Born on November 8, 1922, in Beaufort West, South Africa, Christiaan Barnard was the first surgeon to perform a success-ful human heart transplant.

Address: P.O. Box 988, 8000 Cape Town, Republic of South Africa.

As the 1960s drew to a close, doctors at more than twenty medical centers throughout the world stood ready to make history by performing the first human heart transplant, offering hope to those whose failing hearts had otherwise condemned them to death. At Groote Schuur Hospital in Cape Town, South Africa, Dr. Christiaan Barnard was among those surgeons awaiting the simultaneous availability of a compatible donor and patient. When the moment arrived in December, 1967, he and his team removed the heart of a young accident victim and placed it in the chest of a fifty-four-year-old man. Minutes later, the heart began beating once again, and within hours, news had spread worldwide of one of the century's most remarkable medical milestones.

Christiaan Neethling Barnard is the third of four sons born to Maria Elizabeth de Swart and Adam Hendrik Barnard, a Dutch Reformed clergyman who ministered to the mixed-race population of a small South African town. Because Reverend Barnard was paid only about a third of what his counterpart in the same town earned as pastor of an all-white church, the family was quite poor. But both parents—especially Mrs. Barnard—instilled their children with a drive to succeed and the desire to attend college. At an early age, Christiaan decided to become a doctor, and following his graduation from high school, he enrolled in the University of Cape Town Medical School. (He financed his education with a scholarship and a small allowance from his parents.) After receiving his degree in 1953, he worked briefly as a general practitioner, then accepted a position as a research fellow in surgery at the University of Cape Town Medical School, where he specialized in gastrointestinal defects and diseases.

In 1955, Barnard was offered the chance to study in the United States at the University of Minnesota Medical School under the direction of noted surgeon Dr. Owen Wangensteen. At first, Barnard continued the research he had begun in South Africa on congenital intestinal atresia, an intestinal abnormality occurring in newborns. Soon, however, he became fascinated by heart surgery, which just then was emerging as a major surgical specialty. He observed and occasionally participated in several operations not only at the University of Minnesota, one of the leading centers of such work, but also at the Mayo Clinic and in Houston under the tutelage of pioneering heart surgeons Michael DeBakey and Denton Cooley.

At Minnesota, Barnard managed to cram into three years the work and experience most other students took four or five years to obtain. He returned to the University of Cape Town Medical School in 1958 with a master's degree for his thesis on making and testing an artificial heart valve and a doctorate for his thesis on the causes of intestinal atresia. Thanks to Dr. Wangensteen, Barnard also returned with a heart-lung machine—the only one in all of Africa—so that he could continue to do advanced heart surgery. He set up the prized equipment at nearby Groote Schuur Hospital, an affiliate of the medical school.

As the new director of surgical research at Groote Schuur, Barnard focused his attention on performing various kinds of open-heart operations, especially those that involved replacing damaged heart valves with artificial ones. In doing so, he and his team of surgeons became skilled at running the heart-lung machine and providing effective post-operative care to heart patients. Barnard also experimented with transplantation, successfully duplicating Soviet efforts of the late 1950s to attach a second head onto a dog. But by the late 1960s, he felt ready to tackle another kind of transplant: that of a human heart. The only obstacle to performing such ground-breaking surgery was the simultaneous availability of a compatible donor and patient.

Barnard found his patient in Louis Washkansky, a fifty-four-year-old grocer who had been admitted to Groote Schuur in October, 1967, suffering from progressive heart failure complicated by diabetes and an enlarged liver. By November, doctors estimated Washkansky had only weeks to live, and Barnard approached him to explain what he wanted to try. Without hesitation, Washkansky agreed to undergo the procedure, and Barnard and his thirty-member surgical team went on stand-by status to await a donor. Finally, on the evening of December 2, the doctor received a call from the emergency room at Groote Schuur. Twenty-five-year-old accident victim, Denise Darvall, had been brought in with head injuries so severe she would not survive through the night. Barnard spoke to her father and received permission from him to remove her heart upon death. Once that moment came, the transplant team immediately went to work.

Early in the morning of December 3, while one group of surgeons and nurses attended to Darvall and kept blood flowing through her heart with a heart-lung machine, a second group opened Washkansky's chest and prepared to connect him to a heart-lung machine to maintain blood circulation throughout the rest of his body. Barnard then removed Darvall's heart, hooked it up to yet another heart-lung machine, removed Washkansky's diseased heart, and then began the painstaking task of stitching the donor heart into place. Almost four hours later, Barnard was ready to try to make Darvall's heart beat in Washkansky's chest. A single jolt of electric current was all it took; within fifteen minutes, Washkansky's heart-lung machine was turned off, and his new heart completely took over the job of circulating his blood.

Washkansky recovered quickly from the surgery and was soon talking, eating solid food, and waving at the horde of journalists and photographers camped outside the hospital. Meanwhile, Barnard and his assistants worked to prevent his body from rejecting the heart. They administered massive doses of azathioprine and hydrocortisone plus radiation in the form of gamma rays. Although the treatment did indeed prevent Washkansky's body from mounting a defense against the foreign organ, it also left him open to all kinds of infection. Despite the best efforts of Barnard and his colleagues, Washkansky's condition slowly began to deteriorate. He died of pneumonia on December 21, just eighteen days after his surgery.

By this time, however, Barnard had already been hailed worldwide for his bold attempt to give a dying patient a second chance at life. Though saddened and discouraged by Washkansky's death, Barnard made up his mind to try again when an autopsy revealed no sign that the heart itself had failed. On January 2, 1968, he operated on Philip Blaiberg, a fifty-eight-year-old retired dentist, and gave him the heart of a twenty-four-year-old man who had succumbed to a stroke. While the Washkansky case had sparked international debate on ethical issues involving the definition of death, this one raised eyebrows among South Africans because Blaiberg was white and the donor was of mixed-race ancestry. Barnard brushed aside the criticism and concentrated instead on eliminating post-operative complications of the kind that had killed Washkansky. By cutting back on the amount of anti-rejection drugs they administered and isolating their patient in a germ-free environment, he and his staff were able prevent any life-threatening infections from taking hold. Blaiberg was released from the hospital about eleven weeks after his surgery and lived for some eighteen months with his new heart.

Barnard continued to perform heart surgery until 1983, when

rheumatoid arthritis—first diagnosed while he was at the University of Minnesota—crippled his hands to the point that he could no longer operate; by his own count, he had done about 160 transplants and countless "ordinary" open-heart surgeries. During the 1970s, he also experimented with relatively untried procedures such as heart-lung transplants and the so-called "piggyback" technique in which a second heart (either a human one or that of a baboon or a chimpanzee) is grafted into a patient to assist a damaged heart until it can heal itself or to buy time until a suitable human donor can be found for a complete transplant.

At every turn, Barnard weathered criticism from colleagues in the medical community who looked at the initially poor success rate of heart transplants (due to rejection) and questioned their effectiveness as well as that of the more complicated operations he was performing. Many found transplantation an unacceptable form of treatment and refused to refer patients to Barnard, who argued that it still held out the only hope to many victims of heart disease. As he once observed in a *Saturday Evening Post* article, "If a man is standing there with a noose around his neck, he will do anything for a second chance."

Since giving up surgery, Barnard has kept busy with other health-related issues, including euthanasia and problems of malnutrition and tuberculosis in his native South Africa. He travels throughout the world as a guest speaker, and he has written several novels based on the medical world as well as scientific works on medical topics. He also serves as a research coordinator for a company in Switzerland that manufactures anti-aging cosmetics, a role that has left him open to criticism from those who feel his endorsement of such products demeans his former profession. But without a doubt he remains best known as the surgeon who skyrocketed to fame as the first to perform a successful human heart transplant and thus provide a measure of hope to those who would otherwise certainly die.

Barnard himself now downplays his "first," pointing out that luck and circumstances had as much to do with it as surgical skill—he found a donor at just the right moment and, unlike doctors in the United States (where the world's second heart transplant was performed just three days after Louis Washkansky's operation), he worked in a country relatively free of regulations and the threat of lawsuits. "I never tried to think of myself as the greatest surgeon," he remarked to Catherine Gilfether in a Newhouse News Service report published in the *Grand Rapids Press.* "I was not a bright man, but I had tremendous dedication. I was not scared. No, I was not courageous either. I was just very adequately prepared and the chances of success were very, very big."

Sources

➤ **Books**

Barnard, Christiaan, and Curtis Bill Pepper, *Christiaan Barnard: One Life,* Macmillan, 1969.

➤ **Periodicals**

Grand Rapids Press, "Heart Transplant Pioneer Recalls His 'Moment of Truth,'" February 17, 1991, p. F11 (opening quote).

Health, "A Conversation with Christiaan Barnard," February, 1982, p. 6.

Maclean's, "Interview with Dr. Christiaan Barnard," January 9, 1978, pp. 4–9.

People, "His Hands Stiffened by Arthritis, Christiaan Barnard Explores a Second Career in Television," April 17, 1978, pp. 38–40; "Christiaan Barnard Endorses Cosmetics and the Famous Heart Surgeon Gets Creamed," April 14, 1986, pp. 101–106.

Saturday Evening Post, "Christiaan Barnard: South Africa's Premier Surgeon," March, 1977, pp. 62–64.

Time, "The Ultimate Operation," December 15, 1967, pp. 64–72; "Barnard's Bullet," August 9, 1971, p. 37.

Clara Barton

"I *may be compelled to face danger, but never* fear *it."*

Clara Barton's experiences as a battlefield nurse during the Civil War later inspired her to establish the American Red Cross. She was born on December 25, 1821, in North Oxford, Massachusetts, and died on April 12, 1912, in Glen Echo, Maryland.

For the last forty years or so of her life, Clara Barton was a name known to all—a name that was "associated in the public mind with goodness and mercy," as a writer for the *New York Times* observed in an editorial written at the time of her death. It was her tireless devotion to the wounded on some of the bloodiest battlefields of the Civil War that first earned Barton the enduring affection and gratitude of her fellow citizens. But it was her pioneering work among the victims of natural disaster that won her international acclaim as the founder of the American Red Cross.

Clarissa Harlowe Barton was born into a middle-class Massachusetts family on Christmas Day of 1821. Her father, Stephen Barton, was a successful farmer and businessman, a representative to the state legislature, and a noted humanitarian who doted on the youngest of his five children and left an indelible impression on her character. Clara's mother, Sarah (Sally) Stone, was distant and somewhat eccentric, with an iron will and a fiery temper.

Barton grew up eager to be of service to others. She opted for teaching, one of the few professions open to women in her day. Popular and effective with her students, she taught for more than a dozen years, first in her hometown and then in Bordentown, New Jersey. There she clashed with a principal who was jealous of her success and took every opportunity to make her life miserable. In early 1854, on the verge of a nervous breakdown, she quit her job and moved to Washington, D.C. With the help of a relative who had served in Congress, Barton found work copying secret papers for the U.S. Patent Office, thus becoming the first woman clerk in the federal government. In 1857, however, she was forced to resign from her position when her strong anti-slavery stance put her at odds with the new pro-slavery president, James Buchanan. Returning to Massachusetts, Barton continued to do copy work for the patent office by mail. She was called back to her old job in Washington following Abraham Lincoln's election in 1860.

When the Civil War broke out in April, 1861, Barton was shocked to discover that virtually no preparations had been made to care for the wounded, many of whom bled to death, starved, or developed infections and gangrene before they could be transported to hospitals. At first, Barton opened up her own apartment to as many of them as she could and cared for them herself. She then sought permission to go directly into the field, a request that met with overwhelming resistance from those who felt women lacked courage and stamina and would just "get in the way." She persisted, however, and in mid-1862 at last received official permission to serve as a battlefield nurse.

The next three years saw Clara Barton destroy forever the notion that female nurses had no business on the front lines. Working primarily in Virginia and Maryland, she fed, clothed, and bandaged "her boys" with supplies she gathered and organized into wagon trains that followed troops of the Union Army into battle. This earned her the nickname "Angel of the Battlefield" for her compassion and unflinching bravery. "I saw many things that I did not wish to see and I pray God I may never see again," Barton later wrote of the especially gruesome aftermath of the Battle of Antietam. Yet she never hesitated to go where she was needed, declaring that "while our soldiers can stand and *fight*, I can stand and feed and nurse them." They in turn adored her, and even those she met who never benefitted directly from her care granted her their respect and protection.

As the war drew to a close, Barton's attention shifted to the problem of tracking down missing men. Soliciting help from veterans through newspaper ads, she managed to collect information on more than twenty-two thousand soldiers. When she learned of the infamous Andersonville prison camp in Georgia, where thirteen thousand Union prisoners died and were buried in unmarked graves, she led the effort to have the camp turned into a national cemetery. Barton supervised all the work herself, seeing to it that the bodies were reinterred in deeper graves and that each received a marker.

To raise money for her projects, Barton traveled extensively from 1866 to 1868, lecturing about her life and work during the war. By the end of 1868, emotional and physical strain again left her close to a nervous breakdown. On the advice of her doctor, Barton agreed to go abroad and take a long rest. Her inactivity was rather short-lived, however; while visiting Switzerland in late 1869, she met Dr. Louis Appia, a physician who asked for her help in convincing the U.S. government to ratify the Treaty of Geneva, which as one of its many provisions called for the creation of an international relief organization known as the Red Cross. Barton promised to do whatever she could as soon as she felt ready to work again.

Within just a few months, her rest came to an end when she agreed to help organize Red Cross relief efforts in response to the Franco-Prussian War. She was greatly impressed by what she witnessed at the aid stations on the front lines. After the war ended,

Barton stayed to oversee rebuilding efforts. Wherever she went, she stressed the importance of people helping themselves and not relying strictly on handouts, a policy she believed would restore their dignity as well as their material comfort. This later became one of the guiding principles of the American Red Cross.

In 1873, Barton came down with rheumatic fever and returned to the United States to convalesce. As she slowly regained her health and considered how she might be of service again, Barton recalled her promise to the International Red Cross. Contacting Dr. Appia, she asked his permission to establish an American chapter. He responded by naming her the group's U.S. representative. Barton then began campaigning for ratification of the Treaty of Geneva, which American officials opposed because they felt that the United States should not be involved in the affairs of other countries. Barton disagreed but realized she would have to try another tactic to win approval for the treaty and, by extension, the Red Cross. So she began to promote it as a peacetime relief organization that would respond to natural disasters such as floods, fires, or earthquakes.

In May, 1881, Barton established the first American Red Cross chapters and was elected president of the organization. That fall, volunteers faced their first major test when a forest fire in northern Michigan left thousands injured and homeless. The Red Cross solicited donations nationwide and sent in relief workers, gaining valuable publicity and good will for its efforts. The following spring, in March, 1882, Congress at last ratified the Treaty of Geneva, thanks in large part to Barton's perseverance and her demonstration of how useful the Red Cross could be.

Beginning in 1883, Barton devoted herself completely to the Red Cross, serving not only as its chief administrator but also as a participant in relief operations throughout the country. In 1884, she sailed to Europe as the U.S. delegate to the Red Cross conference in Geneva—the only woman present in that capacity. Over the objections of some key members who did not want the Red Cross to stray from its original purpose of providing only wartime relief, Barton's idea of offering help to victims of natural disasters was officially adopted into the group's charter as the "American Amendment."

Barton served as president of the Red Cross for more than twenty years, overseeing day-to-day operations and raising funds. She continued to perform relief work herself—sometimes staying at a particular disaster site for months at a time—until she was well into her seventies. Her true strengths however were in promoting the organization and hiring talented people to staff it and run the various programs. In her spare time, Barton also lectured, lobbied for women's rights, and wrote a book about the Red Cross. During the 1890s, she also introduced the concept of foreign aid to the American public by spearheading relief efforts directed overseas following a famine in Russia and a massacre in Armenia.

Beginning around 1900, however, power struggles within the Red Cross led to a decline in Barton's influence. Devastated by accusations that she was a poor administrator and had misappropriated funds, she at one point considered leaving the United States and moving to Europe. The squabbling continued even after the charges against her were dropped for lack of evidence, and in 1904, a tired and heartbroken Barton resigned from her lifetime appointment as president of the American Red Cross. She died of pneumonia on April 12, 1912, at her home in Glen Echo, Maryland. In attendance at services there and in her native North Oxford, Massachusetts, was a gray-haired contingent of "her boys" from the Civil War, whose loyalty to the "Angel of the Battlefield" had never wavered.

Sources

➤ **Books**

Barton, Clara, *The Story of My Childhood*, Arno, 1980.

Boylston, Helen Dore, *Clara Barton, Founder of the American Red Cross*, Random House, 1955.

Hamilton, Leni, *Clara Barton*, Chelsea House, 1988.

Pryor, Elizabeth Brown, *Clara Barton, Professional Angel*, University of Pennsylvania Press, 1987 (opening quote).

Ross, Ishbel, *Angel of the Battlefield: The Life of Clara Barton*, Harper, 1956.

➤ **Periodicals**

New York Times, "Clara Barton Dead in Her Ninetieth Year," April 13, 1919, pp. 12–13.

Leonard Bernstein

"**M**usic is something terribly special. It doesn't have to pass through the censor of the brain before it can reach the heart."

An internationally acclaimed conductor, composer, and teacher, Leonard Bernstein was born on August 25, 1918, in Lawrence, Massachusetts. He died in New York City on October 14, 1990.

Address: c/o Carson Office, 101 West 55th St., 9-B, New York, NY 10019.

"Exuberant, willful, driven"—these were the words *People* magazine used to describe Leonard Bernstein, widely regarded as the most gifted American musician of this century. His flamboyant conducting style was his trademark and the basis of his reputation, but he also left a legacy as a brilliant composer, an extraordinary teacher, and an accomplished pianist. Responding once to suggestions that perhaps he spread himself a bit *too* thin, he proclaimed, "I don't want to give in and settle for some specialty—it would bore me to death." As a *New Republic* reporter observed, Bernstein was "one of the few figures in American musical life who fully deserved to be called maestro."

One of three children of Russian-Jewish immigrants Samuel and Jennie Resnick Bernstein, Leonard Bernstein first fell in love with the piano at the age of ten after his parents agreed to store an old upright model for a relative. Music had never figured prominently in the elder Bernsteins' lives, so they were quite surprised when their son insisted on taking lessons. As Lenny's fascination with the piano grew and he announced his intention to make music his career, a dismayed Samuel Bernstein refused to continue paying for lessons; he had expected his son to work with him in the family beauty-supplies business. Although he relented somewhat when Lenny began earning money by playing with a dance band, he never really approved of his son's choice. The bitterness between the two men lingered for many years.

Determined to pursue his passion, Bernstein took courses in piano and composition at Harvard University, from which he graduated in 1939, and then studied conducting at the Curtis Institute of Music in Philadelphia. Summers were spent at the Berkshire Music Center in Tanglewood, Massachusetts, where Bernstein worked for a man he would later describe as his mentor—Boston Symphony Orchestra conductor Serge Koussevitzky. (Bernstein maintained a lifelong association with the renowned Tanglewood facility, returning there often to teach.) In the summer of 1943, a little more than a year after his graduation from the Curtis Institute, he left Tanglewood and a position as Koussevitzky's assistant to accept a position as assistant conductor of the New York Philharmonic Orchestra.

Bernstein was only twenty-five when he burst on the national music scene in a way that might have come straight out of a movie script. On November 13, 1943, only a few months after joining the Philharmonic, he received a last-minute call to substitute for an ailing guest conductor. Still recuperating from a party held the night before to celebrate the successful debut of his *I Hate Music* song cycle at a Town Hall recital, Bernstein stepped up to the podium and, without time for rehearsal, masterfully led the orchestra through a difficult program. His efforts earned him a tremendous ovation from the audience and an enthusiastic front-page review in the next day's *New York Times*.

The 1940s also marked Bernstein's emergence as a composer of note. Besides *I Hate Music,* he wrote a symphony, *Jeremiah,* which the New York City Music Critics' Circle named the most distinguished new American orchestral work of the 1943–44 season. His most striking success of the decade was his score for the ballet *Fancy Free.* With Bernstein conducting, it premiered in April, 1944, and garnered much praise; then it was adapted for the Broadway stage as the hit musical *On the Town.*

After a brief stint as conductor of the New York City Symphony, Bernstein spent the remainder of the 1940s and most of the 1950s as a visiting conductor for several different orchestras. At the same time that he was enhancing his reputation as a skillful interpreter of others' music, Bernstein was turning out some of his greatest work as a composer. He wrote a variety of classical pieces during the 1950s, among them some song cycles and a short opera entitled *Trouble in Tahiti,* as well as the music for the film *On the Waterfront,* for which he received an Academy Award nomination. His most memorable contributions were the scores for two hugely popular Broadway musicals, *Wonderful Town* and *West Side Story.* Indeed, it is as the composer of *West Side Story* that Bernstein became a household name, a first for an American symphony conductor.

The 1950s also saw Bernstein develop into a teacher best described as "spellbinding, erudite and passionate," to quote from *U.S. News and World Report.* His forte was bringing music to the masses via television, initially on the "Omnibus" program and then as host of the New York Philharmonic's Emmy Award-winning "Young People's Concerts." As Victor Navasky explained in the *Nation:* "[Bernstein] was not, like so many who came before him, a remote pedagogue determined to preserve 'classical' music's high status. . . . He lured us onto the stage with him, and instantly it was as if we were in his living room and he was patting the piano bench saying, 'Come on, sit down next to me, and I'll show you something incredible.' And he did . . . holding us with his every word until, miraculously, we actually began to understand how music worked and what made it so beautiful."

In 1957, Bernstein again joined forces with the New York Philharmonic, becoming co-conductor (with Dimitri Mitropoulos) and then music director the following year, the first American-born person to head a top symphony orchestra. (Central Europeans had dominated the field for many years.) Under his supervision, the Philharmonic enjoyed unparalleled success and prestige; concert subscriptions nearly tripled, and the orchestra's recordings sold millions of copies. Bernstein's presence at the podium virtually guaranteed a sellout crowd, even though the lushly romantic and traditional pieces he favored were out of fashion in an age of atonal avant-garde compositions.

Besides broadening the appeal of classical music via television, Bernstein tried to draw more people to live performances by making the experience less formal and therefore less intimidating. Thursday evenings, for example, were set aside for a special "Preview" series of Philharmonic concerts at which the dress and the mood were both casual, with the tieless conductor usually turning to the audience to chat about an upcoming selection. Bernstein also introduced free concerts in the parks, and unlike many of his colleagues, he never scorned jazz and popular music as too "lowbrow"; he often incorporated such pieces into his programs and made a point of demonstrating their merit.

Bernstein retired as director of the New York Philharmonic in 1969, citing a desire to spend more time on his own music. He remained on as laureate conductor, however, and also continued a close association with the Israel Philharmonic as well as the Vienna Philharmonic. In addition, an extensive series of guest conductorships throughout the 1970s kept him on the road almost constantly.

Meanwhile, Bernstein was forced to cope with several personal crises that threatened his professional reputation and drained him of creative energy. A longtime political liberal, he was harshly and publicly criticized for his support of the Black Panthers, a controversial Black-American political and social organization. Another blow came in 1976, when he separated from his wife of twenty-five years, Felicia Montealegre Cohn, who learned shortly afterward that she had terminal cancer. Her death in 1978 sent Bernstein first into a deep depression, then into a period of near-manic activity. For the most part, his musical compositions from this troubled decade did not fare well with critics or audiences, some of whom also felt his conducting had begun to suffer as a result of his chaotic personal life.

The 1980s ushered in a new era for Bernstein, as he emerged from the turmoil of the 1970s to ascend to a new level of recognition and respect. In 1985, he received a Lifetime Achievement Grammy Award, and in 1988, he marked his seventieth birthday as guest of honor at dozens of tributes and celebrations, including a star-studded gala at Tanglewood. "I have no further requests of the fates . . . except for time," he declared. "I've achieved more than I had any right to expect. Nobody has been as lucky as I have."

Within a few months, however, it was apparent that Bernstein's years of heavy smoking were taking their toll; his emphysema worsened and other related ailments began to plague him. On October 14, 1990, just days after announcing his retirement from conducting, Bernstein died of a heart attack brought on by lung failure. Reflecting on his contributions, Michael Walsh of *Time* noted that Bernstein was "the signal musical figure of his age, at once the best, the brightest and the most exasperating." In short, concluded Walsh, "he lived his life the way he composed and conducted: passionately and wholeheartedly, as an outsize, outrageous combination of creative joie de vivre and destructive self-indulgence. His death . . . has left the music world a quiet place."

Sources

➤ **Books**

Bernstein, Leonard, *Findings*, Simon & Schuster, 1982.

➤ **Periodicals**

Connoisseur, "Bernstein's Last Hurrah," September, 1991.

Dance Magazine, "Farewell to Lenny," December, 1990; "'Remembering Leonard Bernstein," January, 1991.

Harper's, "The Tragedy of Leonard Bernstein," May, 1983.

Maclean's, "A Rhapsodic Life," October 29, 1990, p. 78.

Musical America, "Leonard Bernstein, 1918–1990," January, 1991.

Nation, "Lenny's Life," November 5, 1990, pp. 511–512.

New Leader, "The Star of American Music," January 10, 1983, pp. 13–14.

New Republic, "Maestro," November 5, 1990, p. 10.

New York, September 12, 1988, p. 80; October 29, 1990, p. 91.

New York Times Magazine, "Catching Lenny," December 19, 1971; "Bernstein Triumphant," August 31, 1986.

Newsweek, "He's So Lucky to Be Lenny," September 5, 1988, pp. 54–59; "An Affair to Remember," October 29, 1990, pp. 79–80.

Opera News, "Leonard Bernstein, 1918–1990," December 8, 1990.

People, "America's Maestro Bows Out," October 29, 1990, pp. 44–47.

Rolling Stone, November 29, 1990.

Time, "The Best and the Brightest," October 29, 1990, p. 113.

U.S. News and World Report, October 29, 1990, p. 21.

Mary McLeod Bethune

"O ur aim must be to create a world of fellowship and justice where no man's skin color or religion is held against him. 'Love thy neighbor' is a precept that could transform the world if it were universally practiced."

Educator Mary McLeod Bethune championed interracial harmony and equal opportunity for Black Americans. She was born on July 10, 1875, in Mayesville, South Carolina, and died on May 18, 1955, in Daytona Beach, Florida.

Mary McLeod Bethune was a member of the generation of Black-American leaders who lived and worked in an era that began in the grim days after the Civil War and ended at the dawn of a new age of militancy. In many ways, she served as a bridge between the beliefs of conservatives like Booker T. Washington and more militant figures like W. E. B. Du Bois. Like Washington, she agreed that the most pressing problem facing Black Americans was obtaining job skills that would lead to economic success. But like Du Bois, she felt that civil and social inequities had to be remedied at the same time economic ones were; she could not accept Washington's optimistic view that Whites would one day grant civil rights to Blacks as a "reward" for demonstrating their worth to society. "The Freedom Gates are half-ajar," she declared not long before her death. "We must pry them fully open."

Mary Jane McLeod Bethune was the fifteenth of seventeen children born to former slaves Samuel and Patsy McIntosh McLeod, who eked out a living as farmers on a small plot of land purchased from the family to whom Patsy McLeod had once belonged. Like the rest of her brothers and sisters, Mary went to work picking cotton at a very early age. Attending school was out of the question, for there were no public institutions nearby that accepted Black students. When Mary was nine, however, she began attending a new Presbyterian Church mission school about five miles from the McLeod farm. "It was a humble one-room school," she later recalled. "The blackboard was only painted cardboard. But that didn't matter. For there I saw letters make words. I was reading! At home, I gathered the other children around me to teach them what I knew."

At the age of twelve, Mary graduated from the mission school and, with the help of a scholarship, was able to continue her education at Scotia Seminary, a Presbyterian facility in Concord, North Carolina. There she spent the next seven years taking high school- and junior college-level courses. Eager to serve as a missionary in Africa, she obtained another scholarship for study at the Moody Bible Institute in Chicago. Upon completing her training in 1895, however, twenty-year-old Mary was rejected for missionary service on the grounds that she was too young. Disappointed and discouraged, she headed back home to contemplate how else she might be of service to others.

Over the next few years, Mary taught at several small schools for Black Americans throughout the South, including one in Sumter, South Carolina, where she met and married a fellow teacher named

Albertus Bethune. Eventually relocating with him to Savannah, Georgia, she gave birth to a son and briefly retired from teaching, then moved restlessly from one mission school to another in search of a place she felt she could do the most good.

In 1904, Bethune heard that a major railroad construction project under way along the east coast of Florida had attracted hundreds of Black men (many accompanied by their families) hoping to find work. In most instances, they lived there in squalor and poverty. Crime and racial violence were commonplace. Learning that conditions were especially desperate around the resort town of Daytona Beach, Bethune visited the area to see for herself. There she encountered widespread ignorance and indifference to her suggestion that she establish a school for the workers' children.

Undaunted, Bethune resolved to find a way to provide an education to those she knew might never have another opportunity to go to school. That September, she rented a dirty, ramshackle frame building in Daytona Beach with money she earned by making sweet potato pies, ice cream, and fried fish and selling them to construction crews. She scrubbed and scoured until it was clean, then turned her attention to gathering equipment and supplies. Too poor to buy anything, she instead made ink from the juice of wild elderberries, fashioned pencils out of slivers of charred firewood, and scrounged through the garbage of the city's best hotels to retrieve discarded kitchenware, linens, broken furniture, and other items. She also went door to door in residential neighborhoods and took her pleas to churches, clubs, and other groups, begging for whatever people could spare. "I considered cash money as the smallest part of my resources," she later wrote. "I had faith in a loving God, faith in myself, and a desire to serve."

On October 3, 1904, the doors of the Daytona Normal and Industrial School for Negro Girls opened for classes with a grand total of six students—five girls and Bethune's son. The emphasis was on practical knowledge: besides reading, writing, and arithmetic, students were taught cooking, sewing, and other vocational skills. In less than two years, the school grew to about 250 students (some of whom also boarded there) and a faculty of five.

But with success came a need for more space. Financially, it was a constant struggle just to keep the existing school afloat; Bethune still sold food to construction crews and salvaged junked items, and a student choir earned a little money by giving concerts in and around Daytona Beach. Eventually, Bethune managed to scrape together a down payment on thirty-two acres of swamp and dump property surrounding her school building. She and her students then cleaned up the mess and, thanks to secondhand material and labor furnished mostly by her students' fathers in exchange for tuition credit, a building known as Faith Hall rose on the reclaimed land in 1907.

The school grew slowly but steadily after that, aided in large part by donations Bethune secured from nationally prominent businessmen and philanthropists who were impressed by her determination and vision. Through the years, several other halls were built, and the school's offerings expanded to include adult education programs and various exhibits, shows, and even contests to encourage nearby residents to keep their houses and yards clean and neat. The scramble for funds also continued on a regular basis; for example, students planted and sold vegetables and raised livestock to provide the school with a steady income.

In the early 1920s, Bethune decided to safeguard the future of her dream by affiliating the Daytona Industrial and Normal School with the Methodist Episcopal Church. The church then merged it with the Cookman Institute, a Jacksonville, Florida-based boys' school, forming what came to be known in 1928 as Bethune-Cookman College. Bethune stayed on as president until 1942, but during the 1930s her other interests and activities increasingly took her off campus. A dynamic speaker and prolific contributor to magazines and newspapers, she was in demand as an authority on education and civil rights issues. (She was especially outspoken on the topic of making it easier for Black Americans to exercise their right to vote, which she believed was the mark of true freedom.) She also served as a vice-president of the National Association for the Advancement of Colored People (NAACP) and the National Urban League's commission on interracial cooperation.

Bethune spent much of her time during this period in Washington, D.C. It was there, for example, that she established and headed the National Council of Negro Women in 1935 and gained national prominence as an advisor on minority affairs to President Franklin Delano Roosevelt. (She also became close friends with Eleanor Roosevelt, and they sometimes made appearances together on behalf of causes they both supported.) Her government service began in 1936, when the president appointed her director of Negro affairs for the National Youth Administration, a position in which she supervised the development of recreational facilities and vocational training programs for young Black men and women. On the eve of World War II, when the booming defense industry refused to hire Black workers, she persuaded President Roosevelt to create the Federal Committee on Fair Employment Practice, which outlawed such discrimination. During the war itself Bethune worked as special assistant to the secretary of war and was charged with selecting candidates for the first officers' training school for the Women's Army Corps. In 1945, as a special representative of the Department of State, she traveled to San Francisco to attend the organizing conference of the United Nations.

As she headed into her seventies, Bethune ignored repeated warnings from her doctor urging her to slow down. Instead she kept busy literally until her dying day; just two months before her eightieth birthday, she collapsed and died of a heart attack after putting in a full day of work at home in Daytona Beach. She was buried on the grounds of her beloved college, which at the time of her death in 1955 boasted an enrollment of more than one thousand and a faculty of one hundred. Today, Bethune-Cookman College has over two thousand students and nearly two hundred faculty members.

In one of her last published articles, a piece written for *Ebony* magazine, Bethune reflected on what she thought would be her legacy to Black Americans. Among the things she cited were love, hope, faith, courage, racial dignity, a thirst for education, and a desire to live together harmoniously. But most of all, she noted, "If I have a legacy to leave my people, it is my philosophy of living and serving. As I face tomorrow, I am content, for I think I have spent my life well."

Sources

➤ **Books**

Halasa, Malu, *Mary McLeod Bethune*, Chelsea House, 1989.

Holt, Rackham, *Mary McLeod Bethune*, Doubleday, 1964.

Peare, Catherine Owens, *Mary McLeod Bethune*, Vanguard Press, 1951.

➤ **Periodicals**

Christian Century, "Mrs. Bethune's Death Marks Changing Negro

Leadership," June 8, 1955, p. 676; "The Miracle Years of Mrs. Bethune," February 1, 1956, pp. 140–141.

Ebony, "My Last Will and Testament," August, 1955. Reprint, November, 1990, pp. 128–134 (opening quote).

Journal of Negro History, "Mary McLeod Bethune," October, 1955, pp. 393–395.

Newsweek, "Faith in a Swampland," May 30, 1955, p. 47.

New York Times, May 19, 1955, p. 29.

Reader's Digest, "An Unforgettable Character: Mary Bethune," February, 1952, pp. 146–151.

Time, "Matriarch," July 22, 1946, p. 55.

Stephen Biko

"We are aware that the white man is sitting at our table. . . . We want to remove him from our table, strip the table of all the trappings put on it by him, decorate it in true African style, settle down and then ask him to join us on our terms if he wishes."

A champion of freedom and equality through nonviolence, Stephen Biko was the founder and leader of the Black Consciousness movement in South Africa. Born on December 18, 1946, in King William's Town, South Africa, Biko died on September 12, 1977, in Pretoria, South Africa.

During the late 1960s, with many of its older leaders in jail or under government orders to remain out of the public eye, the South African Black political movement stood poised on the brink of a new era. Into the vacuum created by the enforced silence of men such as Nelson Mandela stepped Stephen Biko, a thoughtful and articulate university student whose message about the importance of Black self-reliance quickly gained a foothold, especially among young Black South Africans like himself. He quickly became one of the most powerful and influential Black figures in the country, a man to whom not only his own people looked with hope, but also those Whites inside and outside South Africa who opposed apartheid. Less than a decade after he first rose to prominence, Biko paid for his activism with his life. And to some observers, the last chance for a peaceful accommodation between Blacks and Whites in South Africa may well have died with him.

Stephen Biko was born and grew up in the eastern Cape Province, attending a number of primary and secondary schools there before enrolling at the University of Natal in 1966. He intended to study medicine, but he soon became interested in politics and began to devote more and more of his time to organizing student groups. Probably the most important of these was the all-Black South African Students' Organization (SASO), an offshoot of the National Union of South African Students (NUSAS). The mostly-White membership of NUSAS consisted of liberal, English-speaking university students who, unlike South Africans of Dutch descent (Afrikaners), opposed apartheid and supported the concept of racial justice. Believing that NUSAS—no matter how good its intentions—was too overwhelmingly White to serve the best interests of Black South Africans, Biko formed SASO in 1968, and through it his philosophy of "Black Consciousness" spread throughout South Africa.

Similar in many ways to the American Black Power movement of the 1960s, Black Consciousness represented a new style of leadership for South Africa. "The biggest mistake the black world ever made was to assume that whoever opposed apartheid was an ally," Biko once wrote. "One has to overhaul the system in South Africa before hoping to get black and white walking hand in hand to oppose a common enemy." To that end, he urged Black South Africans to break their ties with liberal Whites and multiracial organizations and establish a strong, separate identity based on principles of self-worth and self-reliance. In his view, Blacks could only accomplish this in isolation from sympathetic Whites, whose eagerness to help was more often than not an obstacle to true Black achievement. (South Africa's system of apartheid ensured that even antiracist Whites were not free to live out their ideals of racial harmony.) Once Black South Africans had successfully overcome the demoralizing effects of racism by fostering Black awareness and pride, they would then be in a better position psychologically to confront the White power structure. Although Biko sought peaceful change, he often expressed fears that the situation in South Africa had deteriorated to the point where violence was probably inevitable.

Biko was expelled from the University of Natal in 1972, ostensibly on account of his poor grades but more than likely because of his unacceptable political activities. Despite his efforts to stay in the background of the Black Consciousness movement and develop a more collective leadership, the charismatic Biko had emerged as a natural spokesman for his philosophy, and the South African government took note. In March, 1973, he was banned from speaking in public or for quotation in any publication or broadcast and was also prohibited from traveling outside his home district of King William's Town, a rather remote area about thirty miles inland from the seaside city of East London. Yet he continued to gain international recognition and wield considerable influence, playing host to a steady stream of diplomats, professors, politicians, and journalists from all over the world who publicized and legitimized his struggle for freedom. He also established and ran Black Community Programs, a group of self-help projects in such fields as literacy training, health education, and job preparation, and served as honorary president of the Black People's Convention. In his spare time, he studied law via the correspondence school of the University of South Africa. And he regularly defied the travel ban to visit friends and colleagues in other parts of the country.

On August 18, 1977, during one of his unauthorized trips outside King William's Town, Biko was stopped by government security police at a roadblock, arrested, and taken to Port Elizabeth for questioning. Since this was certainly not the first time he had been harassed and detained, no one was unduly alarmed when he was not immediately released. Everyone—including Biko himself—assumed he was too famous and too important to be harmed; they felt the government would never risk causing trouble at home and abroad if something were to happen to him.

But on September 6, while still in police custody, Biko was

stripped of all his clothes, handcuffed and put into leg irons, then chained to an iron grille and subjected to twenty-two hours of interrogation during which time he was tortured and beaten. Although he subsequently displayed obvious signs of having suffered severe brain damage, including frothing at the mouth and lapsing in and out of consciousness, Biko received no special care either from his jailers, who thought he was faking an illness, or from prison doctors, who repeatedly failed to diagnosis the extent of his injuries. On September 11, his condition having worsened, the still-naked and unconscious Biko was thrown into the back of a Land Rover and driven nearly eight hundred miles to Pretoria. He died a day later—the twentieth Black South African to die in police custody that year.

In announcing the news to the world, South African authorities maintained that their previously hale and hearty, thirty-year-old prisoner had died after a seven-day hunger strike. His family and friends were highly suspicious, however, because he had made a pact with them that no matter what he was forced to endure if he were arrested, he would never take or endanger his own life. (It was common knowledge that police routinely attributed the deaths of jailed political activists to suicide, hunger strikes, or unlikely "accidents.") After weeks of contradictory statements by South African officials that underscored the mystery surrounding Biko's death, a likely scenario finally emerged at an inquest held in November, 1977. But because no one who testified was willing to name the person (or persons) who delivered the fatal blows, the judge ruled that Biko's death could not be attributed to any criminal act or omission and therefore his head injuries must have occurred during a scuffle with police. A subsequent re-examination of the case in 1985 found two government doctors who had examined Biko guilty of negligence; one received a reprimand and the other was barred from practicing medicine until late 1991, when he submitted a written apology to the South African medical society.

While Biko's death did not spark widespread riots and bloodshed as many had feared, it provoked a torrent of criticism inside and outside South Africa. It also gave the Black Consciousness movement its first martyr and was grimly symbolic of the ultimate consequence of apartheid for all who dared oppose it. But as Biko revealed in an interview held just a few months before his death, despite his confidence in his ability to defuse tense situations involving the police, he had accepted the fact that his activism put him in danger. "The bond between life and death is absolute," he declared. "You are either alive and proud or you are dead, and when you are dead, you don't care anyway. And your method of death can itself be a politicizing thing. . . . So if you can overcome the personal fear for death, which is a highly irrational thing, you know, then you're on the way."

Sources

➤ Books

Arnold, Millard, *Steve Biko: Black Consciousness in South Africa*, Random House, 1978.

Woods, Donald, *Biko*, Paddington Press, 1978 (opening quote).

➤ Periodicals

Canadian Forum, December, 1977-January, 1978, pp. 15–20.

Christian Century, "Steve Biko: Liberator and Martyr," November 2, 1977, pp. 997–999.

Ebony, "Cry Freedom," December, 1987, pp. 60–66.

Nation, "Steve Biko Is Dead," October 15, 1977, pp. 356–357.

New Republic, "Biko on Death," January 7, 1978, pp. 11–13.

Newsweek, "'Steve Biko Is Dead,'" September 26, 1977, pp. 41–42; "A Tragic Turn to Terrorism," October 10, 1977, pp. 50–51; "Biko's Last Days," November 28, 1977, p. 74; "A No-Fault Verdict," December 12, 1977, pp. 67–69; "Black Pride," November 13, 1978, p. 117; "The Biko Case: A Slap on the Wrist," July 15, 1985, p. 34.

New York Times, "Young Black Leader Dies in Detention in South Africa, Raising Fears of New Unrest," September 14, 1977, p. A3; "South African Doctor Writes Apology in the Death of Biko," October 21, 1991, p. A9.

People, "Newsman Donald Woods Still Seeks Justice for Stephen Biko in the Film 'Cry Freedom,'" November 23, 1987, p. 64.

Time, "Death of a Prisoner," September 26, 1977, p. 35; "Inquest into a Curious Death," November 28, 1977, p. 53.

➤ Other

The 1987 film *Cry Freedom*, based on the book *Biko* by South African journalist Donald Woods, dramatizes Biko's life and death and recounts the friendship that existed between the two men. Also available is a 1988 video documentary entitled *Biko: Breaking the Silence.*

Jim and Sarah Brady

"Congress just doesn't listen to the groups that don't have a lot of money or power. Maybe that's what we're going to spend our lives doing—making people aware."—Sarah Brady*

Jim and Sarah Brady are gun-control activists. Jim was born on August 29, 1940, in Centralia, Illinois. Sarah was born on February 6, 1942, in Missouri.

Address: Handgun Control, Inc., 1225 I St. N.W., Washington, D.C. 20005.

ife was going extremely well for Jim and Sarah Brady in the
opening months of 1981. Jim had recently been named press
secretary to newly-elected President Ronald Reagan, and
Sarah enjoyed a satisfying career with the Republican National
Committee. They were parents of a toddler son they adored, and
they were increasingly popular figures on the Washington, D.C.,
social circuit. Then, on March 30 came the shattering event that
turned their comfortable existence upside down. As President
Reagan left the Washington Hilton Hotel with his entourage following an appearance before a convention of labor leaders, he was the
target of an assassination attempt by a disturbed young man named
John W. Hinckley, Jr., who fired several shots at close range. Bullets
struck the president, a secret service agent, a policeman, and Jim
Brady. Initial news reports indicated that Jim had died of his
injuries, but the exuberantly cheerful and energetic man affectionately known as "Bear" to his family and friends was not about to
give up that easily.

In the years since that tragedy, Jim Brady has struggled against a
myriad of difficulties, most notably paralysis in his left leg and arm,
short-term memory loss, and slurred speech. At his side has been
Sarah, who in 1985 became actively involved with Handgun Control, Inc., a Washington, D.C.-based group that lobbies for stricter
gun-control laws. As Jim slowly regained his health, he too joined
the fight, and today the Bradys comprise what a *Vanity Fair* reporter
calls "the most potent partnership in the battle for gun control and
the most effective weapon so far against the National Rifle Association's stranglehold on Congress."

James Scott Brady was born and grew up in southern Illinois, the
only child of a railroad yardmaster and his social worker wife. A
born leader who was active in many different sports, clubs, and
organizations during his youth, Jim attended the University of
Illinois in Champaign-Urbana, receiving his B.S. degree in communications and political science in 1962. After a brief stint in law
school, he worked as a campaign manager for several Illinois
politicians and also served as executive vice-president of a Chicago
public relations firm. At a Republican party gathering in Washington, D.C., in 1970 he met Sarah Kemp, then employed by the
Republican National Committee. The daughter of a former FBI
agent, she had grown up in Alexandria, Virginia, and graduated
from the College of William and Mary in 1964. She then taught
school for several years before becoming involved in Republican
party activities on Capitol Hill.

After conducting a long-distance romance for three years, Jim and Sarah married and settled in Washington, remaining active in Republican politics throughout the 1970s. In March, 1980, after serving as press secretary for former Texas governor John Connally during his failed bid for the Republican presidential nomination, Jim switched over to the Ronald Reagan camp as director of public affairs and research. His quirky sense of humor and frathouse antics sometimes got him into trouble with his superiors, but his free-wheeling personality and straightforwardness endeared him to the Washington press corps. He went on to serve as chief spokesman of the transition team following Reagan's election victory in November, 1980, and was subsequently named press secretary after the new president took office in January, 1981.

Jim Brady had been on the job only a few months when he was shot by the would-be assassin's bullet, which struck him in the forehead and then exploded into several dozen fragments that pierced his brain and caused extensive damage. By late May, however, having survived some life-threatening complications (including blood clots in his lungs and leaking spinal fluid), he was able to begin therapy. But he remained in the hospital until Thanksgiving, and even after his release his ordeal was far from over; he needed almost around-the-clock care and still faced an onslaught of dangerous complications. He was in constant pain and battled frustration and restlessness as he tried to learn to deal with his disabilities.

For the first few years after the shooting, Jim and Sarah Brady's lives were focused almost exclusively on Jim's recovery and on spending time with their son. Gun-control advocates approached Sarah from time to time about lending her support to their cause, but she hesitated to get involved, not only because she was busy, but also because she was afraid people would accuse her of capitalizing on the tragedy of her husband's shooting. And as someone who had been around guns all of her life—her father used to take her target-shooting as a child, and he, her brother, and her uncle were all hunters—she was not opposed to the idea of possessing and using them for sport.

But in the mid-1980s, while on vacation in Illinois, Sarah was jolted into activism when young Scott Brady crawled into the front seat of a friend's pickup truck and came across a gun that he playfully pointed at his mother. At first, she thought it was a toy, but then to her horror she realized that what her son held was not a toy but a real, loaded handgun.

Back in Washington, a shaken and angry Sarah began to rethink her position on gun control. One day, she picked up the newspaper and read about the McClure-Volkmer bill, a piece of legislation pending in the Senate and backed by the National Rifle Association (NRA) that would have essentially overturned the Gun Control Act of 1968, which had banned the mail-order sale of guns, established a licensing and inspection program for firearms dealers, and prohibited licensed dealers from selling guns to convicted criminals, fugitives from justice, and people who had been officially judged mentally incompetent. Outraged at the thought that the act might be rendered ineffective, Sarah Brady called Handgun Control, Inc., a lobbying group formed in 1974 by the father of a San Francisco shooting victim, and asked what she could do to help.

One of her first acts was to put the NRA on notice that she was going to make it her "life's ambition to see that we get some decent gun laws." Friends and colleagues thought she was crazy—especially as a woman—to take on what is widely acknowledged to be the most powerful, the best funded, and the most vindictive lobbying group in Washington. "But I didn't allow that to stop me," Sarah Brady later said. "I think that my being a woman is a plus. Women are more able to stick to a task until it is completed. And when something angers them, when they see an injustice, they are more anxious to stay with it and beat it."

At first, she was the only Brady to take up the cause; Jim, who had returned to work for the Reagan administration in November, 1982, on a part-time basis, could not speak out given the president's opposition to gun control. (Much of his free time was also taken up with activities concerning the rights of the disabled.) But in 1988, during the last months of the Reagan presidency, Jim emerged from his silence to help Sarah and Handgun Control defeat the NRA's attempt to repeal a new Maryland law banning the manufacture and sale of so-called "Saturday-night specials," small, cheap handguns often used by urban criminals—and by the young man who had shot him.

The following year, the fight began in earnest for the Brady Handgun Violence Prevention Act, popularly known as "the Brady bill," a piece of legislation that had been around in various forms since 1987. Its key provision required a national seven-day waiting period for handgun purchasers to allow time for a background check. After it was defeated in a floor vote in the House of Representatives, Jim went before the Senate in November, 1989, to argue for its passage, accusing congressmen of being "gutless" for not standing up to the NRA and other "special-interest groups that whine about a little inconvenience [like a waiting period] and other such lamebrain nonsense." Every day, he went on to tell the senators, "I need help getting out of bed, help taking a shower, and help getting dressed, and—damn it—I need help going to the bathroom. . . . I guess I'm paying for their 'convenience.'"

Despite this impassioned plea, the Brady bill was bottled up in the House of Representatives throughout 1990 and never made it to the floor for a vote. It was reintroduced in Congress in January, 1991, and received an unexpected boost in March when NRA member Ronald Reagan came out in support of the bill. The House passed the bill in May and the Senate passed it in July, the proposed seven-day waiting period trimmed to five days in a compromise move. The Handgun Control forces were ecstatic at this apparent victory, but their joy evaporated in November, when President George Bush objected to other provisions in the massive anticrime package of which the Brady bill was only a part. Unable to gather enough support to overturn a promised presidential veto, Congress gave up trying to pass the crime package, and the Brady bill died along with it.

While they have not yet achieved their goal on the federal level, the Bradys have enjoyed greater success on the state and local level. Thanks in part to their efforts, stricter gun-control laws are now on the books not only in Maryland but also in California, Virginia, Oregon, Delaware, New Jersey, Connecticut, Iowa, and Rhode Island. As the chairman of Handgun Control, a post she has held since 1989, Sarah (who has come to be known as "the NRA's worst nightmare") feels there is still much to be done in the areas of gun safety and education, curbing handgun sales among private owners, and making sure existing gun control laws are not overturned.

To that end, the Bradys stay on the move, lobbying legislators, making speeches, and developing strategies with other gun-control advocates. Sometimes they appear together, and sometimes separately; Jim is also active with the National Organization on Disability and the National Head Injuries Foundation, so his agenda often includes meetings and speaking engagements on behalf of those groups. He still must endure often-excruciating pain, regular physical therapy sessions, and the frustrations that stem from being dependent on others, but the challenge of a good fight has done much to revive his energy and spirits since he teamed up with Sarah on the handgun control issue.

Those who have come to know Sarah and Jim Brady marvel at their lack of self-pity and bitterness. By and large, they take life one day at a time, for as Sarah Brady says, "I've learned not to look into the future." Her happy-go-lucky husband seconds that thought, adding, "You've got to play the hand you're dealt. You can't spend your time on anger."

Sources

➤ **Books**

Dickenson, Mollie, *Thumbs Up: The Life and Courageous Comeback of White House Press Secretary Jim Brady*, Morrow, 1987.

➤ **Periodicals**

Ladies' Home Journal, "Brady's Battle," March, 1991, pp. 61–62.

Ms., "Sarah Brady," January/February, 1989, pp. 84–86 (opening quote).

New York Times Magazine, "Target: The Gun Lobby," December 9, 1990.

Time, "Plea from a Wheelchair," December 4, 1989, p. 49; " . . . And the Case Against Them: The Head of Handgun Control Says Weapons Are Killing the Future," January 29, 1990, p. 23; "Gunfight on Capitol Hill," May 6, 1991, p. 27.

TV Guide, "Under Fire: Movie about Brady Shooting Heats Up Gun-Control Debate," June 15, 1991, pp. 12–13.

USA Weekend, "The Gun Battle," February 15–17, 1991, pp. 4–5.

Vanity Fair, "The Brady Offensive," January, 1991.

Washingtonian, "Smiling Again," March, 1991.

➤ **Other**

A dramatization of Jim Brady's story entitled "Without Warning: The James Brady Story" aired on HBO in 1991.

Christy Brown

"I 've had no choice but to be an observer, always on the outside looking in. You can see plenty from a comfortable wheelchair if you just sit back and pay attention."*

Almost totally crippled by cerebral palsy, Christy Brown learned to use his left foot to express himself through painting and writing. He was born on June 5, 1932, in Dublin, Ireland, and died on September 6, 1981, in Parbrook, England.

C hristy Brown was the tenth of Paddy and Bridget Brown's twenty-two children, thirteen of whom survived to adulthood. The birth was a difficult one for both the baby and his mother; Christy experienced breathing problems that damaged the part of the brain that controls muscle coordination. The Browns took their son to a succession of doctors, none of whom could discover exactly what was wrong or offer any hope that he might improve. Many pointed out that given the severity of his physical disabilities, he was likely to be mentally defective as well.

Unwilling to accept that diagnosis, Mrs. Brown vowed that her son would not be pushed aside as an imbecile. Whatever time she could spare away from her other responsibilities was devoted to Christy. She showed him picture books for hours on end, telling him the names of the different animals and flowers and trying to make him repeat them. The best the little boy could do was occasionally gurgle or grunt in response. "I was lonely," he later recalled, "imprisoned in a world of my own, unable to communicate with others, cut off, separated from them as though a glass wall stood between my existence and theirs."

This isolation ended with a remarkable breakthrough when Christy was five years old. One day while a few of the Brown children were doing some arithmetic problems on an old slate, Christy, who was propped up on the floor nearby, suddenly grabbed a piece of chalk from his sister with his left foot and made what he described as "a wild sort of scribble with it on the slate." Everyone in the room fell silent and stared at him; he had never used his foot before. Coming in from the kitchen, his mother immediately sensed what her son was trying to do. She took another piece of chalk and carefully drew the letter *A* on the floor in front of Christy and asked him to copy it. He strained to make his foot work but only succeeded in drawing another very crooked line. Mrs. Brown encouraged him to keep trying. He had produced one side of the *A* and half of the other when the chalk broke. The frustrated little boy just wanted to give up; his mother's hand on his shoulder urged him to finish. "Out went my foot," Christy later recounted. "I shook, I sweated and strained every muscle. My hands were clenched, my fingernails bit into the flesh. I set my teeth so hard that I nearly pierced my lower lip. . . . But—I drew it—the letter *A*."

Christy's life was never the same after that. Within a year, Mrs. Brown had taught her son to print the entire alphabet. She also taught him to read and write. Because he still could not speak clearly enough to be understood by anyone but family members (and sometimes not even them), Christy's left foot became his main means of communication. It gave him some mobility, too, for he learned to use it and a few other muscles he could control to propel himself around the house on his backside.

With the help of his brothers, Christy was at last able to go outside and play. They took him everywhere, pushing him around in an old wooden go-cart Mr. Brown had built from scrap materials. Dubbed the "chariot," it gave the youngster his first chance to experience life outside the four walls of his home and made him feel like a normal boy. When the chariot broke and could not be fixed, Christy was shattered. Outside with his brothers and his friends, he was happier than he had ever been before and almost forgot about his handicaps; forced to stay inside, he was cruelly reminded of his limitations, and the realization left him severely depressed.

His melancholy continued throughout the rest of the summer and into the fall, worsened by mounting feelings of nervous energy and mental tension. Christy longed for some sort of creative outlet that would keep him busy. His wish came true at Christmas that year when he traded his gift of toy soldiers for a box of paints that his brother Paddy had received but didn't want. Holding the brush between his toes, Christy worked day after day in his room, painting family portraits, still lifes, landscapes, and abstract works on pieces of paper tacked to the floor. As he became immersed in this fascinating new pastime, Christy felt his depression ease. By the age of twelve, he had become skilled enough to win a nationwide coloring contest.

Within a few years, however, even painting wasn't enough to combat the feelings of misery and resentment that often overwhelmed the teenager. Christy then began to write, producing melodramatic westerns, wistful love stories, and violent detective thrillers inspired by movies he had seen as a child. While it provided some relief from the monotony of his days, writing did not cure his deepening loneliness and depression.

When he was eighteen, Christy underwent experimental treatments for cerebral palsy at a special clinic affiliated with the Dublin Orthopaedic Hospital. The grueling regimen of physical therapy helped him to speak more clearly, but his overall coordination showed little improvement, even when he made the ultimate sacrifice and agreed not to use his left foot in an attempt to force his other muscles to develop. Doctors later concluded that he had begun therapy too late in life for it to bring about significant changes in his condition.

While his stay at the clinic did not bring about the much-hoped-for cure, it did help Christy come to grips with his affliction. In the twisted limbs and distorted faces of the infants and children he met at the clinic, he truly saw himself for the first time: a man who would never be physically normal but who could think, feel, paint, and especially write. This revelation left him full of ideas that he wanted to pass along to others. Determined to keep his promise not to use his left foot, he convinced his younger brother Eamonn to write for him as he dictated. Together they worked for a year to compile the manuscript of Christy's life story. The young man was not satisfied with the results, however; he felt as if he had created "a forest of words" rather than a good book. Deciding he needed the advice of an educated person on how to write more clearly and constructively, he showed his manuscript to one of his doctors, Robert Collis, who encouraged him to write in a simpler, more straightforward fashion. (Not until much later did Christy find out that, in addition to being a physician, Collis also happened to be a noted writer, playwright, and teacher.)

The lessons in writing and literature Christy received from Dr. Collis were soon supplemented by those of a private tutor—the first formal education the young man had ever received. Working with another brother, Francis, Christy produced several revisions of his life story, none of which pleased him. One day, in a fit of frustration, he took the pencil from Francis and began writing himself instead of dictating. "I wrote and wrote, without pause, without consciousness of my surroundings, hour after hour," Christy recalled. "I felt a different person. I wasn't unhappy anymore. . . . I was free, I could think, I could live, I could create." In 1954, after more than four years of effort, he finally saw his autobiography published under the title *My Left Foot*.

Christy used the money from the sales of this book and subsequent writings plus a monthly stipend from the Disabled Artists' Association to travel all over Ireland and live "life in the raw," as he put it. Having learned to use the toes of his left foot to type on an electric typewriter, he produced a steady stream of articles, stories, and poems over the next twenty-five years. In 1970, he published his first novel, the autobiographical *Down All the Days*, a much-praised account of Irish family life as seen through the eyes of one of its members, a handicapped but remarkably observant and sensitive boy. It became an international bestseller and made its author a celebrity.

Two years later, on October 6, 1972, Christy married Mary Carr. Despite occasional bouts of depression and anger over his dependence, he continued to write and paint; the nine years of his marriage were among the most prolific and happiest of his life. But on September 6, 1981, he was eating dinner at home when he choked to death on a piece of food. While he had not yet attained the literary greatness some critics thought was well within his reach, Christy Brown had without question realized another dream that had once seemed impossible: "to be remembered not for your human frailties or mannerisms, but for something you did, achieved, left behind, something that reached and touched the lives of total strangers."

Sources

➤ **Books**

Brown, Christy, *My Left Foot,* Simon & Schuster, 1955.

Dictionary of Literary Biography, Volume 14: *British Novelists Since 1960,* Gale, 1983.

➤ **Periodicals**

New York Times, September 8, 1981, p. D19.

Newsweek, "The Miracle," June 8, 1970, pp. 98–98A (opening quote).

Reader's Digest, "Unforgettable Christy Brown," June, 1982, pp. 71–77.

➤ **Other**

My Left Foot, a film based on Brown's autobiography, was released in 1989.

Pearl Buck

"*A writer must be involved in the mainstream of life in order to write. . . . When I become involved and find a situation that is not right, then I must try to do something to change it.*"

Born on June 26, 1892, in Hillsboro, West Virginia, Pearl Buck won acclaim as the author of *The Good Earth* and as an advocate for mixed-race children and other causes. She died on March 6, 1973.

Address: Pearl S. Buck Foundation, P.O. Box 181, Perkasie, PA 18944.

The daughter of Presbyterian missionaries Absalom and Caroline Sydenstricker, Pearl Buck was born in West Virginia but spent virtually the entire first half of her life in China. Unlike most missionary families, the Sydenstrickers made their home among the Chinese rather than with the other Westerners in the isolated foreign compound, so young Pearl was able to immerse herself totally in the language and culture of her adopted land. In later years, she would often say that growing up in such an environment had left her "mentally bifocal"—able to appreciate and love two very different cultures, each on its own terms.

After graduating in 1914 from Randolph-Macon Women's College in Lynchburg, Virginia, Pearl returned to China and taught at a missionary school for Chinese boys until her 1917 marriage to American agriculturalist Lossing Buck. She often accompanied her husband into the countryside, where she learned about the peasants and their customs. She also tried her hand at writing and sold some nonfiction articles on China to American magazines.

In 1921, Buck gave birth to a daughter, Carol. Complications following the pregnancy left her unable to bear more children, a situation worsened by the realization that Carol was retarded and probably would need to be institutionalized some day. In the hope that their daughter might benefit from having a playmate, the Bucks adopted a little girl, Janice. It soon became obvious, however, that Carol was not going to improve, and caring for her began to drain Buck emotionally and physically.

Desperate for some free time to work on the novel she had been wanting to write for several years, Buck journeyed to the United States in 1929 and convinced the Presbyterian Mission Board to lend her the money she needed to institutionalize Carol at a New Jersey training school for two years. In January, 1930, she returned to China and immediately started writing what she referred to as her "Wang Lung" novel, the epic tale of a Chinese peasant's relationship to his family and the land that sustains them. Upon its publication in 1931, *The Good Earth* met with critical and popular acclaim, zooming to the top of the best-seller lists and staying there longer than any book had before. It went on to win the Pulitzer Prize in 1932.

It was not until she visited New York City later in the year, however, that Buck realized she had become a celebrity. At a series of events held in her honor, she met numerous writers, editors, artists, and musicians who—unlike her husband and most other members of the missionary community—shared her interests in literature, history, and current events. By 1935, she had permanently relocated to the United States, divorced Lossing Buck, and married Richard Walsh, the head of the John Day Company, which had published her novel. They quickly settled into family life together, adopting three baby boys and a baby girl in the first two years of their marriage. (During the 1950s, they adopted four older biracial children.)

Buck continued writing throughout the 1930s, producing additional novels, articles, stories, speeches, and pamphlets as well as two highly acclaimed biographies, one of her mother (*The Exile*) and a companion volume on her father (*Fighting Angel*). By the end of the decade, she was one of the most popular and widely translated authors in the world. Her fame and prestige were further enhanced when she received the 1938 Nobel Prize for literature. By this time in her career, however, Buck's interests had begun to shift elsewhere, and while she remained a best-selling writer for the rest of her life, she never again matched the critical success she enjoyed with *The Good Earth*, *The Exile*, and *Fighting Angel*. More and more, she felt compelled to write and speak out on behalf of various humanitarian concerns—racism, the betterment of international relations, the problems of retarded and handicapped children, and the treatment of orphans.

Buck first became aware of racism's influence in American society during a visit to Harlem shortly after *The Good Earth* was published. Invited to meet with a group of Black-American professionals, Buck described her own experiences as a member of the White minority in China and then attended an exhibit featuring paintings by local artists. The scenes of lynchings, poverty, and despair horrified her; never had she imagined that such cruelty existed in her native country. Following this painful realization, Buck made a point of educating herself about Black Americans, reading everything she could find and then using her knowledge to focus national attention on their plight.

During World War II, her concerns about racism intensified as she watched the United States form exceptionally close ties with European allies and virtually ignore China, then embroiled in not only a civil war but also a brutal war against Japan. On the home front, she was appalled by the internment of Japanese-Americans and spoke out against the racist attitudes that tolerated such treatment. These convictions were at the heart of her speeches and articles calling for an end to discrimination and colonial rule throughout the entire world. Since the United States had assumed a leadership position among democracies, she was especially critical of its failure to back up words with deeds. As she wrote in a 1958 letter to Philippine leader Carlos P. Romulo: "Can we be surprised if we are mocked as we deserve to be when we declare all men free and equal and then deny the affirmation every day of our lives in the way we behave toward our own minorities? . . . Can we be surprised [when] nations doubt the validity of our ideals?"

Buck's interest in the problems of retarded and handicapped children sprang directly from her own experiences with her daughter Carol. She knew that having such a child often led to feelings of shame and despair, which parents hesitated to discuss with others. After hearing the heartwarming story of a young couple who decided to keep a baby girl they had adopted and then learned was retarded, Buck decided to write about Carol for the very first time. Appearing initially as an article in *Ladies' Home Journal* and later in book form, "The Child Who Never Grew" generated an outpouring of letters from parents of retarded children expressing relief that they were not alone in their struggle.

At about this same time Buck became interested in yet another cause—the treatment of orphans, especially those of mixed race. As a well-known advocate of adoption, she was often approached by people seeking homes for orphans. In late 1948, she received word about two half-Asian infants considered "unadoptable" because the strict laws of the time required a child to match the adoptive couple in religion, race, and physical appearance. Buck agreed to help find an agency that would place them. But every agency she called turned her down, citing the need to match babies with parents. Angry and frustrated, she resolved to start her own agency specializing in mixed-race children.

Together with some friends who shared her belief that it was more important for a child to have a permanent home than parents who "matched," Buck launched the Welcome House concept and established a foster care facility near her Pennsylvania farm. The immediate goal of Welcome House was to find adoptive homes for American-born biracial children, but long-range plans included changing restrictive adoption laws and fighting the racial prejudice of judges and social workers. Welcome House eventually expanded to dozens of homes where mixed-race children lived in a family-type atmosphere until adoptions could be arranged. Later, Buck turned her attention to the biracial offspring of American service-men stationed overseas, particularly in Asia. Established during the early 1960s and still active, the Pearl S. Buck Foundation clothes, feeds, educates, and seeks employment for these often-abandoned children in their native countries.

As she approached her eightieth birthday in June, 1972, Buck looked forward to another year full of book projects, articles, and television appearances (many inspired by the re-opening of China following President Richard Nixon's visit early that year); she even made plans for a trip to the country she had not seen in nearly forty years. At the last minute, however, she received word from the Chinese Embassy in Canada that her request for a visa had been denied due to the "attitude of distortion, smear and vilification" she had long displayed toward the people of China and its leaders. Several months later, Buck fell ill with what was later diagnosed as cancer. She died on March 6, 1973, at her home in Danby, Vermont, and was buried on the grounds of her Pennsylvania farmhouse, now the headquarters of the Pearl S. Buck Foundation.

While a few of her books are likely to endure—*The Good Earth* and her parents' biographies among them—Pearl Buck's real legacy is in the work she did to break down the barriers separating one race from another, one country from another, and one person from another. "She was herself a missionary in the fundamental meaning of the word," declared Thomas Lask in the *New York Times*. "Less concerned with theological orthodoxy . . . , she felt it her duty in life to search out and defend the humanity common to all . . . : Orientals and Westerners, black Americans and children of mixed blood, the mentally retarded and the powerless."

Sources

➤ **Books**

Block, Irvin, *The Lives of Pearl Buck: A Tale of China and America,* Crowell, 1973.

Buck, Pearl, *My Several Worlds: A Personal Record,* John Day, 1954.

Doyle, Paul A., *Pearl S. Buck,* Twayne, 1965, rev. ed., G. K. Hall, 1980.

Harris, Theodore F., *Pearl S. Buck: A Biography,* two volumes (Volume 2 is a collection of her letters), John Day, 1969.

LaFarge, Ann, *Pearl Buck,* Chelsea House, 1988.

Stirling, Nora, *Pearl Buck: A Woman in Conflict,* New Century Publishers, 1983.

➤ **Periodicals**

Christianity Today, March 30, 1973, p. 29.

New Republic, "An Island in Time," March 24, 1973, pp. 28–29.

New York Times, March 7, 1973, p. 1; March 10, 1973, p. 34.

Newsweek, March 19, 1973, p. 49.

Time, "Earth to Earth," March 19, 1973, p. 81.

Chris Burke

"I don't consider myself a star yet. This is only a start.*"*

The first actor with Down syndrome to be cast as a regular in a television series, Chris Burke was born on August 26, 1965, in New York City.

F rank and Marian Burke's son Christopher was only a few hours old when a doctor came to them with some frightening news: the baby had been born with Down syndrome, a chromosomal abnormality characterized by moderate to severe mental retardation and physical attributes such as upward-slanting eyes, a broad and somewhat flattened skull, wide hands, and short fingers. He would probably never learn to read or write, explained the doctor, and he might not even be able to dress or feed himself. The best course of action under the circumstances was institutionalization, preferably before they became too attached to him.

Disbelief mingled with fear as the Burkes struggled to understand and accept this grim prognosis. "A lot of things ran through our minds," Marian Burke later noted. "But committing our son was never an option." Instead, they took Chris home from the hospital, determined to shower him with the same loving attention they had given to their other three children. At that time, parents of babies with Down syndrome had virtually no one to turn to for advice and encouragement; doctors had not yet discovered how much infants benefitted from early exercise and stimulation, and since many people were ashamed to admit that they had a retarded child, there were few support groups or organizations that could offer assistance. So the Burkes developed a program of their own for Chris, making up games to help him learn to talk, involving him in sports to improve his coordination, and working with flash cards to teach him to read.

Chris began attending New York City's Kennedy Child Study Center at the age of four and later went to special schools in Massachusetts and Pennsylvania. Although he had trouble with math and the concept of money and making change, he studied hard to master reading. His favorite activity, however, was anything that put him in the spotlight; he spent hours dancing and learning to lip-sync popular songs.

The idea of acting first attracted Chris's attention when he was eight years old. Rummaging through a box of old photographs, he came across some glossy promotional portraits of his brother and sisters dating back to the days when they had done some modeling and acting in television commercials. He immediately announced to his parents that he, too, wanted to be on television. Although the Burkes had always avoided discouraging their son in any way, they gently pointed out that there probably wouldn't be many parts for him. But Chris—perpetually cheerful, charming, and overflowing with self-confidence—refused to give up his dream. His first role, a nonspeaking one, was as a shepherd in a school Christmas pageant. From that he graduated to a one-line role in another school play, *The Emperor's New Clothes.*

More than a decade passed, during which time Chris completed school and moved back in with his parents, who felt he was not quite able to handle living on his own. He also began looking for a job but met with one rejection after another. Chris then spent two unhappy weeks in a sheltered workshop before landing a volunteer position at a school for children with severe disabilities. An exceptionally gentle and loving person who related well to the school's multi-handicapped students, he was eventually hired for a salaried job as an elevator operator.

Still very much on Chris's mind, however, was his desire to become an actor. In 1984, he had watched a television program featuring a ten-year-old actor named Jason Kingsley who had Down syndrome. Excited to see a boy so much like himself working in the profession that had fascinated him for so many years, Chris immediately wrote Jason a fan letter. Jason's mother, television writer Emily Kingsley, was so moved by Chris's note that she wrote back a few weeks later, and the two became pen pals.

In 1987, Kingsley received a call from writer-producer Michael Braverman asking her to recommend a teenage actor with Down syndrome for a small part in a made-for-television movie, the pilot for a possible new series. Kingsley suggested Chris, who auditioned in New York and Hollywood and eventually got the part. Although disappointed when the pilot did not lead to a series, Chris was thrilled to have been given a chance to fulfill his dream and looked forward to his next role.

Back in Hollywood, Braverman hadn't forgotten the likable young man who was so eager to act. So he went to work creating a television series around Chris, fashioning an hour-long drama about a working-class family with a son who has Down syndrome. Braverman's goal was to highlight the issues such a family confronts on a daily basis and demonstrate how love, understanding, patience, and humor help them cope.

In January, 1989, Chris was summoned to Hollywood to shoot the pilot episode of "Life Goes On," the title given to Braverman's show. There was more than a little uneasiness on the set; as the central character, eighteen-year-old Corky Thatcher, Chris had a heavy workload and many lines. But he pulled it off without a hitch, completing his most difficult scene in only one take and winning the admiration and respect of the crew and his fellow cast members. The show debuted on September 12, 1989, and while never a ratings blockbuster, it has been a consistent favorite of the critics and especially of handicapped people, who look to Chris as proof that being "different" does not mean "incapable." Working with a dialogue coach who helps him interpret scenes and memorize lines, Chris as Corky has gone to dances, endured the teasing of cruel classmates, pressed his parents for more independence, and fallen in love. "I think it's beautiful that people like me can watch our show and see what Corky can do," Chris says.

Chris takes his status as a role model for disabled children and young adults very seriously. As a result of his success on "Life Goes On," he is much in demand as a spokesman for various causes that emphasize what people with handicaps can achieve if given a chance. He is perhaps most visible as a goodwill ambassador for McJobs, a program sponsored by McDonald's restaurants that employs people with mental and physical disabilities.

Today, Chris Burke leads the kind of life he once dreamed about and that few—especially those with Down syndrome—can ever hope to attain. A bubbly, irrepressible optimist, he continues to revel in his good fortune and has no reason to believe it will end with "Life Goes On." In his bedroom hangs a sign that reads, "Obstacles are what you see when you take your eyes off the goal." "I love that saying a lot," declares the young man who rejects the term *Down syndrome* in favor of *Up syndrome.* "To tell you the truth, I'm just like James Stewart, because I never studied to be an actor." Notes his mother, Marian Burke: "He will always amaze me. What impresses me most is not what he has achieved, but rather his attitude about life. He is . . . able to find something to smile at or feel good about in almost every situation. . . . Truly, Chris has been much blessed."

Sources

➤ **Books**

Burke, Chris, *A Special Kind of Hero,* Doubleday, 1991.

➤ **Periodicals**

New York, "Grace Notes," September 18, 1989, p. 67.

People, "For Chris Burke, the First Actor with Down Syndrome to Star on TV, *Life Goes On* in a Big Way," October 16, 1989, pp. 61–69 (opening quote).

Reader's Digest, "A Part for Chris," February, 1991, pp. 155–160.

Redbook, "A Mother's Story: 'My Son Will Always Amaze Me,'" November, 1989, pp. 48–52.

Ben Carson

*"*It doesn't matter if you come from the inner city. People who fail in life are people who find lots of excuses. It's never too late for a person to recognize that they have potential in themselves.*"*

Ben Carson overcame poverty, racism, and a violent temper to become a world-renowned neurosurgeon. He was born on September 18, 1951, in Detroit, Michigan.

Address: Johns Hopkins Hospital, 600 North Wolfe St., Baltimore, MD 21205.

I n April, 1987, a West German doctor traveled to Baltimore's Johns Hopkins Hospital to consult with pediatric neurosurgeon Ben Carson on an especially difficult case. Already highly respected for his ability to save the lives of sick children whose conditions others had judged hopeless, Carson now faced the prospect of separating congenitally united (Siamese) twins, joined together at the back of the head, an extremely complicated and risky operation that had always left one or both patients dead or severely brain damaged.

While this may have been the greatest challenge of his career, Carson had already faced great ones on his road to becoming a doctor. As a youngster, he was branded a failure; as a teenager, he seemed destined to fall victim to the violence of his inner-city neighborhood. Thanks in large part to his mother, his own determination, and his strong religious faith, however, he avoided becoming just another statistic and is now an acknowledged expert in pediatric neurosurgery at one of the most prestigious medical facilities in the world.

Benjamin Solomon Carson is the youngest of two sons born to Sonya Copeland Carson and Robert Solomon Carson. His parents divorced when he was eight, and except for a two-year period when he, his mother, and his older brother, Curtis, lived with relatives in Boston, he grew up in Detroit. The family was very poor. Sonya Carson had left school after the third grade, married at thirteen, and worked long hours as a domestic to support herself and her sons. Ben felt a sense of hopelessness and despair about their situation that was reflected in his poor performance at school and his hair-trigger temper, which exploded at the slightest provocation.

Sensing that Ben's academic problems stemmed from a lack of motivation, not a lack of intelligence, Sonya Carson devised a plan. She limited his television viewing to just a couple of shows a week (which she selected) and ordered him to read two books a week and submit written reports to her. (What her son didn't realize at the time was that she herself could barely read what he wrote.) At first, Ben hated reading, but soon he found himself hooked and eagerly shared what he learned with his mother. As he later recalled, "Once I discovered that between the pages of those books . . . we could go anywhere and we could meet anybody and we could do anything, that's when it really started to hit me." And when he read about the work of a missionary doctor who had gone overseas to help sick people, he had a goal: he, too, would become a doctor.

By the end of sixth grade, about a year-and-a-half after his mother had instituted her reading plan, Carson had zoomed from the very bottom of his class to the top. Still of concern, however, was his fiery temper. "I would just fly off the handle, and the only thing that was important to me, if somebody made me mad, was to make them unhappy," he explains. "If that meant hitting them with a rock or a brick or a baseball bat, that's what I wanted to do." Sometimes it was the racist taunts of White youths in his neighborhood that set him off; other times it was the teasing of a friend.

One day when he was fourteen, Carson became enraged when one of his buddies tuned in a different station on a radio they were listening to and refused to change it back. Grabbing a knife, he plunged it into his friend's stomach, where it struck a metal belt buckle and snapped off. The other boy fled in terror, and a shaken Carson returned home and agonized over what he had just done. "It was then that I realized that if I continued in that vein, I was going to kill somebody or somebody was going to kill me," he says. He locked himself in the bathroom for several hours and prayed for help, eventually concluding that "if people could make me angry, they could control me. Why should I give someone else such power over me?"

Feeling that he was no longer at the mercy of his temper, Carson applied himself to his studies with a renewed sense of purpose. Except for a brief period when his grades slipped because he was spending too much time "hanging out" and not enough time hitting the books, he received all A's and in 1969 graduated third in his high school class. With his pick of several scholarships to choose from, he opted to continue his education at Yale. From there he went on to the University of Michigan Medical School, initially planning to specialize in psychiatry. But during his first year, he found himself more fascinated by the physical disorders of the brain than the mental and emotional ones, so he switched to neurosurgery.

After completing medical school, Carson headed to Baltimore, where he was accepted into the prestigious residency program in general surgery at Johns Hopkins Hospital. He then became Hopkins's first Black-American neurosurgery resident, in a training program that lasted five years. In 1983 an offer came to serve as chief resident at Queen Elizabeth Medical Centre in Perth, Western Australia. Because there were so few neurosurgeons in that country, Carson's workload was much heavier than it would have been in the United States, and he was able to gain several years' worth of operating-room experience in only twelve months. He returned to Johns Hopkins in 1984 and was soon promoted to Director of the Department of Pediatric Neurosurgery, becoming at the age of thirty-three the youngest doctor in America to hold such a position.

In the years since then, Carson has become an internationally known expert on treating severe neurological disorders, particularly in children. (Only about twenty percent of his patients are adults.) Besides performing "routine" operations such as removing brain tumors or correcting vascular defects, he has combined his knowledge and surgical skill with the latest technological innovations to tackle many cases that other doctors have either given up on or refused to handle.

In the mid-1980s, for example, he revived a very risky procedure known as a hemispherectomy, which involves removing half of a patient's brain to prevent seizures of the type brought on by a rare and chronic form of encephalitis. Because of the high mortality rate associated with hemispherectomies, most doctors had stopped doing them. But Carson developed new techniques that have led to astonishing successes in patients who were otherwise doomed to suffer from as many as 120 seizures a day. He has also developed new methods for helping children with usually fatal brain-stem tumors, and he was the first doctor to perform brain surgery on a fetus inside the womb. His guiding principle in all he does is a simple one: "If the patient will be no worse off from the surgery than by letting the disease run its course unimpeded, there's nothing to lose by going forward—and possibly a great deal to gain."

Never was this more true than in the case of West German infants Patrick and Benjamin Binder, the congenitally united twins Carson operated on in September, 1987. Although they had separate brains, they were joined at the back of the head and shared blood vessels at that point. In similar cases, one child usually dies or is left severely mentally impaired by heavy blood loss and other complications during surgery. But the boys' mother refused to sacrifice one of her sons to save the other. Carson pondered this dilemma for several months, then settled on a radical new approach that borrowed from cardiac surgery techniques: stop the babies' hearts and drain their blood, then work quickly (taking no more than one hour) to repair all of the damaged and tangled blood vessels before restoring circulation.

The entire procedure took twenty-two hours and required the services of a seventy-person medical team. At the critical point when the twins' hearts were stopped and their blood had been drained, Carson began performing the delicate task of separating them. Less than a minute short of the hour limit, he completed the separation and closed up Patrick Binder's head while another doctor tended to Benjamin. The easy-going, soft-spoken Carson subsequently became a bit of a celebrity when he met with television and print journalists to explain the surgery on behalf of the Hopkins team. Before long the inspiring story of his climb up from poverty and despair had spread across the country.

Carson is now in constant demand as a speaker at colleges, churches, and schools, where he admonishes young people "to do the best you can with what you have." He believes very strongly that doctors have a responsibility to contribute more to society than just their medical skills, and with that in mind he makes time to meet monthly with several hundred Baltimore-area teenagers to talk about seeking achievement and recognition through academics—especially science—rather than entertainment or sports.

At commencement exercises for the class of 1988 at his alma mater, Detroit's Southwestern High School, Ben Carson shared his upbeat philosophy of life with the graduates and their families. "It's important that you know there are many ways to go," he said. "There are opportunities everywhere. You just have to be willing to take advantage of them. Think big! Set your sights as high as Mount Everest. Nobody was born to be a failure. If you feel you're going to succeed—and you work your tail off—you will succeed!"

Sources

➤ **Books**

Carson, Ben, and Cecil B. Murphey, *Gifted Hands: The Ben Carson Story*, Zondervan, 1990.

Carson, Ben, *Think Big*, Zondervan, 1992.

➤ **Periodicals**

Black Enterprise, "Merging Medicine with Technology," October, 1988, p. 70.

Christianity Today, "Surgeon on a Mission: With Prayer and Self-Discipline, Ben Carson Overcame Poverty to Become America's Leading Pediatric Neurosurgeon," May 27, 1991, pp. 24–26.

Detroit Free Press, "Doctor Tells Teens to Take a Risk," November 9, 1990, p. 4B.

Detroit News, "A Modern Joseph Tells Teens: Don't Be Victim," November 11, 1990; "Doctor Who Separated Siamese Twins Will Address WSU Grads," June 6, 1991, p. 5B.

Ebony, "Surgical Superstar," January, 1988, pp. 52–58; "The Love That Changed My Life," May, 1990, p. 38.

People, "The Physician Who Healed Himself First," Fall, 1991 (special issue), pp. 96–99 (opening quote).

Reader's Digest, "Ben Carson: Man of Miracles," April, 1990, pp. 71–75.

Jimmy and Rosalynn Carter

"Being out of the political arena . . . has given the news media a different perspective of what we . . . tried to do . . . in the White House."— Jimmy Carter

Former President Jimmy Carter was born on October 1, 1924, in Plains, Georgia, and former First Lady Rosalynn Carter was born on August 18, 1927, just outside Plains.

Address: The Carter Center, 1 Copenhill, Atlanta, GA 30307.

On November 2, 1976, Jimmy Carter became the first southerner elected to the presidency of the United States since before the Civil War. A one-term Georgia governor heralded by *Time* magazine in 1971 as a symbol of the New South, Carter rose from near obscurity to lead the Democratic party to victory over Republican President Gerald Ford by persuading a nation fed up with political scandal that he was the man to restore trust in government. His "working partner" in that pledge was his wife, Rosalynn, the most active and influential First Lady since Eleanor Roosevelt. While their time in the White House was marked by more disappointments than successes, the Carters have devoted themselves since then to a variety of public service activities that have garnered the respect of national as well as international leaders.

James Earl Carter, Jr., is the oldest of four children born to Lillian Gordy Carter, a nurse, and James Earl Carter, Sr., a farmer, businessman, and civic leader in the small Georgia town of Plains. James Earl, Jr., or "Jimmy," as he prefers to be called, was a somewhat shy and studious youngster who excelled in school. After graduating from high school at the age of sixteen, he attended Georgia Southwestern College in nearby Americus for a year and then spent the following year at the Georgia Institute of Technology in Atlanta before gaining admission to the U.S. Naval Academy in Annapolis in 1943.

It was during one of his visits home to Plains that the young cadet made an especially favorable impression on his sister Ruth's best friend, Rosalynn Smith. Born just outside of town on her mother's family farm, Rosalynn, like Carter, was also the oldest of four children. Her father, Wilburn Edgar Smith, was a mechanic and school bus driver who died of leukemia when Rosalynn was only thirteen. His death left the family in dire financial straits and forced Rosalynn to take over many of the household responsibilities while her mother, Allethea Murray Smith, struggled to make a living for herself and her young children. Despite the demands placed on her at home, Rosalynn was valedictorian of her high school graduating class. She then enrolled in a secretarial course at Georgia Southwestern College, using money her mother had managed to set aside expressly for the higher education of her children.

Jimmy Carter and Rosalynn Smith first dated during the summer of 1945 and were married on July 7, 1946, after each had graduated from their respective schools. Commissioned an officer in the U.S.

Navy, Jimmy then embarked on what both he and Rosalynn assumed would be a lifetime career in the service. Over the next seven years, his assignments took them from Virginia to Hawaii to Connecticut to New York, where he was accepted into the Navy's then-new nuclear submarine program; he also studied nuclear physics and engineering at Schenectady's Union College. During this hectic period, Rosalynn gave birth to four sons (Amy, the only Carter daughter, was not born until 1967) and learned to cope with the ups and downs of being a navy wife whose husband was often away at sea.

In 1953, however, the Carters' lives took an unexpected turn when Jimmy received news that his father had died. After much soul-searching, he decided—against Rosalynn's wishes—to resign from the navy and go back to Plains. There he rebuilt and expanded the family business (which included a seed and fertilizer supply store, a peanut farm, and a peanut warehouse) while Rosalynn kept the books. Gradually he began to get involved in civic and church affairs on a local, regional, and state basis, and in 1962 he ran for the Georgia state senate. He won that election as well as his re-election bid in 1964, then sought the Democratic nomination for governor in 1966 but lost to Lester Maddox.

Jimmy Carter made a second try for the governorship in 1970 and this time was victorious. Rosalynn, who had stayed out of the limelight during his previous campaigns in favor of working behind the scenes and tending to the family business, forced herself to overcome her natural shyness and go out on the trail in support of her husband. Once installed in the governor's mansion, she slowly gained self-confidence in her new role as Georgia's First Lady and became active in a number of causes, especially those having to do with the mentally retarded and the mentally ill. Jimmy Carter, meanwhile, lived up to his billing as a true son of the New South by opening up the government to Blacks and women, reforming the appointment system for members of the Cabinet and judiciary, improving the prison system, and reorganizing state agencies to eliminate some of the bureaucracy. He also came out strongly against racial discrimination, a stand that had already caused him a bit of trouble back in conservative Plains.

As early as 1972, Jimmy Carter had begun to give some thought to the idea of running for president in 1976, and with that dream in mind he made a point of familiarizing himself with foreign affairs. In 1974 he also made valuable contacts around the country as the national campaign committee chairman of the Democratic National Committee. Later that same year, shortly before his term as governor was up, he officially announced his candidacy for the 1976 Democratic presidential nomination.

For twenty-two months in 1975 and 1976, the Carters worked tirelessly to make sure he became the Democrats' choice, traveling together and separately to get the word out about the man whose name usually prompted the question, "Jimmy who?" More than a dozen other men were also interested in the job, including such notables as Henry "Scoop" Jackson, Morris Udall, George Wallace, Jerry Brown, and Hubert Humphrey. But Carter took them all on fearlessly in thirty of the thirty-one primaries, eighteen of which he won. By the time of the Democratic National Convention in July, 1976, Jimmy Carter—thanks to some last-minute delegate-switching—was able to secure the nomination on the first ballot.

His Republican opponent for the presidency was Gerald Ford, the former vice-president who had become president following the resignation of Richard Nixon. The issue of trust in government dominated the campaign, and Washington "outsider" Carter ran on a populist platform that blended conservative language and liberal goals. His standard introduction was brief and to the point—"Hi, I'm Jimmy Carter from Plains, Georgia, and I'm running for president"—as was his slogan: "I will never lie to you." He vowed to counteract what he saw as years of government mismanagement, both fiscal and moral. (Carter made no secret of the fact that he was a born-again Christian and an active Southern Baptist.) Well aware that people were still a bit leery of someone so inexperienced and untested, he also tried to sharpen his image by agreeing to a *Playboy* interview and a series of three televised debates with Ford.

After enjoying an initial lead in the popularity polls, Carter saw his ratings take a tumble in the fall. The *Playboy* interview had proven to be a major blunder; his candid admission that he had "looked on a lot of women with lust" and had "committed adultery in my heart many times" backfired and made him the brunt of jokes. He also did poorly in his first debate with Ford. But he staged an impressive comeback in the second and third debates, and by the time election day arrived on November 2, the outcome was too close to call. Carter won by a relatively narrow margin of less than two million popular votes.

For a while after taking office in January, 1977, the Carters enjoyed the heady euphoria of a new administration with its fresh faces and fresh hopes. Among the new president's immediate actions were pardoning Vietnam War draft resisters (a promise he had made during the campaign), gradually withdrawing some U.S. troops from Korea, putting an end to the practice of denying foreign communists entry into the country, and establishing a cabinet-level Department of Energy to spearhead conservation efforts. He also proposed welfare and tax reform to stimulate the economy and create more jobs and took the first steps toward fashioning a comprehensive environmental protection package. In keeping with his pledge to establish a more "folksy" presidency, he eliminated limousine service for his staff, turned down the White House thermostats, and revived the Roosevelt-era tradition of "fireside chats" with the American people.

In the meantime, the First Lady, having made it clear to voters that she and her husband were partners ("I come with him" is how she put it on the campaign trail), served as a combination chief adviser and roving ambassador, meeting world leaders on his behalf and sometimes explaining his policies to them. In addition, she attended cabinet meetings as an observer, helped plot political strategy, and traveled the country soliciting reactions to her husband's policies. She also continued her work on behalf of the mentally ill and took up the cause of the elderly and their needs and fought for passage of the Equal Rights Amendment.

Before long, Rosalynn's apparent status as the most powerful unelected public figure in the nation had angered and alarmed those who felt she was overstepping her bounds as First Lady. But as she told a *People* magazine reporter, "You can either not do anything public and stay out of sight or go and do those things that you think are important. I'm not one to just sit back. . . . I feel the responsibility to do something. . . . I've just always worked with Jimmy this way, ever since he ran for governor in 1966. . . . Now that he is the President, am I supposed not to be interested? I don't advise him on things that I don't know anything about."

By the middle of 1977, Carter himself had begun to lose some of his popularity, especially after his appointee at the Office of Management and Budget, longtime friend Bert Lance, was suspected of involving himself in some shady practices while serving as head of a Georgia bank. Lance eventually resigned in the face of intense media scrutiny and criticism, casting a shadow on the president's promise that he would restore honesty and morality in government.

Things got off to a rocky start in other ways for the president. The role of Washington outsider, which had served him so well during the campaign, was proving to be a liability as he tried to garner support for his measures in a Congress where he had few allies. His strong stand on human rights created resentment at home and abroad. Ongoing arms talks with the Soviet Union fell apart when he unexpectedly scrapped the treaty that had been in progress since the previous administration and called for even greater arms reductions, a move that left the Soviets angry and suspicious. Tensions rose over the Panama Canal as Panamanians demanded an end to U.S. control over the waterway; concluding that the goodwill of Latin American countries was worth more than maintaining control over the canal, Carter negotiated a controversial treaty that will turn over ownership to the Panamanians on December 31, 1999. Closer to home, Americans battled rising oil prices that led to double-digit inflation, high unemployment, and soaring interest rates.

The highlight of Carter's presidency came in 1978. On August 5 of that year, disturbed by the slow progress of peace talks in the Middle East, he invited Israeli prime minister Menachem Begin and Egyptian president Anwar Sadat to join him in September at the presidential retreat in Camp David, Maryland. For nearly two weeks, the three men worked in isolation from the press to come to some sort of a peace agreement. They emerged on September 17 having made remarkable progress but with no definite agreement in hand. Finally, after months of intense negotiations, Begin and Sadat signed what came to be known as the Camp David Accord on March 26, 1979, a ground-breaking document that guaranteed peace between Israel and Egypt.

The Camp David Accord supplied a much-needed boost to Carter's flagging popularity, but already another crisis was brewing that signaled the beginning of the darkest year of his presidency. In February, 1979, Muslim fundamentalists led by the Ayatollah Khomeini took over Iran and drove the Shah (the former ruler) and his family out of the country. No other world leader was eager to give the Shah sanctuary for fear of angering the Iranians, so for several months he and his family wandered throughout the world seeking asylum wherever they could find it. Then the Shah grew ill with cancer that required treatment available only in the United States. As a humanitarian gesture, Carter agreed to allow him to enter the country. On November 4, 1979, outraged Iranians responded by storming the U.S. Embassy in Teheran and taking ninety hostages, sixty-three of whom were American employees.

As weeks stretched into months with no apparent sign that the Iranians intended to release their prisoners, Americans at home— infuriated by the sight of militant Iranians burning U.S. flags and chanting insults—grew impatient as they waited for Carter to do something to secure the hostages' freedom. At first, he worked through an Algerian mediator, but progress was almost nonexistent. Finally, in April, 1980, he authorized the use of military force in a secret rescue mission that ended in disaster when several helicopters crashed and eight Marines were killed. Once again, negotiations stalled for a while, but when they resumed, the president himself played a key role.

Other crises preoccupied him that same year. In January, for instance, the Soviets invaded Afghanistan. Carter responded by canceling cultural exchanges between the United States and Russia, banning new sales of high tech goods, curtailing Soviet fishing rights in U.S. waters, cutting grain sales, and boycotting the Summer Olympics, which were to be held in Moscow. Although most of these actions won the support of the American people, they made little impression on the Soviets, who showed no signs of leaving Afghanistan. And cutting grain sales ended up having an adverse effect on U.S. farmers and made some Americans think twice about the desirability of economic sanctions.

As the 1980 presidential election neared, Democrats rallied to support Carter, who was still desperately pursuing ways to bring the hostages home from Iran. By this time, however, the majority of Americans had lost confidence in the man from Georgia and his ability to manage the economy and solve the hostage crisis. So at the polls that November, they elected Ronald Reagan in a landslide. Just moments after the new president was sworn into office on January 20, 1981, Iran released the hostages after 444 days of captivity.

The stinging defeat was a bitter disappointment to both the Carters, who felt hurt and rejected by the American people they had pledged to serve. They quietly returned to Plains, only to discover a major financial crisis awaited them there—the peanut warehouse, which during their stay in Washington had been operated by a blind trust, was nearly one million dollars in debt. In the end, Carter had to sell the business to straighten out the financial mess.

Gradually, the Carters emerged from their low-profile existence in Plains. In 1983, for example, Jimmy published his memoirs, *Keeping the Faith,* and Rosalynn followed in 1984 with hers, *First Lady from Plains.* A skilled carpenter, Jimmy Carter joined Habitat for Humanity in 1982 and regularly participates in many of their building projects for the poor throughout the country, often accompanied by Rosalynn when she is not busy with her own projects, which focus on mental health issues.

Both Carters became actively involved in the planning of the Carter Presidential Library and Carter Center at Atlanta's Emory University during the early 1980s. As conceived by the former president, the Carter Center is primarily a think tank and research facility where statesmen, scholars, and experts in national and international problems can meet to study and formulate policy and, most important, find a common ground on which to discuss peace. More recently, Carter himself has served as a sort of "citizen-diplomat" who mediates world conflicts and referees elections in emerging democracies.

Today, the Carters, especially Jimmy, have grown somewhat philosophical about the criticism they endured while in the White House. "I know what we tried to do," says Jimmy. "I know what we failed to do. . . . There was never any allegation of lying or greed or selfishness or abandonment of peace or human rights or environmental quality." To their great disappointment, some of the accomplishments of their administration—the environmental protection programs, the expanded mental health programs, and the re-establishment of human rights as a principal part of U.S. foreign policy—did not survive the Reagan era, either as a result of budget cuts or a difference in priorities and attitude.

From the perspective of the 1990s, Jimmy Carter and his presidency are enjoying increasingly better reviews from historians, political commentators, and even the public, which has come to admire his stands on the problems of the homeless and the hungry, on the arms race, on physical and mental health, and on peace. He is pleased to be on the "comeback trail," especially after life dealt such a curve back in 1980. "We had to shift the path we had laid out for ourselves, which was 4 more years in the White House, and like everybody should do we tried to find an alternate path that was not necessarily inferior," Carter explains. "No matter what role in life one plays, if your business goes bankrupt, if you get fired from your job, or your spouse dies, people have to have within themselves some stability, a foundation on which they can build. . . . Then they can look to the future with confidence that they have talent and ability and can utilize those in a liberating, exuberant, unpredictable, adventurous way."

Sources

➤ **Books**

Carter, Jimmy, *Keeping the Faith: Memoirs of a President*, Bantam, 1983.

Carter, Jimmy, and Rosalynn Carter, *Everything to Gain: Making the Most of the Rest of Your Life*, Random House, 1987.

Carter, Rosalynn, *First Lady from Plains*, Houghton, 1984.

Wade, Linda R., *Encyclopedia of the Presidents: James Carter*, Children's Press, 1989.

➤ **Periodicals**

Esquire, "Whatever Became of Jimmy Carter?," July, 1984, pp. 78–84.

Good Housekeeping, "Jimmy and Rosalynn," January, 1992 (opening quote).

Newsweek, "Out on Her Own," June 13, 1977, pp. 15–18.

New York Times Magazine, "Peanut Farmer for President," December 14, 1975; "The Importance of Being Rosalynn," June 3, 1979.

People, "Downstairs She Is History's Most Influential First Lady: 'Up Here, We're Just Family,'" December 24, 1979, pp. 32–35; "Inside the White House (Cont'd): Jimmy Sleeps Well, Amy's Mad at Mom and Rosalynn's Content," January 7, 1980, pp. 70–75; "Former First Lady Rosalynn Carter Is the Second Big-Time Author from Plains," April 30, 1984, pp. 80–85; "Ex-President Jimmy Carter Keeps the Faith on a Mission of Hope to a New York Slum," September 17, 1984, pp. 40–45.

Reader's Digest, "America's First 'Good Ole Girl,'" June, 1980, pp. 195–200.

Time, May 31, 1971; "Man of the Year: I'm Jimmy Carter," January 3, 1977, pp. 11–22; "Assessing a Presidency," August 18, 1980, pp. 10–15; "'We Enjoyed Living in This House,'" January 26, 1981, pp. 27–28; "The Man from Plains Sums It Up," October 11, 1982, pp. 62–64.

USA Weekend, "How Jimmy Will Save the World," March 15–17, 1991, pp. 4–5.

U.S. News and World Report, "Rosalynn Carter Takes On the President's Critics," April 9, 1979, pp. 49–50; "Memoirs, Speeches, Relaxation—What's Ahead for Carter," November 17, 1980, p.

63; "Carter's Own Post-Mortem: Successes, Mistakes—and His Future," November 17, 1980, pp. 91–93; "Jimmy Carter: Back Home and On the Mend," March 30, 1981, pp. 28–29; "Life After the White House: How First Families Adjust," June 25, 1984, pp. 39–40; "Chapter 2 for Jimmy and Rosalynn," June 1, 1987, p. 62.

George Washington Carver

"It has always been the one great ideal of my life
to be of the greatest good to the greatest number of 'my people' possible.''

Born near Diamond, Missouri, in late 1864 or early 1865,
George Washington Carver was a pioneer in agricultural education and a creative scientist who helped revolutionize farming practices in the American South. He died on January 5,
1943, in Tuskegee, Alabama.

F ame came to George Washington Carver relatively late in life, when he was nearly sixty years old. From then until many years after his death, he was hailed as the foremost Black-American scientist of the day, as an innovative thinker who, among his other accomplishments, developed more than three hundred uses for the peanut. The story of his struggle to achieve success against tremendous odds as well as his gentle humor and saintly image made him a folk hero among Black as well as White Americans. Recently, historians have begun to separate the man from the myth in an attempt to assess Carver's true legacy. The picture that has emerged is one of a skilled teacher and scientific popularizer whose many practical efforts to raise the standard of living of poor, mostly Black farmers in the American South have been largely overshadowed by the legend of the creative scientist.

George Washington Carver was born into slavery sometime during the final months of the Civil War. His mother, Mary, was a slave who belonged to Missouri homesteaders Moses and Susan Carver, a childless couple. Though opposed to slavery, they had purchased Mary out of a desperate need for help on their farm. George's father, whose name is unrecorded, was believed to have been a slave on a nearby homestead; he died in an accident around the time his son was born. During a wartime raid on the Carver farm, Mary and her infant son were kidnapped and taken to the neighboring slave state of Arkansas. A man hired by Moses Carver to bring them back was able to track down only the baby; Mary was never heard from again. As a result, the Carvers raised the orphaned George and his older brother, Jim, as their own.

George's frequent childhood bouts with various respiratory illnesses left him unable to do heavy farm work. Instead, he helped with such tasks as cleaning the house, doing the laundry, and tending to the garden, where he soon displayed a talent for nurturing plants. The Carvers did what they could to see that he received some education. By the time he was twelve, George had progressed beyond the resources available in a rural setting and had to move to a nearby town to attend school. He stayed for about a year, rooming with a Black-American couple and visiting the Carvers only on weekends. Then he left with another family in 1878 for Fort Scott, Kansas.

Thus began a period of restlessness and wandering that lasted more than twelve years and took young Carver back and forth across several midwestern states. Along the way, he managed to finish high school while supporting himself by doing odd jobs, including knitting, sewing, embroidery work, and laundry. In 1884, officials at a Kansas City college admitted him on the basis of a mail-in application, then turned him away at the door when they saw he was Black. Bitter and frustrated, Carver decided to try homesteading. He farmed for two years in west-central Kansas before abandoning his claim and working his way east to Indianola, Iowa. There he enrolled in Simpson College in September, 1890, to study painting.

Carver soon realized, however, that no matter how much he loved to paint, he would never be able to support himself as an artist. Contemplating a more practical subject to pursue, he opted for agriculture. After receiving his bachelor's degree in agriculture in 1894 from the Iowa State College of Agricultural and Mechanical Arts (at that time one of the finest schools of its kind in the country), he enrolled in the master's program and received a faculty appointment to teach freshman biology courses.

As he gained fame in academic circles for his teaching skills, Carver was offered positions at many other colleges and universities throughout the country. From Booker T. Washington came a personal request to head the new agricultural school at Alabama's Tuskegee Institute, the leading industrial school for Blacks in the United States. Its philosophy of providing practical vocational training to help students achieve social and political rights through economic success meshed perfectly with Carver's own desire to improve the lot of Black farmers through education. He accepted Washington's offer and officially joined the faculty in 1896.

Carver's responsibilities at Tuskegee were wide ranging. In addition to heading the agriculture department and teaching a full schedule of classes, he directed the institute's agricultural experiment station, managed its two farms, and temporarily served as its veterinarian. He also ran agricultural extension services throughout rural areas of the South, served on numerous faculty committees, and supervised the beautification of the campus. But it was in the classroom that Carver truly excelled; he not only instructed but inspired his students with practical experiments and hands-on work and observation that emphasized the concrete over the abstract. He also shared with them his reverence for the beauty and miracle of nature, which for him was inextricably linked with a deeply mystical religious notion of God as the creator of it all.

Through his work at the experimental station and as director of the extension service, Carver—who usually worked alone with almost no funds and no equipment—fulfilled his dream of helping the South's poorest farmers. For example, he showed them how to cultivate crops other than cotton (which still dominated the region at the time), using methods that did not require them to purchase expensive equipment, seeds, or fertilizers. He issued regular bulletins on his findings, delivering practical and easy-to-understand advice geared toward laypeople rather than the scientific community. He also set up classes and conferences at the institute designed specifically for farmers. To reach those who could not come to Tuskegee, Carver went out into the countryside in a wagon he outfitted with demonstration materials and equipment.

Carver's involvement in so many different activities taxed his abilities to the limit. A dreamer and a dabbler at heart, he displayed shortcomings as a manager that frustrated Booker T. Washington and gradually led to tension between the two men. The agriculture department was reorganized several times during the early 1900s, and each reorganization left Carver with fewer responsibilities and a bruised ego. By 1915, he had withdrawn from teaching to concentrate solely on research and public speaking, the latter an outgrowth of his success with the extension service.

Around this time, Carver also turned his attention to what was called "creative chemistry"—developing products that could be commercialized. Washington's death in 1915 brought Tuskegee a new president, Robert Russa Moton, who got along well with Carver and encouraged him to spend as much time as possible in the laboratory. Recognizing the professor's popular appeal, Moton also groomed Carver to succeed Washington as an ambassador of sorts, someone who could attract much-needed publicity and contributions to Tuskegee.

Carver soon began to garner national and even worldwide attention for his work. Honors from several prestigious organizations were followed by a consultantship to the U.S. Department of Agriculture on overcoming food shortages during World War I, an invitation from Thomas Edison to join him in work at his laboratory in New Jersey, an appointment as a spokesman for peanut growers and processors, and an appearance before a congressional committee (on behalf of the peanut industry) that was so entertaining and thorough that he charmed the committee members and as well as the American public, which read about his testimony in countless newspaper and magazine articles. Carver's name became a household word, and by the early 1920s he found himself hailed as a genius and in great demand as a lecturer and as a spokesman for a wide variety of groups.

Carver was showered with awards and honors throughout the 1920s and 1930s, including the NAACP's Spingarn Medal in 1923. His fame continued to grow as he sought commercial markets and producers for his many inventions and, during the Depression, researched diet, nutrition, and economical ways of feeding a family. He was a strong proponent of self-sufficiency and making the best of limited resources. He also abhorred waste and developed many ways of recycling discarded material into useful items. But Carver quickly grew bored with old projects when a new one came along and did not often perfect a product or process to make it truly marketable. As a result, few of his inventions made it out of the laboratory.

Carver was nevertheless immensely popular, even among conservative southern Whites, who found him acceptable because he rarely spoke out on race relations. He felt that one's personal example of hard work and success was the best way to change people's minds about race. Equally appealing were his deep religious faith and belief in divine revelation (which put him at odds with much of the scientific community but endeared him to the public) and his image as a kindly, humble eccentric with a knack for explaining his subject matter in simple but vivid terms.

Beginning around 1935, age and declining health began to take their toll on Carver, whose symbolic status had by then reached mythic proportions. His last major project was to establish the George Washington Carver Museum and Foundation as a way to preserve his legacy and provide a way for others to carry on his work. Following his death on January 5, 1943, Carver was buried on the Tuskegee campus, his home for almost fifty years.

Viewed from a modern perspective, Carver's fame was in large part the creation of the White press, which overlooked his substantial success as an educator and instead embellished his accomplishments in creative chemistry to show that Black Americans could achieve despite segregation and racism. Carver himself never objected to being used as a token of Black-American success; as a man who was easily wounded by any kind of criticism, he thoroughly enjoyed the praise and attention he received. The popular image of him also ignored the fact that he could at times be arrogant, secretive, and difficult to work with. Yet he was an inspiration to many Black Americans who strove to become something other than what White society expected or wanted them to be. He also changed some people's minds about the supposed inferiority of Black Americans and, as a frequent victim of segregationist laws and overt prejudice during his many travels throughout the country, he served as a constant reminder that racism was still a factor in American life, even for someone as beloved and celebrated as George Washington Carver.

Sources

➤ **Books**

Adair, Gene, *George Washington Carver*, Chelsea House, 1989 (opening quote.)

Elliot, Lawrence, *George Washington Carver: The Man Who Overcame*, Prentice-Hall, 1966.

Holt, Rackham, *George Washington Carver: An American Biography*, rev. ed., Doubleday, 1962.

Manber, David, *Wizard of Tuskegee*, Crowell, 1967.

McMurry, Linda O., *George Washington Carver: Scientist and Symbol*, Oxford University Press, 1981.

➤ **Periodicals**

Christian Century, "Death Comes to Dr. Carver," January 20, 1943, p. 68.

Commonweal, "One of Our Greatest Americans," April 16, 1943, pp. 645–647.

Nation, January 16, 1943, pp. 75–76.

Newsweek, January 18, 1943, pp. 67–68.

Reader's Digest, "No Greener Pastures," December, 1942, pp. 71–74.

Time, "Black Leonardo," November 24, 1941, pp. 81–82; January 18, 1943, p. 89.

Mary Cassatt

"There are two ways for a painter: the broad and easy one or the narrow and hard one."

Born on May 22, 1844, in Allegheny City, Pennsylvania, Mary Cassatt defied the social conventions of her day to become one of America's foremost artists. She died June 14, 1926, in Mesnil-Theribus, France.

I n the spring of 1877, French artist Edgar Degas visited the studio of a thirty-three-year-old American painter named Mary Cassatt. A leading figure in the radical group of painters known as the Impressionists, Degas had seen evidence in one of the young woman's paintings that she obviously felt as he and his colleagues did about color and technique. Would she be interested in exhibiting with their next show?

Cassatt had long resented the rigid artistic standards of the day, which insisted on clean lines, muted tones, smooth surfaces, and classical themes. She admired the luminous palette, unblended brushstrokes, and ordinary subject matter of the Impressionists. Consequently, she didn't even have to think twice about her answer. "I accepted [Degas's invitation] with joy," Cassatt later told her first biographer, Achille Segard. "I hated conventional art. I began to live." Thus she became the first—and only—American to join the Impressionists during their most productive years.

Mary Stevenson Cassatt was born in 1844 in Allegheny City, Pennsylvania, an area that is now part of Pittsburgh, and grew up in Philadelphia. She was the fifth child of Katherine Kelso Johnston and Robert Simpson Cassatt, a well-to-do real estate and investment broker. Her upbringing was fairly typical for the era and her social class; at school, she prepared for life as a wife and mother, which included lessons in how to run a home as well as in such genteel pastimes as embroidery, music, sketching, and painting. To broaden their children's education, the Cassatts took them to live in Europe for several years during the early 1850s.

In 1860, sixteen-year-old Mary enrolled in the Pennsylvania Academy of the Fine Arts in Philadelphia. Despite the fact that women—especially upper-class women—were not encouraged to pursue careers, she wanted to be a professional artist. By 1862, however, she had grown frustrated with the program's slow pace and inadequate course offerings; she also resented the patronizing attitude of the male teachers and most of her fellow students. She concluded that the best way for her to learn about art would be to go to Europe and study the works of the old masters on her own.

Overcoming the strong objections of her family (her father once declared he would rather see his daughter dead than living abroad as a "bohemian"), Cassatt left for Paris in 1866 to take private art lessons and copy masterpieces in the Louvre. Over the next few years, she traveled throughout France and stayed briefly in Rome. Her first break came in 1868, when one of her portraits was accepted at the prestigious Paris Salon, an exhibition run by the French government's Academy of Fine Arts. (To protect her family from embarrassment, Cassatt submitted the painting under the name "Mary Stevenson.") Her debut effort was very well received, as was another portrait she submitted in 1870.

Not long after the Franco-Prussian War began in 1870, Cassatt reluctantly returned home and immediately encountered obstacles that threatened to put an end to her career. Living with her parents in a small town well outside Philadelphia, she had problems finding supplies and people willing to model for her. To make matters worse, her father announced that he would provide for her basic needs but not for anything connected with her work. In an attempt to raise some money, Cassatt left some of her paintings with an art dealer in New York, but he was unable to interest any buyers. She then took them to a dealer in Chicago, where they were all destroyed in the catastrophic fire of 1871.

Cassatt was close to despair when the archbishop of Pittsburgh contacted her in late 1871 and commissioned her to paint copies of two works by the Italian master Correggio. Since the originals were on display in Parma, Italy, Cassatt accepted the assignment and left immediately for Europe. She used the money she had earned to resume her career in Europe. The Paris Salon accepted one of her paintings for the 1872 exhibition, and again she found herself the toast of the continent. Over the next year or two, she visited Spain, Belgium, and Rome to continue her studies. After the Paris Salon accepted two more of her works in 1873 and 1874, Cassatt settled permanently in the French capital.

Feeling increasingly constrained by the inflexible guidelines of the Salon, Cassatt decided to paint how and what *she* wanted, not just what was fashionable or commercial. Critics soon charged that her colors were too bright and that her portraits were too accurate to be appropriately flattering to the subject. When she spied some pastels by Degas in a Paris art dealer's window, she knew she was not alone in her rebellion against the Salon. "I used to go and flatten my nose against that window and absorb all I could of his art," she once wrote to a friend. "It changed my life. I saw art then as I wanted to see it."

Following Degas's invitation, Cassatt exhibited eleven of her paintings with the Impressionists in 1879. The show was a tremendous success commercially and critically, as were subsequent exhibitions in 1880 and 1881. By this time, she and Degas had become close friends whose strong personalities frequently clashed but whose artistic sensibilities were usually in accord.

Unlike many of the other Impressionists, who favored landscapes and street scenes, Cassatt became famous for her charming portraits, primarily of women in casual domestic surroundings. According to a *Newsweek* writer, she "painted what she knew best, the gracious life of the Victorian American abroad—a chat at tea, a sedate carriage ride through a Parisian park, a reflective hour in a sunlit garden. But most often this woman who never married painted the warmth of maternity." Indeed, about one-third of Cassatt's total output depicted mothers and their children. Like her technique, her treatment of this rather conventional subject matter was refreshingly different; as a *Newsweek* writer observed, her mothers and children are "not the madonnas and cherubs of the Renaissance or the adoring couples of conventional portraiture. They are, instead, two separate beings living in easy harmony." Commenting in *American Artist*, Gemma Newman noted that "her constant objective was to achieve force, not sweetness; truth, not sentimentality or romance."

Not long after her first triumphs with the Impressionists, Cassatt was forced to give up painting to care for her mother and sister, who fell ill after moving to Paris in 1877. The sister died in 1882, but Mrs. Cassatt regained her health so that her daughter was able to resume painting by the mid-1880s.

As Cassatt's style evolved, she began to move away from Impressionism and its characteristic exuberance to a simpler, more straightforward approach. After her last exhibition with the Impressionists in 1886, she no longer identified herself with any particular movement or school. She experimented with a variety of techniques and demonstrated a versatility few of her contemporaries shared.

The 1890s became Cassatt's busiest and most creative period and marked her emergence as a role model for young American artists who came to Europe seeking her advice about their studies. As the new century began Cassatt shifted emphasis from her own work to that of others. She had long championed her fellow Impressionists and rarely missed the chance to encourage wealthy Americans to support the fledgling movement by purchasing artwork. Now she tackled the role in earnest, serving as an advisor to several major collectors. Cassatt's only stipulation was that whatever they purchased would eventually be passed along to American art museums. The results of her expert guidance can be seen today in the core collections of some of the country's premier institutions.

In 1910, Cassatt accompanied her brother Gardner and his family on a trip to Egypt. Overwhelmed by the magnificent ancient art she saw there, she lost confidence in her abilities and the value of her own work; her brother's unexpected death from an illness he contracted during the journey proved to be another devastating blow. The two events combined to affect her physical and emotional health, and she was unable to paint until around 1912. By 1915, diabetes forced her to give up working entirely to preserve what little vision she had left. Cassatt spent the remaining eleven years of her life in almost total blindness, bitterly unhappy with the cruel twist of fate that had taken away her greatest source of pleasure. She died on June 14, 1926, at her beloved country home, Chateau de Beaufresne.

Mary Cassatt's legacy is one of courage, independence, and talent that forever guarantee her a place near the top of her profession. But to the artist herself, who thought "perhaps" her paintings would survive her, her efforts had been inadequate. "I have not done what I wanted to," Cassatt remarked toward the end of her life, "but I tried to make a good fight."

Sources

➤ **Books**

Cain, Michael, *Mary Cassatt*, Chelsea House, 1989.

Carson, Julie M. H., *Mary Cassatt*, McKay, 1966.

Hale, Nancy, *Mary Cassatt*, Doubleday, 1975.

McKown, Robin, *The World of Mary Cassatt*, Crowell, 1972.

Wilson, Ellen, *American Painter in Paris: A Life of Mary Cassatt*, Farrar, 1971.

➤ **Periodicals**

American Artist, "The Greatness of Mary Cassatt," February, 1966; "An American in Paris: Mary Cassatt," March, 1973.

American Heritage, "Mary Cassatt," December, 1973.

Horizon, "Cassatt: The Shy American," March, 1981, pp. 56–62.

Newsweek, "The Proper Impressionist," February 14, 1966, p. 86; "Lady from Philadelphia," October 12, 1970, pp. 102–105.

New York Times, June 16, 1926, p. 25.

Reader's Digest, "Mary Cassatt: Pioneer Woman Painter," November, 1959, pp. 228–232.

Time, "Portrait of a Lady," February 4, 1966, p. 78.

Chai Ling

"When I stood in Tiananmen Square in front of many, many people, it was like standing before a great mountain, or a sea. . . . It was a spiritual feeling. It was like music. I'd always felt inferior because I could never really understand music. But I felt music come from my own heart in the Square."

Born c. 1966 in Shandong, China, Chai Ling is one of the most prominent leaders of the Chinese democracy movement.

On June 3, 1989, Chinese tanks and troops took their positions in and around Tiananmen Square in the capital city, Beijing, where some of the most massive anti-government demonstrations since the revolution were taking place. Primarily a student movement when it emerged earlier that spring, the protest had grown to encompass peasants, workers, journalists, and others who sought democratic freedoms and an end to corruption. Thousands were assembled in the square on that fateful day as twenty-three-year-old Chai Ling, commander-in-chief of the most influential student group, passionately urged her fellow protesters to stand firm. "This nation is our nation, these people are our people, this government is our government," she declared. "If we do not speak, who will? If we do not act, who will?"

Chai, whose parents are both party members and doctors for the People's Army, never considered herself very political until she entered Beijing University, a traditional center of student activism in China. She first became involved with the democracy movement in early 1987 and participated in several demonstrations. Around that same time Chai met another activist, engineering student Feng Congde, whom she later married. In April, 1989, as a graduate student in child psychology at Beijing Normal University, Chai joined the sit-in on Tiananmen Square. A speech she had written became the group's manifesto, and soon she was elected their leader.

Looking back on the events that captured the world's attention during the spring of 1989, Chai says she is not sure how she came to be at the forefront of a movement that began with such hope and ended with such brutality. "I did not seek leadership," she told Robin Morgan in a *Ms.* magazine interview. "The group chose me. Maybe because they couldn't agree on anyone else and I had less ego than the men. Maybe they made a bad choice."

She and the other protesters had made it clear from the very start that they wanted the uprising to be nonviolent. Led by Chai, they negotiated with the troops in an attempt to avert bloodshed. They even walked through the square at one point and asked students to give up their weapons, which included bricks as well as several guns and Molotov cocktails provided by soldiers who were sympathetic to their cause. "At the last moment," Chai recalls, "I spoke to the students, reminding them that ours is a peaceful movement. We had the Goddess of Democracy, the beautiful statue that we made. To take up arms would turn it all into tragedy."

Alarmed by growing support for the students and the eruption of similar demonstrations in other Chinese cities, the government decided to take action. On June 3, gunfire rang out across the square. The lights had been turned off, so it was difficult for Chai and the others to see exactly what was happening. "I could hear bullets flying and people screaming," she told Paula Chin of *People* magazine. "We climbed to the upper tiers of the People's Monument and could see the tanks lined up at the edge of the square. Then it was suddenly silent. We huddled together, holding hands and singing. We knew we might die, but we also felt that our sacrifice would be the most glorious moment in China's history."

By the next day, the protest was over, crushed by the troops and tanks that had effectively cut off Tiananmen Square from the rest of the city. An unknown number of students had been killed, and many more had been arrested. Chai, one of twenty-one activists named on the government's "most wanted" list, managed to slip away from the square and immediately went into hiding along with her husband. In a taped message that was smuggled out of China, she reported what she knew of the military's assault on the protesters.

Chai remained on the run for the next ten months. To her surprise, hundreds of Chinese people from all walks of life came forward to offer aid, providing her with food and shelter, moving her from province to province to throw authorities off her trail, and eventually spiriting her out of the country. (She still declines to comment specifically on the details surrounding her escape, noting only that many underground organizations sprang up after the events of June 4 for the purpose of helping dissidents.) On April 3, 1990, she appeared on French television with her husband to announce that they were both safe and sound.

In an interview held about two weeks later, Chai spoke at somewhat greater length to a *New York Times* reporter about the events at Tiananmen Square and her life as a fugitive. After expressing her gratitude to the ordinary people who risked their own lives to protect hers, she revealed her thoughts on the student movement. "Today my feeling is that I am not 100 percent satisfied with what we did," she said. "We did not go far enough, take our actions far enough. For example, we were not in contact with people abroad and had little understanding of the impact we had. But I think that, after forty years of repression, this was the most pacific and reasonable revolt imaginable."

Chai is still recovering physically and mentally from her ordeal and adjusting to the idea that she may be forced to remain in exile for many years—perhaps for the rest of her life. She worries about her parents and her younger brother and sister, and she is not sure if her marriage will endure. (Feng Congde left France and is living in Boston; Chai settled in New Jersey as a visiting scholar at Princeton University, but she thinks she might eventually want to live in New York.) "In such a short time, I've experienced so much," she explained to Morgan. "Life and death. . . . And the loss of freedom and home and then becoming famous."

Despite the uncertainty that clouds much of her life, Chai Ling is determined to remain active in the democracy movement, which is being kept alive by an international network of Chinese student organizations. She speaks to government officials around the world about the plight of imprisoned student activists, and she is also working on a book "to tell the world what really happened" in Tiananmen Square. "Every time I close my eyes, I see nightmarish scenes that prevent me from sleeping," she remarked in the *New York Times*. "I feel the souls of the dead are seeking my help." The prospect of one day being able to return home is what keeps her on course. As she told Chin, "More than anything, my strength comes from love, a love for the Chinese people—and my poor, miserable country."

Sources

➤ **Books**

Shen Tong and Marianne Yen, *Almost a Revolution*, Houghton, 1991.

➤ **Periodicals**

Economist, "The Din of Democracy Disturbs Deng's Peace," April 28, 1990, pp. 33–34.

Glamour, "1990 Women of the Year," December, 1990, pp. 96–101.

Ms., "Chai Ling Talks with Robin Morgan," September/October, 1990, pp. 12–16 (opening quote).

New York Times, "China Protest Leader Escapes," April 4, 1990, p. A13; "Tiananmen Protest Leader Credits 'Lots of People' for Escape to West," April 14, 1990, p. 3; "Chinese Dissident Relives the 1989 Massacre," January 20, 1991, p. B6.

Newsweek, "Beijing Bloodbath," June 12, 1989; "Reign of Terror," June 19, 1989; "'What I Saw Is Bodies, Bodies': Eyewitness Accounts of the Battle of Beijing," June 19, 1989.

People, "One Year Later, the Pasionaria of Tiananmen, Chai Ling, Implores the World Not to Forget the Bloodbath," June 18, 1990, pp. 44–45.

Reader's Digest, "China: The Hope and the Horror," September, 1989.

Time, "Despair and Death in a Beijing Square," June 12, 1989; "Defiance," June 19, 1989; "China's Dark Hours," June 19, 1989.

Winston Churchill

**N**ever give in! Never give in! Never, never, never, never, never—in nothing great or small, large or petty—never give in except to convictions of honor and good sense."

Universally acclaimed as one of the greatest statesmen who ever lived, Winston Churchill served Great Britain for over sixty years in various capacities, including prime minister during World War II. He was born on November 30, 1874, at his family's ancestral home near Woodstock, England, and died on January 24, 1965, in London, England.

Apoor student whose father feared he was retarded, an aristocrat who was reviled by many of his peers as a traitor to his class, a career politician who shouldered the blame for one of his country's worst military disasters during World War I and then went on to engineer its victory during World War II— Winston Churchill was an extraordinary man who time and again faced disappointment and adversity with courage, strength, and determination. He was a larger-than-life presence in his native England for more than fifty years and on the international scene for half of that, displaying a genius and vision that "made greatness casual and prodigious deeds commonplace," to quote a *Newsweek* reporter. To many, Churchill's death in 1965 at the age of ninety signaled the end not only of an exceptional life but of an era that produced leaders the likes of which we may never see again.

Winston Leonard Spencer Churchill was the eldest of two sons of Lord Randolph Churchill, a British politician, and Jennie Jerome, an American heiress whose father was a noted Wall Street speculator and part owner of the *New York Times*. Born at Blenheim Palace, the family home of his ancestors, the dukes of Marlborough, Churchill was a child of privilege. But he was a sickly boy and a poor student who preferred games and play to school; only his father's influence gained him entrance to the best prep schools in England, including Harrow, where he consistently finished at the bottom of his class every term. He detested the rules and regulations governing life at Harrow and despised most of the subjects he was forced to study, except for English grammar and literature and debate and public speaking.

Churchill's grades were so poor upon his graduation from Harrow that it was clear he would never be accepted at Oxford or Cambridge. He did like to play with toy soldiers, however, and showed some talent and imagination in lining them up for battle. So Lord Randolph encouraged his son to apply to the Royal Military College at Sandhurst, the West Point of England. After failing the entrance exams twice, Churchill barely passed on the third try (thanks to some intensive tutoring) and was assigned to the cavalry. At Sandhurst, he blossomed into an excellent rider and an eager student who devoured all the information he could about military matters. He graduated with honors in 1895 and was commissioned as an officer in the 4th Hussars, a cavalry regiment made up of gentlemen-soldiers known for their skill at war games and their love of "the good life."

Churchill soon grew restless and bored, and in late 1895 he asked for leave to go to Cuba, where a revolt against Spain was under way. He stayed for a few months, hoping to get a chance to fight but serving instead as a foreign correspondent for a London newspaper. Returning to England in 1896, he set off with the Hussars that fall for a lengthy stint in India, where he spent much of his first year or so playing polo and pursuing independent studies in history, philosophy, and economics. In search of more excitement, he joined a different regiment and this time saw action in a local rebellion both as a soldier and a war correspondent. His riveting reports from the front created a sensation back home, and in 1898 he gathered them into a best-selling book that led him to consider a career as a military writer. Later that same year, he served with yet another regiment in North Africa during the Sudan campaign, once again acting as both soldier and correspondent. Upon his return to England, Churchill resigned from the army to write another best-seller, this time on British military efforts in the Sudan. At the urging of some Conservative politicians, he also ran for a seat in the House of Commons but lost the election.

In the fall of 1899, war broke out between the Dutch Boers and the British in South Africa. Churchill headed there as a correspondent and was captured by the Boers not long after his arrival. In December, he managed a dramatic and dangerous escape from the prison camp where he was being held and eventually made his way into neutral territory. As news of his ordeal became known, Churchill was hailed as a hero, but before long he was being criticized for blasting the poor performance of the British military in a series of articles he wrote on his experience. Despite his views on the army, he soon joined up again so that he could get back into action in South Africa. After the war wound down, he returned to England and gave politics another try, this time defeating his opponent.

Twenty-six-year-old Churchill took his seat in the House of Commons in February, 1901, and immediately made a name for himself with his forceful opinions and penchant for siding with the Liberals on many issues (especially those dealing with social reform), a practice that angered his fellow Conservatives. Tensions gradually mounted to the point where Churchill left the party and declared himself a Liberal. He then served in a succession of government posts (which outraged many of his former Conservative colleagues, who accused him of selling out both his party and his class to realize his own ambitions), culminating in his appointment as first lord of the admiralty in 1911. In this position, similar to that of the U.S. secretary of the navy, Churchill was one of the few government leaders to recognize that Germany was preparing for war and that Great Britain should do the same. Although his warnings fell largely on deaf ears, he boldly went about the business of modernizing the Royal Navy and making suggestions for improving other branches of the service, even pushing for the development of a strange armored vehicle that was dubbed "Winston's Folly"—better known later as a tank.

On August 4, 1914, thanks to Churchill's foresight and perseverance, England entered World War I with the best navy in the world. The first lord of the admiralty remained intensely involved in military matters, even working out strategies with the help of various technical advisors. But in the spring of 1915 came a disastrous blow when combined British and French forces botched an assault on Turkish troops at Gallipoli, a peninsula that lies between the Aegean Sea and Istanbul, Turkey. Churchill had hoped that such an unexpected strike on the enemy's flanks would ease fighting on the European front and open the door to an invasion from the south. Casualties were very heavy, and outraged Britons unfairly held Churchill personally responsible for the defeat. He was forced to resign and take a lesser cabinet post, which he left some six months later after being excluded from a special war council.

Although he was still a member of Parliament, Churchill joined the army and served until the spring of 1916, at which time he returned to London on leave to participate in an official debate on the navy. Back in the House of Commons, he was subjected to a torrent of insults and abuse from his political enemies. But when his old friend, David Lloyd George, was asked to form a new government in July of that year, Churchill accepted his offer to mobilize Britain's industries for the war effort as minister of munitions. After the conflict ended in November, 1918, he was named minister of war and charged with helping British troops make a speedy and smooth transition to civilian life. He then served as secretary for the colonies and given the responsibility of ending Arab rebellions in Britain's outposts in the Middle East.

In 1922, Churchill lost his seat in the House of Commons following an election in which the Liberals were trounced by the relatively new Labour party. He ran again several times before he was finally victorious in late 1924, this time with backing from the Conservatives, who again embraced him as a member. During the two years he was out of office, however, Churchill was far from inactive. He wrote *The World Crisis,* a six-volume history of World War I, which was very well received. He also produced a number of landscape paintings, a hobby he had taken up to ease the tensions resulting from the Gallipoli affair. And he spent a great deal of time at his country house with his wife, Clementine (whom he had married in 1908), and their children.

Upon his return to Parliament in 1924, Churchill was appointed chancellor of the exchequer, the post his father had once held. As the man in charge of the economy, he angered British workers with his stubborn refusal to back down during a general strike in 1926. He subsequently alienated his fellow Conservatives for displaying the same quality in his dealings with them, and by the end of the decade he was again an extremely unpopular figure.

During the early 1930s, Churchill opened himself up to criticism as a warmonger for repeatedly warning in speeches and articles about the threat posed by Adolf Hitler and Nazi Germany. Pacifist sentiment was very strong in postwar England, and no one wanted to hear about the need to prepare for another conflict. To absolutely no one's surprise, he was excluded from the government Neville Chamberlain formed in 1936 and stood virtually alone in Parliament in opposing Chamberlain's policy of appeasing Hitler.

On September 1, 1939, Germany invaded Poland, a country whose borders England and France had pledged to defend. On September 3, following Hitler's refusal to withdraw his troops, Great Britain declared war on Germany. Reappointed by Chamberlain to his former position as first lord of the admiralty, Churchill immediately began assessing the status of the fleet. Meanwhile, things looked very bad for the allies during the first few months of the war as Denmark and Norway fell and the Soviet Union signed a nonaggression pact with Germany. Harshly criticized for his timid and inept leadership, Chamberlain resigned as prime minister in May, 1940, and King George VI asked Churchill to form a new government. Thus, at the age of sixty-five—an age when most people are looking forward to retirement—the somber yet determined statesman embarked on what would prove to be the most challenging journey in his life and in the history of his nation. "I have nothing to offer but blood, toil, tears, and sweat," he remarked upon taking office. "Let us go forward together with our united strength."

Churchill's first months as prime minister continued to bring nothing but discouragement. Holland and Belgium fell to the

Germans, and trapped British troops retreated to Dunkirk in the north of France. In May, 1940, they braved constant bombing attacks while fleeing across the English Channel on anything that would float. Although much of their equipment had to be left behind, more than three hundred thousand soldiers managed to make it back safely, scoring a moral if not a military victory for the British. But just a month later came frightening news of the fall of France. Great Britain now stood alone against the Nazis, almost certainly the next target for invasion.

That entire summer of 1940, from late June well into September, the country was subjected to the "Blitz," Germany's savage and relentless air war. Bombs rained down on England, especially London, as Hitler tried to undermine British resolve, despite the prime minister's assertion that his nation would "never surrender." Donning a special "siren suit" of his own design, Churchill regularly ventured out into the streets of London after (and sometimes during) air raids to tour bomb sites and offer moral support to the local residents. They in turn welcomed the man they affectionately called "Winnie" with warmth and cheers, marveling at his gallantry, unflagging optimism, and total lack of fear. Thus did Churchill successfully rally his citizens to the cause and instill them with confidence during an extremely difficult period, which he described as "their finest hour."

When he was not busy bolstering the spirits of his fellow Britons, Churchill—an impatient perfectionist with a seemingly inexhaustible supply of energy—was directing virtually every aspect of England's war effort. He personally ran the army, navy, and the air force and never hesitated to become involved in other areas that interested him, an unorthodox style of management that nevertheless had the full backing of the country. He frequently traveled to the war zone to confer with military commanders and also met regularly with other world leaders, forging an especially strong bond of friendship with President Franklin Roosevelt in the months before the United States entered the war.

By late 1941, however, the British press had begun to question Churchill's suitability for the job of prime minister, suggesting that at sixty-seven he was too old, particularly if he insisted on running everything. Despite the fact that both the Soviet Union and the United States had entered the war against Germany, things continued to go badly for the Allies. In the Pacific, Japan had already captured Malaya, Burma, and Singapore and was sinking one major

American and British ship after another. In North Africa, the Germans and the Italians were defeating the British and inflicting heavy losses. Equipment was in increasingly short supply, and the United States was unable to help because it was facing enough of a struggle supplying its own troops.

A humble Churchill decided to go before Parliament and ask for a vote of confidence in his leadership. He frankly expressed his opinion that things were going to get worse before they got better, but he reiterated his belief that Great Britain and its allies would eventually win. By a vote of 464 to 1, members of Parliament reaffirmed their belief in "Winnie" and his ability to lead the nation.

As Churchill had predicted, the setbacks continued well into 1942 as the Allies sustained heavy losses in the Pacific, North Africa, and along the Russian front; German U-boats wreaked havoc in the Atlantic. But in October of that year, the tide began to turn in North Africa following the British victory at El Alamein and a subsequent invasion by British and American troops. By mid-1943, additional victories had made it clear that Germany was slowly on the way to defeat. Then came the Allied invasion of Europe on June 6, 1944, and almost a year later, on May 7, 1945, Germany's surrender.

While the end of the war brought a tremendous sense of relief to the embattled populace of Great Britain, it also allowed old political rivalries to resurface as the need for cooperation evaporated. In addition, despite their great personal affection for Churchill, most Britons were tired of the Conservative party, which they held responsible for the war. Eager for fresh faces and fresh ideas, voters turned out Churchill and his party in July, 1945.

Coming as it did at a time when he was still savoring the Allied victory in Europe, this rejection deeply wounded Churchill, who took it as a sign of ingratitude. He reluctantly "retired" to his country estate and once again took up painting and writing, compiling a six-volume history of World War II that is considered a standard reference work on the subject. But he remained active in politics, too, both on the national and international scenes. He was especially outspoken on the subject of the Soviet Union and constantly warned about the dangers associated with the spread of communism throughout Eastern Europe and beyond. In March, 1946, during a speech in Fulton, Missouri, Churchill added a new phrase to the language when he described how nations under Soviet control were imprisoned behind an "Iron Curtain" that had cut them off from the rest of the world.

By 1951, Britons had grown tired of the Labour party, which had been unable to deliver on most of its promises of a brighter future. Voters again turned to the Conservatives, and at the age of seventy-seven, Churchill assumed the post of prime minister for the second time, serving until he voluntarily resigned in 1955. Now *Sir* Winston—he was knighted by Queen Elizabeth in 1953, the same year he also received the Nobel Prize for literature for his book *The Second World War*—truly entered retirement, still technically a member of Parliament but basically no longer active (or even interested) in politics. He spent most of his time in the country surrounded by his children, his grandchildren, his dogs, and his racing horses, painting and puttering and gracefully accepting the numerous honors that came his way, including the distinction of being named the first honorary citizen of the United States.

On January 15, 1965, the ninety-year-old statesman suffered a stroke. For nine days he clung to life, but early in the morning of January 24 came word that he had died at his London home. Tributes poured in from throughout the world, for as a *Newsweek* reporter noted, "there was the feeling that somehow Winston Churchill had a hand in shaping the course of virtually every life. He was the one man who had infinite confidence when few others could see any reason to hope at all. He was the rock that could not be shaken." After a state funeral of a scale and splendor usually reserved for monarchs, Churchill was buried on the grounds of the parish church near his birthplace.

With the death of one of the last great figures of World War II came a sense that the world itself had changed in some way, that the era of such personally powerful and dynamic leadership had also ended. As a writer for *Time* put it, "Today's rulers seem, in comparison, faceless and mediocre. Churchill was an aristocrat, a brilliant dilettante, a creator in a dozen roles and garbs. He was a specialist in nothing—except courage, imagination, intelligence. He was never afraid to lead, and he knew that a leader must sometimes risk failure and disapproval rather than seek universal acclaim." Concluded another writer for *Time:* "If Churchill was sometimes wrong, on the great issues of his times he was most often right. History will forgive his faults; it can never forget the indomitable, imperturbable spirit that swept a people to greatness."

Sources

➤ Books

Albierg, Victor L., *Winston Churchill*, Twayne, 1973.

Churchill, Randolph Spencer, *Winston S. Churchill*, Vol. 1, *Youth, 1874–1900*, Vol. 2, *Young Statesman, 1901–1914*, Houghton, 1966.

Churchill, Winston, *My Early Life: A Roving Commission*, Scribner, 1930.

Churchill, Winston, *The Second World War*, six volumes, Houghton, 1948–53.

Gilbert, Martin, *Churchill: A Life*, Holt, 1991.

Keller, Mollie, *Winston Churchill*, F. Watts, 1984.

Manchester, William, *The Last Lion: Winston Spencer Churchill*, Vol. 1, *Visions of Glory, 1874–1932*, Little, Brown, 1983, Vol. 2, *Alone, 1932–1940*, Little, Brown, 1987.

Reynolds, Quentin, *Winston Churchill*, Random House, 1963.

Rodgers, Judith, *Winston Churchill*, Chelsea House, 1986.

Taylor, Robert Lewis, *Winston Churchill*, Doubleday, 1952.

➤ Periodicals

Atlantic Monthly, March, 1965, pp. 49–101 (special issue devoted to Churchill).

Newsweek, "London: Death of a Titan," February 1, 1965, pp. 38A–42D (opening quote).

New York Times, "Churchill Dies at 90 at Home in London," January 24, 1965; "Winston Churchill: His Life and Times" (special section), January 25, 1965, pp. 39–46.

Reader's Digest, "Man of the Century: A Churchill Cavalcade," December, 1964, pp. 205–248; January, 1965, pp. 205–247.

Time, "Man of the Year," January 6, 1941, pp. 23–26; "Through War and Peace," January 2, 1950; "Churchill," January 29, 1965, pp. 31–33; "Requiem for Greatness," February 5, 1965, pp. 26–35.

U.S. News and World Report, "All in One Life's Span," February 1, 1965, pp. 46–48.

Jacques Cousteau

"**S**ometimes we are lucky enough to know that our lives have been changed. It happened to me that summer's day when my eyes opened to the world beneath the surface of the sea."

Born on June 11, 1910, in St. Andre-de-Cubzac, France, Jacques-Yves Cousteau is a world-renowned oceanographer, environmentalist, filmmaker, and writer.

Address: Cousteau Society, Inc., 425 East 52nd St., New York, NY 10022.

I n 1936, a twenty-six-year-old French naval officer named Jacques Cousteau saw his dreams of a career in aviation come to an end when a serious automobile accident crushed his chest and left one arm so badly broken and infected that doctors advised amputating it. Ten months of agonizing physical therapy restored much of his strength, but the remaining lameness in his arm and his permanently bowed back forced the young man to drop out of flight school. Once a promising pilot, Cousteau now viewed the future with deep disappointment.

His life until that fateful time had been exciting and unconventional. The son of Daniel P. Cousteau, a lawyer, and Elizabeth Duranthon, he was born in his parents' ancestral village near Bordeaux and quickly whisked off to Paris, where his father served as business manager and private secretary to a rather eccentric American millionaire who liked to travel. As a result, the Cousteaus were almost constantly on the move. During an unusually lengthy stay in New York City, young Jacques attended school (as "Jack" Cousteau) and learned to speak and write English fluently.

Cousteau continued his secondary education in France and eventually entered the naval academy. "There was no fanaticism in my choice, and no naval tradition in my family," he told James Dugan of *Holiday* magazine. "I thought it was a good way to go places." After graduating second in his class in 1933, he entered the French Navy as a second lieutenant, serving his first year aboard a training ship that cruised around the world. Following a stint in Shanghai and a voyage along the coast of Indochina, he returned to France to attend naval aviation school. Just a few weeks before graduation, however, came the accident that dashed his hopes of becoming a pilot.

When he had recovered sufficiently to go back on active duty, Cousteau was sent to a gunnery unit in Toulon, a major port on the Mediterranean Sea. He soon made friends with a fellow officer who suggested that he try swimming to help regain the use of his arm. Having heard stories about local spear fishermen who wore Tahitian pearl divers' goggles to hunt underwater, Cousteau borrowed a pair and ventured into the harbor. The creatures and plant life he could see so clearly for the very first time fascinated him in a way that nothing else ever had. He wanted to see more—to dive deeper and stay under longer—but with only goggles, flippers, and a snorkel fashioned out of garden hose, such a feat was impossible.

He vowed then and there to invent the equipment that would give him complete freedom in this magical new world.

Cousteau focused his initial efforts on developing a self-contained underwater breathing apparatus that would eliminate the need for bulky hoses and other awkward contraptions. His experiments were temporarily interrupted at the beginning of World War II, but after the fall of France and the dismantling of its navy, he was able to resume his work. "The Germans considered me a harmless nut, and I did all I could to reinforce the impression," Cousteau explained to James Stewart-Gordon of the *Saturday Evening Post*. "I dived in the worst weather, and used the excuse that I was spearfishing to help out the slender rations we were allowed." This ruse enabled him to carry out espionage activities for the French resistance and also diverted the Germans' attention from his research.

Finally, in late 1942, with the help of a French engineer who had designed an automatic gas-feeder valve, Cousteau invented the Aqua-Lung. It was a mouthpiece attached by a special hose to a tank of compressed air worn strapped on the back. Testing his new device in the Mediterranean in mid-1943, he reveled in the feeling of being a "man-fish." As he later recalled in a *Time* magazine article, "I experimented with all possible maneuvers—loops, somersaults, barrel rolls. I stood upside down on one finger. . . . Delivered from gravity and buoyancy, I flew about in space." With this single invention, noted the *Time* reporter, Cousteau created "a mass sport out of a pastime that once belonged to an adventuresome few."

Toward the end of the war and for several years afterward, Cousteau continued his oceanographic research under the auspices of the French Navy. As founder and head of its Undersea Research Group, he conducted minesweeping operations in the Mediterranean and helped explore shipwrecks. The experience he gained through these activities enabled him to perfect new equipment and techniques, including underwater television cameras and color-corrected flash photography. Yet these successes were not enough; more than anything, Cousteau longed for his *own* oceangoing ship, one that would give him the freedom to cruise where he wanted and explore whatever caught his eye. Given the expenses involved, such an undertaking seemed out of the question.

Around 1950, however, two businessmen approached Cousteau and offered to provide him with enough money to purchase a ship for marine research; their only stipulation was that he never publicize their names. The Frenchman agreed to the terms and soon bought a British mine sweeper that had been converted to a ferry after the war. He then rebuilt the ship to his specifications, outfitting it for diving expeditions and oceanographic studies. But he decided to keep the name its former owner had given it in honor of the sea nymph who kept Odysseus on an island for seven years, a name the new owner still found quite appropriate: *Calypso*. In partnership with one of his anonymous backers, an Englishman, Cousteau subsequently created a nonprofit foundation called Calypso Oceanographic Expeditions to help finance his travels. He also broadened his research efforts by establishing two additional organizations—the Campagnes Oceanographiques Francaises and the Centre d'Etudes Marines Avancees—both of which focused on operating research ships, developing equipment for underwater use, and studying the effects of diving on man.

Cousteau asked for and was granted an unpaid leave from the navy to test his ship's capabilities. The *Calypso*'s first trip was to the Red Sea, where the crew and scientists on board worked together to gather samples of plant and animal life and experiment with very-deep-water color photography. This was followed soon after by a four-year expedition across the oceans of the world, a journey sponsored by the National Geographic Society and the French Academy of Sciences. Cousteau spent part of this time writing *The Silent World*, a philosophical look back at his undersea adventures since his first dive in the late 1930s. Published in 1953, it brought him international acclaim and a much-needed financial boost. A documentary version, filmed by Cousteau and others aboard the *Calypso* during the ocean expedition, was released in 1956 and went on to win the grand prize at the Cannes Film Festival as well as an Academy Award.

Cousteau finally resigned from the navy the following year to devote full time to his ever-growing list of projects and related business concerns, "a bewildering web of profitmaking, nonprofit and governmental enterprises," according to the *Time* reporter. Known today as the Cousteau Group, this umbrella organization now encompasses activities in more than a dozen separate fields, among them diving-equipment development and manufacturing, oceanographic research, marine engineering, film and television production, and ecology. In general, Cousteau has used the profits from his inventions, books, and films along with grants from the National Geographic Society, universities, government agencies, and other institutions to subsidize his research efforts. But he has often been forced to leave his ship and come ashore to raise funds for one venture or another.

Aboard the *Calypso*, Cousteau has accomplished what is perhaps his greatest work: introducing the world to the beauty and mystery of life underwater. Beginning with the 1966 National Geographic special "The World of Jacques-Yves Cousteau" and continuing with a dozen films broadcast under the series title "The Undersea World of Jacques Cousteau," his Emmy Award-winning television documentaries have fascinated millions of viewers with their close-ups of marine life and archaeological treasures accompanied by Cousteau's poetic narration. Some have criticized him for shortchanging science in his programs, a charge Cousteau does not deny but for which he also does not apologize. "Our films have only one ambition—to show the truth about nature, and give people the wish to know more," he once told a reporter for the *New York Times Magazine*. "I do not stand as a scientist giving dry explanations. I'm an honest observer."

At one time, Cousteau spent as much as eight months of every year at sea. Now, the constant struggle to raise funds keeps him on land for much of the year, either at his apartment in Paris or his home in Monaco, where he still serves as director of the Oceanographic Institute and Museum, a post he has held since leaving the navy. With him always is his wife, Simone Melchior Cousteau, who has never missed a voyage of the *Calypso*. Son Jean-Michel is an administrator with the Cousteau Group. Another son, Philippe, who collaborated with his father on many films and television programs, died in a 1979 plane crash.

In recent years, Cousteau has emerged as an outspoken and respected environmentalist whose chief concerns are protecting the ocean from destructive fishing methods and pollution caused by industrial waste. The Cousteau Society, founded in 1975, is the branch of the Cousteau Group that is responsible for publicizing ecological problems, financing projects, and pressuring governments to take action. "We are fighting not for survival but for quality of life, for happiness," declared Cousteau in Axel Madsen's biography of him. "People can only be happy if they marvel at nature, if they marvel at creation, if they marvel at what surrounds them. If they love creation, if they protect it, if they extend their minds to other people's jobs and to animals' lives and to other planets. An extension of mind is an extension of everything."

Sources

➤ **Books**

Dugan, James, *Undersea Explorer: The Story of Captain Cousteau*, Harper, 1957.

Greene, Carol, *Jacques Cousteau: Man of the Oceans*, Children's Press, 1990.

Iverson, Genie, *Jacques Cousteau*, Putnam, 1976.

Madsen, Axel, *Cousteau: An Unauthorized Biography*, Beaufort Books, 1986 (opening quote).

Munson, Richard, *Cousteau: The Captain and His World*, Morrow, 1989.

➤ **Periodicals**

Holiday, "Pioneer Undersea Explorer," September, 1955.

New York Times Magazine, "Portrait of Homo Aquaticus," April 21, 1963; "Cousteau Searches for His Whale," September 10, 1972.

Saturday Evening Post, "The Wet World of Jacques-Yves Cousteau," November, 1973.

Time, "Poet of the Depths," March 28, 1960, pp. 66–77.

U.S. News & World Report, June 24, 1985, p. 68.

Marie Curie

"**I** believe that Science has great beauty. A scientist in his laboratory is not a mere technician: he is also a child confronting natural phenomena that impress him as though they were fairy tales."

Nobel Prize-winning physicist Marie Curie was born on November 7, 1867, in Warsaw, Poland. With her husband, Pierre Curie, she discovered the elements radium and polonium and launched the study of modern physics. She died on July 4, 1934, near Sallanches, France.

Whenever Marie Curie was asked in her later years when she was going to write her autobiography, she responded, "[My life] is such an uneventful, simple little story. I was born in Warsaw of a family of teachers. I married Pierre Curie and had two children. I have done my work in France." A brilliant physicist and tireless researcher who was the first woman to win a Nobel Prize, she was always exceedingly modest about her achievements and emphasized that they belonged to science, not to her. Yet as Mollie Keller put it in her biography of Curie, "this tiny woman with her decigram of radium turned the world upside down, forever changing the way we look at, understand, and use our environment."

Marie Curie was born Marya Sklodowska, the fifth and youngest child of Bronsitwa Boguska, a pianist, singer, and teacher, and Ladislas Sklodowski, a professor of mathematics and physics. Bronsitwa Sklodowska died of tuberculosis when Marya was not quite eleven, leaving Ladislas Sklodowski as his daughter's chief role model. Even as a very young girl she was fascinated by his physics equipment, and like him she was introspective, quiet, and studious.

Marya was an outstanding student who graduated at the top of her high school class when she was only fifteen. She then spent eight years working as a tutor and a governess to earn enough money to attend the Sorbonne in Paris. In her spare time, she studied mathematics and physics on her own and attended a so-called "floating" university, a loosely-organized, clandestine program conducted by Polish professors in defiance of the Russians then in charge of the educational system. Finally, in November, 1891, Marya left Poland and registered at the Sorbonne under the French version of her first name, "Marie."

Despite living under conditions so spartan that she grew ill on several occasions from lack of food and sleep, Marie graduated first in her class in the spring of 1893. A year later, she obtained her master's degree in mathematics, then remained in Paris to conduct some experiments for a French industrial society. Finding the Sorbonne's facilities inadequate, Marie set out to learn where she might find the necessary laboratory space and equipment. Her search led her to Pierre Curie, a highly acclaimed professor at the School of Physics. The two scientists shared many of the same beliefs and habits and were immediately drawn to each other. They married on July 26, 1895, thus launching one of the most significant partnerships in scientific history.

Marie and Pierre Curie were inseparable, working side by side in the laboratory during the day and studying together in the evening. Even the arrival of their daughter, Irene, in 1897 barely interrupted their routine. By this time, Marie had decided to pursue her doctorate in physics, and for her thesis she chose to focus on the source of the mysterious rays given off by uranium, a phenomenon scientist Henri Becquerel had first observed in 1896.

Curie set up her equipment in a small, glass-walled shed at the School of Physics. Despite the primitive conditions—dirt floor, drafty windows, and perpetual dampness—within just two months she had made two important discoveries: the intensity of the rays was in direct proportion to the amount of uranium in her sample, and nothing she did to alter the uranium (such as combining it with other elements or subjecting it to light, heat, or cold) affected the rays. This led her to formulate the theory that the rays were the result of something happening within the atom itself, a property she called *radioactivity*. Subsequent tests she performed on the minerals chalcocite, uranite, and pitchblende revealed higher-than-expected levels of radioactivity and led her to conclude that a new, more powerful element had to be responsible.

Curie began working on this problem during the spring of 1898, and by summer her husband had abandoned his own research to help her. Confining their study to pitchblende because it emitted the strongest rays, they developed a painstaking refining method that required them to process tons of the mineral to obtain just a tiny sample of radioactive material. At last they uncovered a new radioactive element they named polonium in honor of Marie's native Poland. They then identified an even stronger radioactive element, which they named radium. Although they announced their discovery to the world on December 26, 1898, it was March, 1902, before they were able to isolate enough radium to confirm its existence and thus earn Marie Curie her doctorate (the first awarded to a woman in Europe) and both Curies the 1903 Nobel Prize in physics.

With this honor came immediate international fame—disrupting the two scientists' personal and professional lives for quite some time—and enough money to ease some of their financial burdens. (They had supported the radium research with their own money.) After the birth of her second daughter, Eve, in December, 1904,

Madame Curie rejoined her husband in the laboratory. Then came news that the French government wanted to reward the Curies by creating a new professorship in physics at the Sorbonne for Pierre and building a new laboratory for Marie. But before the deal could be finalized, Pierre was killed when he absentmindedly stepped into the path of a horse-drawn wagon on a Paris street.

After her husband's death, Madame Curie assumed his physics professorship at the invitation of the Sorbonne, making her the university's first woman faculty member. In addition to teaching, Curie also continued to spend time in the laboratory, determined to isolate pure polonium and pure radium to remove any remaining doubts about the existence of the two new elements. Her success in doing so garnered her another Nobel Prize in 1911.

By 1914, Curie was the head of two laboratories, one in her native Warsaw and one at the Sorbonne, known as the Radium Institute. Unable to continue her experiments after the outbreak of World War I and eager to be of service, she received approval to operate X-ray machines on the battlefield so that the wounded could receive immediate treatment. It was exhausting and dangerous work, but within two years she had established two hundred permanent X-ray units throughout France and Belgium.

After the war ended, Curie campaigned to raise funds for a hospital and laboratory devoted to radiology, the branch of medicine that uses X rays and radium to diagnose and treat disease. An American journalist named Marie Meloney heard about Curie's efforts and invited her to tour the United States to publicize the project. Although she dreaded the thought, Curie accepted and sailed for America in 1921. The tumultuous reception she received left her frightened and exhausted, but she did manage to return to France with enough radium, money, and equipment to outfit her new laboratory.

Realizing that her status as a celebrity gave her the power to have an impact on causes she favored, Curie began speaking at meetings and conferences throughout the world, gradually becoming more comfortable in the spotlight. She found that people were very willing to support her work, and she had great success as a fundraiser for the Radium Institute. Curie also lent her name to the cause for world peace by serving on the council of the League of Nations and on its international committee on intellectual cooperation.

As the 1920s drew to a close, Curie began to suffer almost constantly from fatigue, dizziness, and a low-grade fever. She also experienced a continuous humming in her ears and a gradual loss of eyesight that was helped only partially by a series of cataract operations. Even though a number of her colleagues who had worked with radium were displaying many of the same symptoms and others had died at relatively young ages of cancer, for a very long time Curie could not bring herself to admit that the element she and her husband had discovered could possibly be at fault. Eventually she did accept the fact that radium was dangerous, but she continued to work with it anyway. In the early 1930s, however, Curie's health noticeably worsened, and doctors finally discovered the cause: pernicious anemia caused by the cumulative effects of radiation exposure. The news was kept from the public as well as from Curie herself, and on July 4, 1934, she died at the mountain sanitorium where she had gone to convalesce.

Curie lived long enough to see her investigation into the "mysterious rays" emitted by uranium give birth to an entirely new scientific discipline, atomic physics. And in the years since its discovery, radium has been put to use in many different ways. Despite the fact that she was not directly involved in any of these developments, Marie Curie is nevertheless a part of every one, "like the fifteenth century navigators who set out to the west and sighted continents of an extent that they could not conceive," as Waldemar Kaempffert observed in the *New York Times.* "Few persons contributed more to the general welfare of mankind and to the advancement of science than the modest, self-effacing woman whom the world knew as Madame Curie," declared another *New York Times* reporter. "Her epoch-making discoveries ... , the subsequent honors that were bestowed on her ... and the fortunes that could have been hers had she wanted them did not change her mode of life. She remained a worker in the cause of science, preferring her laboratory to a great social place in the sun."

Sources

➤ **Books**

Curie, Eve, *Madame Curie,* Doubleday, 1938. Reprint. Da Capo, 1986.

Giroud, Francoise, *Marie Curie: A Life,* translated from French by Lydia Davis, Holmes & Meier, 1986 (opening quote).

Keller, Mollie, *Marie Curie,* F. Watts, 1982.

➤ **Periodicals**

New York Times, "Madame Curie Is Dead; Martyr to Science," July 5, 1934; "Science: The Trail That Was Blazed by Madame Curie," July 8, 1934, section 8, p. 9.

Dalai Lama

"Once your mind is dominated by anger, it becomes almost mad. You cannot take right decisions, and you cannot see reality. But if your mind is calm and stable, you will see everything exactly as it is. I think all politicians need this kind of patience."*

Born on July 6, 1935, in Taktser, Tibet, the Dalai Lama is the spiritual leader of Tibetan Buddhists and former ruler of Tibet.

Address: Thekchen Choeling, McLeod Ganj—176219, Dharamsala, Distt. Kangra, Himachal Pradesh, India.

In 1937, Tibetan monks began scouring the countryside northeast of the capital city of Lhasa on a holy mission of the utmost importance: the search for the new Dalai Lama, the fourteenth earthly reincarnation of the Buddhist Lord of Compassion. As dictated by centuries of tradition, the monks relied on dreams, oracles, and omens to lead the way, and at last they converged on a farmhouse in the village of Taktser.

Inside they found a two-year-old boy whom they subjected to an exhaustive series of tests. His performance convinced the monks that they had indeed found the reincarnation of the thirteenth Dalai Lama, who had died in 1935. After lengthy negotiations with the Chinese overlord who ruled the region, the monks finally secured permission to take the boy to Lhasa. And it was there, on February 22, 1940, that four-year-old Lhamo Dhondrub—renamed Jetsun Jamphel Ngawang Lobsang Yeshe Tenzin Gyatso, Holy Lord, Gentle Glory, Eloquent, Compassionate, Learned Defender of the Faith, Ocean of Wisdom—was formally installed as the fourteenth Dalai Lama, the spiritual and temporal leader of Tibet, an isolated Himalayan nation long cloaked in mystery and exoticism.

The Dalai Lama was the fourth of five children born to peasants Chokyong Tsering and Sonam Tsomo. But once he was whisked off to Lhasa and the thousand-room Potala Palace that was home to the Tibetan ruler, he saw very little of his family, except for an older brother who lived with him and served as his only playmate and later as one of his chief aides. (A regent was charged with actually governing the country until the Dalai Lama reached the age of eighteen.) A precocious and fun-loving boy, he was raised and educated by Buddhist monks who saw to it that their future leader was well versed in religious matters. On his own, he also studied English, mathematics, and geography, and whenever possible indulged his love of taking apart and repairing all kinds of machines.

Throughout most of the first half of the twentieth century, Tibet enjoyed a relatively peaceful relationship with neighboring China. Beginning in 1949, however, the newly victorious Communist forces began to threaten the Tibetans, and in 1950 they invaded the country and quickly overwhelmed it. The Dalai Lama spent the rest of the decade walking a diplomatic tightrope, trying to preserve the ancient Tibetan religious and political structure in the midst of an expanding Chinese presence that was pushing for "modernization." Although he abhorred violence and counseled cooperation and persuasion, he could not defuse the tensions between the two countries. By the late 1950s a guerrilla war was under way as Tibetans sought revenge for increasingly brutal Chinese attacks against monks and monasteries.

The showdown finally came in March, 1959, when the Dalai Lama was more or less ordered to attend a theatrical performance at a nearby Chinese army camp. In the past, Tibetan leaders who had accepted such "invitations" had disappeared; the same fate now seemed to await the Dalai Lama. Tens of thousands of Tibetans surrounded his palace in an attempt to protect him, and the Chinese responded by sending in troops and artillery. Fearful that war was imminent and that the death of their leader would mean the end of Tibet, the Dalai Lama's family and advisors persuaded him to leave the country. Disguising himself as a soldier, he escaped from the palace on the night of March 17 and, accompanied by his mother, sister, and about one hundred followers, he set off on a torturous journey through the mountains to India. He arrived nearly two weeks later, ill with dysentery and saddened by the knowledge that China had attacked and defeated the Tibetans only two days after he fled.

Within a year, the Dalai Lama established his government-in-exile at Dharamsala, a mountain village in northern India. Thousands of Tibetans eventually joined him there and at other nearby refugee camps as the Chinese systematically set out to eradicate Tibetan culture. "We decided that our number-one priority must be to stand on our own feet, and work hard for self-sufficiency," he later explained to E. Richard Sorenson in *Smithsonian*. "We planned and founded large communities to preserve Tibetan culture and atmosphere, where we could establish monasteries and build Tibetan schools so our children could learn our history, language and philosophy. But we also decided that we needed modern education. We wanted to progress as a modern nation." To that end, the Dalai Lama himself studied various Western languages, scientific developments, and world affairs.

In addition to overseeing the survival of Tibetan culture, the Dalai Lama began almost immediately to rally world opinion against the Chinese occupation of his country. At first, the Indian government, fearing repercussions from China, refused to allow him to travel abroad to plead his cause. But in 1967 they relented, and since then he has spent much of his time visiting world leaders (both secular and religious) to keep alive interest in Tibet's plight. In 1979, after an eight-year struggle to obtain a visa, he made his first visit to the

United States. During a seven-week tour that was billed as nonpolitical so as not to offend the Chinese, the Dalai Lama spoke in churches, synagogues, Buddhist centers, and universities across the nation, describing conditions in his country and explaining what Tibetan Buddhism might have to offer to the West with its emphasis on compassion and nonviolence.

The Dalai Lama's quest has been a constant source of irritation to the Chinese, who have taken steps to discredit him and his work. Throughout the 1960s and well into the 1970s, they tried to obliterate his influence in Tibet and annihilate traditional Tibetan culture, often by torturing and killing monks and destroying monasteries and religious artifacts. This savagery eased somewhat during the late 1970s when more moderate leaders came to power in China and expressed a willingness to allow the Dalai Lama to return to Tibet with all of his previous rights and privileges restored. "I told them that this is not the case, the problem is six million people," he remarked in an interview with Associated Press reporter Jeffrey Ulbrich that appeared in the *Grand Rapids Press*. "It's their rights and their culture. And unless that basic problem is solved, the question of my return is meaningless."

In the meantime, sporadic violence still plagues Tibet, as do rumors of continued torture and jail sentences. In the late 1980s, rioting broke out in Lhasa for several years in a row around the anniversary of the Chinese invasion, resulting in dozens of deaths and eventually the imposition of martial law. Clashes between Tibetan pro-independence forces and the Chinese have also erupted during recent visits of the Dalai Lama to the United States, where he has received increasingly warm welcomes from government officials, including members of Congress and, in April, 1991, President George Bush.

Despite his fears for the future of Tibet—and much to the dismay of some younger, more restless Tibetan refugees who have grown impatient with his support of civil disobedience over violence to achieve peace and freedom—the Dalai Lama has remained firm in his resolve to pursue reconciliation with the Chinese. His latest proposals fall short of total independence; he would like to leave defense and foreign affairs to the Chinese and put all internal matters in Tibetan hands, creating "a zone of peace with complete demilitarization." But his definition of peace is not just the absence of war. Instead, he advocates "a genuine peace without fear, genuine in the sense of cooperation, or the sense of some kind of security, and working together. That's not the mere absence of war. That's much more positive, much more conceptive. [It] comes through mental peace, so first peace must be created here, in our minds. Then as a reflection of that inner peace, peace atmosphere in the family, peace atmosphere in the community, in the country and on an international level."

The Dalai Lama's lifelong dedication to speaking out against China's political, social, religious, and economic oppression of Tibet, as well as his own personal warmth, humility, and compassion, have made him an international symbol of hope and inspiration to those who advocate a kinder and more spiritual approach to solving world conflicts. In 1989, those very qualities led the Nobel committee to award him its Peace Prize. His reaction to the news was typically humble: "My case is nothing special. I am a simple Buddhist monk—no more, no less."

After more than thirty years in exile, the Dalai Lama is well aware that changes in Tibet have made his position outdated if not totally obsolete in the event he and the Chinese can reach some sort of an agreement. Declaring "there is too much devotion toward me," he believes that he would probably be "an obstacle to developing a genuine democracy in Tibet" and should therefore remain outside any new government. But for the moment, he told Sorenson, "the Dalai Lama is very useful, very helpful for Tibet. That is why I am serving. But when the institution of the Dalai Lama is no longer of use the Dalai Lama will disappear. . . . Tibetans who have returned to Tibet say I should not go unless I am very sure I would have a free hand. Only then could I do something for my country from within its borders. . . . The main condition is that my return give satisfaction to the Tibetan people. I am their spokesman: my return is for them to decide. They are my boss."

Sources

➤ **Books**

Dalai Lama, *My Land and My People*, McGraw, 1962.

Dalai Lama, *Freedom in Exile*, HarperCollins, 1990.

Dalai Lama, *My Tibet*, photographs by Galen Rowell, Mountain Light Press/University of California Press, 1990.

Piburn, Sidney D., *The Dalai Lama: A Policy of Kindness*, Snow Lion Publications, 1990.

➤ **Periodicals**

Grand Rapids Press, "Dalai Lama Longs for Tibet Home, But Chinese Scorn His Kind Ways," December 9, 1990, p. E5; "Dalai Lama's D.C. Visit May Cause Political Storm in U.S., China," April 4, 1991, p. B6; "Dalai Lama Visits Bush; China May Be Miffed," April 17, 1991, p. A6.

Life, "The Dalai Lama," June, 1988, pp. 21–25.

Maclean's, "A God-King in Exile," October 15, 1990.

Newsweek, "The God-King's Visit," September 17, 1979, p. 115.

New York Times Book Review, "We Must Change Our Lives," September 30, 1990; "'There Is Too Much Devotion Toward Me,'" September 30, 1990, p. 49.

Smithsonian, "To Tibet's Dalai Lama, Exile Is a Haven—and an Opportunity," March, 1984, pp. 82–90.

Time, "'I Am a Human Being: A Monk,'" September 17, 1979, p. 96; "Tibet's Living Buddha," April 11, 1988, pp. 58–60; "A Bow to Tibet," October 16, 1989, p. 44.

U.S. News and World Report, "The Days of a Holy Man," October 29, 1990, pp. 92–94.

Vanity Fair, "The Silent Killing of Tibet," May, 1991.

Clarence Darrow

*"*F*ew of us are capable of judgment, just as few of us ever think, and few can ever mete out justice to our fellows, no matter how sincerely we try. And to reconcile the law with justice and human progress is sometimes impossible."*

A champion of labor and the oppressed and among the first to argue that criminals are often products of their environment, Clarence Darrow was one of America's most celebrated lawyers. He was born on April 18, 1857, in Kinsman, Ohio, and died on March 13, 1938, in Chicago, Illinois.

Described by a *Time* magazine writer as a "defender of underdogs" and a "winner of lost causes," Clarence Darrow served as defense counsel in some of the most famous trials in U.S. history. He specialized in fighting for those he felt had been "condemned for getting out of step with the crowd, not for doing evil," and in doing so he made many powerful enemies among the more conservative elements of society. Because he was vehemently opposed to the death penalty, he also defended murderers whose guilt was rarely in doubt and who therefore faced certain execution. He was unquestionably a humanitarian, but he was no idealist; in fact, he had a fairly low opinion of the human race and its chances for improvement. As a self-proclaimed "pessimist with hope," however, Darrow believed in working within the system to bring about changes in the ways some groups or individuals were treated by the law, especially those who had battled poverty or oppression.

Clarence Seward Darrow was the son of Emily Eddy and Amirus Darrow, a furniture manufacturer and dealer. Amirus Darrow had originally trained as a minister, but just before his ordination he experienced a crisis of faith that led him to question the existence of God and the notion of life after death. He passed these same doubts along to his son, who later became known as much for his fiery agnosticism as for his brilliant legal mind.

After completing his primary and secondary education in his Ohio hometown, Darrow briefly attended Allegheny College in Meadville, Pennsylvania, then taught school for several years before enrolling at the University of Michigan Law School. He left there a year later without a degree and, as was customary at the time, went to work for an attorney to complete his education. Following his admission to the bar in 1878 at the age of twenty-one, he practiced law in several small Ohio towns for a decade before heading to Chicago and the promise of a more exciting career.

Not long after his arrival in Chicago, Darrow became involved in attempts to free eight anarchists who had been charged with murder after a May, 1886, bomb explosion at a workers' rally in Haymarket Square killed eleven people. He also took part in Democratic politics, through which he met and became close friends with John Peter Altgeld, at that time a state supreme court judge and later the governor of Illinois. With Altgeld's help, Darrow secured a job in the city of Chicago's legal department in 1889 and quickly rose to the position of chief counsel and head of the department. Three years later, he resigned to become general attorney for the Chicago and North Western Railway Company.

In 1894, however, Darrow gave up a potentially lucrative future in corporate law to represent (without pay) the president of the American Railway Union, socialist Eugene V. Debs, and other union leaders arrested for staging a crippling railroad strike from May through July of that year. Darrow succeeded in having conspiracy charges against his clients dismissed, but the U.S. Supreme Court upheld lower court rulings stating that Debs and his fellow union members had ignored a judge's order to return to work. Despite the fact that Debs was forced to serve six months in jail while his co-defendants each served three months, Darrow was lauded as a hero and gained national acclaim as a champion of labor.

Over the next seventeen years, Darrow concentrated almost exclusively on labor law. He took on a number of cases across the country in which union membership and the right to strike were challenged by management. He also generated national headlines in several high-profile trials involving other labor-related issues. For example, as the official arbitrator in the 1902 Pennsylvania coal strike, Darrow stunned the American public when his cross-examinations revealed the difficult and dangerous working conditions miners faced and the extent to which coal companies relied on child labor. But his most famous case during this period was that of William D. "Big Bill" Haywood, a member of the Western Federation of Miners and head of the newly organized Industrial Workers of the World (IWW). In 1907, Darrow successfully defended Haywood against a charge that he had conspired with two other union officials to kill the former governor of Idaho, Frank Steunenberg. As part of his argument, the famed lawyer documented the fact that mining company management and local government officials had joined forces to harass union sympathizers.

Darrow's career in labor law came to an end in 1911 when he took on the case of brothers Joseph and James McNamara, socialists accused of dynamiting the *Los Angeles Times* building in October, 1910, and killing twenty-one people inside. Although he was strongly opposed to the use of violence to settle labor disputes, Darrow agreed to defend the McNamaras but then persuaded them to plead guilty and accept a pre-trial sentencing agreement. (By doing so, he hoped to avoid a jury trial that he was sure would end in conviction and the death penalty for his clients.) The deal outraged labor leaders, who felt it ruined the socialist candidate's chances in an upcoming Los Angeles election. Practically on the eve of that election came accusations that Darrow, through an intermediary on his staff, had attempted to bribe a juror into voting for the McNamaras' acquittal. Tried twice on bribery charges and found not guilty both times, Darrow—penniless and with his reputation in shambles—returned to Chicago and never again argued another labor case.

Back in Chicago, Darrow worked to establish a new private practice. During World War I, he defended many people accused of disloyalty for refusing to serve in the armed forces or because they were communists or socialists. (He personally supported the war but did not agree that those who opposed it were necessarily disloyal.) After the war, he turned to criminal law and again found himself in the spotlight when two sensational trials during the mid-1920s gained nationwide attention.

In 1924, Darrow was hired to defend Nathan Leopold and Richard Loeb, two well-to-do, young Chicago men who kidnapped and murdered fourteen-year-old Bobby Franks just for "fun" and to see if they could get away with it. After ordering his clients to plead guilty, Darrow then concentrated on saving them from a likely death sentence by introducing mounds of psychiatric evidence to back up his claim that while they were growing up "something slipped and disfigured their personalities." Depicting a criminal as a victim of his environment rather than an inherently evil monster was then a new and untested approach; it proved successful when Leopold and Loeb were judged insane and sentenced to life in prison.

Darrow's next big trial of the decade occurred the following year. In Dayton, Tennessee, John Scopes was indicted for violating a state law that prohibited the teaching of Charles Darwin's theories of evolution in the public schools because they were at odds with Christian fundamentalist thought. Squaring off in the courtroom for the so-called "monkey trial" were Darrow (who had volunteered to represent Scopes) and, for the prosecution, the equally renowned lawyer and orator William Jennings Bryan. Their impassioned arguments ranged far beyond the basic facts of the case, however; in some of the most dramatic and eloquent language ever recorded in the annals of legal history, the lifelong agnostic Darrow and the devoutly religious Bryan debated the existence of God and the truthfulness of the Bible. This emotional showdown between supporters and opponents of Christian fundamentalism and academic freedom attracted worldwide attention. Although Darrow lost—Scopes was convicted and fined $100—he took the fight all the way to the Supreme Court of Tennessee, which dismissed the case on a technicality. The state subsequently repealed the evolution law.

Darrow closed out his career with several civil rights cases, including a 1926 trial in Detroit in which he successfully defended members of a Black-American family accused of murdering a Ku Klux Klansman who, as part of a mob, had tried to drive them out of their new home in a White neighborhood. Darrow retired from his law practice in 1929 but was persuaded to return to court in 1932 for one last criminal case, that of a U.S. Navy lieutenant, his mother-in-law, and two sailors charged with murdering a Hawaiian man who was under indictment for assaulting the lieutenant's wife. The defendants admitted their guilt and were convicted of manslaughter rather than murder. They had their ten-year prison sentences reduced to one hour in the custody of the territorial sheriff.

Darrow spent the remaining years of his life in near seclusion. He died of heart disease at the age of eighty, respected by some and despised by others as a colorful rebel who was always willing to take on unpopular causes in the firm belief that they were the right ones to back—regardless of their impact on his career and his finances. (He often did not receive a fee for his services and was even known to pay some costs out of his own pocket.) As a *Nation* reporter noted, Clarence Darrow brought "a measure of humanity into the law" and could always be counted on as "the man who could work miracles for the defense."

Sources

➤ **Books**

Darrow, Clarence, *The Story of My Life,* Grosset & Dunlap, 1932.

Gurko, Miriam, *Clarence Darrow,* Crowell, 1965.

Stone, Irving, *Clarence Darrow for the Defense,* Doubleday, 1941. Reprint. New American Library/Dutton, 1971.

Weinberg, Arthur, editor, *Attorney for the Damned: Clarence Darrow in the Courtroom,* University of Chicago Press, 1989.

➤ **Periodicals**

Nation, March 19, 1938, p. 316.

New Republic, "Clarence Darrow," March 23, 1938, p. 179.

Newsweek, March 21, 1938, pp. 32–34.

New York Times, March 14, 1938, p. 15 (opening quote).

Time, March 21, 1938, p. 34.

➤ **Other**

The Scopes trial was dramatized in the play *Inherit the Wind,* (1955, by Robert E. Lee and Jerome Lawrence), which was also made into a movie. The Loeb-Leopold case was dramatized in *Compulsion,* (1956, by Meyer Levin).

Tom Dooley

"I *have spent six years of my life among different men, and always I find that the similarities outweigh the differences. Each life is infinitely precious as a life. Everywhere."*

Born on January 17, 1927, in St. Louis, Missouri, Tom Dooley was a medical missionary in Southeast Asia. He died of cancer on January 18, 1961, in New York City.

s the second son of a comfortably well-to-do St. Louis family headed by Thomas Anthony Dooley, Jr., a steel company executive, and his wife, Agnes Wise, Thomas Anthony Dooley III seemed destined from early youth "to live off his assets— ready cash, good looks, and a flair for amusing people with his dexterity at the piano and a frisky wit," as one of his colleagues later wrote. Brash, outgoing, and always in search of a good time or a bit of adventure, he took everyone by surprise when he announced after graduating from high school that he intended to study medicine. Even his parents doubted that he had the patience to stick with such a long and difficult program.

In the fall of 1943 Dooley enrolled at Notre Dame as a pre-med major. During his years there—interrupted by a stint in the navy during World War II—he compiled a less-than-spectacular scholastic record. He nevertheless managed to win admittance to the St. Louis University School of Medicine, where he continued to show little real promise. He still preferred parties to books, and most of his professors and fellow students figured he would eventually drift into a cushy private practice among the city's socialites.

Dooley received his degree in 1953 and re-entered the navy to serve an internship in the medical corps. After assignments at naval hospitals in California and Japan, he was sent aboard the *U.S.S. Montague*, which was charged with helping the French evacuate Vietnamese refugees as they fled south to escape the advancing forces of the communist Viet Minh. From August, 1954, until May, 1955, Operation Passage to Freedom shepherded more than six hundred thousand people from Haiphong in the north to Saigon in the south. Dooley was the only medical officer assigned to the task force, and as such he had to oversee the care of all those who sought the Americans' help.

Officially, his responsibilities included screening refugees for communicable diseases and vaccinating them, as well as providing food and sanitary facilities at the camp he built and ran to house them while they waited for their chance to head south. Unofficially, Dooley and his staff of four enlisted men also treated numerous injuries, among them rat bites and war wounds, and operated to repair broken bones that had never been set. Finding his own medical supplies inadequate for such an undertaking, he scrounged whatever he could from other ships in the harbor and requested donations from pharmaceutical companies back in the United States. The young doctor's job was made even more difficult given the prejudices and suspicions of his patients, most of whom had been bombarded for years with anti-American propaganda. All in all, it was exhausting, often thankless work, but Dooley repeatedly refused the navy's offer to replace him. He stayed with the evacuation effort until the Viet Minh marched into Haiphong, routinely treating upwards of three hundred people over the course of a typical eighteen-hour work day.

Back amid the comforts of home some months later, a restless and often angry Dooley reflected on the wretchedness he had observed in Vietnam and the need for ongoing medical help throughout all of Southeast Asia. When a fellow naval doctor suggested that putting his thoughts down on paper might help reduce his frustrations, Dooley produced *Deliver Us from Evil*, a straightforward account of his months in Haiphong. Published in late 1955, the book became a bestseller, and Dooley soon found himself in demand as a lecturer. Wherever he spoke, he emphasized the desperate situation facing people in countries like Vietnam. Before long, a plan began to take shape in his mind: *he* would go back to Southeast Asia himself and set up a medical mission. Resigning from the Navy in the spring of 1956, he set out to beg for or purchase as many supplies as he could, using money from donations as well as the earnings from his book.

In August of that same year, accompanied by several shiploads of supplies and three of the four medical corpsmen who had served with him in Vietnam, Dooley arrived in Laos and set up a hospital in the tiny village of Nam Tha. There he once again treated people by the thousands, including some Chinese refugees who slipped over the nearby border. He lavished special attention on children, who in turn worshipped the man they called "Dr. Tom" or "Dr. America."

Eager to set up additional facilities, Dooley returned to the United States in 1957 to raise more money and drum up more supplies. In a grueling lecture tour that took him across the country—the first of many such tours he would make over the next few years—the energetic young doctor spoke anywhere he thought he might find support. He also made appearances on national and local radio and television programs. At every opportunity, Dooley shared his dream of a worldwide organization that would send out medical teams to undeveloped corners of the globe, wherever they were needed. "We believe we can win the friendship of the people only by working beside them, humans-to-humans, toward goals they understand and seek themselves," he explained. "Our instrument for this shall be medicine." His dream soon became reality in the form of

MEDICO (short for Medical International Cooperation), a nonprofit volunteer agency dedicated to providing medical care to remote areas. By the end of 1960, MEDICO had seventeen projects operating in twelve countries, including seven hospitals in Southeast Asia.

Though widely admired in the United States for his efforts, Dooley was a somewhat controversial figure among some of the other American doctors working in Asia. They complained about his arrogance and insensitivity, and they accused him of being a "hit-and-run" doctor who spent too much time on the road and too little time seeing patients. They also faulted him for failing to use— or not knowing how to use—the most modern equipment and treatment procedures and for not having fully-trained medical personnel assisting him.

In response to his critics, Dooley freely admitted that he was far from being a meek or humble man. He also agreed that he tended to favor simple methods and that he preferred staffing his hospitals with young American volunteers who were not doctors. But he insisted that his approach was the appropriate one given the conditions he faced: widespread malnutrition, primitive sanitary facilities, and patients who still believed in witchcraft and were suspicious of outsiders. "What we strive for is *cure,* not prevention of disease," he declared. "Our patients sleep on mats and they do not have sheets. It may sound like seventeenth-century medicine, but it is better than the fifteenth-century medicine these natives were used to."

In 1958, Dooley turned over his hospital at Nam Tha to the Laotians and, under the auspices of MEDICO, established a new one about twenty miles away in Muong Sing. (Another lecture tour and proceeds from his second book, *The Edge of Tomorrow,* helped finance this undertaking.) He had been there about a year when he noticed a painful lump on his chest. However, it wasn't until a visiting doctor stopped by in July, 1959, that Dooley bothered to have the lump removed and sent in for analysis. An urgent telegram advising him to come home contained the grim diagnosis: malignant melanoma, a fast-spreading and deadly cancer.

Dooley underwent surgery in August and soon was back on the road promoting his third book, *The Night They Burned the Mountain,* and soliciting more donations. In an eight-week tour that took him to thirty-seven cities, he raised nearly one million dollars. More worn out than usual from his frantic schedule, Dooley feared something was wrong even though periodic check-ups revealed nothing new. By mid-1960, however, he had developed severe back pain and a lump in his neck; doctors confirmed that the cancer had spread to his spine. Realizing that his time was indeed running out, Dooley continued his fund-raising efforts with near-manic energy and made frequent visits back to his hospital in Muong Sing. "I am not going to quit," he declared. "I will continue to guide and lead my hospitals until my back, my brain, my blood and my bones collapse."

In November, 1960, Dooley was fitted with a torturous back brace to help support his disintegrating vertebrae. Thin, exhausted, and in constant pain, he nevertheless made one last trip through Southeast Asia before returning to the United States on Christmas Day and checking into New York's Memorial Hospital on December 27. There he spent the next few weeks slipping in and out of a coma until the evening of January 18, 1961, the day after his thirty-fourth birthday, when he died quietly in his sleep.

Tom Dooley achieved enduring international fame in little more than five years, a period during which he "seemed to be consuming a lifetime in one concentrated burst of amazing vitality," to quote Shirley Seifert in *Coronet*. Although he and his methods were occasionally the subject of criticism, he won the affection and respect of millions with his charm, sincerity, and enthusiasm. But most of all, observed a writer for *Christian Century*, "What endeared [Tom Dooley] to the world of his admirers was not his youth and his colorful personality but the fact that in him was seen a rare thing, the total surrender of life to the service of fellow men."

Sources

➤ **Books**

Dooley, Agnes W., *Promises to Keep: The Life of Doctor Thomas A. Dooley*, Farrar, Straus, 1961.

Dooley, Tom, *Deliver Us from Evil*, Farrar, Straus, 1955.

Dooley, Tom, *The Edge of Tomorrow*, Farrar, Straus, 1957.

Dooley, Tom, *The Night They Burned the Mountain*, Farrar, Straus, 1959.

Elliott, Lawrence, *The Legacy of Tom Dooley*, World, 1969.

Monahan, James, *Before I Sleep: The Last Days of Dr. Tom Dooley*, Farrar, Straus, 1961.

➤ **Periodicals**

Christian Century, "The Good Die Young," February 1, 1961, p. 132.

Coronet, "The Untold Story of Tom Dooley," August, 1961, pp. 58–64.

Life, "Tom Dooley at Work," April 18, 1960.

Newsweek, "The Doctor's Last Days," November 23, 1959, p. 106; "Doctor of the Jungle," January 30, 1961, p. 70.

New York Times, "Dr. Dooley Dead; Built Laos Clinics," January 19, 1961.

Reader's Digest, "Before I Sleep: The Last Days of Dr. Tom Dooley" (condensation of book of the same title), January, 1962, pp. 216–251; "Promises to Keep: The Life of Doctor Thomas A. Dooley" (excerpt from book of the same title), February, 1963, pp. 213–216 (opening quote); "Unforgettable Tom Dooley," June 1976, pp. 108–112.

Time, "Jungle Physician," August 31, 1959, p. 50; "What Few Have Done," January 27, 1961, p. 32.

W. E. B. Du Bois

"*The problem of the twentieth century is the problem of the color line.*"

Born on February 23, 1868, in Great Barrington, Massachusetts, educator, writer, and human rights activist Du Bois championed the cause of freedom and equality for Black Americans during the first half of the twentieth century. He died in Accra, Ghana, on August 27, 1963.

On August 28, 1963, more than two hundred thousand people gathered in the nation's capital for the March on Washington for Jobs and Freedom, a huge demonstration of support for the civil rights movement that ended with Martin Luther King, Jr.'s famous "I Have a Dream" speech. During the march, word circulated throughout the crowd that death had come just the day before to W. E. B. Du Bois, a man who had long warned Black Americans about the danger of remaining submissive in the belief that White society would voluntarily grant them equal rights. One of the demonstrators compared Du Bois to Moses, another great leader who did not live to see the promised land. Yet with his "acid pen, brilliant mind and strident tongue," to quote a *Christian Century* writer, Du Bois had indeed given shape and direction to the protests of the 1960s.

William Edward Burghardt Du Bois was born and raised in Great Barrington, Massachusetts, the son of Alfred Du Bois, a restless wanderer who left town within a year after his son's birth, and Mary Salvina Burghardt. Left alone to support herself and William, Mary Du Bois worked as a maid until a stroke left her partially paralyzed. Relatives and neighbors then helped by donating food and clothes, and William pitched in by chopping wood, shoveling coal, delivering groceries, and doing other odd jobs.

Du Bois was a brilliant student and received a bachelor's degree from Fisk University in 1888; he earned a second one from Harvard University in 1890. He then went on to graduate school and doctoral studies in Germany at the University of Berlin. Upon returning to the United States in 1894, Du Bois taught briefly at Wilberforce University in Ohio before accepting an offer to teach at the University of Pennsylvania in Philadelphia and conduct sociological research on a local Black neighborhood plagued by poverty, violence, and crime. Working entirely alone, he gathered a tremendous amount of information via thousands of personal interviews and published his findings in *The Philadelphia Negro: A Social Study*, the first sociological analysis of a Black-American ghetto. In it, he advanced the then-revolutionary conclusion that Black Americans had few chances for advancement not only because Whites denied them such basic rights as equal employment and fair housing but also because middle-class Blacks did little to help poor Blacks. Furthermore, he wrote, Black Americans would emerge from oppression only when Blacks provided their own role models, strong leadership, and a political voice.

In 1897, Du Bois was named professor of history and economics at Atlanta University in Georgia. He remained there for twelve years, establishing Black sociology as a legitimate field of study and organizing a series of annual conferences on the problems of Black America. These conferences—which he continued to lead for some eight years after leaving the university—contributed greatly to making him a nationally known figure.

In 1900, while in France attending the Paris Exposition (for which he had created a prize-winning display on Black-American life), Du Bois met with a group of thirty-two men and women who shared his interest in advancing the civil rights of Africans and their descendants around the world. It was the first meeting of what came to be known as the Pan-African Association. Although it disbanded some two years later, its goal of promoting international unity among Blacks lived on in the person of its chairman, Du Bois.

Throughout this period, Du Bois regularly contributed pieces on various political and social issues to major magazines and newspapers. In 1903, some of these essays were published in a collection entitled *The Souls of Black Folk,* which touched off a feud between Du Bois and Booker T. Washington, then the most prominent and popular Black leader in the country. Du Bois was harshly critical of Washington's policy of compromise and accommodation, which encouraged Black Americans to put aside their desire for social and political equality and focus instead on achieving economic success. Convinced that such a submissive attitude would just leave Blacks mired in second-class servitude, Du Bois called on Black-American intellectuals (whom he referred to as "the Talented Tenth") to lead the struggle for equal rights.

Washington and his supporters responded by trying to discredit Du Bois, who eventually decided that it was up to him to provide new Black leadership. In mid-1905, he and about thirty other like-minded men and women banded together in what became known as the Niagara Movement. It expanded slowly for several years despite Washington's efforts to crush it, then began to fall apart as members drifted away to join other civil rights organizations.

In 1909, however, a group of White and Black social workers and reformers (including Du Bois) formed the National Association for the Advancement of Colored People (NAACP) to carry on the goals of the Niagara Movement. Du Bois, the only Black American on the organization's board of directors, was named head of publicity and research and as such he edited *Crisis,* the NAACP's official publication, shaping its tone and content and effectively increasing membership. After Booker T. Washington's death in 1915, many looked to Du Bois as the leading Black figure in the country. Yet his relationship with the other members of the NAACP board was often strained due to his outspokenness and his ties with radical activists.

The 1920s was a decade of triumph as well as turmoil for Du Bois. He was in great demand for lectures, conferences, and exhibitions. He continued to write and actively promoted the careers of numerous young Black-American writers, musicians, and singers. And he remained at the forefront of the fight for civil rights. But when race riots erupted across the United States shortly after the end of World War I, some people blamed Du Bois because he had encouraged returning Black-American soldiers to keep up the fight for democracy at home. Also, both he and the NAACP found themselves at odds with the Universal Negro Improvement Association (UNIA) and its charismatic founder, Marcus Garvey, whose philosophy blended Pan-Africanism, Black nationalism, and Booker T. Washington's teachings on self-improvement. Garvey ultimately fell from favor when he allied himself with the Ku Klux Klan to promote racial separation, but as a result of his actions, Black Americans lost interest in Africa and Africans, thus undermining the Pan-African movement.

During the 1930s, Du Bois's radicalism intensified as he observed the devastating effects of the Depression on Black Americans. In the pages of *Crisis,* he championed what he called "voluntary segregation"—the idea that Black Americans should pool their resources to help their fellow Blacks because Whites were not about to do so. His position upset the NAACP leadership, which opposed segregation in any form. After the board of directors voted that no officer was allowed to criticize the policies, work, or other officers of the NAACP in *Crisis,* Du Bois resigned as editor in May, 1934, and returned to Atlanta University. Appointed to a lifetime position as chairman of the Department of Sociology, he resumed his research, taught graduate courses, founded the social science journal *Phylon,* and wrote books, articles, and newspaper columns. A trip abroad in 1936 gave him the opportunity to compare U.S. society with that of other nations, particularly the Soviet Union, whose concern for the working class greatly impressed him. His admitted communist sympathies and emphasis on Black studies made some of his colleagues uncomfortable, however, including Florence Read, president of Spelman College, Atlanta University's college for women. In the mid-1940s, she successfully persuaded the university to revoke Du Bois's lifetime appointment.

Then came an unexpected offer from the NAACP to return as director of research. Du Bois immediately became involved in a wide variety of activities and continued to speak out forcefully on behalf of Pan-Africanism. His vigor surprised the NAACP leadership, which had expected the seventy-six-year-old scholar to serve as little more than a figurehead. Tensions increased between Du Bois and the board of directors, and in 1948, they again voted to oust him.

Two years after leaving the NAACP, Du Bois ran for (and lost) a seat in the U.S. Senate as a candidate of the American Labor Party. He also headed several organizations the government regarded as subversive due to their ties with the Soviet Union. Charged with failing to register as a foreign agent, he was put on trial in November, 1951. The proceedings attracted worldwide attention as the government made every effort to humiliate and intimidate Du Bois. He was quickly acquitted, but the charges against him were not as quickly forgotten. The police and the FBI harassed him, and the State Department prevented him from traveling abroad throughout most of the rest of the decade. Invitations to lecture and write dwindled to almost nothing, and his influence slowly declined. By the end of the decade, Du Bois's voice had been effectively silenced.

In October, 1961, having lost all hope that Black Americans would ever know freedom in their own country, Du Bois accepted an offer from President Kwame Nkrumah to move to Ghana and begin work on an *Encyclopedia Africana*. In a symbolic parting gesture, the ninety-three-year-old activist officially joined the American Communist party. When the U.S. government subsequently refused to renew his passport, Du Bois renounced his citizenship. Upon his death in Ghana, he was granted a state funeral and buried on the grounds of the Government House.

During Du Bois's lifetime, support for his ideas was limited primarily to a small group of liberals; most Black Americans considered him too radical and too scholarly to appreciate the reality of their everyday lives. As a writer for *Christian Century* pointed out, however, the demonstrators gathered in Washington on the day after Du Bois's death gave new voice to the words he had first penned more than fifty years earlier: "We claim for ourselves every right that belongs to a free-born American—political, civil and social—and until we get these rights, we will never cease to protest and assail the ears of America with the story of its shameful deeds towards us."

Sources

➤ **Books**

Du Bois, W. E. B., *The Souls of Black Folk: Essays and Sketches*, A. C. McClurg, 1903. Reprint. Random House, 1990.

Du Bois, W. E. B., *Darkwater: Voices from Within the Veil*, Harcourt, 1920. Reprint. Kraus Reprint, 1975.

Du Bois, W. E. B., *Dusk at Dawn*, Harcourt, 1940. Reprint. Transaction Publishers, 1991.

Du Bois, W. E. B., *In Battle for Peace: The Story of My 83rd Birthday*, Masses and Mainstream, 1952. Reprint. Kraus Reprint, 1976.

Du Bois, W. E. B., *The Autobiography of W. E. B. Du Bois*, International Publishers, 1968. Reprint. Kraus Reprint, 1976.

Hamilton, Virginia, *W. E. B. Du Bois: A Biography*, Crowell, 1972.

Stafford, Mark, *W. E. B. Du Bois*, Chelsea House, 1989 (opening quote).

➤ **Periodicals**

Christian Century, "Du Bois Dies in Ghana," September 11, 1963, p. 1092.

Ebony, "Ten Greats of Black History," August, 1972, pp. 35–42.

New York Times, August 28, 1963, p. 33.

Time, September 6, 1963, p. 56.

Albert Einstein

"O ne cannot help but be in awe when [one] contemplates the mysteries of eternity, of life, of the marvelous structures of reality. It is enough if one tries merely to comprehend a little of this mystery each day. Never lose a holy curiosity."

One of the greatest theoretical physicists who ever lived, Albert Einstein revolutionized scientific thought with his theory of relativity and discoveries that form the basis of quantum physics. Born on March 14, 1879, in Ulm, Germany, he died on April 18, 1955, in Princeton, New Jersey.

Albert Einstein was a man of contrasts. He was, for instance, a scientific genius who deliberately distanced himself from others (including his own family) in order to carry out his ground-breaking research in solitude. At the same time, he was a public figure who gave generously of his time and energy to causes he supported, enduring harsh criticism and even risking death as a result of the stands he took on some of the major issues of his day. Some also see tremendous irony in the fact that the work of such a great humanitarian provided the theoretical basis for one of the most destructive man-made forces in the world, the atomic bomb. Yet his commitment to the right of every human being to freedom, truth, justice, and opportunity was unyielding and allowed for no ambiguity. "The most important human endeavor is the striving for morality in our actions," he once wrote. "Our inner balance and even our very existence depend on it. Only morality in our actions can give beauty and dignity to life."

Albert Einstein was the son of Pauline Koch Einstein and Hermann Einstein, owner of a company that made and sold electrical equipment. No one in the family was particularly gifted in science or math, and for some time it appeared that Albert wasn't either—in fact, he didn't show much aptitude for anything. He couldn't talk until he was three, and for a number of years after that he still had trouble speaking fluently. In elementary school his performance was dismal at best, leading some people (including his parents) to suspect that he was retarded. From the time he was a small child, however, Albert preferred to learn on his own; in his early teens he taught himself advanced mathematics and science. He followed this pattern of independent study throughout the rest of his life.

Graduating from the Swiss Federal Polytechnic School in Zurich in 1900 with a degree in physics, Einstein worked at a series of temporary jobs before landing a permanent position in 1902 as a technical expert with the Swiss Patent Office. For the next seven years he evaluated proposed inventions by day and conducted his own research in the evenings and whenever else he had some free time, applying his work toward a doctorate at the University of Zurich. He also married a former classmate at the Polytechnic, Mileva Maric, and together they had a daughter and two sons.

As early as 1902 Einstein had become consumed with the task of linking time and space, matter and energy. In 1905, at the age of twenty-six, he published a paper outlining his special theory of relativity, which demonstrates mathematically that the speed of light is constant (roughly 186,000 miles per second) and *not* relative to its source or to the speed of an observer. That same year he published papers on four other topics of note: quantum law and the emission and absorption of light (research that won him the 1921 Nobel Prize in physics), Brownian motion, the inertia of energy, and the electrodynamics of moving bodies.

Upon its publication, the special theory of relativity met with scorn among those scientists who bothered to pay attention to it at all. But as the young theoretician published his other equally-controversial papers—most of them on topics so advanced only a handful of physicists understood them—more and more of his colleagues began to notice the genius in their midst. Einstein suddenly found himself in demand at universities all over Europe. In 1913, after teaching at nearly a half-dozen institutions, he accepted a prestigious appointment as head of the Kaiser Wilhelm Physical Institute, special professor at the University of Berlin (with all the research time he wanted), and member of the Royal Prussian Academy of Sciences. He moved to Berlin in April, 1914, leaving his family behind in Zurich. He and his wife divorced in 1919, at which time he married a cousin, Elsa Einstein.

Comfortably ensconced in his new position and free of the distractions of family life, Einstein was able to devote himself entirely to research. Building on some of his earlier findings, he developed what is probably the best-known equation in science, the general theory of relativity: $E=mc^2$. In stating that energy (E) equals mass (m) times the square of the speed of light (c^2), Einstein proposed that an ounce of matter contains as much energy as that given off by the explosion of nearly a million tons of TNT. His theory also challenged one of Newton's laws by predicting that observations of astronomical phenomena would prove that gravity can bend even light. Published in 1916, the theory was validated in 1919 by British astronomers who noted in photographs of a solar eclipse that the apparent positions of star images surrounding the sun changed position during the eclipse, the light from them deflected by the gravitational effects of the sun.

Although Einstein's work was without a doubt the most important thing in his life, it was not his only concern. A pacifist who believed in the "internationality" of science, he was disappointed by the outbreak of World War I and appalled by his colleagues' involvement in programs to develop weapons, airplanes, and poison gas. Denounced as a traitor, he was spared any serious consequences only because he was so famous.

During the 1920s, as Germany struggled to get back on its feet after a humiliating defeat and a punitive peace treaty following World War I, Einstein became a target of anti-Semitic criticism and even occasional death threats when he began speaking out on behalf of the Zionist movement and its demands for a Jewish homeland in Palestine. The public and some members of the European scientific community turned against him, but Einstein resolved to stay in Germany and work for world peace. To demonstrate the depth of his commitment, he renounced the Swiss citizenship he had held since 1901 and once again took up German citizenship.

As conditions in his homeland deteriorated throughout the decade, Einstein spent more and more of his time abroad giving lectures and raising money for the Palestine Foundation Fund. In between trips he focused his research efforts on the problem that would occupy him for the rest of his life: the unified field theory (also known as the grand unified theory), a concept that would mathematically reconcile the apparent contradictions between general relativity and quantum mechanics and thus explain the behavior of everything in the universe.

During the 1930s, the rise of Adolf Hitler made life in Germany very uncomfortable and even dangerous for Einstein, who continued to speak out for peace and against rearmament and the rising tide of anti-Semitism. In January, 1933, while teaching at the California Institute of Technology in Pasadena, Einstein learned that Germans had elected Hitler as their new chancellor. Saddened by this turn of events, he once again renounced his citizenship and accepted a permanent position at the Institute for Advanced Study in Princeton, New Jersey.

Einstein's repeated warnings about the Nazi threat fell largely on deaf ears once he settled in the United States. Even his fellow pacifists scoffed and called him a traitor to the cause of world peace when he recommended that Europe re-arm itself and build up its military forces to counter what he was sure were German preparations for war. Feeling that no one was interested in what he had to say, he withdrew into his research.

In 1939, however, several other prominent scientists persuaded him to end his silence and sign a letter they had written urging President Franklin Delano Roosevelt to fund an atomic bomb project before Germany did. (Because he harbored so many reservations about creating such a weapon, Einstein also wrote a follow-up letter of his own stating that it should not be used against people.) His plea was instrumental in convincing Roosevelt to approve the so-called Manhattan Project, and although Einstein himself was never personally involved, his general theory of relativity provided the theoretical explanation for the research that spawned the first atomic bomb. Its use against the Japanese in August, 1945, horrified him. He later became chairman of the Emergency Committee of Atomic Scientists, a group that encouraged countries to focus on developing peaceful uses for nuclear energy.

Einstein officially retired from the Institute for Advanced Study in 1945 but continued to work on his elusive unified field theory. Several times he announced he was close to a breakthrough, but eventually he was forced to admit that he could not come up with a practical way of confirming his ideas through experimental evidence.

During the late 1940s, Einstein began to suffer from health problems that doctors attributed to a heart aneurysm. He ignored their advice to take it easy and kept busy with his research, raising money for war relief organizations, lobbying on behalf of the World Government Movement, speaking out for human rights and for civic and academic freedoms jeopardized by anti-communist hysteria, decrying the escalation of the arms race, and lending his support to Zionism. In 1952, after the death of Israel's founder and first president, Chaim Weizmann, Einstein declined an offer to succeed him. His health took a turn for the worse in early 1955, and on April 18—having adamantly refused to undergo surgery—he died when his weakened heart artery ruptured. Per his instructions, there was no funeral, no grave, and no monument; his brain was donated to science and his body was cremated, and the ashes were scattered over a nearby river.

Despite the fact that he was a very public figure, Einstein was in many ways a personal enigma. Close to only a handful of people and never one to divulge his innermost thoughts and feelings even to them, he lived a simple and secluded life that revolved around his work, the most significant portion of which he completed well before he had turned thirty. He was puzzled and rather annoyed by the fuss others made over him but learned to use it to advance his causes. In short, declares Jamie Sayen in the book *Einstein in America,* "Einstein was a unique phenomenon: a theoretical scientist whose area of expertise was far removed from the everyday concerns of his fellow mortals, a man without interest or training in the workings of politics who, nevertheless, by the sheer force of his character, came to play a critical role in the public life of his epoch as preeminent moral figure of the Western world."

Sources

➤ **Books**

Bernstein, Jeremy, *Einstein*, Viking, 1973.

Clark, Ronald W., *Einstein: The Life and Times*, World Publishing, 1971 (opening quote).

Dank, Milton, *Albert Einstein*, F. Watts, 1983.

Einstein, Albert, *Out of My Later Years*, Greenwood Press, 1970. Reprint of 1950 edition.

French, A. P., editor, *Einstein: A Centenary Volume*, Harvard University Press, 1979.

Ireland, Karin, *Albert Einstein*, Silver Burdett, 1989.

Sayen, Jamie, *Einstein in America: The Scientist's Conscience in the Age of Hitler and Hiroshima*, Crown, 1985.

➤ **Periodicals**

Atlantic, "Albert Einstein: Appraisal of an Intellect," June, 1955.

Newsweek, "Unanswered Question," May 2, 1955, pp. 86–87.

New York Times, "Einstein Sees Lack in Applying Science," February 17, 1931, p. 6; April 19, 1955.

New York Times Magazine, "Einstein, at 75, Is Still a Rebel," March 14, 1954.

Reader's Digest, "The World of Albert Einstein," May, 1953, pp. 76–78.

Saturday Evening Post, "What Life Means to Einstein," October 26, 1929.

Time, "Death of a Genius," May 2, 1955, pp. 50–54.

Duke Ellington

"M *usic is my mistress, and she plays second fiddle to no one."*

Often described as America's greatest jazz composer, Duke Ellington was also a renowned bandleader, arranger, and pianist. He was born on April 29, 1899, in Washington, D.C., and died on May 24, 1974, in New York City.

D uring a career that spanned more than fifty years, Duke Ellington almost singlehandedly changed the way people throughout the world regarded the uniquely American form of music known as jazz. In his hands, jazz became serious art, as lyrical and as complex as any symphony. From his popular standards of the 1930s and 1940s to his sacred pieces of the 1960s, he infused all of his compositions with a distinctive sound that drew on jazz's African roots to "catch the character and mood and feeling of my people," as he once explained. Although he preferred the term *Negro music* to describe his works in the belief that *jazz* defined them too narrowly, Ellington is regarded as a jazz virtuoso by the many admirers of his vast and exciting repertoire.

Edward Kennedy Ellington enjoyed a happy, carefree youth as part of a loving and close-knit, middle-class family in Washington, D.C. From his father, James Edward Ellington, who worked days as a blueprint maker for the U.S. Navy and evenings as a caterer and waiter, he inherited a love of music and a sense of style and charm. From his mother, Daisy Kennedy Ellington, he gained inner strength through religion and pride in himself and in his race. Although baseball was his first real passion, Edward took piano lessons on and off for a few years until he was around ten, when his teacher gave up on him because he liked to experiment too much with unusual chords and sounds. But he continued to learn on his own, imitating and memorizing songs he heard others play.

By the time he was in high school, Ellington—dubbed "Duke" by a friend who thought the dapper young man with the fancy manners and flawless speech deserved an appropriate nickname— was fairly sure he wanted to be a musician. He began to put in long hours of piano practice and mastered the popular tunes of the day. He also frequented local pool halls, where many of the best Black-American jazz and ragtime pianists played informally. Before he had even finished high school, Ellington had decided to abandon his plans to study commercial art and instead went to work as a professional pianist. He then formed and managed several different bands that played regularly around the Washington area. By 1920, he had assembled a single group of superbly talented musicians who shared his serious attitude about music and performing. Unlike many bandleaders of that era, he treated them well, kept them working steadily, and paid them generously. They in turn rewarded him with exceptional loyalty and dependability. Some stayed with him for several decades.

In late 1922, Ellington and a few of his bandmates headed north to New York City's Harlem neighborhood, then in the midst of a creative period known as the Harlem Renaissance. Beginning with a few brief engagements at small clubs that catered mostly to Black-American audiences, "Duke Ellington and the Washingtonians" (as they were then billed) soon moved on to steady engagements at bigger clubs with exclusively White audiences, culminating in 1927 with an invitation to play at the Cotton Club, Harlem's premier nightspot. By the end of the decade, "Duke Ellington and His Orchestra" (as they had begun to call themselves) were a sensation not only in Harlem but across the country, thanks in part to the live radio broadcasts of their performances, which brought them recognition and acclaim from coast to coast. Their hot "jungle" sound—featuring animal-like growls and wah-wah effects produced by trumpets and trombones fitted with plungers—was a tremendous hit, as was Ellington himself, whose elegant attire and sophisticated manner of speaking seemed to epitomize Harlem's glamorous nightlife.

During this same period, Ellington launched his songwriting career in earnest. He had penned his first compositions as a teenager; now he began to write not only for his own band but also to sell to music publishers. He eventually wrote or co-wrote more than two thousand compositions of various lengths, and it is estimated that he was responsible for roughly ninety percent of the material his band recorded.

The 1930s saw Duke Ellington and His Orchestra claim the title of the most popular Black jazz band in the United States. Dropping the jungle sound to experiment with other variations on jazz, they produced music that was more complex and original yet still very appealing. The slow and dreamy "Mood Indigo" (1930) was Ellington's first big hit and typical of his new direction. He followed it with "Creole Rhapsody," a much longer and more serious work that foreshadowed many of his later compositions. But his major contributions during this era were to pop music, including such songs as "It Don't Mean a Thing If It Ain't Got That Swing," "Sophisticated Lady," "Solitude," "In a Sentimental Mood," and "I Let a Song Go Out of My Heart." Ellington eventually grew tired of performing these hits only at the Cotton Club, however, so beginning in 1931 he took his orchestra on the road for several successful tours of the United States and Europe. They also appeared in several short films and made frequent radio broadcasts and recordings.

The early 1940s marked the creative peak of both Ellington and his band. Their popularity soared to an all-time high both in the United States and overseas as they incorporated elements of the new "swing" style jazz into their music. (Light, fast, and very rhythmic, swing was created especially for dancing.) Their chart-topping hits during these years included "Don't Get Around Much Anymore" and the orchestra's theme song, "Take the 'A' Train." Another important milestone came on January 23, 1943, when Duke Ellington and His Orchestra became the first Black jazz group to perform at Carnegie Hall, launching an annual tradition that continued into the early 1950s. Besides being huge commercial successes, the concerts forever changed the way the public viewed both Ellington and his fellow band members. With a new long composition serving as the centerpiece of each performance, Ellington came to be regarded as an innovative composer and the skillful leader of a group of serious and talented musicians.

After the highs of the first half of the decade came some lows that lasted well into the next decade. Jazz and swing declined in popularity, and even Ellington had to struggle to keep his band together through a series of unprofitable tours and sporadic club dates. By the early 1950s, both he and his orchestra seemed bored and discouraged; their performances were criticized as lackluster and uninspired, several longtime members quit, and Ellington experienced an unusual creative slump that affected the quantity as well as the quality of his compositions. By the middle of the fifties, many observers thought his best days were behind him and that his band was finished.

In the mid-1950s, however, Ellington launched an amazing comeback. He began to compose pieces that reflected a more modern approach to jazz and tailored them to the strengths of his younger musicians. His renewed sense of energy and creativity in turn sparked interest in him as a performer and a recording artist. Evidence that the Duke was definitely still a force to be reckoned with came in spectacular fashion at the Newport Jazz Festival in July, 1956. Playing a few new compositions as well as rearrangements of old ones, he and his orchestra gave one of their most explosive concerts ever, touching off frenzied dancing in the aisles and landing Ellington on the cover of *Time* magazine.

From then until his death in 1974, Ellington stayed at or near the top of the jazz world. His surge of songwriting creativity endured well into the 1960s as he concentrated mainly on longer works, including three sets of religious pieces he called "sacred concerts." Incorporating both jazz and classical elements, they advanced his reputation as a serious composer. At the same time, he continued to turn out shorter pieces and even scored a few films. He also toured frequently with his band, made recordings, and performed regularly at clubs and festivals. In recognition of his many achievements, Ellington was showered with awards, including a special Grammy Award in 1968, the Presidential Medal of Freedom in 1969 (presented at a White House ceremony in honor of his seventieth birthday), and the French Legion of Honor in 1973 (the first ever given to a jazz musician).

Age began to take its toll on Ellington and his orchestra at the beginning of the 1970s. A few of the oldest members died or retired, and Ellington himself was diagnosed with lung cancer in early 1973. Although the disease left him weak and tired, he refused both rest and medical care, choosing instead to keep working until he collapsed on stage in January, 1974. He died in the spring of that year while undergoing treatment for pneumonia.

Today, Duke Ellington's orchestra thrives under the leadership of his son, Mercer Ellington, and his music lives on thanks to other bands, singers, and even Broadway productions that feature his work. In taking a popular form of music and transcending it to produce serious art, he left behind what is widely acclaimed as jazz's most distinctive and impressive body of composition. Of perhaps greater significance, though, is the fact that through his music he celebrated the lives of Black Americans, "elevat[ing] a people others wanted to denigrate, utiliz[ing] a heritage many sought to discard," as *Ebony* magazine noted. And by his own personal example of dignity and pride, Duke Ellington quietly, yet firmly, challenged unflattering racial stereotypes and discrimination.

Sources

➤ **Books**

Collier, James Lincoln, *Duke Ellington*, Oxford University Press, 1987.

Ellington, Duke, *Music Is My Mistress*, Doubleday, 1973 (opening quote).

Frankl, Ron, *Duke Ellington*, Chelsea House, 1988.

► **Periodicals**

Crisis, June, 1974, pp. 197–200.

Ebony, January, 1974 (excerpt from *Music Is My Mistress);* "A Tribute to Duke Ellington, 1899–1974," September, 1974, pp. 43–54; "Why We Must Preserve Our Jazz Heritage," November, 1990, pp. 159–164.

Esquire, "Jazz," December, 1975, pp. 138–144.

High Fidelity/Musical America, "The Duke in the Recording Studio," November, 1974, pp. 65–78.

New York Times, "Duke Ellington, Master of Music, Dies at 75," May 25, 1974.

Time, "Undefeated Champ," June 3, 1974, p. 83.

Anthony S. Fauci

"No matter what you decide on, there will be those who praise you and those who will go so far as to call you a murderer. The saving grace is that, fundamentally, I'm a scientist. . . . Do the science correctly, and ultimately you will be doing good for people."

Affiliated with the National Institutes of Health, Anthony S. Fauci directs AIDS research. He was born on December 24, 1940, in Brooklyn, New York.

Since becoming the director of the National Institute of Allergy and Infectious Diseases (NIAID) in 1984, Anthony S. Fauci has been on the front lines in the war against AIDS. The political and emotional currents that swirl around this deadly disease have made an already difficult job even more so. Not only is Fauci charged with directing the efforts to discover and evaluate treatments and ultimately a cure, he must also wage a constant battle for research funds, spearhead educational efforts, and defend the government against charges that it hasn't done enough to stop or at least slow down the epidemic. But in the delicate balancing act between meeting scientific goals and addressing humanitarian needs, the nation's AIDS chief has garnered the praise and respect of people inside and outside the government for his adroit and compassionate approach.

Brooklyn native Anthony Stephen Fauci is one of two children born to Stephen Fauci, a pharmacist, and Eugenia Fauci. After graduating from a Jesuit high school in Manhattan known for its demanding curriculum, he attended Holy Cross College in Worcester, Massachusetts, from which he received a B.A. degree in 1962. Fauci then went on to medical school at Cornell University and later completed his internship and residency at the university's medical center in New York City.

Fauci's affiliation with the National Institutes of Health (NIH) began in 1968, when he went to work for NIAID (one of the eleven institutes that make up NIH) as a research fellow in the Laboratory of Clinical Investigation. He held several posts within NIAID during the early 1970s and was appointed its deputy clinical director in 1977 and chief of the immunology laboratory in 1980, a position he retains to this day. In 1984, Fauci was promoted to director of NIAID, and in 1988 he took on additional responsibilities as associate director of NIH for research on AIDS and head of the NIH Office of AIDS Research. Since then, fifteen-hour work days have become commonplace for the man fighting what some regard as the plague of the twentieth century.

Fauci characterizes his current research on AIDS as a logical extension of his earlier studies on the human immune system and illnesses that result from the abnormal function of the body's natural defenses. During the 1970s, for example, he was part of a team of doctors who examined the origination, development, and treatment of several rare, incurable, and usually fatal immune-related diseases such as polyarteritis nodosa, Wegener's granulomatosis, and lymphomatoid granulomatosis. Fauci developed highly effective cures for these diseases, while at the same time learning a great deal about the immune system.

Since taking over the reins at NIAID, Fauci has devoted his attention to both AIDS and HIV (human immunodeficiency virus), which causes a variety of infections and other symptoms leading to the onset of full-blown AIDS. His research has pinpointed how AIDS destroys the body's defenses and thus makes a person susceptible to numerous other deadly infections and diseases, including certain forms of pneumonia and cancer. Using that information he has helped formulate treatments designed to bolster the immune systems of those suffering from AIDS so that they are not as likely to develop such illnesses. He has also identified a protein substance secreted in the human bloodstream by a type of immune cell that turns a latent AIDS infection into an active one. According to Fauci, this discovery suggests that HIV-positive patients who want to ward off AIDS symptoms for as long as possible should avoid doing anything that might cause that protein to be secreted, including using recreational drugs and contracting sexually transmitted diseases.

Other major areas of investigation at NIAID are the development and testing of drugs to treat people who already have AIDS and the creation of a vaccine to prevent the disease. Most experts, including Fauci, believe that an effective vaccine is still many years away, but trials of promising drugs are conducted on a regular basis. It is this latter aspect of the government's AIDS research that has come under attack most often; AIDS activists have repeatedly charged that the testing and approval process for new drugs is far too slow and cumbersome and that people are dying as a result. Some of the angrier and more radical AIDS advocates (such as members of the AIDS Coalition to Unleash Power or ACT UP) have even gone so far as to say the government is guilty of murder for not taking more aggressive action.

In the middle of this highly emotional controversy is Fauci, who as a scientist must balance his reluctance to hand out drugs before they are fully tested with his realization that some of what the activists have said is true. In the late 1980s, he began meeting regularly with AIDS advocates to discuss their frustrations and concerns. One program that resulted from those conversations is the AIDS Clinical Trial Group, a chain of centers for drug testing. Under this system, which is intended to circumvent typical government bureaucracy, experimental drugs will be distributed to as many AIDS-infected patients as possible at the same time that scientists conduct more traditional evaluations of the drugs' effectiveness. As Fauci explained to a *New York Times* reporter, "Now we are going to reserve a certain amount of money so we don't have to wait eight months while people decide who's going to do it and how they are going to do it. We are going to say, 'You, do it!'"

AIDS activists have also been critical of the fact that virtually everything scientists know about the disease is based on studies of homosexual White males. Since AIDS has spread beyond that group, Fauci has pledged to include more Black and Hispanic Americans, women, and children in clinical trials in order to assess their responses to various treatments.

As an administrator with what one colleague described as "an unusual gift for conciliation and compromise and a profound capacity to listen," Fauci has been able to do what few other federal officials have managed: gain the respect of government leaders, AIDS activists, *and* his fellow scientists. President George Bush has lauded him as a hero and even tried to persuade him to accept an appointment as director of NIH when that post was vacated in 1989. (Fauci declined because he felt he could contribute more by staying in research.) At the Sixth Annual Conference on AIDS, held in San Francisco in June, 1990, many attendees greeted U.S. administration officials with boos and catcalls but interrupted Fauci's speech with cheers and gave him a standing ovation at the end of his talk. Other AIDS researchers rate him as one of the top medical scientists in the world.

Fauci defends his investigators as "good people doing the best they can." He also defends the rights of AIDS activists "to be heard and to be part of the process" and acknowledges that many scientists and government officials need to be more sensitive. Grimly noting that over a million Americans are HIV-positive and thus likely to develop AIDS, he concludes that "the worst is still ahead."

And for that reason alone, declares Fauci, "we have got to work together."

Sources
➤ **Periodicals**

New York Times, "AIDS Advocates Are Angry at U.S. But Its Research Chief Wins Respect," September 4, 1990, p. A14.

People, "Anthony Fauci," December 31, 1990-January 7, 1991, pp. 68–69 (opening quote).

Science, "Bush Goes 0 for 2 with Anthony Fauci," November 17, 1989, p. 880.

Jose Feliciano

"I *have tried to change the image of blind performers. I don't wear glasses, just like deaf people don't wear earmuffs."*

Jose Feliciano is a guitarist, singer, and songwriter who overcame blindness and poverty to excel as a pop music performer. He was born on September 10, 1945, in Lares, Puerto Rico.

I n 1968, twenty-three-year-old Jose Feliciano was already a hit with Spanish-speaking audiences in the United States and Latin America when he exploded on the English-language pop scene with his stylized versions of two well-known songs: the Doors' "Light My Fire" and the "Star-Spangled Banner." The creator of a highly personal and exciting blend of rock, soul, jazz, blues, classical, and Latin sounds and rhythms, he has won accolades for his virtuoso guitar playing and is the only performer to have won pop music Grammy Awards in two language categories. The fact that he is blind is something he tends to downplay, for he has never let it slow him down or stand in the way of achieving fame.

A native of Puerto Rico, Feliciano is the second of eleven boys, three of whom did not survive to adulthood. His family was very poor—the elder Feliciano was a farmer—and in 1950 they moved to New York City in search of a better life. Because of his blindness (attributed to congenital glaucoma), young Jose was unable to participate in sports and other activities, so at a very early age he turned to making music.

When he was only three, for example, he was beating out rhythms on a tin cracker can to accompany his uncle. At six, he taught himself to play the concertina (a type of accordion) by listening to records, and at nine, he learned the guitar, again by listening to records for as many as fourteen hours every day. He eventually mastered a number of other instruments, including the banjo, mandolin, harmonica, organ, piano, harpsichord, conga drums, bongo drums, and timbales.

At first, Feliciano's chief musical influence was the Latin American sound his father urged him to imitate. But soon he was drawn to the work of soul stars Ray Charles, Sam Cooke, and Otis Redding. With the advent of rock and roll later in the 1950s, he began to admire performers such as Chuck Berry, Fats Domino, and Elvis Presley and was inspired by them to sing as well as play the guitar. He became familiar with still more varieties of music (especially classical) thanks to schoolteachers who recognized his talent. As a result, Feliciano developed a truly unique style that nearly defies categorization—a mixture that a *Time* magazine reporter once described as a cross between "Johnny Mathis and Ray Charles with a Latin American flavor and a classical-tinged guitar backing."

Feliciano's career as a performer blossomed almost as early as his flair for music. He made his first public appearance at the age of nine at El Teatro Puerto Rico in Spanish Harlem, and soon he was playing at local events, talent shows, and school assemblies. At seventeen, he dropped out of high school to help support his family with the money he earned by performing at coffeehouses in Greenwich Village. Soon he was booked for engagements elsewhere in the East and Midwest, where his combination of Spanish and American folk songs, rock, old standards, and novelty tunes were a hit with audiences, who also marveled at his dexterity on the guitar.

His popularity was noticed by a record company executive, and at seventeen Feliciano was signed to a recording contract. However, most of his releases were in Spanish and aimed at the Latin American market. So, while he was slowly making a name for himself in the United States with well-received appearances at the 1964 Newport Jazz Festival and other venues, he was becoming a pop sensation throughout Central and South America, where he was the star of his own syndicated television show.

It was not until mid-1968 that Feliciano scored his first big breakthrough in the English-language market. His soulful re-make of the Doors' hit "Light My Fire" quickly rocketed to the top of the charts, as did the album on which it was included, a spring release entitled *Feliciano!* A series of sellout nightclub, theater, and concert performances soon followed, and by that fall, the young singer-musician was in demand for television programs, personal appearances, and other activities.

Perhaps the most memorable performance he gave that year came in October, when he sang a stylized version of the "Star-Spangled Banner" before the fifth game of the World Series between the Detroit Tigers and the St. Louis Cardinals. His blues-rock version of the national anthem—the first of many such non-traditional interpretations at sporting events—prompted a deluge of calls to the Tiger Stadium switchboard and created a major controversy across the country. Purists found Feliciano's "Spanish soul" treatment of the anthem shocking and unpatriotic, while others thought it gave the song a refreshing new twist. His subsequent recording of the "Star-Spangled Banner" made it to the number eighteen slot on the pop music charts, and the furor surrounding the entire affair made Feliciano's name a household word by the end of 1968. At that year's Grammy Awards ceremonies, he was named best male pop singer and best new artist.

Throughout the rest of the 1960s and well into the 1970s, Feliciano continued to enjoy stardom as a recording artist, performer, and composer. He scored several films and also wrote and sang the theme song to the popular television series "Chico and the Man." He released several more hit records ("Feliz Navidad," now a Christmas standard, came out in late 1970), made numerous radio and television appearances (including a few specials of his own), and performed at concerts in cities all over the world. Although his album production slowed down late in the decade, he was still a major concert draw and frequent television guest.

Since then, however, Feliciano has branched out into other aspects of the music business while maintaining his stature as a performer primarily in the Latin American market. In 1990, for example, at the invitation of science fiction writer Ray Bradbury, he composed music to accompany Bradbury's play, *The Wonderful Ice Cream Suit.* He has also made appearances with various symphony orchestras, including the London Symphony, the Los Angeles Philharmonic, and the Vienna Symphony. And in August, 1991, Feliciano began a stint as a Saturday morning disc jockey at a radio station in Westport, Connecticut, not far from his home. Besides playing a mix of old and new songs (some in Spanish and some in English), he chats with callers, relates "insider" anecdotes about musicians, and occasionally picks up an acoustic guitar and sings a song or two on the air. "I'm having a great time," he told Associated Press reporter Denise Lavoie for an article that was published in the *Grand Rapids Press.* "I love it all—the singing, the talking, the performing. . . . I'm not the type of disc jockey who's going to give you the weather, but I can talk about certain things other people might not know about."

In addition to these activities, Feliciano still spends a lot of time on the road doing shows—including twenty to thirty benefit concerts a year for charity organizations that serve the blind—but he has given up extended tours. Instead, he writes and records in his studio and revels in the joy of just "being a dad." (He and his wife, Susan, have a young daughter and son.) As he remarked many years ago to a *Newsweek* reporter, "I always wanted to be a star. I used to listen to the radio and say 'that's where I want to be.'" With six Grammy Awards and over forty gold and platinum records to his credit, Jose Feliciano has indeed seen his childhood dream come true. Says he:

"Only in America could something like that happen to somebody like me."

Sources

➤ **Periodicals**

Detroit News, "After Lighting His Fire in 1968, Jose Feliciano Is Back to Help Lend a Hand," September 6, 1991, p. 1B.

Grand Rapids Press, "Jose Feliciano Adds Disc Jockey to Repertoire," December 20, 1991, p. B6 (opening quote).

Newsweek, "The Happy One," September 23, 1968, p. 109.

Time, "Latin Soul," September 27, 1968, p. 78.

TV Guide, "Whatever Happened to . . . ," February 17, 1990, pp. 14–16.

Alexander Fleming

"**I** had no suspicion that I had got a clue to the most powerful therapeutic substance yet used to defeat bacterial infections in the human body. But the appearance of that culture plate was such that I thought it should not be neglected."

Alexander Fleming was the discoverer of penicillin. He was born on August 6, 1881, in Lochfield, Scotland, and died on March 11, 1955, in London, England.

"**H**ad my laboratory been as up to date and as sterile as those that I have visited [in the United States], it is possible that I would have never run across penicillin." Thus did Alexander Fleming modestly downplay his own role in the discovery of a substance that even the most cautious scientists of his day enthusiastically referred to as a "wonder drug" for its ability to cure a wide range of often-fatal bacterial illnesses. Although more than ten years passed between the time he first identified penicillin and another team of researchers successfully purified, tested, and produced it in mass quantities, Fleming conducted the initial experiments that served as the basis for all of their work. Penicillin's success ushered in an age of life-saving antibiotics, such as streptomycin, aureomycin, terramycin, and bacitracin, that "vastly changed not only the practice of medicine but also human expectations and attitudes about health," according to Edwin Kiester, Jr., in the *Smithsonian.*

One of eight children of Hugh Fleming, a farmer, Alexander Fleming grew up in the Scottish countryside. An outstanding student who faced limited career opportunities in his native country, he left home at the age of thirteen to live with an older brother in London. There he attended a polytechnic school and worked as an office boy for several years before deciding to become a doctor. Supported by scholarships as well as an inheritance from an uncle, Fleming enrolled at St. Mary's Hospital Medical School, later a part of the University of London. He performed brilliantly, winning numerous class prizes and taking honors in physiology, pharmacology, medicine, pathology, forensic medicine, and hygiene. Immediately upon receiving his licentiate from the Royal College of Physicians in 1906, Fleming accepted a research position in bacteriology at St. Mary's. As a staff member in the Inoculation Department (later renamed the Wright-Fleming Institute of Microbiology), he worked as an assistant to Sir Almroth Wright, a distinguished British physician who pioneered the use of vaccine therapy to fight bacterial infections such as typhoid. In 1908, Fleming passed his final medical examinations and was awarded the Gold Medal of the University of London in recognition of his academic excellence.

Following his graduation, Fleming divided his time between a research post at St. Mary's and a professorship in bacteriology at the University of London. The laboratory was his first love, however, and it was there that he spent most of his time. He even managed to continue his research during World War I as a member of the Royal Army Medical Corps. Disturbed by the high rate of death from infected wounds, Fleming began to question the effectiveness of treating dead or damaged tissue with certain antiseptics. In a series of ingenious experiments, he proved that the antiseptics then in use actually did more harm than good by killing the white cells of the immune system and thus making it easier for infection to develop.

After the war, Fleming returned to St. Mary's and resumed his study of bacteriology, focusing primarily on identifying some naturally occurring substance that could fight bacteria without harming healthy tissue or weakening the body's self-defense mechanisms. (Conventional medical wisdom had maintained for years that no drug given internally could destroy an infection without also killing the patient.) In 1921, he took a major step in that direction when he discovered that human tears and nasal mucus as well as egg whites all contained a similar chemical that dissolves some bacteria. He called the new antibiotic lysozyme and published several articles on its capabilities, but most scientists dismissed his findings.

Despite the lack of enthusiasm among his colleagues, Fleming continued his search for a better antibiotic. One day during the fall of 1928, he was in his basement laboratory checking some staphylococci bacteria cultures. One culture in particular caught his eye; accidently left uncovered for several days, it had been contaminated by a mold spore that had blown in through the room's only window. Fleming was about to rinse off the dish when he noticed something highly unusual. In the area surrounding the greenish-blue spot of mold, the staphylococci had completely disappeared. Elsewhere on the plate, it was still thriving.

Intrigued, Fleming immediately began to grow more of the mold so that he could study its amazing properties. Over the next eight months, he discovered that it secreted a powerful substance, which he named "penicillin" after the *Penicillium Chrysogenum notatum* mold from which it originated. That substance destroyed not only staphylococci but a number of other deadly bacteria, including streptococci and pneumococci. Testing small doses first on laboratory animals and later on himself, he also learned it was not toxic. The *Penicillium* mold proved to be extremely difficult to grow in the laboratory, however, and the meager amount of penicillin that could be extracted from a culture was unstable and tainted with foreign proteins. Fleming turned to a biologist friend for help, but neither scientist was able to come up with a way to produce enough pure penicillin to treat someone who was actually ill and thus demonstrate its potential as an antibiotic.

Hoping to interest others in tackling the problem, Fleming presented a report on his experiments at a meeting of bacteriologists in May, 1929. Unfortunately, the presentation coincided with a surge of interest in the new sulfa drugs, which were then being heralded as the cure-all for infectious diseases. So the miraculous accomplishments of an airborne mold attracted little attention, and Fleming moved on to other research. But he did not give up on penicillin; just in case someone stepped forward with an idea, he kept a strain of the original mold growing in a corner of his laboratory.

By the late 1930s, it was clear that the sulfa drugs had been greatly overrated; they were not as effective as first believed, and they exhibited some toxic side effects, including kidney damage. With the prospect of another world war looming on the horizon, there was a sudden and urgent need for a new substance to combat wound infections. At Oxford University, Australian-born pathologist Howard W. Florey searched through some old professional journals for clues to a possible breakthrough. In 1938, he came across Fleming's report on penicillin and paid a visit to the Scotsman, who gave him a sample of the *Penicillium* mold he had been keeping alive in his laboratory.

Working with Ernst Chain, a chemist who had fled Nazi Germany, Florey verified all of Fleming's observations and encountered precisely the same problem: the mold produced very small amounts of penicillin, and extracting and purifying it before it lost its effectiveness was difficult. But some tests they ran on a few white mice infected with staphylococci proved that it did indeed work. Because the scientists had such a difficult time collecting enough penicillin to treat a human, however, their early tests in that area were less conclusive; several patients near death from infection responded quickly and dramatically when given a dose of penicillin but eventually died when the supply ran out before they were completely cured. Florey and Chain then concentrated all their efforts on producing enough purified penicillin to demonstrate its power on humans, and by 1941 they could document nearly two hundred cases in which penicillin therapy had destroyed infections that otherwise would have been fatal.

The next step was to develop a way to mass produce penicillin and thus interest major drug companies in manufacturing it. Unable to secure funding from Oxford for additional research, Florey and Chain turned to the United States, where they found the financial and technical help they needed. At the Northern Regional Research

Laboratory in Peoria, Illinois, British and American scientists working together discovered a new growing medium for the mold that produced two hundred times more penicillin per liter than the old medium. By mid-1943, factories in England and the United States had geared up to produce some four hundred million units of penicillin in a five-month period, a number that jumped to over nine billion units per month by the end of the year. Although initial production was designated for military use only, penicillin became available to the civilian population in 1944.

As co-discoverers of this wonder drug, Fleming and Florey were showered with honors. Both were knighted in 1944, and in 1945, Fleming, Florey, and Chain shared the Nobel Prize in medicine. None of them profited financially from the sale of penicillin, however. Fleming routinely gave any money he received to St. Mary's for research, even a $100,000 award of merit a group of American pharmaceutical firms presented to him in gratitude for his contribution to medical science. Due to the rather dramatic circumstances surrounding his accidental find, Fleming more so than Florey or Chain became an international celebrity. But he was always quick to credit the others with developing penicillin into a substance that doctors could use to treat their patients.

Despite the commotion caused by his sudden fame, Fleming continued to spend as much time as possible working quietly in his laboratory, his efforts focused on examining the bacteria-fighting capabilities of other molds. In 1946, he was named director of the Wright-Fleming Institute, a position he held until November, 1954, when he retired to pursue his own research. On March 11, 1955, he died of a heart attack in London.

As time passed, the limitations of penicillin became more apparent. It could not cure *all* infections, for example, and it triggered allergic reactions in some people that were occasionally severe enough to result in death. But for untold millions, bacterial illnesses such as pneumonia, blood poisoning, gangrene, and even strep infections were no longer the dreaded killers they once had been. Taking that fact alone into account, declared the eminent British physician Lord Horder upon Alexander Fleming's death, the discoverer of penicillin "conferred a benefit upon humanity that is quite incalculable."

Sources

➤ Books

Fox, Ruth, *Milestones of Medicine,* Random House, 1950.

Macfarlane, Gwyn, *Alexander Fleming: The Man and the Myth,* Harvard University Press, 1984.

Tames, Richard, *Alexander Fleming,* F. Watts, 1990.

➤ Periodicals

Newsweek, March 21, 1955, p. 72.

New York Times, "Fleming, Pioneer in Penicillin, Dies," March 12, 1955, p. 19.

New York Times Magazine, "The Mold That Fights for the Life of Man," January 2, 1944 (opening quote); "Man of Science and of Penicillin," July 29, 1945.

Science Digest, "Sir Alexander Fleming and the Story of Penicillin," September, 1953, pp. 84–90.

Smithsonian, "A Curiosity Turned into the First Silver Bullet Against Death," November, 1990, pp. 173–187.

Time, "20th Century Seer," May 15, 1944, pp. 61–68; "The First Was the Best," March 21, 1955, pp. 46–48.

Lou Gehrig

"I *may have been given a bad break, but I have an awful lot to live for. With all this, I consider* myself the luckiest man on the face of this earth."

Regarded as one of the greatest baseball players of all time, Lou Gehrig appeared in a record 2,130 consecutive games for the New York Yankees before he was diagnosed with amyotrophic lateral sclerosis (ALS), also known as "Lou Gehrig's Disease." He was born on June 19, 1903, in New York City and died there on June 2, 1941.

On June 2, 1925, a husky, young baseball player named Lou Gehrig faced another day on the New York Yankee bench as back-up first baseman to veteran Wally Pipp. Frustrated at not being able to play every day, the promising but unproven rookie had repeatedly begged manager Miller Huggins to send him back to the minors. Huggins refused, pointing out that Gehrig still had a lot to learn about baseball, and one of the best ways to do that was by watching his fellow players. Then fate intervened: Pipp developed a headache after being hit on the head by a pitch during batting practice, and Huggins tapped an eager but nervous Gehrig to replace him in the lineup. By the end of the day, he had thrilled the crowd by posting a double, two singles, a run, eight putouts, and one assist. And for the next fourteen years, the only player at first base for the Yankees was Lou Gehrig, a man honored not only for his athletic skills but also for his modesty, perseverance, and courage in the face of the devastating illness that ended his brilliant career.

Born and raised in a poor, overcrowded New York City neighborhood, Henry Louis Gehrig was the son of German immigrants Heinrich and Christina Gehrig. He began playing baseball at the age of five after receiving a catcher's mitt for Christmas. Although he was left-handed and the mitt was for a right-hander, Gehrig became skilled enough by the time he reached seventh grade to play not only on his school team but also in the city's parks and recreation department league.

A strong-willed woman who labored as a cook and a maid and took in laundry to help support her family, Christina Gehrig wanted more than anything for Lou to get a good education. So, at an age when many of his friends left the classroom to go to work, Gehrig went on to high school, where he was expected to give up baseball and prepare himself for college. After doing well in his pre-engineering courses, he persuaded his mother that he could study and play sports, too. He went out for both soccer and baseball, performing rather miserably in the latter until he tried using a left-handed glove for the first time. He soon improved enough to become the starting first baseman for the team.

By his senior year, Gehrig was one of his school's best all-around athletes, turning in solid performances in baseball, football, basketball, soccer, and gymnastics. His proudest moment came when his baseball team won the New York City championship and went on to a high school world series contest in Chicago. The New Yorkers beat the Chicagoans, thanks in part to Gehrig's ninth-inning grand-slam home run.

After graduation, Gehrig enrolled at Columbia University and continued to play baseball. It was at one of his college games in April, 1923, that he first captured the attention of a Yankee scout when he hit a game-winning home run that sailed completely out of the field and landed some 450 yards away on the library steps. Against his mother's wishes, he left school two months later and signed with the Yankees, then winners of two consecutive American League pennants and boasting a strong lineup that included slugger Babe Ruth, one of Gehrig's idols.

His first two years with the Yankees gave little hint that Gehrig would one day become one of baseball's best players. While his hitting was strong, his knowledge of defensive positioning, pitching strategies, base-running techniques, and other aspects of the game was almost nonexistent. As Paul Gallico noted in a *Reader's Digest* article, Gehrig was also "awkward, inept and downright clumsy"— in short, far from a natural talent. He listened, watched, and absorbed all he could, but his youth and inexperience kept him in the minors, where he worked to perfect his swing and put in more playing time at first base.

Then came the 1925 season, which opened with Gehrig determined to make the team. After his big break came on that June day when Wally Pipp was hit by an errant pitch, Gehrig hustled to prove that he deserved to stay in the lineup. He worked hard on his game and finished his first full season with the Yankees with a .295 average and 21 home runs. Despite Gehrig's contributions, the Yankees finished a disappointing seventh in the pennant race, primarily because Babe Ruth sat out most of the year.

The 1926 season saw the fortunes of both Gehrig and the Yankees improve. Batting fourth as part of the so-called "Murderers' Row" lineup of powerhouse hitters (which included Ruth), Gehrig raised his average to .313, launching the first of twelve consecutive seasons in which he hit .300 or better. In addition, the Yankees recovered from their poor finish the year before to capture the American League pennant and take the St. Louis Cardinals to seven games in a losing effort to win the World Series.

For most of the next decade, the Yankees dominated baseball, racking up five World Series victories and posting phenomenal individual and team statistics. Gehrig, a veritable "first-base-covering machine," to quote Gallico, usually held the number two or three position in every major category, including overall batting average, home runs, and runs batted in (RBIs), and on four occasions he was voted the American League's Most Valuable Player. Probably his best year was 1934, when he led the league with a .363 average, 49 home runs, and 165 RBIs, beating out Babe Ruth for the first time since joining the Yankees. Yet his lack of self-confidence always made him question his true abilities and fear that failure was just around the corner. And as a shy, soft-spoken, and extremely modest man, he was no match for Ruth, whose flamboyance generated headlines in a way Gehrig never did. He labored quietly in Ruth's formidable shadow until 1936, when he began playing second fiddle to a new Yankee sensation, Joe DiMaggio. Consequently, Gehrig never experienced the adulation of the fans in the way that some of his flashier teammates did.

Durable and dependable, Gehrig came to be known as the "Iron Horse" for his apparent indifference to pain and fatigue. He played day in and day out, through illness and injury (including a concussion on one occasion and severe back pain on another), and on August 17, 1933, he passed the major-league record for consecutive games played (1,307). After that, Gehrig did not allow himself to be X-rayed following an injury because he was afraid doctors might find a chip or a break that would force him to sit out for a while. Several years later, X rays of his hands revealed that he had indeed suffered seventeen fractures that had healed by themselves.

In 1938, Gehrig's consecutive-games streak hit two thousand. But at mid-season, he went into a hitting slump that he couldn't seem to shake. In addition, his coordination began to fail, his hands trembled, and he often felt overwhelmed by fatigue. Yet he refused to miss a game, and consequently he experienced one of his poorest seasons ever: a .295 average, 29 home runs, and 114 RBIs.

With the opening of the next season, it was clear that even a winter of rest had not cured his slump. He continued to display physical symptoms that affected both his fielding and his hitting. While the fans assumed the thirty-six-year-old Gehrig was just showing signs of age, his teammates knew that it was not normal for a good ballplayer to lose all of his skills at once; they suspected something else far more serious behind his sudden clumsiness. Meanwhile, Gehrig privately battled fear and depression as he watched his game deteriorate despite the fact that he relentlessly drove himself to work harder. Finally, on May 2, realizing that he was more of a hindrance than a help to the team, Gehrig voluntarily benched himself, ending his consecutive-game streak at 2,130.

In June, Gehrig went to the Mayo Clinic, where doctors quickly diagnosed the source of his difficulties as amyotrophic lateral sclerosis, a rare, degenerative condition affecting the spinal cord that leads to muscular weakness throughout the body and death within two to four years. Returning to New York, Gehrig calmly remarked to reporters, "I guess I have to accept the bitter with the sweet. If this is the finish, I'll take it."

On July 4 of that year, more than sixty thousand fans and dozens of players, officials, sportswriters, and political dignitaries gathered in Yankee Stadium for Lou Gehrig Appreciation Day. The veteran first baseman was showered with gifts, and speaker after speaker rose to pay tribute to his kindness and decency and express appreciation for the thrills he had given to baseball lovers for so many years. There to salute him, too, were his former teammates from the 1927 world champion Yankees. As wave after wave of cheers roared throughout the stadium, Gehrig himself finally stepped up to the microphone, tears flowing down his cheeks. In a voice choked with emotion, he faced the now-silent crowd and simply yet movingly thanked everyone for their affection and support, acknowledging his "bad break" but declaring himself "the luckiest man on the face of this earth."

Gehrig served out the rest of the Yankees' 1939 season as the team's nonplaying captain. In an unprecedented move, the baseball writers waived the normal waiting period and at the end of the year voted him into the Hall of Fame. By then, Gehrig had accepted an offer from New York mayor Fiorello La Guardia to serve on the city's parole board and work with young people in trouble with the law. A year later, however, he had to give up even that job when he became too weak and exhausted to go into the office. He fell into a coma and died at home on the evening of June 2, 1941, just two weeks short of his thirty-eighth birthday. The next day, flags flew at half-mast in New York City and at baseball stadiums around the country in honor of the man who, at the time he was forced to retire from the game he loved, held forty-five batting, fielding, and endurance records. While many of those records have since been broken, the endurance record still stands in testimony to the dedication of the "Iron Horse."

Sources

➤ **Books**

Robinson, Ray, *Iron Horse: Lou Gehrig in His Time,* Norton, 1990.

Rubin, Robert, *Lou Gehrig: Courageous Star,* Putnam, 1979 (opening quote).

➤ **Periodicals**

Newsweek, July 3, 1939, pp. 22–24; June 9, 1941, p. 49.

New York Times, "Gehrig, 'Iron Man' of Baseball, Dies at the Age of 37," June 3, 1941.

Reader's Digest, "Lou Gehrig's Epic of Courage," February, 1942, pp. 8–11.

Time, "Iron Horse," May 15, 1939, pp. 32–34; "Iron Horse to Pasture," July 3, 1939, p. 24; June 4, 1941, p. 63; June 16, 1941, p. 63.

➤ **Other**

Lou Gehrig's life story was dramatized in the 1942 film *The Pride of the Yankees.*

Elizabeth Glaser

"**I** had convinced myself that at some moment when our lives seemed utterly hopeless an angel would suddenly appear to set everything right. Well, there weren't going to be any angels. . . . If anything was going to be done, I was the one who would have to do it."

Elizabeth Glaser is co-founder of the Pediatric AIDS Foundation. She was born about 1948.

Address: Pediatric AIDS Foundation, 2407 Wilshire Blvd., Santa Monica, CA 90403.

I n the spring of 1986, the lives of Elizabeth Glaser and her actor-director husband, Paul Michael Glaser, were shattered by the news that their four-year-old daughter, Ariel, had tested positive for the AIDS virus. Further testing soon revealed that their year-and-a-half-old son, Jake, was also infected, as was Elizabeth Glaser herself. Her initial shock and fear soon turned to disbelief and anger when she discovered how little doctors knew about the effects of AIDS on children or the best ways to treat it. Out of that grim reality arose the Pediatric AIDS Foundation, a group she and two friends established in 1988 to educate the public about AIDS in children and to raise money for research. Since then, Glaser—by nature a very private person—has become what a *Glamour* magazine writer calls "a formidable public presence" as she lobbies in Washington for federal funds and persuades Hollywood celebrities to help support her efforts.

Elizabeth Meyer Glaser grew up in Hewlett Harbor, New York, and obtained a master's degree in early childhood education at Boston University. During the early 1970s, she moved to Los Angeles, where in June, 1975, she met Paul Michael Glaser, at that time just a few months away from stardom in the television series *Starsky and Hutch.* They married in August, 1980, and a year later, they welcomed their first child, a daughter they named Ariel. It had been a difficult pregnancy, and Ariel was delivered by caesarean section. Elizabeth then hemorrhaged so severely that she required a transfusion of seven pints of blood.

Home with her baby a few weeks later, Glaser read a newspaper article about a new virus called AIDS that could be transmitted by blood transfusions. Panic stricken, she immediately telephoned her doctor, who told her she had nothing to worry about. For the next few years the Glasers enjoyed an unusually happy family life and Paul's blossoming career as a director. Son Jake was born in October, 1984, and Elizabeth's vision of the future was an idyllic one that included a houseful of children and grandchildren.

The following spring, the Glasers took up residence in Miami for a few months while Paul directed his first feature film, *Band of the Hand.* Ariel then began experiencing stomachaches and cramps that doctors were at a loss to explain, even after they had run a battery of tests. She also tired easily and grew very pale.

Back in Los Angeles later that year, Ariel's pediatrician checked her for a variety of unusual blood disorders, including lupus and leukemia, but the results all came back negative. Then he suggested testing for AIDS. Glaser wasn't especially alarmed; after all, the other tests hadn't revealed anything, and there was no way Ariel could have contracted AIDS. But in the spring of 1986, two separate blood tests eliminated all doubts: Ariel indeed had AIDS. Tests on the rest of the family indicated that both Jake and Elizabeth were also infected but free of symptoms. Doctors surmised that Elizabeth had probably picked up the virus from the transfusions she received following Ariel's birth and then passed it along to her daughter during breast-feeding and to her son in the womb. "In our worst nightmares, we could never have imagined the devastation of those few days," Elizabeth later wrote. "Our entire world had been crushed. . . . It was too much to comprehend."

To bolster Ariel's fragile immune system, doctors advised that she immediately begin gamma globulin treatments and receive antibiotics to ward off infections. They also recommended that Paul and Elizabeth keep silent about the diagnosis because of the harassment other AIDS families (like that of Ryan White) had experienced. So the Glasers decided to tell only a few of their closest friends and others they felt should know. At that time, people had many questions about AIDS—especially regarding transmission of the virus—to which there were no answers. As a result, some parents refused to allow their children to be around Ariel and Jake. Elizabeth's yoga teacher told her never to come to class again. Several psychiatrists declined to take on Ariel as a patient because they were afraid of jeopardizing their practices if word got out about her condition. And officials at the private school Ariel was scheduled to attend banned her for a while until they formulated an AIDS policy.

For the next few years, making sure the diagnosis remained a secret became a near-obsession for the Glasers, who were terrified that the news would leak out and they "would be treated like plague victims for no reason." Elizabeth in particular resented the lack of strong leadership from the Reagan administration during the early months of the epidemic, which she feels added to the fear and hysteria that gripped the country. "It is what all families battling AIDS had to face then," she later noted. "You are told that you and your children may die. You are told that there are no answers now. And then as you are struggling not to completely fall apart, you realize that very few people are going to reach out to help or comfort you."

By mid-1987, Ariel's condition had worsened considerably, and the Glasers asked doctors to start treating her with AZT, a promising drug already widely used by adults but still several months away from being approved for children. Finally, just before Christmas, Ariel was able to begin taking AZT in pill form. It had no effect on her health, however, and in March, 1988, she came down with pneumonia and had to be hospitalized. Doctors then discovered that her brain had atrophied, a common AIDS complication in children but not in adults. The Glasers were told to prepare for the worst, and for the first time Elizabeth confronted the possibility of her daughter's death. With that painful acknowledgment came the realization that she "could no longer sit quietly in Santa Monica. . . . I had to do more."

Ariel recovered from her bout with pneumonia, and Elizabeth set about making good on her vow to "shake things up." She educated herself on various AIDS issues of local and national interest and met with doctors and politicians to devise a strategy for winning over influential leaders in Washington, D.C. Aware from her own painful experience that little research was being done on AIDS in children, she decided to focus on that aspect of the battle in particular, teaming up with two friends to form the Pediatric AIDS Foundation.

While in Washington, Elizabeth learned that some doctors had reported positive results in children taking AZT intravenously rather than orally. Once again, the government had not yet approved intravenous AZT for use in children, and it was therefore unavailable to Ariel, who by this time could no longer walk or talk. "To a mother losing her child, it made no sense," says Glaser. "I couldn't accept that there was something that might help my child live that they wouldn't give me because regulations stood in the way. I used every connection. . . . Finally, we were sent the intravenous AZT." Within a few weeks after Ariel began treatments in the spring of 1988, she regained her ability to walk and talk. But by July, she began to lose ground again, and on August 12, 1988, she died.

At first, grief over her daughter's death left Glaser emotionally drained and depressed. But soon she realized that her son's life might depend on what she could do to make sure that children were not forgotten in the fight against AIDS. "I wasn't trying to make people care about AIDS because it happened to my family," she later recalled. "I was just trying to make people care." In fact, the Glasers still had not made public the cause of Ariel's death and the fact that Jake and Elizabeth were both HIV positive. But in August, 1989, they were forced to reveal their secret when they learned that a supermarket tabloid was planning to run a distorted account of their ordeal. To their surprise and relief, the much-feared backlash never materialized. Instead, friends and colleagues offered their love and support and wholeheartedly embraced the goals of the Pediatric AIDS Foundation.

Since then, Elizabeth has focused her energies on raising money and channeling it as quickly as possible into research. (The record album *For Our Children,* a collection of children's songs performed by famous pop and rock musicians, is one of the group's most successful fund-raising projects to date.) Studies funded by the Pediatric AIDS Foundation have investigated why the disease so viciously attacks the central nervous systems of its youngest victims and how to prevent infected mothers from passing along the virus to their babies. Also on the organization's agenda are various educational programs and an assistance plan for hospitals treating pediatric AIDS patients.

More than ten years after she first contracted AIDS, Elizabeth Glaser remains in stable health, as does her son. She draws strength from her role as an advocate for other AIDS victims with less influence and also relies on the memory of her daughter to sustain her when she feels she is about to falter. "I've always been someone who fought for a happy ending," she explains. "Even though I cannot erase the death of my child, all I'm doing right now is giving my best shot at fighting for a happy ending." Yet there is an underlying sadness to her determination. "As proud as I am about what we have accomplished," says Glaser, "I still hate the fact we had to do it at all."

Sources

➤ **Books**

Glaser, Elizabeth, and Laura Palmer, *In the Absence of Angels: A Hollywood Family's Courageous Story,* Putnam, 1991 (opening quote).

➤ **Periodicals**

Glamour, "Women of the Year, 1990," December, 1990.

Ladies' Home Journal, "In the Absence of Angels" (excerpt from book), March, 1991.

New York Times Book Review, "The Youngest Victims of AIDS," March 3, 1991, pp. 14–15.

People, "Hollywood Helps a Brave Couple Raise Money for Children Dying of AIDS," November 13, 1989, pp. 58–59; "In the Absence of Angels" (excerpt from book), February 4, 1991, pp. 84–93; "After the Tragedy, a Call to Arms," February 4, 1991, pp. 94–96.

Mikhail Gorbachev

*"**M**y life's work has been accomplished. I have done all I could. I think that in my place, others would have given up a long time ago."*

Winner of the 1990 Nobel Peace Prize for his leading role in ending the Cold War and promoting disarmament, former Soviet president Mikhail Gorbachev also sparked revolutionary political changes in his native country and throughout Eastern Europe. He was born on March 2, 1931, in Privolnoye, Russia.

On March 11, 1985, a new era in Soviet and world history began with the election of Mikhail Gorbachev to the USSR's top leadership position, that of general secretary of the Communist party. From the outset, it was clear that Gorbachev was "no Cold War dinosaur," as one reporter put it. A fifty-four year-old product of the communist establishment, Gorbachev was much younger and better educated than his predecessors and radiated an infectious energy and drive. He was also the first general secretary to have come of age after the terror and paranoia that marked the Josef Stalin era. His presence on the national and international scene hinted at major changes to come, and over the next six-and-a-half years Gorbachev did his best to live up to that impression. In the process, he launched a veritable revolution whose outcome is still very much in doubt.

Born in a village near the city of Stavropol, in the heart of one of southern Russia's most fertile agricultural regions, Mikhail Sergeevich Gorbachev is the son of Sergei Andreevich Gorbachev, a mechanic on a state-run collective farm, and Maria Panteleevna Gorbachev, also a farm worker. Life for nearly everyone in the village revolved around harvest times; Mikhail and most of his classmates usually spent their vacations from school helping in the fields.

In 1950, Gorbachev left home to study law at Moscow University, where he joined the Komsomol, or Young Communist League, an organization that served as a training ground for the future leaders of the Communist party (and thus of the Soviet Union). Soon he was devoting more time to politics than to his studies, and in 1954 he was elected head of the university's Komsomol chapter. Following his graduation in 1955, Gorbachev, who had hoped to stay in Moscow and work for the central government, was instead sent back to Stavropol and a minor position with the local Komsomol group.

Over the next two decades, Gorbachev steadily made his way up the political hierarchy (mostly in various agriculture-related posts), first at the local and regional level and, beginning in 1970, at the national level. In that year, he became a representative to the Supreme Soviet, the USSR's parliament. The following year, he was named to the powerful Central Committee, the inner circle of people in charge of running the government. In 1978, the Central Committee elected Gorbachev to the post of agricultural secretary, and in 1979 he was made a nonvoting member of the Politburo, the Central Committee's policy-making body. A year later, he was promoted to full membership in the Politburo.

In late 1982, one of Gorbachev's mentors, KGB chief Yuri Andropov, became head of the Soviet Union upon the death of Leonid Brezhnev, whose tenure as general secretary had been marked by widespread government inefficiency, corruption, and a sense that the nation had been drifting along without true leadership. Andropov immediately tapped Gorbachev to be his chief aide, and together the two men initiated some bold reforms, including purging dishonest and incompetent officials from the party, cracking down on alcoholism, absenteeism and poor performance in the workplace, and taking steps to decentralize key industries.

Andropov's death in 1984 after only fourteen months in office dealt a serious blow to these efforts, especially after Brezhnev loyalist Konstantin Chernenko was named to succeed him. Gorbachev nevertheless remained a powerful figure in the Politburo and gradually assumed many of Chernenko's public duties as the elderly leader's health began to fail. On one memorable trip to Great Britain in December, 1984, Gorbachev—by this time the heir-apparent to the ailing Chernenko—charmed conservative Prime Minister Margaret Thatcher and Western reporters with his intelligence and sophistication, his self-confident demeanor, his ready smile, and his sense of humor. (His wife, Raisa, earned points for her stylish dress and ability to speak some English.) At the conclusion of their talks, an obviously impressed Thatcher declared, "I like Mr. Gorbachev. We can do business together."

Three months later, in March, 1985, the world learned it would have a chance to "do business" with Gorbachev when the announcement came that he had been elected general secretary of the Communist party and leader of the Soviet Union following Chernenko's death. From the moment he took office, Gorbachev made it clear that he intended to proceed vigorously with a complete overhaul of the Soviet system from top to bottom, focusing on changes that would get the economy moving, scale back the bureaucracy, and rejuvenate the party.

To that end, he renewed the crackdowns on corruption, alcoholism, and incompetency and instituted cash incentives and bonus consumer goods for industrial and agricultural workers who improved productivity. He tackled the issue of decentralization and fostered greater independence among local factory managers by giving them more authority to decide schedules and quotas. He introduced new technology and stressed the importance of quality, of delivering goods in a timely fashion, and of anticipating and meeting consumer demand for specific products—concepts almost totally foreign to Soviet citizens.

To revitalize the government and the party, Gorbachev forced many of the older and more conservative leaders to retire or accept lesser positions that effectively removed them from power. He also replaced many lower-level bureaucrats and party officials. And unlike his typically dour and aloof predecessors, he tried to gain the respect and even the affection of the Soviet people by speaking to them in a down-to-earth manner that combined a genuine sense of concern with a blunt frankness.

Gorbachev's impact on the international scene was equally forceful. His top priority was improving the somewhat chilly relations between the Soviet Union and the West, particularly the United States; the detente of the 1970s had given way to a new arms race in the 1980s when the Reagan administration decided to proceed with the controversial Strategic Defense Initiative or "Star Wars" project, a complex system of defense against nuclear missiles. Realizing that any attempt by the Soviet Union to create a similar system of its own would probably devastate the country economically and shatter his plans for reform and recovery, Gorbachev surprised the world by proposing sweeping arms cuts on both sides, including a ban on nuclear weapons by the year 2000. On four separate occasions, he met with President Reagan to hammer out a weapons treaty that was finalized in December, 1987, during the Soviet leader's first visit to the United States.

Earlier that same year, Gorbachev announced a new series of domestic reforms, including expanded freedoms and the democratization of the political process, all of which were to be achieved through his policies of social and economic restructuring, or *perestroika*, and openness, or *glasnost*. (Some of the very first hints of *glasnost* had appeared in late 1986, when Gorbachev ended the exile of Nobel Peace Prize-winning dissident Andrei Sakharov, who had been banished in 1980 for speaking out against the government.) Before long, Soviet writers were taking advantage of their new freedom to examine, discuss, analyze, and even criticize the past and the present openly without fear of reprisal.

Gorbachev continued to amaze the world throughout the rest of the decade. In April, 1988, for example, he announced his decision to pull Soviet troops out of Afghanistan, where they had been entrenched in a bloody and futile guerrilla war for nearly ten years. In December, during a dramatic speech before the United Nations, he proposed deep cuts in the Soviet military budget, the withdrawal of 50,000 Soviet troops from Eastern Europe, and a 500,000-man reduction in the army's overall strength. It was also in 1988 that Gorbachev first expressed his intention to end the Communist party's control of the day-to-day operations of the country and create new, elected political institutions.

Social and political reforms continued at a dizzying pace throughout 1989. In March, the Soviet people voted in the first democratic elections in their nation's history; later, they watched on television as their newly elected legislators debated Soviet policy. In April came news that the antireligion laws of the 1960s had been rescinded. But by far the most breathtaking changes of that year occurred outside the Soviet Union as communist regimes in Poland, Hungary, East Germany, Czechoslovakia, Bulgaria, and Romania disintegrated (most peacefully) amid impassioned calls for political and economic reforms. Unlike his predecessors, who had always been more than willing to use force to crush any signs of discontent in Eastern Europe, Gorbachev made it clear that he felt the Soviet Union had no moral right to interfere in the affairs of other countries. Behind the scenes he did his best to discourage violent crackdowns on demonstrators and persuaded a few of the more hard-line communist leaders to resign. Perhaps the most dramatic moment of the year came on November 9 with the opening of the Berlin Wall, for nearly thirty years a grim reminder of the hostility and suspicion dividing East and West. Gorbachev was universally acclaimed as the man who had finally brought the Cold War to an end.

Though Gorbachev basked in the adulation of the Western democracies at the close of the 1980s, at home he was the target of widespread criticism and dissatisfaction. The giddy excitement and optimism that had characterized his first few years in office evaporated as the Soviet people were forced to deal with inflation and chronic shortages of basic consumer goods that rivaled those of the World War II era. In 1990, emboldened by the democracy movements in Eastern Europe, the Baltic states and Ukraine began agitating for independence, and ethnic and religious violence erupted in Armenia and Azerbaijan. Faced with the growing threat of anarchy and the need to strike a balance between hard-line conservatives and radical reformers like Boris Yeltsin, president of the Russian republic, Gorbachev began to back away from many of his more drastic proposals (especially his plan to dismantle the central economy and create a free-market system) and assume a far more moderate position, suggesting to some Western observers that he had succumbed to the hard-liners' demands.

In the midst of this domestic chaos came news that Gorbachev had won the 1990 Nobel Peace Prize for his bold moves to improve the international political climate. The Soviets greeted the news with indifference and even some hostility, but Gorbachev expressed hope that such an important reaffirmation of his policies would energize him for the battles still ahead.

Throughout the first half of 1991, the Soviet Union teetered on the brink of self-destruction, and Gorbachev continued to retreat from his earlier policies, increasing speculation that the reactionary wing of the Communist party was indeed gaining influence over him. In January, just three months after the Nobel announcement, troops opened fire on demonstrators in Lithuania and killed fourteen people, tarnishing Gorbachev's reputation as a peacemaker and prompting fears of violent crackdowns elsewhere or even civil war. (The Soviet chief insisted he had been asleep when it happened and did not know anything about it until he woke up.) In a nationwide referendum held in March, the country approved Gorbachev's proposed Union Treaty, an arrangement that would have transferred sweeping powers from the central government to the republics while preserving the USSR. After several months of squabbling over the terms of the treaty, Gorbachev and leaders of some of the republics finally reached agreement and made plans to sign the new union into effect on August 20.

But on August 18, a group of hard-line communists staged a coup and held Gorbachev and his family under house arrest at their summer home in the Crimea. In Moscow, Yeltsin called on his Russian supporters to resist the takeover. For three days angry Muscovites squared off against a contingent of tanks the coup plotters had assembled around Yeltsin's headquarters; similar confrontations between Soviet troops and citizens occurred elsewhere in the country. It quickly became clear, however, that there was little support for the hard-liners, and by August 21 the coup had failed. Gorbachev immediately headed back to Moscow to resume power.

Over the next four months, Gorbachev repeatedly tried to reassert his authority, and for a time it appeared that he might succeed. He resigned as head of the Communist party and urged its disbandment for the role it had played in the failed coup. Abandoning his earlier moderate stance, he also pledged his renewed support for radical reform. But it was too little, too late; Yeltsin had gained the upper hand as a result of his heroics during the coup, and one republic after another declared its independence. Gorbachev nevertheless fought to preserve at least a form of economic and military unity, warning of "catastrophe for all mankind" if the union splintered. By the end of December, however, the USSR was no more. In its place stood the Commonwealth of Independent States (CIS), a loose federation made up of eleven of the fifteen former Soviet republics. The Russian republic was acknowledged as the successor to the Soviet Union, thus strengthening the perception of Yeltsin as the man in charge. On December 25, 1991, a bitter and humiliated Gorbachev formally resigned as head of the Soviet Union.

Although it is too early to tell how history will ultimately judge Mikhail Gorbachev, most analysts agree that he will be remembered as one of the pivotal figures of the twentieth century, more for what he did for the world than for his own people. He took office announcing his intention to reform communism, not destroy it, and his biggest failure was stubbornly sticking to that goal even after it was clear that the system was so corrupted that there was virtually nothing worth saving. As a result, the Soviet people saw their standard of living decline rather than improve during his tenure. But his legacy also includes bringing an end to the Cold War and allowing freedom and democracy to take root in countries that had known only totalitarianism for more than four decades. For making those things possible Mikhail Gorbachev will no doubt be remembered as a leader who was swept aside by the very forces he unleashed—a man who, notes Gail Sheehy, "changed the world and lost his country."

Sources

➤ **Books**

Butson, Thomas G., *Gorbachev: A Biography,* Stein & Day, 1985.

Butson, Thomas G., *Mikhail Gorbachev,* Chelsea House, 1986.

Gorbachev, Mikhail, *The Coming Century of Peace,* Richardson & Steirman, 1986.

Gorbachev, Mikhail, *Perestroika: New Thinking for Our Country and the World,* Harper, 1987.

Gorbachev, Mikhail, *The August Coup: The Truth and the Lessons,* HarperCollins, 1991.

Kaiser, Robert G., *Why Gorbachev Happened: His Triumphs and His Failure*, Simon & Schuster, 1991.

Mikhail S. Gorbachev: An Intimate Biography, compiled by the editors of *Time* Magazine, Time, 1988.

Olesky, Walter, *Mikhail Gorbachev: A Leader for Soviet Change*, Children's Press, 1989.

Sheehy, Gail, *The Man Who Changed the World: The Lives of Mikhail S. Gorbachev*, HarperCollins, 1991.

➤ **Periodicals**

Detroit Free Press, "Swept Away," December 22, 1991.

Detroit News, "Gorbachev's New Mood," February 17, 1991; December 13, 1991 (opening quote); "Legacy of a Reformer," December 22, 1991.

Newsweek, "No Prize for Compromise," October 29, 1990, pp. 49–50; "The End," January 6, 1992, pp. 12–17.

Time, "The Unlikely Patron of Change," January 1, 1990, pp. 42–45; "The Year of the People," January 1, 1990, pp. 46–53; "The Gorbachev Touch," January 1, 1990, pp. 54–55; "No Peace for the Prizewinner," October 29, 1990, pp. 57–58; "The End of the U.S.S.R.," December 23, 1991, pp. 18–22; "'I Want to Stay the Course,'" December 23, 1991, pp. 24–27; "Farewell . . . and Hail," January 6, 1992, pp. 56–59; "'I Have Big Plans,'" January 6, 1992, p. 61; "Mikhail Gorbachev, Private Citizen," March 9, 1992, pp. 34–35.

U.S. News and World Report, "The Last Hurrah," November 19, 1990, pp. 34–42.

Alex Haley

"**R**oots *is the simple story of all black people.
Every one of us goes back ancestrally to
someone who lived in one of those African villages, was
caught, brought across the ocean and worked on a
plantation, went through the Civil War. That's the
saga of the whole race.*"

Alex Haley's *Roots* earned praise for fostering better race
relations and for reaffirming pride in Black-American heritage. He was born on August 11, 1921, in Ithaca, New York, and
died on February 10, 1992, in Seattle, Washington.

I n 1964, while visiting the National Archives in Washington, D.C., journalist Alex Haley impulsively asked to take a look at the 1870 census records for Alamance County, North Carolina, his grandmother's childhood home. Turning the reels of microfilm, he spotted the familiar names of his great-grandparents and their children, among them six-year-old Elizabeth. "That really grabbed me," Haley later recalled. "That was Aunt Liz. I used to sit on her front porch and play with her long gray hair. The experience galvanized me. Grandma's words became real."

What began as a casual interest in his ancestry quickly turned into an obsession. On October 1, 1976, the results of Haley's twelve-year effort to document his past were published as *Roots: The Saga of an American Family*. The book rocketed to the top of the bestseller list and, in January, 1977, an Emmy Award-winning television mini-series adaptation attracted 130 million viewers, a then-record two-thirds of the possible audience. (It still ranks among the thirteen highest-rated programs of all time.) Its popular appeal was almost matched by its critical reception; in the first two years after its publication, *Roots* garnered a special Pulitzer Prize, a National Book Award, and nearly three hundred other honors. But Haley's success could not be measured strictly in terms of copies sold or number of viewers. As a writer for *Time* magazine declared, his true accomplishment was showing Americans of both races that "the ties that link them to their ancestors also bind them to each other."

Alex Murray Palmer Haley was the oldest of three sons of Bertha George Palmer and Simon Alexander Haley, a college professor who taught at various institutions throughout the South. During the school year, Alex and his brothers lived with their parents, but summers were spent in Henning, Tennessee, at the home of their maternal grandparents. It was there that Alex grew particularly close to his grandmother and his great-aunts, spending hours on the front porch listening to their simple but dramatic accounts of an African ancestor named "Kin-tay" who had been kidnapped and sold into slavery in America during the late 1700s.

After graduating from high school at age fifteen, Haley briefly attended college before joining the U.S. Coast Guard in 1939. To alleviate the boredom of cruising at sea for weeks at a time, he read extensively and also took up writing, at first mostly love letters that he composed on behalf of his less-talented shipmates. Eventually he tried to sell some maritime adventure stories to various American magazines, usually without much luck. (Years later, when his celebrity status left him with little time to write, he would book passage on a freighter and revel in the opportunity to work without interruptions.) An occasional success kept his hopes alive, however, as did the Coast Guard's decision to create the public relations position of chief journalist just for him. Upon his retirement from the service in 1959, Haley decided to become a free-lance writer.

Several very lean years followed until magazines such as the *Reader's Digest* began buying Haley's articles on a fairly regular basis. His first big break came when *Playboy* asked him to interview jazz trumpeter Miles Davis for a piece that launched the magazine's well-known interview feature. That assignment led to another *Playboy* interview with Black-American Muslim leader Malcolm X, who then chose Haley to collaborate with him on his "as-told-to" autobiography. Completed just a few weeks before Malcolm X's assassination in 1965 and published later that same year, *The Autobiography of Malcolm X* received excellent reviews and became an enduring bestseller.

With his reputation now secure, Haley was able to earn a very comfortable living lecturing and taking on only those writing assignments in which he was most interested. But already the desire to spend more time investigating his family history was proving to be irresistible. Financed by occasional advances from his publisher, Doubleday, and the *Reader's Digest*, Haley began accumulating mounds of information from libraries, archives, and other research centers. Consultations with a linguist eventually helped him link the many "k" sounds in the language spoken by his ancestor Kintay to the Mandingo people of Gambia in West Africa.

On a trip to Gambia in 1967, Haley met with a *griot*, or oral historian, of the Kinte (pronounced Kin-tay) clan in the Mandingo village of Juffure. What followed, he later said, was "a moment which, emotionally, can never again be equaled in your life." Through an interpreter, the *griot* told the story of the Kinte clan, going back centuries to recite details about marriages, births, deaths, and other events. Eventually he reached the late 1700s and related the tale of Kunta Kinte, a young man who left his village one day to chop some wood and was never heard from again. "Goose pimples came out on me the size of marbles," Haley recalled. "He just had no way in the world of knowing that what he told me meshed with what I'd heard from the old ladies on the front porch in Henning, Tennessee." Getting out his own notes, he shared his grandmother's stories with the *griot*, and soon everyone present realized that Kunta

Kinte and Kin-tay the African were probably one and the same person.

Haley pressed on with his research to document his findings, discovering records that supported the story of Kunta Kinte's kidnapping and passage to America on a British slave ship. But when he finally began to tackle the monumental task of transforming what he had gathered into a compelling narrative, he found it a struggle to bring his family's story to life on the printed page. After more than a decade of work, his dream of creating "a buoy for black self-esteem—and a reminder of the universal truth that we are all children of the same creator" seemed impossibly out of reach.

The turning point finally came on board a ship bound for America from Liberia, a trip Haley made to help him understand what Kunta Kinte must have experienced while crossing the Atlantic. Even though he spent his nights in the cargo hold, stripped to his underwear and lying on a rough-sawn board, he could not imagine the horror of that long-ago journey. Deeply depressed by mounting financial difficulties, a fast-approaching deadline for submitting his manuscript, and his inability to describe Kinte's ordeal, Haley stood by the ship's railing and considered slipping quietly into the sea. As he looked down at the water, though, he heard the voices of his ancestors urging him to continue working on his book. That night, he went back into the hold and "felt for the first time that I *was* Kunta Kinte," as he told an *Ebony* magazine reporter. "From that moment on, I had no problem with writing."

The book *Roots* and its two immensely popular television adaptations (the one that aired in 1977, just a few months after the book was published, and a sequel that aired in 1979) renewed an interest in Black history and genealogy that had first surfaced during the 1960s. It also sparked passionate discussions about race relations in America. According to many commentators, the tale of Kunta Kinte took what people already *knew* about slavery (mostly from White sources) and made them *feel* it from a Black viewpoint, creating among Whites an unexpected shock of identification with Blacks and prompting among Blacks a startling realization of what they have had to overcome. And while some reviewers were uncomfortable with the author's blend of fact and fiction, primarily because it made *Roots* impossible to evaluate purely as history or purely as entertainment, by and large they readily acknowledged the power of what one called the story's "mythic veracity" as well as its ability to sensitize people to the Black-American situation. As *Newsweek* critic Paul D. Zimmerman concluded, "Instead of writing a scholarly monograph of little social impact, Haley has written a blockbuster in the best sense—a book that is bold in concept and ardent in execution, one that will reach millions of people and alter the way we see ourselves."

After *Roots*, Haley kept busy lecturing, making personal appearances on radio and television programs, and writing. (Among his more recent and as yet unpublished projects were his father's family history, a detailed account of his twelve-year struggle to research and write *Roots*, and a profile of Henning, Tennessee, as it was during the years he spent his summers there.) In February, 1992, Haley was in Seattle for a speaking engagement when he suffered a fatal heart attack. His body was returned to Henning and buried on the grounds surrounding his grandparents' home (now a state museum), just a few steps from the porch where he used to listen to the gripping saga of Kunta Kinte.

Despite the accolades he received for *Roots*, Haley felt that the greatest reward of all was the respect and affection fellow Black Americans granted him for providing the family history slavery had denied them. He therefore made sure that everything he did advanced Black Americans as a people. "The money I have made . . . means nothing to me compared to the fact that about half of the black people I meet—ranging from the most sophisticated to the least sophisticated—say to me, 'I'm proud of you,'" he once told a reporter for *Ebony*. "I feel strongly about always earning that and never letting black people down."

Sources

➤ **Books**

Dictionary of Literary Biography, Volume 38: *Afro-American Writers After 1955: Dramatists and Prose Writers*, Gale, 1985.

Roots: The Saga of an American Family, Doubleday, 1976.

➤ **Periodicals**

Ebony, "Alex Haley: The Man Behind *Roots*," April, 1977, pp. 33–41; "Alex Haley in Juffure," July, 1977, pp. 31–42; "We Must Honor Our Ancestors," August, 1986; Reprint, November, 1990, pp. 152–156.

Essence, "Alex Haley's Roots Revisited," February, 1992.

Newsweek, "In Search of a Heritage," September 27, 1976, pp. 94–96 (opening quote).

New York Times, February 11, 1992, p. B8.

People, "Having Left L.A. to Settle in His Native Tennessee, Alex Haley Turns Out His First Book Since *Roots,*" December 12, 1988, pp. 126–128.

Publishers Weekly, September 6, 1976, pp. 8–12.

Reader's Digest, "My Search for Roots: A Black American's Story," April, 1977, pp. 148–152; "What *Roots* Means to Me," May, 1977, pp. 73–76.

Time, "Why *Roots* Hit Home," February 14, 1977, pp. 69–77; "*Roots'* Roots," December 25, 1978, p. 30; February 24, 1992, p. 68.

Barbara Harris

"**A** *fresh wind is indeed blowing. . . . To some the changes are refreshing breezes. For others, they are as fearsome as a hurricane.*"

Born in Philadelphia, Pennsylvania, in 1930, Barbara Clementine Harris is the first female bishop in the history of the U.S. Episcopal Church and the international Anglican community of which it is a part.

Address: Episcopal Diocese of Massachusetts, 138 Tremont St., Boston, MA 02111.

I n February, 1989, a 2,000-year-old tradition came to an end when Barbara Harris was ordained suffragan (assistant) bishop of the U.S. Episcopal Church following her election to the post the previous September. Part of the worldwide Anglican Communion, which grew out of the Church of England and now includes twenty-eight independent national churches in 164 countries, the Episcopal Church immediately came under fire from within and without for its decision. Not only was Harris a woman—making her election "sacrilegious" to those who believe bishops are successors to the original twelve apostles and should therefore be male—she was also black, divorced, and lacked a college degree, seminary training, and experience as a full-time priest in her own church.

Harris freely admits that her "faith journey," as she calls it, has been somewhat unorthodox. Raised in the middle-class Germantown section of Philadelphia, she regularly attended Episcopal services with her family (her mother was the church choir director and organist) and was actively involved in the parish, even serving for a time as a lay chaplain. After graduating from high school, Harris went to work for Joseph V. Baker & Associates, a black-owned public relations firm, and within ten years she was named president. She left in 1968 for a position in community relations with the Sun Oil Company and in five years became head of the department. When she resigned from Sun Oil in 1980, Harris was a senior consultant in public relations.

Much of Harris's free time during the 1960s was devoted to the civil rights movement. She participated in various demonstrations and voter-registration drives and even accompanied Dr. Martin Luther King on his 1965 "freedom march" from Selma to Montgomery, Alabama. Later in the decade, as her increasingly radical politics put her at odds with the conservative church she had attended since childhood, she began looking around for a congregation that shared her views. She settled on the Church of the Advocate, an inner-city Episcopal parish that was home to the black power movement in Philadelphia. Its rector, Paul Washington, became her mentor and one of her staunchest supporters. There Harris helped the poor in the surrounding community, volunteered in the soup kitchen, and served as a prison chaplain.

Harris firmly allied herself with Episcopal activists in July, 1974, when she led a procession of women who had come to the Church of the Advocate to witness the illegal ordination of eleven female priests. Performed by three retired bishops, the ceremony was in direct violation of church rules, which did not allow women to serve as priests. (The church voted to change this rule two years later and subsequently legalized the ordination of the eleven women.)

At about this same time, Harris—after much soul-searching—made up her mind to pursue a career in the priesthood, a move that puzzled her friends and business colleagues but one she felt was a natural outgrowth of her political and social activism. Working with an advisor, she put together an innovative program of study that required her to devote evenings, weekends, and vacations to some college course work and other special training. Harris completed the program in about four years, earning the same number of credits as a typical seminarian, and passed her exams "with flying colors." She was ordained a deacon in September, 1979, and then a priest in October, 1980. Eager to devote full time to her new duties, she quit her job with Sun Oil.

Harris's first assignments included serving as a part-time priest in a Philadelphia church and as a prison chaplain. In 1984, she joined the Episcopal Church Publishing Company as executive director. Over the next four years, she gained national recognition as columnist, editor, and publisher of *The Witness*, an independent church journal with a reputation for championing various liberal causes. Harris continued the tradition, using her columns to attack social, political, and economic injustice and to support feminism, gay rights, prison reform, the Sandinista government in Nicaragua, and the anti-apartheid movement in South Africa. She was also highly critical of the teachings and practices of the Episcopal Church, which she characterized as "male-dominated" and "racist." In 1988, Harris left *The Witness* when Paul Washington retired from the Church of the Advocate and she was named to replace him on a temporary basis.

That same year, Anglican bishops from around the world met for their once-a-decade conference in Canterbury, England. High on the agenda was the question of ordaining female bishops. Despite the strong objections of conservatives—most of whom still did not approve of female priests, let alone female bishops—the assembly voted to adopt a compromise ruling that recognized the right of each national church to decide for itself whether to ordain female bishops. Added to the ruling was a cautionary statement acknowledging that such ordinations could lead to disunity in the worldwide Anglican community, perhaps even a full-fledged split between the U.S. Episcopal Church and less radical national churches in Britain, Africa, and the Asia-Pacific region.

Activists in the U.S. Episcopal Church welcomed this long-awaited decision and immediately seized the opportunity to nominate a woman candidate for suffragan bishop in the diocese of Massachusetts. Their choice was Barbara Harris, who faced the formidable task of garnering enough support among the clergy and the lay delegates to come out ahead of five other candidates—three white men, a black man, and a white woman.

Harris was already well known as a result of her association with *The Witness,* and she had also made a name for herself as a tireless advocate for the poor and oppressed and as a "woman whose voice and presence can fill a cathedral." But some expressed reservations about her business background, her lack of a college degree and seminary training, and her limited pastoral experience. Of concern, too, was the threat to Anglican unity and the ongoing efforts to build closer relations with the Roman Catholic Church if a woman were elected bishop.

Harris's supporters argued that her critics were less bothered by her credentials than by the fact that she was outspoken, black, female, and divorced. (In some Anglican churches, divorced men are barred from entering the priesthood but may be allowed to continue to serve if they are divorced after becoming a priest; Harris's five-year marriage ended in 1965.) As for the unity issue, they pointed out that her ordination would at last open the church to "the other half of the human race" and send a positive message to those who have traditionally been alienated by a church with a reputation for being "predominantly starchy, male and white." Harris kept an uncharacteristically low profile during the controversy, declining comment on her background and her personal beliefs.

Finally, on September 24, 1988, the fifty-eight-year-old priest was elected bishop by a slim margin after eight ballots. "A barrier was broken that was for centuries considered inviolable," declared Matthew R. Lawrence in *Christian Century.* Following additional debate and dire warnings about the future of the Anglican church, committees representing Episcopal dioceses throughout the country ratified the vote in January, 1989. Harris was ordained in a three-hour ceremony held in Boston on February 11, 1989.

Since then, Harris has attempted to settle quietly into her new position as second in charge of the largest diocese in the U.S. Episcopal Church. Proclaiming her desire to be "a bishop for the whole church," she has carried on much of the work she was doing as a priest—helping parishes develop programs, resources, and solutions to problems and serving on committees that deal with pastoral care (including hospital and prison ministry and outreach services to people with AIDS) and social justice issues. She also has the added responsibility of performing confirmations and ordaining new bishops. Reflecting on her goals in an interview with Lynn Rosellini of *U.S. News & World Report*, Harris says, "I certainly don't want to be one of the boys. I want to offer my peculiar gifts as a black woman . . . a sensitivity and an awareness that come out of more than a speaking acquaintance with oppression."

While most of the rest of the Anglican community (including the Church of England) and even some Episcopal dioceses in the United States have refused to acknowledge her ordination, Harris spends little time worrying about the conservatives she once labeled "factious fathers who fear mitered mamas." As she remarked to Rosellini, "I could be a combination of the Virgin Mary, Lena Horne and Madame Curie, and I would still get clobbered by some." Instead, she prefers to focus on what she will be able to accomplish as a "Christian social activist following what I believe my Lord would have me do." "I'm proud of the church for doing this," she told a crowd of well-wishers after her election. "And I'm praying for God's will to be done and the grace to fit into whatever happens."

Sources

➤ **Periodicals**

Christian Century, "Helping the Holy Spirit Elect a Bishop," October 19, 1988, pp. 917–919; "Harris's Credentials Are Scrutinized," December 21–28, 1988, pp. 1175–1176; "Harris Approved," February 1–8, 1989, pp. 104–105.

Christianity Today, "Episcopalians Test Lambeth Ruling," October 21, 1988, pp. 47–49; "Consecration of Bishop Stirs Episcopal Dissent," March 17, 1989, pp. 41–43.

Commonweal, "When the Spirit Leads," March 10, 1989, pp. 133–135.

Ebony, "The First Woman Episcopal Bishop," May, 1989, pp. 40–42.

Essence, October, 1989, p. 66.

New Choices, "The Bold Ones: Four American Pioneers Who Are Changing Our World," July, 1989, pp. 37–41.

Time, "The Bishop Is a Lady," December 26, 1988, p. 81; "To Each Her Own: Combining Talent and Drive, Ten Tough-Minded Women Create Individual Rules for Success," Fall, 1990 (special issue).

U.S. News & World Report, "The First of the 'Mitered Mamas,'" June 19, 1989, pp. 56–57.

Vaclav Havel

"**E**ven a single, apparently powerless man who dares to tell aloud the truth and is prepared to sacrifice his life wields surprisingly more power than thousands of anonymous voters under different conditions."

Czechoslovakian playwright and dissident Vaclav Havel became his country's president in 1989 after a bloodless revolution ended more than four decades of communist rule. He was born on October 5, 1936, in Prague, Czechoslovakia.

Over the course of several tumultuous months in 1989, citizens of Central and Eastern Europe rejoiced as one after another their totalitarian governments crumbled amid popular demands for reform, freedom, and democracy. Sometimes the disintegration occurred with little or no bloodshed, and sometimes it did not. One of the most notable examples of the former was Czechoslovakia, where the uprising was led by internationally respected playwright and dissident Vaclav Havel. An inspiration to his fellow citizens for his courage and defiance in the face of repeated arrests, imprisonment, and harassment, he was chosen not only to lead them out of the dark past but also to guide the way to a brighter future. Thus, in a process that rivaled one of his very own "dramatic excursions into the twilight zone where the rational becomes the absurd," as a writer for *U.S. News and World Report* observed, "an 'enemy of the state' has been unanimously elected President by a parliament packed with the people who had thrown him in jail."

Vaclav Havel spent his early youth as the child of privilege. His father, also named Vaclav, was a successful restauranteur and real estate developer, and as a result young Vaclav and his mother, Bozena Vavreckova Havel, enjoyed a luxurious lifestyle complete with governesses, maids, cooks, and chauffeurs. In 1948, however, communists seized control of Czechoslovakia, and under the new economic system the Havels' restaurant and other properties were confiscated. Denied the chance to further his education by a Stalinist regime intent on punishing those from affluent backgrounds, young Vaclav worked in a chemical factory, drove a taxi, and took night classes at a technical school hoping one day to qualify for admission to a university. He also read voraciously and tried his hand at writing, producing primarily critical essays but also an occasional bit of verse and drama.

After failing on numerous occasions to secure admission to college, Havel decided to indulge his fascination with the theater by signing on as a stagehand with a Prague-based performing company in 1959. A year later he went to work for the leading avant-garde troupe in town, the Theatre on the Balustrade, starting out as a stagehand and electrician but soon moving up to a position on the creative staff, serving as an assistant to the artistic director until 1963, literary manager from 1963 until 1968, and finally resident playwright.

In this latter role, Havel turned out a number of satirical/

absurdist works that poked fun at Czech society and politics, including *The Garden Party, The Memorandum,* and *The Increased Difficulty of Concentration.* All debuted at the Theatre on the Balustrade and later met with success throughout Europe and the United States. During the spring of 1968, Havel was allowed to travel to New York City to attend the first American production of *The Memorandum,* which later won an Obie Award as the best Off-Broadway foreign play of the year.

Havel was by this time well known to audiences on both sides of the Atlantic as writer "transfixed by the plight of man trapped in an inhuman bureaucracy," to quote from a *U.S. News and World Report* article. But he saw his artistic freedom evaporate soon after the Soviet Union invaded Czechoslovakia in August, 1968, and demanded an end to the liberalization that had been sweeping the country for several years. Havel took a leading role in the protests that followed, calling on students and workers to unite under the banner of human rights and urging his fellow writers and intellectuals to resist attempts at censorship and other forms of repression. But the crackdown was swift and severe, and by the end of the decade, hard-line communist bureaucrats—the very people Havel liked to ridicule in his plays—were firmly back in charge.

In the aftermath of the Soviet invasion, Havel's work was banned and his passport was revoked. In addition, his telephones were bugged, his mail was intercepted and opened, and his apartment was routinely broken into and searched. He refused to be silenced, however, and continued to write whenever possible for publication and production in the West, his plays smuggled out of the country by a loyal network of friends and other supporters. For some inexplicable reason, Havel was allowed to keep the royalties he earned abroad. Consequently he became quite well-to-do and enjoyed a number of material privileges, including a Mercedes that he drove to his "official" job stacking barrels in a brewery. Havel also began devoting more and more of his time to politics, and by the mid-1970s he had become his country's leading dissident as well as an internationally acclaimed playwright.

Havel first went to prison for his activism in early 1977 as a result of his involvement with a human rights organization known as Charter 77. Made up of about three hundred writers, intellectuals, musicians, and church officials, Charter 77 issued a manifesto charging the Czech government with failing to honor its agreement to abide by the 1975 Helsinki Covenant on Civil and Political Rights.

Havel, one of the group's three main spokespersons, was arrested and jailed for several months. Later that same year, he was arrested again and received a fourteen-month suspended sentence for sending his banned writings abroad to be published.

In 1978 Havel and some other Charter 77 members formed a new organization, the Committee for the Defense of the Unjustly Persecuted. This in turn led to his arrest on charges of subversion, and in 1979 Havel began serving a four-year term at hard labor, having refused an offer by the government to let him emigrate to the United States and thus avoid imprisonment. (Tens of thousands of his countrymen had already done so since the 1968 crackdown.) "The solution of this human situation does not lie in leaving it," explained Havel about his decision to reject the government's offer. "Fourteen million people can't just go and leave Czechoslovakia empty."

During his long incarceration, Havel became a cause celebre in the worldwide community of writers and human rights activists for his strong stand against the Czech regime. Their protests won him an early release from prison after he grew seriously ill from pneumonia and a lung infection near the end of his sentence (possibly as a result of deliberately inadequate medical treatment). As soon as he regained his health, Havel resumed writing and speaking out against the government. He also published *Letters to Olga*, a collection of his prison correspondence to his wife that has been hailed as a masterpiece of dissident literature.

Throughout the 1980s, Havel lived under virtual house arrest; his every movement was monitored, his visitors were screened and sometimes harassed, and his homes and car were repeatedly vandalized. In January, 1989, he was arrested yet again, this time for laying a wreath in Prague's Wenceslas Square in memory of a Czech student who had set himself on fire there twenty years earlier to protest the Soviet invasion. Found guilty of inciting a public protest and ignoring orders to leave the square, Havel was sentenced to eight months in jail. This time, his fellow citizens vented their outrage directly at the prime minister and managed to have his sentence reduced to four months.

Havel's release from prison in mid-1989 coincided with the growing demand for freedom and democracy that swept across Eastern Europe in the wake of Soviet leader Mikhail Gorbachev's policies of *glasnost* (openness) and *perestroika* (economic restructuring). Drafted into a leadership role in the Czech reform movement,

Havel presided over the peaceful removal of the communist regime in what came to be known as "the velvet revolution." Hundreds of thousands of demonstrators took to the streets on November 17, 1989, and called for free elections, and on November 24, the government resigned. Just a little over two weeks later, on December 10, the first Czech cabinet in over forty years without a communist majority assumed power, and on December 29, a surprised and rather reluctant Vaclav Havel emerged as the unanimous popular choice for interim president until nationwide elections could be held in mid-1990.

Characterizing the process that led to his being made president as "very strange theater" that was part absurdist, part tragedy, part farce, and part fairy tale, Havel likened himself to "an actor in a play that isn't mine." Although he questioned his suitability for the job and noted that he had never longed for a political post, he vowed to lead his country to free elections "in a decent and peaceful way so the clean face of our revolution is not sullied." Following those elections in July, 1990, the new Czech parliament overwhelmingly voted to retain Havel as president.

Since taking over the reins in Czechoslovakia, Havel has faced the gargantuan task of stimulating a hopelessly backward and moribund economy, eliminating the communist bureaucracy, and overcoming the bitter legacy of totalitarianism. The president's greatest fear is not that things will turn out badly for Czechoslovakia, but that he personally will not live up to the expectations people have of him.

Someday, Havel would like to return to his writing. To those who suggest that the fall of communism may have robbed him of creative inspiration, he replies that, on the contrary, "I think the new era has opened up an immense number of new themes. I feel them importuning me, forcing themselves on me, tempting me. . . . I would particularly enjoy mapping the basic existential ground— not just fear of the future, or fear of freedom, but we're starting to see fear of our own past. . . . That, to me, is dramatically very exciting."

In the meantime, he continues to marvel at the whirlwind of events that took a former enemy of the state and made him president. "I learned in prison that everything is possible, so perhaps I should not be amazed," muses Havel. "But I am. Sometimes I ask my friends if this was all a dream, a colorful and beautiful dream from which I would awake—in prison. But finally . . . I began to feel that it was not a dream, and that what has happened is real and lasting."

Sources

➤ **Periodicals**

Newsweek, "'I Should Not Be Amazed—But I Am,'" January 1, 1990, p. 33; "'The Great Moral Stake of the Moment,'" January 15, 1990, p. 42; "'Parallels with a Prison': What Havel Misses," July 22, 1991, p. 31.

New York Review of Books, "'Uncertain Strength': An Interview with Vaclav Havel," August 15, 1991, pp. 6–8.

New York Times, "Portrait of a Playwright as an Enemy of the State," March 23, 1986.

New York Times Magazine, October 25, 1987.

People, "Life Turns Upside Down for Vaclav Havel, Out of Jail and in as Czech President," January 22, 1990, pp. 44–46.

Time, "Act of Artistic Unfreedom," March 6, 1989, p. 45; "Dissident to President," January 8, 1990, pp. 62–64; "The Revolution Has Just Begun," March 5, 1990, pp. 14–15.

U.S. News and World Report, "The Prisoner Who Took the Castle," February 26, 1990, pp. 33–37; "Disciple of Dissent," July 16, 1990, p. 16.

Vanity Fair, "Havel's Choice," August, 1991.

Stephen W. Hawking

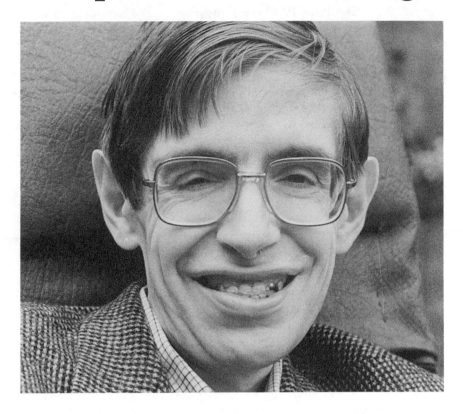

"$\mathbf{I}$ *f you are disabled, . . . it is no good blaming the world or expecting it to take pity on you. . . . If one is physically disabled, one cannot afford to be* psychologically *disabled as well."*

Renowned theoretical physicist Stephen W. Hawking has battled a rare neuromuscular disease while conducting his groundbreaking research. He was born on January 8, 1942, in Oxford, England.

Address: Department of Applied Mathematics and Theoretical Physics, Cambridge University, Silver St., Cambridge CB3 9EW, England.

In 1963, Stephen W. Hawking was a twenty-one-year-old graduate student at Cambridge University when some physical problems he had been experiencing since his undergraduate days began to worsen. As doctors soon determined, his symptoms—slurred speech and an apparent clumsiness that made it difficult for him to tie his shoes or walk without stumbling—signaled the onset of an incurable disorder called amyotrophic lateral sclerosis (ALS). Also known as motor neuron disease or Lou Gehrig's Disease, ALS is a degenerative condition affecting the spinal cord that leads to muscular weakness throughout the body. Death usually comes just two or three years after the initial diagnosis when the chest muscles weaken to the point where the patient can no longer breathe.

Today, Hawking is able to move only a few fingers of one hand—enough to get around in his motorized wheelchair and "talk" by operating a word processor hooked up to a voice synthesizer; nurses, family members, and colleagues attend to his other needs. Yet as so many have observed, including *Commonweal's* Chet Raymo, "within this incapacitated body is contained a remarkably capacitated mind." For while Hawking's body has withered and atrophied, leaving him firmly tied to earth, his mind has proven "capable of somersaulting through space and time," says Ric Dolphin of *Maclean's* magazine. He is frequently ranked among the world's greatest thinkers—Galileo, Newton, Einstein—and his work in theoretical physics has led him to the brink of discoveries that may well explain the universe.

Born three hundred years to the day after Galileo's death, Hawking is the son of E.I. and Frank Hawking, a doctor and research biologist in tropical medicine. The oldest of four children, he grew up in and around London and decided very early on to pursue a career in science. Hawking entered Oxford's University College in 1959 as a mathematics major, then switched to physics. Popular with fellow students and regarded as somewhat of a free spirit, he approached his studies casually, taking few notes and rarely opening a book. But his professors recognized even then that despite his lackluster academic performance, he was "someone far cleverer than most of themselves." After graduating with first-class honors in 1962, he went on to Cambridge University to study theoretical physics and cosmology, a branch of physics that focuses on what Hawking refers to as "the big question: Where did the universe come from?"

Shortly after his arrival at Cambridge came the ALS diagnosis and the overwhelmingly bleak picture it painted of his future. He became deeply depressed, virtually abandoned his studies, and spent many hours alone in his room. "I didn't think there was any point in doing any research, because I didn't feel I would live long enough to get my Ph.D.," he explained to Michael Harwood in a *New York Times Magazine* article.

After progressing rather rapidly at first, Hawking's ALS then stabilized, leaving him only partially disabled and somewhat more optimistic about chances for long-term survival. Resuming his studies, he encountered yet another obstacle when his mathematics skills proved inadequate for the demands of theoretical physics. A turning point came in 1965, when he became engaged to Jane Wilde, an undergraduate language major. "This gave me something to live for," Hawking recalled. "If we were to get married, I had to get a job. And to get a job, I had to finish my Ph.D." About that same time, he also began to gain an appreciation of the mathematics he needed to continue his research. "I started working hard for the first time in my life," he told a *Time* magazine reporter. "To my surprise, I found I liked it."

The young physicist earned his Ph.D. in 1966, submitting a doctoral thesis that set off a lively debate among his colleagues. Working in collaboration with his friend Roger Penrose, a Cambridge mathematician, Hawking developed and applied new mathematical techniques to prove that if Einstein's theory of relativity is correct down to the smallest scale, the matter of a collapsing star crushes together with such force that it forms a "singularity"—an infinitely dense point with no dimensions where all scientific laws governing space and time are distorted by immense gravitational forces. Surrounding the singularity is a "black hole," a region from which not even light can escape due to the singularity's tremendous gravitational pull. Hawking went on to demonstrate that the universe must have sprung from the explosion of a singularity, a conclusion that supported the controversial "Big Bang" theory of the creation of the universe.

Hawking remained at Cambridge after receiving his degree, serving as a fellow of Gonville and Caius College, a member of the graduate staff of the Institute of Theoretical Astronomy, and a research assistant in the department of applied mathematics and theoretical physics. He continued his investigations into black holes and eventually concluded that the forces unleashed during the Big Bang would have created at least a million mini-black holes. He then used quantum theory to challenge the conventional notion that nothing can escape a black hole, proving in a 1974 paper that mini-black holes emit particles and radiation, gradually evaporate, and then explode. His theory has since been accepted by most physicists, and *Hawking radiation* is the term used to describe emissions from black holes.

At the same time his startlingly original insights were holding the scientific community spellbound, Hawking's physical condition was slowly deteriorating. He was able to get around on crutches throughout the 1960s, but by the early 1970s he was confined to a wheelchair. Around 1973, he found he could no longer grasp a pen or a pencil well enough to write, and soon he could not hold a book or even turn the page of one propped up in front of him. Speaking clearly enough to be understood by anyone other than his family and closest associates became virtually impossible; in 1985, a tracheostomy performed to save his life during a severe bout of pneumonia left him completely without a voice.

As a result of his limited mobility, Hawking has been forced to work out his theories almost entirely in his head by thinking pictorially in terms of shapes and models. "I simply can't manage very complicated equations," he told Harwood, "so I have developed geometrical ways of thinking, instead." He comes up with the overview—the "big picture"—then dictates his ideas to his assistants (often graduate students), who follow up with the necessary calculations and paperwork, checking everything against the actual observations of physicists and astronomers. Roger Penrose believes that Hawking's disabilities have actually enhanced his creativity by freeing him to take highly intuitive leaps into territory where someone with more to risk might hesitate to venture.

In 1977, Hawking was promoted to professor of gravitational physics, and in 1980, he became Lucasian Professor of Mathematics, a post once held by Isaac Newton. For the most part, he has been excused from lecturing and teaching responsibilities so that he can concentrate on research. His goal, he says, is "a complete understanding of the universe," and to that end he has devoted his efforts since the late 1970s to the Grand Unified Theory, a concept that also occupied Einstein for the last several decades of his life. This theory would reconcile the apparent contradictions in the two major theories of modern physics: general relativity (which states that gravity controls the universe and does so in a predictable manner) and quantum mechanics (which states that matter behaves randomly at the level of the atom and below). The theory would link general relativity and quantum mechanics to explain the behavior of everything in the universe. According to Jerry Adler of *Newsweek*, unifying the two theories "would deserve not just a Nobel Prize but the last Nobel Prize; as Hawking puts it, 'There would still be lots to do [in physics], but it would be like mountaineering after Everest.'"

Hawking has always been interested in ways to make his work accessible to those without a background in science, and in the early 1980s he began writing a book that he hoped would accomplish that goal. Published in 1988, *A Brief History of Time: From the Big Bang to Black Holes* surveys centuries of thought on the nature of the universe, from Aristotle through Einstein and Hawking's own discoveries. The author's highly readable and often wryly humorous treatment of such a complex topic was phenomenally successful; his book remained on the *New York Times* nonfiction bestseller list for over a year, spending eighteen weeks in first place. Many reviewers have attributed its appeal to the spiritual overtones of Hawking's quest to understand the moment of creation and thus "know the mind of God."

Declaring that he has "a lot of science that I want to do first," Hawking has turned down requests to write another book. When he is not traveling all over the world lecturing and presenting papers to colleagues, he remains in his office at Cambridge. He is "a tough and stubborn man" who, with the help of friends and family, has not allowed disabilities to keep him from his work. "For Stephen Hawking, his wheelchair has became a unique vantage point from which to seek the basic law of nature," says John Boslough in the *Reader's Digest*. "He has became nearly the perfect cerebral being, a small speck of human creation comprehending the whole."

Sources

➤ **Books**

Boslough, John, *Stephen Hawking's Universe*, Quill, 1985.

Bowe, Frank, *Comeback: Six Remarkable People Who Triumphed over Disability*, Harper, 1981.

Hawking, Stephen W., *A Brief History of Time: From the Big Bang to Black Holes*, Bantam, 1988.

➤ **Periodicals**

Commonweal, "Stephen Hawking and the Mind of God," April 6, 1990, pp. 218–220.

Forbes, "Genius Unbound," March 23, 1987, p. 142.

Maclean's, "Glimpses of God," September 19, 1988, pp. 44–47.

Newsweek, "Reading God's Mind," June 13, 1988, pp. 56–59.

New York Times Magazine, "The Universe and Dr. Hawking," January 23, 1983.

People, December 26, 1988-January 2, 1989, p. 99; "Suiting Science to a T (Shirt), Two Chicago Bar Owners Set up a Stephen Hawking Fan Club," September 11, 1989, p. 111.

Popular Science, "A Brief History of *A Brief History,*" August, 1989, pp. 70–72.

Publishers Weekly, October 16, 1987, p. 56.

Reader's Digest, "Inside the Mind of a Genius," February, 1989, pp. 118–123.

Science Digest, "Handicapped People and Science," September, 1984, p. 92.

Time, "Roaming the Cosmos," February 8, 1988, pp. 58–60.

Jim Henson

"I believe in taking a positive attitude toward the world. My hope still is to leave the world a little bit better than when I got here."

Born on September 24, 1936, in Greenville, Mississippi, Jim Henson was the creative genius behind the Muppets. He died May 16, 1990, in New York City.

Address: Henson Associates, Inc., 117 East 69th St., New York, NY 10021.

I n 1956, a young college student and part-time puppeteer named Jim Henson came across an old green coat of his mother's. Always wanting to add new puppets to his menagerie, he fashioned a lizard-like creature out of the material and cut a ping-pong ball in half to make eyes. A year later, the funny-looking fellow—by that time christened Kermit—made his network television debut on Steve Allen's "Tonight!" show, singing "I've Grown Accustomed to Your Face" to another Henson creation, a rather ugly purple monster who first ate his own face and then tried to eat Kermit.

Audiences loved the skit and clamored for more of these so-called "Muppets," the name Henson and his partners gave to their fuzzy, bug-eyed puppets. Beginning with Rowlf the Dog and joined later by a "frogified" Kermit (the character closest to Henson's heart and reportedly his alter ego), Big Bird, Cookie Monster, Bert and Ernie, Miss Piggy, Fozzie Bear, and some two thousand other creatures, the Muppets eventually became a worldwide phenomenon, beloved by adults as well as children. Virtually all of them sprang from the fertile imagination of Jim Henson, a mild-mannered yet intense man with a talent for creating distinctive personalities out of lumps of sculpted foam and fur.

A Mississippi native, James Maury Henson was the son of Elizabeth Marcella Brown and Paul Ransom Henson, an agricultural researcher employed by the United States government. The Henson family left Mississippi when Paul Henson was transferred to Washington, D.C.; Jim grew up in the suburban community of Hyattsville, Maryland. Shy and self-conscious, he liked the idea of performing but dreaded the thought of facing an audience. The perfect creative outlet appeared in the form of his high school's puppet club, which he joined as a scenery designer.

During his senior year, a local television station announced that it was looking for some young puppeteers to staff a morning children's show. Henson, who had been fascinated by the still-new medium ever since he saw his first television program in the late 1940s, eagerly seized the opportunity to get on the air. He and a friend stitched together a rat puppet they named Pierre (because he looked French) and a couple of cowboy puppets and headed for the audition. They got the job, but the show lasted only a few weeks. Despite this less-than-spectacular beginning, Pierre and his creators were soon back on the air helping out on a cartoon show produced by another local station.

Henson worked in Washington, D.C.-area television all through college (he was a theater arts major at the University of Maryland), pairing up with his future wife, Jane Nebel, to do an afternoon variety program and two five-minute nighttime spots, one of which, "Sam and Friends," won an Emmy in 1958 as the best local entertainment show. Until that time, Henson had never seriously considered making puppeteering his career; as he later explained, "It didn't seem to be the sort of thing a grown man works at for a living." He changed his mind in 1958 after visiting Europe, where he discovered that puppetry was still a respected art. Returning to the United States, Henson concentrated on refining his techniques, relying on television monitors to help him synchronize the puppets' mouth movements with simple dialogue and thus improve their appearance on camera.

After graduating from college in 1960, Henson teamed with some other puppeteers to produce television commercials; among his first efforts were dog food spots starring Rowlf. The Muppets then began making guest appearances on a number of network programs, including "The Tonight Show," "The Ed Sullivan Show," and "The Jimmy Dean Show," on which Rowlf was a regular from 1963 to 1966. He was the first Muppet to attract national attention, and his popularity inspired Henson to lobby for a show of his own. He was turned down at all three major networks by programming executives who felt that the Muppets were too sophisticated for young viewers and too childish for adults.

Henson then collaborated with the Children's Television Workshop on a new show intended for broadcast on public television stations across the United States. Entitled "Sesame Street," this innovative blend of education and entertainment aimed at preschoolers first aired in 1969 and featured Muppets in key roles such as introducing films and live performances and conducting lessons on numbers, letters, shapes, colors, and concepts like "up" and "down." Big Bird, Cookie Monster, Oscar the Grouch, Grover, Bert and Ernie, and especially Kermit soon made "Sesame Street" an enormous hit with children, their parents, and critics. It also won two Emmy Awards. As of 1989, it was estimated that more than sixty-eight percent of all households with a child under six tuned in regularly.

Buoyed by the success of "Sesame Street," Henson again approached the networks about a nighttime show featuring the Muppets and was again turned down. He then struck a deal with British broadcasting tycoon Lew Grade, who guaranteed Henson a generous budget, international syndication, and complete artistic control. The result was "The Muppet Show," a weekly half-hour series in which a celebrity guest star interacted with the Muppets in musical numbers or short skits. It also introduced the most charismatic Muppet since Kermit—Miss Piggy, a pushy, temperamental "star" in love with the gentle, wisecracking frog. As the most popular syndicated program in the world, "The Muppet Show" ran from 1976 to 1981, when its creator decided not to do any more new episodes. "I wanted to quit while I was ahead," he later explained. "I didn't want to get stale."

With the success of "Sesame Street" and "The Muppet Show," the 1970s saw a veritable explosion of "Muppet Mania" as the characters were aggressively and effectively marketed on everything from toys, books, and records to clothes and household furnishings and accessories. Sales of Muppet-related merchandise financed the growth of Henson's production company, Henson Associates, and also helped support "Sesame Street" and other Children's Television Workshop programs.

In an interview with John Culhane for a *Reader's Digest* article, Henson searched for the words to explain why so many people were drawn to the Muppets. "I think it's a sense of innocence, of the naivete of a young person meeting life," he said. "Even the most worldly of our characters is innocent. Our villains are innocent, really. And it's that innocence that is the connection to the audience."

In 1979, the tremendous international appeal of the Muppets led Henson to try his hand at feature films. The first effort, *The Muppet Movie*, was a hit, as were *The Great Muppet Caper* in 1981 and *The Muppets Take Manhattan* in 1984. However, his attempts at fantasy— *The Dark Crystal* (1981) and *Labyrinth* (1986)—were critical and box-office disappointments despite their sophisticated, computer-controlled puppets. Henson nevertheless charged ahead throughout the 1980s with ambitious plans for further high-tech creations and other special effects for film and television. Several new television series also premiered, including "Fraggle Rock" for the HBO cable network in 1983 and "The Muppet Babies" Saturday morning cartoon show in 1984.

The 1990s began with Henson still on a creative roll, designing the computerized masks for the Teenage Mutant Ninja Turtles movie, working on several new television projects ("Dinosaurs," "Gulliver's Travels," "Jim Henson's Mother Goose Stories," "The Greek Myths"), and developing numerous movies and specials. But by far the most remarkable announcement came just before the new decade began when it was revealed that Walt Disney Company had agreed to acquire Henson Associates for a reported $100-$150 million, a deal that included copyrights for the Muppets (except for Kermit and the Sesame Street characters) as well as the creative services of Henson himself for the next fifteen years. Rejoicing in his new freedom to pursue design work instead of business problems, Henson declared, "I feel like a kid in a candy store."

Then the unthinkable occurred: on May 16, 1990, the fifty-three-year-old Henson died suddenly from a particularly severe form of pneumonia. Tributes poured in from literally all over the world to the man who was as well known overseas as he was in his native country. More than five thousand fans attended a memorial "celebration of life" in New York City and, mindful of Henson's request for "a friendly little service [with] a song or two . . . and someone [saying] some nice, happy words about me," they waved brightly painted foam butterflies as a Dixieland band played "When the Saints Go Marching In."

With characteristic modesty, Henson once said that he wasn't sure if his Muppets would outlast him. "I don't know how long the characters will continue," he remarked. "If the audience wants them to, then they will. If not, they'll probably go away." Initially, Henson Associates officials—including the founder's five children, who now own the business—considered retiring the characters Henson himself had given voice and life to: Ernie, Rowlf, the Swedish Chef, and, most notably, Kermit the Frog. But as *TV Guide* reporter Timothy Carlson noted in late 1990, "Muppet fans . . . quickly made it clear they didn't want that to happen." Henson's daughter Cheryl admitted, "It was a very touchy thing. . . . We [finally] thought that the Muppets were characters, not people, and that it was much better to say that they don't die." As a result, concluded Carlson, "Though the Muppetmaster is gone, his whimsical, mischievous, lovable creations could hardly be more alive."

Sources

➤ **Periodicals**

American Film, "Jim Henson," November, 1989, pp. 18–21.

Films in Review, "Jim Henson: Muppet Master Breaking New Ground with 'Dark Crystal,'" January, 1983, pp. 41–44.

Newsweek, "Jim Henson, 1936–1990: The Man behind the Muppets Leaves the Stage," May 28, 1990, pp. 79–80.

New York Times Magazine, June 10, 1979, p. 52.

People, "Muppet Master Jim Henson Has Another Brainchild—A Piggyless Project Starring Fraggles and Gorgs," January 17, 1983, pp. 39–41; "Kermit, Miss Piggy, Big Bird, Grover and Kids All over the World Mourn the Loss of Puppetmeister Jim Henson," May 28, 1990, pp. 119–121; "Legacy of a Gentle Genius," June 18, 1990, pp. 88–96.

Reader's Digest, "The Magical, Madcap Muppets," September, 1977, pp. 23–30; "Unforgettable Jim Henson," November, 1990, pp. 124–129.

Rolling Stone, June 28, 1990, p. 36.

School Library Journal, "Jim Henson and the People behind the Muppet Mania," September, 1984, pp. 27–31.

Time, "The Man behind the Frog," December 25, 1978, p. 74; May 28, 1990, p. 71.

TV Guide, "After 35 Years, Henson's Muppet Magic Lives On," November 17–23, 1990, pp. 18–22.

U.S. News and World Report, "Now, Who Can Tell Us How to Get to Sesame Street?," May 28, 1990, p. 12.

Matthew Henson

*"*A*s I stood there at the top of the world and thought of the hundreds of men who had lost their lives in the effort to reach it, I felt profoundly grateful that I . . . had the honor of representing my race in the historic achievement."*

Matthew Henson was the partner of arctic explorer Robert E. Peary. In 1909, the two men made the first successful assault on the North Pole. Henson was born on August 8, 1866, in Charles County, Maryland, and died on March 9, 1955, in New York City.

On April 6, 1988, family members and a host of dignitaries gathered at Arlington National Cemetery for the reinterment of Matthew Henson, co-discoverer of the North Pole. It was seventy-nine years to the day since he and Robert E. Peary had made their way to that frigid site, and while Peary had subsequently reaped the rewards of their triumph, Henson had lived out the rest of his life in near obscurity. On that day at Arlington, Henson at last received the hero's burial denied him upon his death thirty-three years before, thus making amends for what a writer for *Ebony* called "one of the country's most blatant snubs to Black American achievement."

Matthew Alexander Henson was the son of free-born parents who were sharecroppers in Maryland. There are conflicting stories about the circumstances of his youth, but it appears that he was orphaned at an early age and ran away from home when he was about eleven to escape a cruel stepmother. Making his way to Washington, D.C., he lived with an uncle for a while, attended school, and worked in a restaurant. There he heard the exciting tales of a seafarer who called himself Baltimore Jack, and around 1879 Henson decided to give life at sea a try. Heading to Baltimore's waterfront district, he secured a job as a cabin boy on a merchant vessel. For the next six years, Henson traveled around the world and became an accomplished sailor and master of several languages. The ship's elderly captain also taught him to read and write and instilled in him a love of books.

Henson returned to the United States in 1885 and worked all over the northeast at a variety of jobs, including stevedore, bellhop, laborer, and coachman. He eventually settled in Washington, D.C., and landed a job in a hat store. One day in 1887, a young naval officer named Robert E. Peary came in looking for a helmet he could wear on an upcoming engineering survey in Nicaragua. Peary had been advertising for a personal servant to accompany him on his trip, and Henson struck him as the perfect candidate. The prospect of being a valet didn't interest Henson, but the idea of going to Nicaragua did. He accepted Peary's offer on the spot, thus launching a partnership that would endure for the next twenty-two years.

Henson and Peary spent seven months in Nicaragua and battled insects, alligators, oppressive heat, and dense jungle almost every step of the way. Peary soon realized that Henson was far more than a mere valet; the young man quickly became an expert surveyor, and his knowledge of the sea and ability to chart a course through seemingly impenetrable terrain made him an invaluable member of the team.

On the way home, Peary told Henson of a trip he had taken to Greenland in 1886 and of his dream to visit the North Pole—at that time an undertaking as daring and dangerous as space exploration is today—and asked him if he would like to come along. Henson agreed, and in June, 1891, the two men set sail from New York. They were accompanied by Peary's young wife and four others, including Frederick Cook, the expedition's doctor and ethnologist. Once again Henson proved his usefulness, handling all repair work, serving as a blacksmith and carpenter, and even doing the cooking. He was also a skilled hunter and one of the best sledge-builders and dog-drivers in the group, talents that won him the admiration of the Eskimos who joined the party in Greenland. The Eskimos also appreciated the fact that Henson was the only member of the expedition who bothered to learn their language.

Peary and Henson did not reach the pole on that trip, nor did they on subsequent trips in 1893–1895, 1896, and 1897. Most of their activities were confined to unexplored areas of northeastern Greenland, partly due to storms, illnesses, and injuries that slowed their progress. But they gained valuable experience in arctic travel and survival, and their observations confirmed Greenland was an island. They also brought back several large meteorites that created quite a stir. These exploits made Peary (but not Henson) a hero and made him a popular figure on the lecture circuit, which helped him raise money for future expeditions. (He was often accompanied by a fur-clad Henson, howling sled dogs, various pieces of arctic equipment, and dramatic photographs.) When he was not exploring or lecturing with Peary, Henson supported himself at a series of menial jobs, including stints as a janitor and a railroad porter.

Peary and Henson's first serious attempt to reach the North Pole got under way in 1898. During their four-year ordeal, the two men managed to make it farther north than anyone had ever gone before, but early in the expedition Peary was crippled by frostbite that led to the amputation of eight of his toes. They tried again in 1905–1906 and established a new "farthest north" record but still fell about 175 miles short of the pole itself when treacherous broken ice forced them to turn back.

In July, 1908, the two explorers launched what the fifty-two-year-old Peary knew would be his last attempt to reach the North Pole; physically and mentally, he was more than a decade past his prime for such a difficult undertaking and therefore relied heavily on the forty-two-year-old Henson—by far the most competent member of the group—to help keep everything on track. By March 1, 1909, the drive was on for the pole (located 413 nautical miles due north of their starting point) as Peary brought up the rear of his seven-team expedition, which consisted of 24 men (6 Americans and the rest Eskimos), 19 sledges, and 133 dogs. Only the main team—Peary, Henson, and four Eskimos—was scheduled to make the complete journey; the others were responsible for breaking trail and carrying supplies. One by one, at certain points along the way, the support teams were supposed to drop a load of supplies and turn back, thus reducing the number of mouths to feed as they neared the pole. The last support party turned back on April 1, leaving only Peary and Henson's team to press on for the remaining 133 miles.

Over the next five days, Peary and Henson alternated breaking trail. Accounts of the day they finally reached the North Pole— April 6—are somewhat confusing and contradictory. Henson, who was out in front at that point, thought he might have been the first to stand "on top of the world," as he put it, but then a rather annoyed Peary showed up and took some readings that indicated the pole was actually three miles farther north.

While Henson tried to catch a few hours of sleep after their arduous journey, Peary went out with two Eskimos and criss-crossed the area making additional calculations. Tortured by his inability to determine conclusively that they had truly reached the North Pole, Peary returned to camp, rejected his partner's out-stretched hand of congratulations, and brooded about the prospect that he had once again failed to achieve his goal. Henson later remarked that Peary's stony silence in the days following their apparent triumph "nearly broke my heart." Relations between the two old friends were never quite the same again, even though Peary (who had difficulty expressing praise or gratitude) stated publicly on many occasions that he couldn't have gotten along without Henson.

After a brief but extremely bitter controversy that erupted when their onetime friend and traveling companion Frederick Cook falsely claimed that he had reached the North Pole a full year before Peary and Henson, Peary was showered with the attention and honors he deserved as a conqueror of the frozen north. His equally-deserving partner was not, most likely because many Americans at that time found it difficult to accept the fact that Peary had chosen a Black man—the best man, everyone involved agreed—over several White men to make the final dash with him. Subsequent written accounts of the journey, if they mentioned Henson at all, described him merely as Peary's "negro servant."

His career as an explorer at an end, Henson was faced with the prospect of having to earn a living. (Peary had extracted a promise from him not to lecture about their experiences, a promise Henson kept for twelve years until financial hardship forced him to break it.) Beginning in 1913, by order of President William Howard Taft, Henson was employed as a clerk in the New York Customs House, a position he held until he retired in 1936.

It was not until his final years that Henson at last received some recognition for his co-discovery of the North Pole. In 1937, he was admitted to the Explorers Club, and in 1944, Congress awarded a medal to him and the five others who had been on the expedition. He was also saluted at White House ceremonies in 1950 with President Harry S. Truman and again in 1954 with President Dwight D. Eisenhower. Yet in 1955, following Henson's death from a cerebral hemorrhage, his family's request that he be buried at Arlington National Cemetery was denied because he had never been a member of the armed services. Instead, he was buried in New York City, his grave marked by a small monument noting that he had accompanied Peary to the North Pole.

Thanks to the efforts of Harvard University's S. Allen Counter, a longtime admirer of Henson, the polar explorer received a more fitting memorial in 1988. Counter successfully petitioned the federal government to allow the bodies of Henson and his wife, Lucy, to be reburied with full military honors at Arlington. Following the April 6 ceremonies, a black granite monument bearing a gold-leaf likeness of Henson was set in place to mark the gravesite, located next to the final resting place of Robert Peary, the man with whom he had once stood "at the top of the world."

Sources

➤ **Books**

Dolan, Sean, *Matthew Henson*, Chelsea House, 1992.

Henson, Matthew Alexander, *A Black Explorer at the North Pole*, University of Nebraska Press, 1989. Reprint of 1912 edition.

Miller, Floyd, *Ahdoolo: The Biography of Matthew A. Henson*, Dutton, 1963.

➤ **Periodicals**

Ebony, "Matt Henson: Black Explorer Is Part of Controversy in Film 'Race to the Pole,'" November, 1983, pp. 80–84; "A Final Resting Place for Matthew Henson," July, 1988, pp. 108–112.

National Geographic, "Did Peary Reach the Pole?," September, 1988, pp. 386–413; "Descendants of the Expedition: The Henson Family," September, 1988, pp. 422–429.

New York Times, March 10, 1955, p. 27 (opening quote).

People, "No Slouches at Breaking the Ice, Polar Explorers Peary and Henson Each Left Behind a Son in the Arctic," June 1, 1987, pp. 41–42.

Reader's Digest, "Ahdoolo!: The Heroic March of Matthew Henson with Peary to the North Pole" (condensed version of *Ahdoolo: The Biography of Matthew A. Henson* by Floyd Miller), February, 1963, pp. 263–310.

Thor Heyerdahl

"**M**an is man wherever you find him; I feel he cannot be divided or united according to height, color, or pencil lines on a map."

Anthropologist and explorer Thor Heyerdahl has devoted his life to studying patterns of human migration in the belief that ancient Egyptians and South Americans could and did cross the Atlantic and Pacific oceans. He was born on October 6, 1914, in Larvik, Norway.

In 1947, Thor Heyerdahl launched a daring journey across the Pacific that thrilled the public and rocked the scientific world. Setting sail from Peru in a primitive balsa-wood raft called the *Kon-Tiki*, he and his five-man crew traveled 4,300 miles before crashing against a reef just east of Tahiti. Until that day, anthropologists had always insisted that the various Polynesian islands had been settled exclusively by Asians because prehistoric South Americans never could have managed to cross the Pacific. But the *Kon-Tiki's* successful trip—while not proof that such a migration had ever occurred—nevertheless demonstrated that it was indeed possible. Since then, Heyerdahl has gathered a wealth of evidence and undertaken other voyages to support his view that ancient people "put out to sea much more often than modern science has been willing to admit." And in the process, he has also hoped to prove that the national, racial, and religious differences that exist between us are far outweighed by the fact that we are all members of "one human family."

A native of Larvik, Norway, Thor Heyerdahl grew up with a love of the outdoors and an interest in anthropology. His father, also named Thor, was president of a brewery and mineral water plant, while his mother, Alison Lyng Heyerdahl, was head of the local museum. Even as a child, the future scientist and explorer was drawn to Polynesia; he recalls spending many happy hours curled up with some of his mother's books, "looking at these pictures of people living underneath the palm trees, fishing and picking coconuts. As far back as I can remember I was longing to go."

At the University of Oslo, Heyerdahl studied biology, zoology, and geography. In 1936, he left school to do research on the island of Fatu Hiva in the Marquesas, a group of islands in French Polynesia. While trying to determine how certain forms of plant and animal life typically found in South America had ended up on a remote volcanic island in the middle of the South Pacific long before Europeans had visited either place, he came to the unorthodox conclusion that someone else must have brought them to Fatu Hiva.

Over the course of the next year, Heyerdahl immersed himself in the island's culture, scrutinizing language, artifacts, and myths, especially the legend of the sun god Tiki, who was very similar to a pre-Incan South American hero called Kon-Tiki. He also studied the winds and currents and noted that they moved from South America *toward* Polynesia—not the direction one would expect given the prevailing theory that Asians had drifted eastward by sea and come upon Polynesia. By the end of his stay, Heyerdahl had given up biology and zoology to explore the possibility that ancient inhabitants of South America had constructed vessels using native woods and reeds that were capable of crossing the Pacific.

To gather evidence that would back up his theory, Heyerdahl spent the rest of the 1930s and early 1940s learning all he could about ancient civilizations in the Americas (North and South) and Polynesia. He discovered rock carvings and massive stone statues that existed in remarkably similar forms on both sides of the Pacific. He also examined the legend of Kon-Tiki, which tells of a race of Whites who fled pre-Inca Peru and sailed west across the Pacific to avoid being massacred by native tribes. He compared it to Polynesian myths that describe the arrival of a race of Whites from across the sea. But the scientific community ridiculed his efforts and refused to take him seriously.

Heyerdahl finally decided that the only way he could convince other anthropologists that his theory was plausible was to make the Pacific crossing himself in a type of boat prehistoric Indians would have known how to build. So, in April, 1947, he and five other Scandinavians left Peru aboard the *Kon-Tiki*, a forty-five-foot-long balsa raft outfitted with a sail. Skeptics had predicted that the raft would become waterlogged and sink within a few days, but 101 days and 4,300 miles later, the *Kon-Tiki* smashed into a coral reef off the Polynesian island chain of Tuamotu, and the triumphant Heyerdahl and his crew waded ashore.

The daring voyage brought Heyerdahl worldwide renown; his riveting written account of his adventure, *Kon-Tiki: Across the Pacific by Raft* (later published as *The Kon-Tiki Expedition*), was an international best-seller, and his documentary film won an Academy Award. Yet many scientists dismissed the entire event as a publicity stunt and continued to reject Heyerdahl's theory on the basis that the Galapagos Islands, a chain much closer to South America than Polynesia, had never been settled.

So the Galapagos became Heyerdahl's next stop. In 1953, he and two archaeologists conducted the first thorough excavation of the islands. Pottery fragments and other evidence they unearthed indicated that prehistoric South Americans had indeed visited the Galapagos many times but established no permanent settlements due to an inadequate supply of drinking water.

After completing additional research in several South American countries, Heyerdahl then turned his attention to Easter Island, which, at 2,300 miles west of Chile, is the Polynesian island closest to South America. Teaming up with five archaeologists to examine ancient artifacts, he was able to prove with carbon-dating techniques that humans had been there around 380 A.D. (a thousand years earlier than previously thought) and that three different waves of migration had occurred, including a White-race migration whose members were apparently responsible for carving the island's famous stone statues (similar to some in Peru) and introducing several plants native to South America.

Throughout the late 1950s and early 1960s, Heyerdahl spent much of his time writing, researching, lecturing, and presenting his findings to fellow scientists, some of whom gradually came to accept the idea that Polynesia was settled not only by Asians but by significant numbers of South Americans as well. By that time, however, Heyerdahl was already contemplating yet another possible path of migration—from ancient Egypt to Peru. Anthropologists had long noted many striking similarities between the two cultures, including stepped pyramids and giant stone statues, hieroglyphic writing, sophisticated calendars based on astronomical observations, and customs among royalty involving marriage, mummification, and burial. Heyerdahl himself was intrigued by Egyptian tomb paintings of papyrus ships that closely resembled vessels depicted on ancient Inca pottery. (Smaller and more simplified versions of those boats still sail the waters of Lake Titicaca between Bolivia and Peru.) But no one believed that a ship made of papyrus was capable of crossing the Atlantic.

Heyerdahl again decided to challenge the skeptics and prove that such a journey was indeed possible. In May, 1969, he and a crew of six left Morocco in a fifty-foot-long papyrus raft bound for the Caribbean. Named the *Ra* in honor of the Egyptian sun god and the Polynesian word for the sun, it was a replica of the type of vessel ancient Egyptians had sailed around the Mediterranean. The *Ra* traveled 2,700 miles across the Atlantic in eight weeks before heavy seas forced the crew to abandon ship about 600 miles from Barbados. Ten months later, Heyerdahl and a seven-man crew tried again with a slightly shorter, lighter, and stronger version of the original *Ra*. Dubbed *Ra II*, it completed the 3,200-mile trip from Morocco to

Barbados in fifty-seven days, once again demonstrating that ancient civilizations were not necessarily cut off from one another by the oceans.

Since the *Ra* expeditions, Heyerdahl has continued to pursue his theories regarding prehistoric peoples' travel by sea. In 1977, for example, seeking to prove that the Mesopotamians may have spread their culture as far away as India, he sailed a sixty-foot reed boat called the *Tigris* from the mouth of the Shatt-al-Arab River into the Persian Gulf and from there crossed the Indian Ocean to Pakistan. He has also conducted additional archaeological research on land, including explorations of the Maldives (a chain of islands in the Indian Ocean) that suggest they were a popular stopover for prehistoric traders who sailed between China, India, and Africa. More recently, Heyerdahl has spearheaded an ambitious project to excavate a remote area of Peru where twenty-six pre-Incan pyramids—the largest such complex in the Americas—have been left virtually undisturbed for over a thousand years. Anthropologists disagree whether his findings truly support the idea of cultural migration stretching from Egypt to South America to Polynesia, but on two other points they agree: he has successfully attracted much-needed publicity and funds to the fields of anthropology and archaeology and he has inspired a flurry of research activity, especially in the Pacific islands.

At the heart of all Heyerdahl's work is his unwavering belief in the kinship of all people. He deliberately selected "men from many nations, colors, and creeds" to accompany him on the *Ra* expeditions "to show that such differences do not prevent men from cooperating peacefully for survival." As he remarked at the start of the first *Ra* voyage, "there are so many ties between us that we should be able to act more like one human family than creatures of a different species." Not surprisingly, he feels a similar link to the ancient peoples whose cultures he has studied so thoroughly and harbors a deep respect for their accomplishments. "We have the egoistic idea that we in the 20th century are the civilized ones," Heyerdahl once told a *People* magazine reporter. "That people living 1,000 years ago, not to mention 5,000 years ago, were greatly inferior to us. I am opposed to that. The people back then were physically and mentally our equal—if not in many ways better. . . .

We couldn't survive using our brains, as ancient people did. But they would certainly have been capable of watching a television."

Sources

➤ **Books**

Heyerdahl, Thor, *Kon-Tiki: Across the Pacific by Raft,* Rand McNally, 1950. New edition. *The Kon-Tiki Expedition,* 1968.

Heyerdahl, Thor, *Aku-Aku: The Secret of Easter Island,* Rand McNally, 1958.

Heyerdahl, Thor, *The Ra Expeditions,* Doubleday, 1970.

Heyerdahl, Thor, with Christopher Ralling, *Kon-Tiki Man: An Illustrated Biography of Thor Heyerdahl,* Chronicle, 1991.

➤ **Periodicals**

Architectural Digest, "Profiles: Thor Heyerdahl," February, 1987, pp. 102–109.

National Geographic, "The Voyage of *Ra II,*" January, 1971, pp. 44–70 (opening quote).

Newsweek, "In Search of the Sun God," August 7, 1967, p. 11; "Voyage of the Ra," May 26, 1969, pp. 56–58; "Why? Because It Is There," March 10, 1980, pp. 16–17.

People, "Thor Heyerdahl," December 11, 1989, pp. 181–188.

Time, "From Eden to India," November 28, 1977, p. 116.

U.S. News and World Report, "Heyerdahl's Voyage: Modern Sea Epic," July 27, 1970, p. 49; "Thor Heyerdahl: Sailing Against the Current," April 2, 1990, pp. 55–60; "Why I Am Digging at Tucume," April 2, 1990, pp. 56–57.

➤ **Other**

Several of Heyerdahl's expeditions have been documented on film, including his voyages on the *Kon-Tiki* (RKO, 1951), both *Ra* ships (Interwest, 1972), and the *Tigris* (BBC, 1979), as well as his trip to the Galapagos Islands (1955).

Langston Hughes

"**I** didn't know the upper class Negroes well enough to write much about them. I knew only the people I had grown up with, and they weren't the people whose shoes were always shined, who had been to Harvard, or who had heard of Bach. But they seemed to me good people, too."

Born on February 1, 1902, in Joplin, Missouri, Langston Hughes was for several decades the most popular Black-American writer in the U.S. He died on May 22, 1967, in New York City.

One of the most talented and prolific writers to emerge from the Harlem Renaissance of the 1920s, Langston Hughes enjoyed a long and successful career as a poet and author of short stories, novels, magazine and newspaper articles, plays, and numerous other works. His respect for the lives of "plain Black people" resonated throughout everything he produced, as did his gentle, folksy humor and compassion tinged with sorrow. Early in his career, he endured criticism from those who felt he betrayed his race by portraying the less attractive aspects of Black-American life; later, he was rejected by a younger and more militant generation of Black-American writers for his reluctance to display bitterness or take a strong political stand in his writings. Through it all, Hughes remained true to his own vision of a world where most people were basically good and the future still offered hope that all races would one day live together in harmony and understanding.

A native of Joplin, Missouri, who spent most of his youth in Lawrence, Kansas, James Langston Hughes was the only child of James and Carrie Langston Hughes. James Hughes deserted his wife before Langston was born and moved to Mexico to seek his fortune; he did not even meet his son until the child was five years old. While Carrie Hughes went from city to city searching for work, first her mother, Mary Langston, and then some family friends, James and Mary Reed, raised young Langston. In 1915, he joined his mother and her second husband in Cleveland, Ohio, where he attended high school. An excellent student, he wrote verses for the school magazine in a style similar to that of his favorite poets, Carl Sandburg and Walt Whitman, but incorporating Black-American dialects, words, and rhythms.

After graduating from high school, Hughes turned to his long-absent father for financial help so that he could attend New York City's Columbia University and become a poet. The elder Hughes scoffed at the notion of a Black man studying anything so impractical and refused to help unless Langston agreed to study engineering instead. After a brief stint as a teacher in Mexico (during which time he also contributed his first material to NAACP publications, including *Crisis* and *Brownies' Book*, a magazine for children), the young man finally agreed to his father's conditions and enrolled at Columbia in the fall of 1921. But Hughes soon grew bored with his classes and dropped out of school after spring term in 1922 to spend more time with members of the NAACP staff and others who were part of the "Harlem Renaissance," a growing Black-American intellectual and artistic movement.

Supporting himself by doing odd jobs, Hughes soaked up life in Harlem and its environs during this exciting period and published poems on a steady basis, including "The Weary Blues," a brilliant piece that perfectly captured the sounds and rhythms of street talk and music. He also traveled to Africa and Europe, working his way across the Atlantic on board various freighters. (He reported on his experiences in Africa in a popular series of articles written for *Crisis*.) In early 1924, on his third trip overseas, Hughes quit his job and headed for Paris, where he worked as a dishwasher in a nightclub and managed to save enough money to travel to Spain and Italy before returning to New York in November, 1924.

In early 1925, Hughes moved to Washington, D.C., with hopes of attending Howard University. Denied a scholarship, he instead worked at a series of menial, low-paying jobs. Then his luck suddenly began to change. Around mid-year, "The Weary Blues" won an award and attracted the attention of writer and critic Carl Van Vechten, a prominent supporter of Black-American authors and artists, who used his influence to have some of Hughes's poems published in *Vanity Fair* magazine. Van Vechten also persuaded his own publisher, Knopf, to bring out an edition of the young poet's works. Its publication in January, 1926 (under the title *The Weary Blues*), coincided with poet Vachel Lindsay's "discovery" of Hughes. While working as a busboy in a New York City hotel where Lindsay was dining before giving a reading, Hughes slipped him a few of his own pieces, which Lindsay then shared with his audience as the work of a promising young Black-American poet. The exposure quickly made Hughes a celebrity and launched his career as a writer.

With royalties from *The Weary Blues*, payments for various magazine articles, and some prize money, plus financial help from Amy Spingarn, a member of a wealthy family that contributed generously to the NAACP and other Black-American organizations, Hughes was at last able to attend college. He chose Lincoln University, an all-Black school near Philadelphia. Between the time he enrolled in February, 1926, and his graduation in 1929, Hughes spent most of his free time writing. In 1927, Knopf brought out another collection of his poems, *Fine Clothes to the Jew*, an earthy and unsentimental look at life among those at the bottom of society—prostitutes, alcoholics, and the miserably poor. Although the book was a success with literary magazines and the White press, middle-class Black-American intellectuals condemned it as trash and attacked Hughes for perpetuating negative views of Black people.

During the 1930s, Hughes periodically experienced spiritual crises and creative slumps, which seriously affected the quality and quantity of his work. His antidote was often travel, which not only revitalized him but afforded him the opportunity to do research and reach "his people" through poetry readings. Over the course of the decade, he visited Cuba several times (where he met and became lifelong friends with many young writers), Haiti, the Soviet Union, Japan, China, Mexico, and Europe and toured throughout the southern and western United States. When he was able to write, he produced numerous poems, articles, and other works, including a much-praised semiautobiographical novel, *Not Without Laughter;* a collection of short stories, *The Ways of White Folks;* a Broadway play, *Mulatto;* and an autobiography, *The Big Sea.*

The 1930s also saw the awakening of Hughes's political radicalism as he observed the effects of the Depression during his travels. Like so many artists and intellectuals of his era, he was particularly impressed by the Soviet Union and regarded it as a symbol of hope and a model of action. While he was never officially a member of the American Communist party, he did become affiliated with various other left-wing groups, causes, and publications. Gradually, some of his writings took on a more radical tone, which made them difficult to sell to mainstream publishers in the United States. Finally, following a visit to Spain during which he reported on the civil war there for the Associated Press, the Baltimore *Afro-American*, and the Alliance of Antifascist Intellectuals, Hughes came to the realization that he could not be quite as militant as he had been if he expected to be able to earn a living as a writer.

Returning to the United States in 1938, Hughes at first focused on writing and producing plays for the Harlem Suitcase Theater. He then served a brief stint as a screenwriter in Hollywood but found the experience humiliating because he was expected to adhere to the racial stereotypes then common in films. After completing *The Big Sea*, Hughes went back to writing poetry and short stories. Although he was still committed to social justice and racial equality, he toned down his radicalism and opted for a gentler approach incorporating humor and irony. His principal mouthpiece was Jesse B. Semple (also known as just "Simple"), a character who debuted in 1943 in a series of extremely popular short stories that appeared over a twenty-three-year period, first in the *Chicago Defender* and the *New York Post* and later in four separate book collections. A sort of barfly philosopher who shares his troubles with a writer in exchange for a drink, the folksy Simple does not directly challenge racism yet clearly illustrates the difficulties a poor Black man faces in a racist society and the quiet determination necessary to overcome those difficulties.

By the end of the 1940s, more and more Americans were coming to recognize Hughes as one of the country's major writers. In the early 1950s, however, his radical past came under scrutiny by the House Un-American Activities Committee (HUAC), which ordered him to explain his ties to the Communist party. At his hearing, he admitted to his past associations but, unlike many others who were called before the committee, he was not asked to name his fellow "subversives." Despite this rather lenient treatment, Hughes nevertheless felt the impact of the investigation on his career as some groups picketed his lectures and reading tours or canceled them altogether. He was able to continue writing, however, publishing *Montage of a Dream Deferred*, an ambitious series of poems describing a day and a night in Harlem; *I Wonder As I Wander*, the second volume of his autobiography; and *Selected Poems*, a collection he assembled himself that omitted many of his more politically radical pieces.

During the last decade of his life, Hughes continued to write, focusing mainly on plays that proved commercially unsuccessful. He also reviewed the fiction of younger Black-American authors and toured Africa and Europe on behalf of the U.S. State Department as a cultural ambassador. In early 1967, his health began to fail, and on May 22 of that year, he died of uremia.

Although he was often called the poet laureate of his people, Langston Hughes nevertheless endured the criticism of many of his fellow Black Americans for displaying a lack of "responsibility" in his writing. Yet he enjoyed the unconditional love and acceptance of those whose lives he knew best—the "workers, roustabouts, and singers, and job hunters on Lenox Avenue in New York, or Seventh Street in Washington or South State in Chicago—people up today and down tomorrow, working this week and fired the next, beaten and baffled, but determined not to be wholly beaten, buying furniture on the installment plan, filling the house with roomers to help pay the rent, hoping to get a new suit for Easter—and pawning that suit before the Fourth of July."

Sources

► **Books**

Black Writers, Gale, 1989 (opening quote).

Hughes, Langston, *The Big Sea: An Autobiography,* Knopf, 1950.

Hughes, Langston, *I Wander As I Wander: An Autobiographical Journey,* Rinehart, 1956.

Meltzer, Milton, *Langston Hughes: A Biography,* Crowell, 1968.

Myers, Elizabeth P., *Langston Hughes: Poet of His People,* Garrard, 1970.

Rummel, Jack, *Langston Hughes,* Chelsea House, 1988.

► **Periodicals**

Newsweek, "The Death of Simple," June 5, 1967, p. 104.

Time, June 2, 1967, p. 59.

Wilson Library Bulletin, "Hughes, Twain, Child, and Sanger: Four Who Locked Horns with the Censors," November, 1969, pp. 278–286.

Daniel Inouye

"*T*he 17-year-old high-school boy who set out on his bicycle that morning of December 7, 1941, was lost forever amid the debris, and the dead and the dying, of the war's first day."

Daniel Inouye became Hawaii's first U.S. representative and the first Japanese-American elected to the House. A U.S. senator since 1962, he was born on September 7, 1924, in Honolulu.

Address: Hart Senate Office Bldg., Second and C Streets, Washington, D.C. 20510.

Daniel Ken Inouye was a senior in high school and contemplating a career in medicine when the United States entered World War II following the Japanese bombing of Pearl Harbor. A native of Hawaii, he was a *nisei*, the child of a Japanese immigrant to the islands. His father, Hyotaro Inouye, eked out a living as a clerk to provide for his wife, Kame Imanaga (herself a *nisei*), and the four Inouye children. They lived in one of Honolulu's worst slums, but as their oldest son later wrote in his autobiography, "I was too young to realize how underprivileged I was, and foolishly I enjoyed every moment of my childhood. There was always enough to eat in our house—although sometimes barely—but even more important, there was a conviction that opportunity awaited those who had the heart and strength to pursue it."

On the morning of December 7, 1941, the family was dressing for church when news came over the radio of the air raid in progress at Pearl Harbor, several miles from the Inouye home. Everyone ran outside and watched the smoke rise in the sky above the spot where the U.S. Pacific fleet was anchored. Then the telephone rang, and Daniel was asked to report immediately to the Red Cross station where he had been teaching first aid. "It would be five days before I returned—a lifetime—and I would never be the same," Inouye recalled.

Over the next few months, Inouye attended high school during the day and worked a twelve-hour shift for the Red Cross at night, training new volunteers and directing the first-aid program at his school. It was an exhausting schedule, but one he felt compelled to follow. "Like all *nisei*," he said, "I was driven by an insidious sense of guilt from the instant the first Japanese plane appeared over Pearl Harbor. Of course we had nothing to feel guilty about, but we all carried this special burden. We felt it in the streets, where white men would sneer as we passed. We felt it in school when we heard our friends and neighbors called Jap lovers. We felt it in the widely held suspicion that the *nisei* were a sort of built-in fifth column in Hawaii."

In September, 1942, Inouye enrolled in the pre-med program at the University of Hawaii. He also joined a group of young Japanese-American men who had been pressing the U.S. government for the opportunity to serve in the war and thus demonstrate their loyalty. A series of rulings thwarted them at almost every turn, however, as *nisei* were discharged from the National Guard, the ROTC, and the Territorial Guard and forced to surrender their weapons; those already in the service were transferred to non-combat duty. Then in January, 1943, the War Department announced that it would accept fifteen hundred *nisei* volunteers to help form a new combat unit. Nearly a thousand men—including Inouye—signed up on the first day alone. Rejected at first because of his first-aid work and status as a pre-med student, he resigned from the Red Cross, quit school, and tried again. This time, Inouye was accepted and immediately left for training on the mainland as part of the 442nd Regimental Combat Team.

Adopting the motto Go for broke!, the 442nd became the most decorated unit in U.S. history, and young Inouye emerged as one of its most heroic leaders. While fighting in Italy just days before the war in Europe ended, he led his platoon in an assault on a heavily defended German infantry position on a high ridge. As he moved toward the enemy bunkers, Lieutenant Inouye was wounded in the stomach by machine-gun fire. Waving off his men, he managed to lob a grenade into the nearest bunker and cut down the Germans who emerged after it exploded. Continuing his crawl up the hill, he wiped out another bunker. His platoon charged forward, only to meet fierce resistance from a third group of machine gunners. In the meantime, Inouye kept inching his way along the side of the hill and positioned himself to throw another grenade into the third bunker. Just as he drew his arm back, a German soldier stood up and fired a rifle grenade at him, hitting his right elbow and all but tearing his arm off. Inouye pried his grenade from his now-useless right hand and threw it with his left, killing the German. Dragging himself to his feet, he approached the bunker, firing his gun left-handed and taking another hit in the right leg before collapsing and rolling down the hill. Medical personnel evacuated the twenty-year-old Inouye as soon as the area was secure.

Inouye spent the next two years in the hospital recovering from his wounds and the amputation of his arm. Discharged in 1947, he returned to Hawaii, determined to continue his schooling. Medicine was now out of the question, "but I didn't care," said Inouye. "I wanted now to become a lawyer in the hope of entering public life." He obtained his B.A. in 1950 from the University of Hawaii, then went on to George Washington University Law School in Washington, D.C., from which he graduated in 1952.

Throughout his college years, Inouye was active in various student government and veterans' organizations; he worked for the Democratic National Committee while in Washington. After receiving his law degree and returning to Honolulu, he became involved in territorial politics, joining with others to wrest control of the local Democratic party from a communist-dominated union whose radicalism had cemented the Republican plantation owners' hold on the legislature. By 1954, Inouye and his colleagues felt confident enough to take on the Republicans. In that year's elections, the Democrats won a majority of the seats in both the Territorial House and Senate. Inouye himself was elected to the House, serving two terms as majority leader before switching to the Territorial Senate, where he also served as majority leader for a term.

In July, 1959, several months after Hawaii became the fiftieth state, a special election was held to determine who would go to Washington as the island's first member of the House of Representatives. Inouye was the overwhelming choice, becoming the first American of Japanese ancestry to serve in the House. These "firsts," along with his status as a war hero, made the thirty-four-year-old lawyer a celebrity in Washington, but he quickly shunned the limelight to settle into what he termed the "business of learning how to get things done." He easily won reelection to Congress in 1960, and in 1962 he ran for a Senate seat and was elected in a landslide. He has defeated his opponents in every election since then, garnering at least seventy-four percent of the vote each time.

During his long tenure in the U.S. Senate, Inouye has earned a reputation as a party loyalist with a talent for compromise. Praised for his integrity and fairness, he has served in a number of leadership posts and was even mentioned as a vice-presidential candidate on several occasions, especially after his keynote address at the 1968 Democratic National Convention met with nationwide acclaim. Inouye has consistently supported liberal causes (except on defense issues, which tend to bring out a more conservative streak in him), championing the civil rights movement during the Kennedy and Johnson administrations and acting as a spokesman for Asian-Americans. He continued to vote as a moderate or liberal during the Ford, Carter, and Reagan years, backing such causes as abortion rights and gun control as well as legislation favoring organized labor and consumers. It is, however, as a member of the Senate Appropriations Committee that Inouye has wielded the most clout;

as chairman of the Foreign Operations Subcommittee, he is one of just a few people who has directed American foreign policy by allocating aid where he and others on the subcommittee see fit. In this role he has shown himself to be a strong supporter of Israel and a staunch anti-communist.

Nationally, Inouye is best known for his role in two major Senate investigations: as a member of the Watergate committee in 1973 and 1974 and as chairman of the Iran-contra hearings in 1987. Although only a junior member, he made his biggest impact as part of the Watergate committee. While questioning former White House aide John D. Ehrlichman, Inouye—thinking his microphone was turned off—was heard to mutter, "What a liar!" Ehrlichman's attorney in turn attacked the senator, referring to him in public as "that little Jap." Already widely admired for his patience and tenacity in dealing with reluctant witnesses, Inouye received a flood of public support in the wake of this ethnic slur.

Soft spoken and low key, Inouye has always preferred to operate quietly and effectively behind the scenes, "doing his best work where it is least noticed," according to Ronald D. Elving in the *Congressional Quarterly Weekly Report*. "His words have weight. He is one Democrat who does not casually take the Senate floor or adopt a forward position on an issue. When he does, he usually prevails."

Sources

➤ **Books**

Inouye, Daniel K., and Lawrence Elliott, *Journey to Washington*, Prentice-Hall, 1967.

➤ **Periodicals**

Congressional Quarterly Weekly Report, "The Quiet Insider: Hawaii's Daniel Inouye Wields a Private, Personal Power," April 16, 1988, p. 979.
Newsweek, August 10, 1959, pp. 22–24; April 9, 1962, pp. 39–40.

Reader's Digest, "Go for Broke!" (condensed version of *Journey to Washington*), February, 1968 (opening quote).

Time, "New Faces in Congress," August 10, 1959, p. 13; August 27, 1973, p. 18.

Pope John XXIII

"**T**oday more than ever, we are called on to defend above all and everywhere the rights of the human person, and not merely those of the Catholic Church. . . . It is not that the gospel has changed; it is that we have begun to understand it better."

One of the most beloved popes in the history of the Roman Catholic Church, Pope John XXIII sparked an era of wide-ranging renewal within the Church and redefined its role in world affairs. He was born on November 25, 1881, in Sotto il Monte, Italy, and died on June 3, 1963, at the Vatican Palace.

On October 28, 1958, the Roman Catholic Church's College of Cardinals announced the election of a new pontiff: seventy-six-year-old Angelo Roncalli, a veteran of the Vatican diplomatic service. The decision came as a bit of a surprise, for Roncalli was not one of the better known or most accomplished cardinals; most people assumed he was a compromise candidate who would serve briefly and unremarkably as a "caretaker" pope. But virtually from the day he was crowned, Pope John XXIII (the name Roncalli chose for himself) made it clear that he intended to look at the Church with a fresh eye, thus paving the way for a series of sweeping changes the likes of which Roman Catholicism had not experienced for nearly four hundred years. In the process, he won the hearts of millions of people both inside and outside the Church with his immense personal charm and what a *Time* reporter called "a love that broke down barriers."

Angelo Guiseppe Roncalli was the third of thirteen children born to a poor tenant farmer, Giovanni Battista Roncalli, and his wife, Marianna Mazzola Roncalli. At the age of twelve, the future pope (who in later years remarked that he couldn't recall ever wanting to be anything other than a priest) enrolled in a seminary in the town of Bergamo, only a few miles from his native village in northern Italy. Seven years later, he went to Rome for further study, which was interrupted in 1902 by a year of compulsory service in the Italian army.

Ordained a priest in 1904, Roncalli first served as secretary to the new bishop of Bergamo, Giacomo Radini-Tedeschi, an innovative and compassionate man who exerted a powerful influence on his young protege. The bishop's death, which coincided with the outbreak of World War I in August, 1914, was a great personal blow to Roncalli. But he had little time to dwell on his loss, for in mid-1915 he was again drafted into the Italian army. He served for over two years, first in the medical corps and later in the chaplains' corps.

In 1921, Pope Benedict XV summoned Roncalli to Rome to reorganize the Society for the Propagation of the Faith, a group that supported Catholic missions outside Italy. His skillful handling of the position resulted in his appointment to the Vatican diplomatic corps in 1925 and elevation to the rank of archbishop. Roncalli's first assignment was in Bulgaria, where he greatly improved relations with the dominant Eastern Orthodox Church. Later, as papal envoy to the Moslem nation of Turkey, he established many friendly contacts that proved especially useful during World War II, when he passed along valuable information about war plans to the Vatican and arranged safe passage for Eastern European Jews fleeing the Nazis. In late 1944, Roncalli was appointed papal ambassador to France, a country bitterly divided by four years of German occupation and French collaboration and resistance. Roncalli successfully resolved many of the issues that had alienated the French from each other and from the Church, and by the time he left his post in 1953 as a newly appointed cardinal, he was one of the most popular figures in the country.

Back home in Italy, Roncalli settled into his new position as patriarch of Venice, relishing the chance to do what he had always wanted to do: minister "directly to souls" as "a real pastor in the full sense of the word." Five years later, the death of Pope Pius XII brought the cardinal's pleasant semi-retirement to an abrupt end. Although at nearly seventy-seven he felt he was too old to take on such a demanding job, on October 28, 1958, Roncalli accepted the results of a vote by his fellow cardinals electing him as the new pope. In honor of his father and the name of the church in which he was baptized, he took the name John.

To the amazement of those who had not expected much of him, Pope John immediately set out to revolutionize the Church. Uncomfortable with many of the traditional formalities of his position, including the fact that the pope always dined alone and rarely ventured outside the Vatican, he invited guests to join him for dinner, occasionally attended the theater, and made regular (and often unannounced) visits to churches, hospitals, orphanages, prisons, and even the slums of Rome. His goal was to make the Church more meaningful to the everyday lives of Catholics and less mysterious and threatening to non-Catholics; he felt one of the best ways to do that was to let people see for themselves that he was a genuinely concerned and very approachable leader.

Before long, Pope John turned his attention to far more substantial issues. His experiences in the diplomatic corps had convinced him of the need for closer ties not only among Catholics but among Christians and ultimately among all religions in order to bring about a just and peaceful world. Fostering such unity and cooperation—known as ecumenism—thus became one of his chief concerns and the motivating factor behind some precedent-setting decisions, including the creation of a special department within the Vatican to handle the Church's relations with non-Catholics. He was also the first pope to assign Vatican observers to attend important conferences held by other faiths and the first to meet with non-Catholic religious leaders.

In addition to ending the Church's estrangement from other Christian faiths, Pope John also worked to overcome its political isolationism. He met with more world leaders than any of his predecessors and was especially interested in reducing the hostility between the Church and communist nations such as the Soviet Union and its Eastern European allies. Cold war tensions between the superpowers preoccupied him, too, and on several occasions he either volunteered his services as a mediator or personally appealed to government officials for a peaceful resolution to a crisis.

Pope John's most heartfelt plea for justice and peace appeared in an encyclical he wrote, which ranks among the most significant documents in Church history. Released on Easter Sunday 1963, *Pacem in Terris* or *Peace on Earth* was the first such message addressed not just to Catholics but to "all men of good will." In this document, Pope John emphasized that every human being has a right to truth, justice, order, and freedom and that governments have a duty to promote and protect these rights so that their citizens can flourish, "for there can be no exterior peace if it is not the reflected image of interior peace." In addition, he called for an end to the arms race, a ban on nuclear weapons, and more cooperative efforts like the United Nations. Although Pope John was certainly not the first person to advocate these measures, he was the first pope to support democratic ideals without conditions or exceptions as well as the first pope to endorse the work of a secular body such as the United Nations. *Pacem in Terris* was thus acclaimed worldwide for its compassionate and nonpartisan approach to solving problems of interest to all humankind.

By far the most dramatic and enduring event of John's papacy was the convening of a Vatican council, a special conference at which all of the Church's bishops meet to formulate religious doctrine and discuss various issues of concern. The first council to be held in nearly 100 years and only the twenty-first in the 2,000-year history of the Church, Vatican II (as it came to be known) reexamined Catholic teachings in light of twentieth-century changes in science, economics, politics, and morals. The goal of the 2,500 bishops in attendance—as Pope John explained to them at the opening ceremonies on October 11, 1962—was not to reject any basic tenets of the faith but to adapt them to the realities of the modern world and thus endow the Church with a new and more positive spirit. In keeping with the pope's commitment to ecumenism, about forty Protestant and Orthodox clergymen were invited to observe the proceedings, another momentous first in Church history.

Pope John did not live to see the results of Vatican II; already ill at the time the first session began, he died of stomach cancer on June 3, 1963, three months before the council's second session was scheduled to get under way. He nevertheless set in motion a process that ultimately led to a number of profound changes. As a result of Vatican II, priests were allowed for the first time to celebrate mass in languages other than Latin, bishops were granted more authority, and lay people took on bigger roles in Church affairs. The council's ecumenical slant was reflected in a softened attitude toward church-state relations, the issue of religious freedom, and Protestantism. (Until Pope John came along, Protestants were still regarded as heretics.)

An extraordinary man and an even more extraordinary pope, John unleashed forces within the Roman Catholic Church that sparked truly revolutionary changes in its public image and internal direction, "cutting through centuries of legalism and stale traditions to somewhere near the heart of what it means to be a Christian," as James O'Gara declared in the *Commonweal*. And during especially tense and tumultuous period in world affairs, Pope John conveyed a sense of hope that unity and peace were still attainable. "Men have come and gone," he once remarked, "but I have always remained an optimist, because that is my nature."

Sources

➤ **Books**

Hales, E. E. Y., *Pope John and His Revolution,* Eyre & Spottiswoode, 1965.

Hatch, Alden, *A Man Named John,* Hawthorn Books, 1963.

Hebblethwaite, Peter, *Pope John XXIII: Shepherd of the Modern World,* Doubleday, 1985.

John XXIII, *Journal of a Soul,* Doubleday, 1966.

Johnson, Paul, *Pope John XXIII,* Little, Brown, 1975.

Kaiser, Robert B., *Pope, Council, and World: The Story of Vatican II,* Macmillan, 1963.

Walch, Timothy, *Pope John XXIII*, Chelsea House, 1987 (opening quote).

➤ **Periodicals**

America, "The Good Shepherd," June 15, 1963, p. 852; "Looking Back at Pope John," June 29, 1963, pp. 903–905; "The Heritage of Pope John," July 13, 1963, pp. 48–50.

Christian Century, "Pope John XXIII," June 12, 1963, pp. 763–764.

Commonweal, "Pope John," June 14, 1963, pp. 315–316; "Good Pope John," June 28, 1963, p. 366; "Another St. Francis?," June 28, 1963, pp. 367–369; "Voice of the Good Shepherd," June 28, 1963, pp. 369–371; "A Gift of Holiness," June 28, 1963, pp. 371–372; "Break with the Past," June 28, 1963, pp. 372–375.

Newsweek, "Pope John XXIII: Gentle Shepherd of a Revolution," June 10, 1963, pp. 42–48.

New York Times, June 4, 1963.

Time, "Man of the Year," January 4, 1963, pp. 50–54; "Vatican Revolutionary," June 7, 1963, pp. 41–43; "*Vere Papa Mortuus Est,*" June 14, 1963, p. 46.

U.S. News and World Report, "Changes in the Church and World: The Work of Pope John," June 10, 1963, pp. 50–51.

Mother Jones

"*I belong to a class which has been robbed, exploited, and plundered down through many long centuries. And because I belong to that class, I have an impulse to go and help break the chains.*"

Born on May 1, 1830, in county Cork, Ireland, Mother Jones was one of America's first union activists. She died on November 30, 1930, in Silver Springs, Maryland.

A pioneer in the American labor movement, Mother Jones was a feisty, outspoken champion of the men, women, and children who regularly put in twelve- to fourteen-hour days amid conditions so wretched they could justifiably be compared to slavery. Arrested, jailed, and threatened on numerous occasions for what was then termed "agitating," she never wavered in her support for the working poor. "If they want to hang me, let them hang me," she once proclaimed. "But when I am on the scaffold, I'll cry 'Freedom for the working class!'"

Although the exact date of Mary Harris Jones's birth is subject to dispute, she always maintained she was born on May 1, 1830. She was the first child of Mary and Robert Harris, poor tenants on the estate of a well-to-do landowner for whom Robert worked as a hired hand. In 1835, after he ran afoul of the authorities for participating in a series of violent uprisings against the much-hated landlords, Robert Harris fled to the United States. His family—including Mary and her two younger brothers—finally joined him in New York City in 1841. Not long after, the Harrises moved to Toronto, Canada, where Robert joined a crew laying railroad tracks.

Barely able to read and write themselves, Mary's parents made sure their children took advantage of Toronto's free public schools. Mary was an excellent student who progressed rapidly, and within just a few years she became the first member of the Harris family to graduate from high school. Eager to become a teacher but barred from working in the Toronto system because she had been raised in the Roman Catholic Church, she headed for the United States, serving first as a private tutor in Maine for two years and then as a teacher at a convent in Michigan. But Mary found the strict discipline of the religious school intolerable, so she left after only a year to try her hand at dressmaking in Chicago.

Arriving there in 1858, Mary was barely able to earn a living and within two years decided to return to the classroom. Hearing that Memphis was in need of teachers, she went there during the summer of 1860 and immediately landed a job for the fall term. But before school began she married George Jones, a native Tennessean who worked as an iron molder and part-time union organizer. Over the next six years, Mary gave birth to four children, and George left the foundry for a full-time position with the union. The end of the Civil War led to an economic boom in Memphis, and the Joneses lived quietly and comfortably amid the new prosperity. The good times came to an end during the summer of 1867, however, when a yellow fever epidemic swept through the city. As September drew to a close and gave way to October, Mary's children died one by one, followed by her husband.

Completely alone and again faced with the need to earn a living, Mary returned to Chicago and resumed working as a seamstress, earning a small but adequate income sewing clothes, draperies, and furniture coverings for some of the city's wealthiest people. The contrast between their lavish lifestyle and the grim existence of the slum dwellers across town disturbed her, especially since her customers seemed oblivious to the poverty and hunger in their midst. She grew even angrier after the Great Chicago Fire of 1871, a devastating blaze that destroyed one-sixth of the city, including Jones's own working-class neighborhood. The rich had the means to recover from such a loss, thanks to insurance and other resources. But what would happen to everyone else?

Jones was walking through the remains of her old neighborhood one evening when she came across a meeting of the Knights of Labor, a secret organization made up of workers from all professions. Dedicated to the philosophy of cooperative ownership of property—an economic revolution that they hoped to achieve gradually and peacefully—the Knights and their idealism appealed to Jones, who pledged her support on the spot. She quickly became one of the most active members, arranging meetings and speaking to groups of workers all over Chicago. Before long, she had given up sewing in favor of full-time organizing for the Knights, marking the beginning of her sixty-year association with unionism.

At first, Jones was content with the Knights' opposition to strikes and other forms of direct confrontation with management. But as time went on, she grew increasingly impatient and frustrated with their conservatism and inaction. She severed her ties with the group in the mid-1880s and left Chicago to work on behalf of the labor movement as she saw fit—in short, by meeting problems head-on and refusing to negotiate when she felt issues of injustice were at stake. Although it is not clear exactly where she went or what she did over the next few years, Jones definitely remained true to her convictions; by 1890 the name "Mother Jones" was regularly appearing in newspaper accounts of strikes in several different parts of the country. She was especially drawn to miners—she called them "her boys"—and they in turn relied on her for help more than any other outsider. Long hours, low wages, dangerous working conditions, ramshackle living quarters, and repressive social and economic policies were the norm for miners in the late 1800s, and Mother Jones was determined to "raise hell," as she put it.

In 1891, while supporting some Virginia coal miners who had gone on strike, Mother Jones began working as an unofficial organizer for the United Mine Workers of America (UMW); in 1897 she became an official, salaried organizer. According to the accounts of those who saw her in action, she was a flamboyant speaker who shouted, stamped her feet, and used hand gestures to rally the crowd, with some humor and occasional rough language thrown in for emphasis. Sitting down with the miners wherever they congregated, she tried to instill them with dignity, pride, and a fighting spirit. She involved their families, too, organizing wives and sometimes children into "mop and broom brigades," arming them with pots, pans, brooms, and mops and sending them to block strikebreakers from entering the mines. In an era when harassment, beatings, and arrests were common ways of dealing with union organizers and strikers, and when speeches and rallies were often prohibited on orders from a judge, the elderly woman (Jones was over sixty by this time) in the conservative black dress and plain bonnet taunted company guards to shoot her and openly defied their orders to stay away from the miners.

From the early 1890s until around 1920, when rheumatism began to sap her strength, Mother Jones participated in hundreds of strikes across the country, most of them involving "her boys." As she became more widely known and despised by some as "the most dangerous woman in America," judges and guards grew less lenient; she was arrested on several occasions and jailed at least four times, including once in West Virginia when she spent three months in solitary confinement in a military prison. Another time in Colorado she was held without explanation for twenty-six days in the cellar of a county courthouse. She also endured personal attacks on her character ranging from vicious accusations of alcoholism and prostitution to milder charges of being "unladylike." This latter slur Mother Jones dismissed in typically colorful fashion. "A lady is the last thing on earth I want to be," she declared, noting that "capitalists sidetrack the women into clubs and make ladies of them. Nobody wants a lady, they want women. Ladies are parlor parasites."

In addition to her work on behalf of the miners, Mother Jones periodically took up the cause of child labor. Her efforts to draw national attention to the issue failed to bring about any substantial change in the laws, however; children working long hours and being maimed and killed by machinery was "old news" by the turn of the century and did not attract much publicity, even when Mother Jones was the one doing the talking.

In 1920, at the age of ninety, Mother Jones finally decided it was time to take a rest. She had been on the move almost constantly since the early 1870s, and having devoted that entire time to the labor movement, she had little money and no place to live. But the venerable old woman was a virtual legend among mine workers, who willingly opened their homes to her. Eventually she settled in Silver Springs, Maryland, where she lived with a retired mine worker and his wife. It was under an apple tree in front of their house that Mother Jones made one of her last public appearances. Frail and ill, she was carried outside to attend a celebration in honor of her 100th birthday on May 1, 1930. There she gave a rousing speech that listeners felt was every bit as fiery as any she had given thirty years before. Seven months later, on November 30, Mother Jones died. At her request, her body was taken to Mount Olive, Illinois, for burial in Miners Cemetery, the only union-owned cemetery in the country. There, in the presence of thousands of mourners, including more than four thousand mine workers, she was laid to rest near the graves of four men who had been killed in 1898 during a brutal strike at a mine not far away.

In his introduction to Mother Jones's autobiography, completed just a few years before her death, famed attorney Clarence Darrow briefly yet eloquently described the woman who set aside her own personal tragedy and hardship to fight for the rights of American workers. "In all her career, Mother Jones never quailed or ran away," wrote Darrow. "Her deep convictions and fearless soul always drew her to seek the spot where the fight was hottest and the danger greatest. . . . In both the day and the night, in the poor villages and at the lonely cabin on the mountainside, Mother Jones always appeared in time of need."

Sources

➤ **Books**

Atkinson, Linda, *Mother Jones, the Most Dangerous Woman in America*, Crown, 1978 (opening quote).

Jones, Mary, *Autobiography of Mother Jones*, Arno, 1969.

> **Periodicals**

Nation, December 10, 1930, p. 637.

New York Times, "Mother Jones at 100 Years Is Still Fiery; Loudly Denounces 'Capitalists' for Talkie," May 2, 1930, p. 25; "Mother Jones Dies; Led Mine Workers," December 1, 1930, p. 24; December 2, 1930, p. 24, p. 30; December 4, 1930, p. 25; December 6, 1930, p. 17; December 8, 1930, p. 21; December 9, 1930, p. 27.

Michael Jordan

"I *don't feel I've reached my peak as a player. I truly feel like I'll get better as I get older. As long as I have a challenge in front of me, I'm never at the top of my game."*

Born on February 17, 1963, in Brooklyn, New York, Michael Jordan is regarded by many people as the most gifted player in the history of basketball.

Address: Chicago Bulls, 980 North Michigan Ave., Suite 1600, Chicago, IL 60611–4501.

On the evening of June 12, 1991, millions of television sets were tuned to the fifth game of the National Basketball Association (NBA) finals between the Los Angeles Lakers and the Chicago Bulls. Dubbed "The Magic vs. Michael Finals" in reference to the two biggest stars on the court—Earvin "Magic" Johnson of the Lakers and Michael Jordan of the Bulls—the contest thus far had been dominated by Chicago, now only one victory away from claiming its first-ever championship. For Jordan, however, much more than that was at stake. Although he was unquestionably the most electrifying player in the league, he was part of a team that seemed destined to lose the "big" games, and to some people that meant he wasn't quite as good as *true* superstars like Magic, Larry Bird, and Julius Erving, all members of teams that had won NBA titles.

When the Bulls swept past the Lakers that night, a tearful Michael Jordan realized that he had at last overcome whatever remaining doubts there were—including his own—that "great players who never win a title are somehow less great than those who do," as *Time's* Richard Stengel put it. "I think people will now feel it's OK to put me in the category of players like Magic," Jordan told Jack McCallum of *Sports Illustrated.* "The championship, in the minds of a lot of people, is a sign of, well, greatness. I guess they can say that about me now."

Michael Jeffrey Jordan, the second youngest of five children of James and Deloris Jordan, was born in Brooklyn, New York, but grew up in Wilmington, North Carolina, where his father was an equipment supervisor in an electric plant and his mother headed the customer service department at a bank. The elder Jordans always emphasized academics over athletics as the path to success, but when their son Michael displayed an aptitude for sports, they encouraged him to work hard and set realistic goals—plus keep up his grades. An excellent baseball player, Jordan decided in ninth grade to make basketball his top priority instead, even though at 5'9" he was too small for the varsity squad. To compensate for his lack of height, the ferociously determined teenager spent hours every day practicing his jump. By the time he was a junior, Jordan had grown another six inches and improved his basketball skills enough to make the varsity team. (He eventually topped out at 6'6".)

During the summer between his junior and senior years, Jordan was invited to attend the Five-Star Basketball Camp in Pittsburgh, a special training session for the country's best high school players. His outstanding performance there suddenly made him a hot prospect among college recruiters, and early in his senior year Jordan accepted a basketball scholarship to the University of North Carolina at Chapel Hill (UNC).

At UNC, Jordan was named to the starting team, an unusual honor for a freshman. Very competitive and extremely hard working, he became a national sensation on March 29, 1982, when the UNC Tar Heels faced the Georgetown University Hoyas for the National Collegiate Athletic Association (NCAA) championship. In front of one of the largest crowds ever to attend a basketball game in the United States, Jordan made a sixteen-foot jump shot with only seconds remaining in the contest to propel the Tar Heels to a 63–62 victory and their first national championship in twenty-five years.

Jordan continued to amaze basketball fans throughout his college career. His virtuoso performance on the court—soaring through the air, setting a UNC scoring record, rebounding, guarding two men at once, scooping up loose balls, blocking shots, stealing, coming through in clutch situations—brought him All-American honors and led *The Sporting News* to name him the player of the year in 1983 and again in 1984. He also helped the U.S. team capture gold medals at the 1983 Pan American games and the 1984 Olympics.

By this time, college basketball was no longer a challenge for the young man whom more and more people were calling the best player in the country. Jordan left school after his junior year (he later finished his degree in the off-season) to join the Chicago Bulls, perennial losers in desperate need of a superstar to keep the franchise afloat. In every city the team visited, he put on one show-stopping performance after another. Fans soon began to turn out in droves to see "The Michael Jordan Air Show" and were treated to wild, whirling dunks during which he typically soared above players several inches taller than himself, his tongue dangling from his mouth as testimony to his intense concentration. After compiling statistics that added up to the second-best rookie season in NBA history and putting the Bulls in the playoffs, he was named the league's 1985 Rookie of the Year.

Although Jordan continued to dominate the game throughout the rest of the 1980s and was almost singlehandedly credited with reviving interest in professional basketball, he grew increasingly frustrated with his teammates' reliance on him and their apparent inability or unwillingness to go all out for the NBA championship. The Bulls managed to make the playoffs in 1986 (despite the fact that Jordan sat out most of the season with a broken foot) and again in 1987, but they were eliminated both times in the first round by the Boston Celtics. In 1988, Chicago logged its best season in history, and Jordan was named the league's Most Valuable Player, the Defensive Player of the Year, and the 1988 All-Star Game's Most Valuable Player. The team went on to beat the Cleveland Cavaliers in the first round of the playoffs but then lost to the Detroit Pistons in the second round. Despite injuries to key players (including Jordan) during the 1989 season, the Bulls continued to show significant progress as a team. They beat the Cavaliers in round one of the playoffs and upset the New York Knicks in round two before falling to the Pistons in round three.

The 1990s opened on a disappointing note as the Bulls once again fell to the Pistons, this time in the first round of the playoffs. As always, Jordan was a virtual one-man show who played with almost superhuman intensity. The rest of the Bulls played poorly and seemed to lack the spark that motivated their star guard. At one point during the series, an uncharacteristically angry Jordan lashed out at his teammates, accusing them of not playing up to their potential and expecting too much from him. A few of them in turn complained that Jordan was a selfish show-off who never tried to help them improve their game.

Everything finally came together for Chicago during the 1990–91 season. Sensitive to criticism that his own fierce determination to win was hurting rather than helping the Bulls' chances, Jordan made an effort to restrain his own performance and reach out to his fellow players. "I try to be aware of when my team needs my creativity," he explained. "If things are going well, I don't have to score too much. I can stay in the background and get everyone else involved. If I sense we need that extra push, I can pick the time to explode." The Bulls finished first in their division, and Jordan was named the league's Most Valuable Player. Then Chicago proceeded to bulldoze their way through the playoffs, winning fifteen of seventeen games thanks not only to Jordan (who later was unanimously voted the Most Valuable Player) but also to several other team members who came on strong in the home stretch. Overcome with emotion, Jordan told reporters after the victory, "I don't know if I'll ever have this same feeling again. . . . It's been a seven-year struggle for me and for the city of Chicago. And we did it as a team; all season long we did it as a team."

As the most famous basketball player in the world, Jordan is in great demand as a spokesman for various products. Even before he played his first regular-season game with the Bulls, he signed with Nike to promote a special line of basketball shoes introduced in 1985 under the name "Air Jordan"; the line eventually expanded to include items such as tote bags, gym shorts, T-shirts, and sweatsuits. Other companies and products soon followed—Wheaties, Coca-Cola, Gatorade, McDonald's, the Illinois State Lottery—and as of 1991, Jordan was reportedly endorsing more products than any other athlete in the world.

Part of the reason for his tremendous appeal is his wholesome "good-guy" image. Friendly and accessible—"I don't try to isolate myself from anybody," he says—he is active on behalf of various charities through the Michael Jordan Foundation, regularly visits sick children in hospitals, lectures on drug abuse, holds summer basketball camps for impoverished inner-city youths, and gives away game tickets (and sometimes even his basketball shoes) to kids he meets in the rough neighborhood surrounding Chicago Stadium, often stopping to talk with those he senses need someone to take an interest in them. Jordan appreciates the accolades he receives for being such a worthy role model but worries about always having to live up to an image of perfection. "My biggest concern is that people view me as being some kind of a god, but I'm not," he told John Edgar Wideman in an *Esquire* interview. "I try to live a positive life, love to live a positive life, but I do have negative things about me and I do make mistakes."

Looking to the future, Jordan expects to retire in his early thirties to become a professional golfer, a sport he now pursues with a passion in the off-season. But for the moment, there is still basketball (including a spot on the 1992 Olympic team) and the prospect of a second title for the Bulls. In fact, notes one observer, that may be the only goal left for Jordan in the NBA. "Michael Jordan is now his own greatest competition," declares *Time*'s Stengel. "When you make the miraculous routine, the merely superb becomes ordinary. . . . Now that he has won an NBA championship, he doesn't really have anything left to prove—except, of course, that he can do it again."

Sources

➤ **Books**

Berger, Phil, with John Rolfe, *Michael Jordan,* Time Inc., 1990 (opening quote).

➤ **Periodicals**

Detroit Free Press, "Jordan to Win MVP Title Today," May 20, 1991, p. 7D; "Jordan Credits Team Effort for MVP," May 21, 1991, p. 6D; "Jordan Puts an End to Critics' Whispers," June 14, 1991; "Jordan Wins Big Off Court," July 31, 1991; "The True Cost of Those Superstar Smiles," August 19, 1991, p. 4F.

Detroit News, "Promised Land for Jordan," June 13, 1991.

Economist, "Michael Jordan's Magical Powers," June 1, 1991, p. 28.

Esquire, "Michael Jordan Leaps the Great Divide," November, 1990.

Grand Rapids Press, "Michael Wins MVP: 'We Did It as a Team,'" June 13, 1991, p. D1.

Jet, "Michael Jordan Calls Criticism a Bum Rap," May 7, 1990; "Michael Jordan: The Most Exciting Pro Basketball Player Ever," April 29, 1991, pp. 46–48.

Newsweek, "An Air of Superstardom," May 29, 1989, pp. 58–60.

Sport, "Beers with . . . Michael Jordan," May, 1990, pp. 19–21.

Sports Illustrated, June 11, 1990; "Show of Shows," June 10, 1991, pp. 18–23; "Shining Moment," June 24, 1991, pp. 38–49; "Michael Jordan, a Singular Sportsman and Athlete, Stands at the Pinnacle of His Game," December 23, 1991; "For All His Fame and Fortune, Jordan Is, at Heart, Just a Carolina Kid Called Mike," December 23, 1991; "In the Satellite Age, Michael Jordan Has Become the Global Star of a Global Show," December 23, 1991.

Time, "Great Leapin' Lizards!," January 9, 1989, pp. 50–52; "Yo, Michael! You're the Best!," June 24, 1991, p. 47.

U.S. News and World Report, "Liftoff: Rising Above the Ordinary Ambiguities," June 10, 1991, pp. 10–11.

Robert F. Kennedy

*"*S*ome men see things as they are and say, 'Why?' I dream of things that never were and say, 'Why not?'"*

Robert F. Kennedy, younger brother of slain U.S. president John F. Kennedy, was himself assassinated while campaigning for the 1968 Democratic presidential nomination. He was born on November 20, 1925, in Brookline, Massachusetts, and died on June 6, 1968, in Los Angeles, California.

R obert Francis Kennedy was the seventh of nine children born to Joseph Patrick Kennedy, Sr., a multimillionaire business executive and onetime ambassador to Great Britain, and Rose Fitzgerald Kennedy. Outshone by his iron-willed father, two handsome, charming, and accomplished older brothers (Joseph, Jr., and John), and four overpowering sisters, Robert—slight of build and "unblessed by any obvious gifts of scholarship or intellect," according to a *Newsweek* reporter—learned at a very early age that he had to be especially scrappy and determined in order to survive in his fiercely competitive family.

After graduating from prep school, Kennedy enrolled at Harvard University. His education was interrupted during his sophomore year when young Joseph (a navy pilot and the son being groomed for a political career) went down with his plane following a bombing mission over Germany. Several months later, Robert dropped out of school to join the navy. He returned to Harvard in 1946 and graduated in 1948, then obtained his law degree from the University of Virginia in 1951. That same year, he entered government service as an attorney in the criminal division of the U.S. Department of Justice and spent most of the next two years prosecuting graft and income tax evasion cases.

With the death of Joseph, Jr., the Kennedy family pinned its political hopes on the next-oldest son, John, who in 1952 decided to run for the U.S. Senate and asked Robert to be his campaign manager. John won the election, and Robert returned to government service in early 1953, this time as one of fifteen assistant counsels to the Senate Permanent Subcommittee on Investigations. Chaired by Senator Joseph R. McCarthy, the subcommittee quickly gained notoriety for using threats and intimidation to force witnesses to testify about an alleged communist conspiracy in the government and throughout American society. Kennedy resigned from the subcommittee in mid-1953 following a walkout by Democratic members protesting McCarthy's methods. He returned in early 1954 as chief counsel to the Democratic minority, and in early 1955, after McCarthy's downfall, Kennedy became chief counsel to a revamped version of the subcommittee and earned a reputation as a thorough investigator and persistent questioner.

Two years later, these same qualities helped Kennedy land the job of chief counsel to the Senate Select Committee on Improper Activities in the Labor or Management Field, popularly known as the Senate Rackets Committee. As head of a staff of sixty-five, he conducted an aggressive investigation into the Teamsters union, focusing on the organization's officials and their handling of union funds as well as their ties to organized crime. The clashes between Kennedy and Teamsters president Jimmy Hoffa made headlines nationwide, and Hoffa was eventually imprisoned for jury tampering and misusing union funds.

In 1959, John Kennedy announced his intention to run for the presidency of the United States, and again he tapped Robert to manage his campaign. John successfully captured the Democratic nomination and then squeaked past his Republican challenger, Richard Nixon, by a margin of only 119,000 votes out of 68 million cast.

After the election, John appointed his brother attorney general. By virtue of his relationship to the president, Robert wielded an unusual amount of influence; in fact, he was often described as an unofficial "assistant president." He was his brother's chief adviser on domestic and foreign policies, playing a key role in the decision-making process during the infamous Bay of Pigs Invasion and the Cuban Missile Crisis and supporting an expanded U.S. role in Vietnam. He also resumed his investigation of Jimmy Hoffa and the Teamsters and took some controversial stands on a variety of sensitive issues, including civil rights, immigration, crime, labor law, and the federal judiciary. He was especially active on the civil rights front, taking steps to protect demonstrators from harassment and enforcing voting laws and school desegregation in the South.

John Kennedy's assassination in November, 1963, plunged Robert into a profound melancholy for a time. But the experience also seemed to mellow and deepen his character. It made him less conservative politically and more willing to take risks no matter what the consequences. "There's no use figuring out where you're going to be later on; you may not be there at all," he explained. "So the sensible thing is to do the very best you can all the time."

Now that the Kennedy torch had passed into his hands, Robert set about laying the groundwork for his own political future. There was no doubt that he would one day run for the presidency; the only question was when. He served as attorney general under the new chief executive, Lyndon Johnson, until September, 1964, when he resigned to run for a U.S. Senate seat in New York. He easily won the Democratic nomination and went on to defeat the popular Republican incumbent.

As an energetic man of action, Kennedy found the slow-paced process of deliberation and compromise in the Senate rather frustrating, and he bristled at the time-honored rules and traditions and clubby atmosphere. But he worked hard and long to familiarize himself with the issues facing the nation, assembled a large and talented staff, and gradually made a name for himself as an opponent of the administration by espousing a curious blend of liberal and conservative thought. For example, he supported many of President Lyndon Johnson's "Great Society" programs, but he favored more jobs rather than more welfare on the grounds that it was not wise for the government to take on the full burden of caring for the poor. On the subject of Vietnam, at first he adopted a moderate antiwar position and refrained from being too critical of Johnson. Later, he spoke out forcefully against escalation and the bombing of North Vietnam.

In time, Kennedy emerged as a leading voice of dissent and a wildly popular figure among Black and Hispanic Americans, and the young. As early as 1966, with Johnson expected to run for reelection in 1968, the senator began laying plans for a 1972 bid at the presidency. He stood by his decision to remain out of the 1968 fray until antiwar candidate Eugene McCarthy's strong showing in the March New Hampshire primary revealed the extent to which voters were fed up with Johnson and the war. Kennedy then threw his hat into the ring.

At first, his candidacy seemed haunted by the ghost of his brother. Besides the physical resemblance between the two men, there was a sense that Robert had not forged a clear identity of his own, that his campaign had more style than substance, and that his heart really wasn't in it. But within a few weeks after entering the race, that perception underwent a noticeable change. Stung by criticism that he was relying too much on John's legacy, Robert quit invoking his name and memory and began taking an urgent, harder-edged approach that addressed the issues as *he* saw them: ending the war, reducing crime, fostering compassion for the rural and urban poor and finding ways to improve their quality of life, decentralizing government, and encouraging the private sector to become involved in social programs. The result was a campaign that packed a powerful emotional appeal and thus drew huge, frenzied crowds. As a *Time* reporter noted, the charismatic Kennedy had "the capacity to make the past seem better than it ever was, the future better than it possibly can be."

But a barely-acknowledged fear cast a pall over every moment of his quest for the presidency—the fear of assassination. Robert himself shrugged off the danger, refusing police protection and ignoring pleas that he exercise more caution in his public appearances. "I play Russian roulette every time I get up in the morning," he once said. "But I just don't care. . . . If they want you, they can get you."

Throughout April and May, Kennedy scored respectable primary victories in Indiana, Nebraska, and South Dakota, then lost Oregon to McCarthy. (It was the first time a Kennedy had ever lost an election.) The defeat made winning the upcoming California primary that much more crucial, so the candidates—especially Kennedy—pulled out all the stops. The result was a narrow victory for the Kennedy forces and the realization that while Robert was not likely to win the nomination, he would control enough delegates to wield considerable power at the Democratic convention that summer.

Long before that day arrived, however, the nightmare so many had feared came true. Shortly after midnight on June 5, 1968, following his victory speech to cheering California supporters at Los Angeles' Ambassador Hotel, Robert Kennedy left the celebration to attend a news conference in a nearby press room. Passing through a narrow kitchen area, he was shaking hands with a few hotel employees when a disturbed young Jordanian immigrant named Sirhan Sirhan fired several shots, two of which struck Kennedy. The senator clung to life for a little more than twenty-five hours before dying on June 6. He was later buried at Arlington Cemetery, about fifty feet from his brother John's grave.

Because Robert Kennedy was, as a *Newsweek* reporter stated, "a vital young man of unfulfilled promise and uncompleted destiny" from a family that had already sacrificed two sons to the country, his death was viewed as an especially disturbing and tragic loss. Few men in public life had evoked such extremes of hatred and love, yet as a writer for *Christian Century* observed, "To Americans weary of cold war orthodoxies and political platitudes, Robert Kennedy afforded a gracious hope of change for the better." Kennedy himself once declared: "The future does not belong to those who are content with today, apathetic toward common problems and the fellow man alike, timid and fearful in the face of new ideas and bold projects. Rather it will belong to those who can blend passion, reason, and courage in a personal commitment to the ideals and great enterprises of American society. It will belong to those who see that wisdom can only emerge from the clash of contending views, the passionate expression of deep and hostile beliefs. . . . This is the seminal spirit of American democracy. . . . It is this which is the hope of our nation."

Sources

➤ Books

Fairlie, Henry, *The Kennedy Promise: The Politics of Expectation,* Doubleday, 1973.

Halberstam, David, *Unfinished Odyssey of Robert Kennedy,* Random House, 1969.

Kennedy, Robert F., *To Seek a Newer World,* Doubleday, 1967, rev. ed., Bantam, 1968.

O'Neill, William L., *Coming Apart: An Informal History of America in the 1960s,* Quadrangle, 1971.

Schlesinger, Arthur, Jr., *Robert Kennedy and His Times,* Houghton, 1968.

➤ Periodicals

Christian Century, "Robert F. Kennedy," July 10, 1968, pp. 891–894.

Economist, "An American Tragedy," June 8, 1968, pp. 11–12; "Spokesman for Change," June 6, 1968, pp. 17–20.

McCall's, "RFK: My View of Life," August, 1968.

Newsweek, June 17, 1968.

New York Times, June 6, 1968.

New York Times Magazine, "The Making of a Candidate, 1968," March 31, 1968; "Said Robert Kennedy, 'Maybe We're All Doomed Anyway,'" June 16, 1968.

Time, October 10, 1960; February 16, 1962; June 21, 1963; September 16, 1966; "The Politics of Restoration," May 24, 1968, pp. 22–27; June 14, 1968 (opening quote); "Second Thoughts on Bobby," June 21, 1968, p. 48; "R. F. K. Remembered," June 6, 1969, p. 3.

U.S. News and World Report, "RFK: The Man, the Dream, the Tragedy," June 17, 1968, pp. 16–18.

Ron Kovic

"I *realized in Vietnam that the real experience of war was nothing like the comic books or movies I had watched as a kid. . . . These movies had romanticized war, made war seem like a glorious and heroic thing, a wonderful thing to get involved in."*

Born on July 4, 1946, in Ladysmith, Wisconsin, Ron Kovic is a Vietnam veteran whose evolution from zealous patriot to antiwar activist is chronicled in his autobiography, *Born on the Fourth of July.*

In late January, 1968, twenty-one-year-old Ron Kovic, more than halfway through his second tour of duty in Vietnam, wanted more than anything to go home. He had enlisted in the marines shortly after graduating from high school, eager "to make something out of my life," as he later explained in his autobiography. Most of all, he wanted to be a hero, and he figured that serving with the marines would give him that chance. But in the short space of a few weeks, two horrific incidents, followed by a devastating wound that left him paralyzed from the chest down, forever changed young Kovic's view of war and eventually put him at the forefront of the peace movement in the United States.

By his own account, Kovic was a typical kid growing up in a working-class neighborhood of Massapequa, Long Island. A fervent patriot who was especially proud of his Fourth of July birthday, he was tremendously impressed by two marine recruiters who visited his high school during the last month of his senior year and subsequently decided to enlist in the fall of 1964. He carried his dream of becoming a bona fide hero well into his second tour of duty, at which point his life began to fall apart. During an especially confusing encounter with the enemy one night, he panicked and accidentally shot and killed a fellow marine. Racked with guilt, Kovic tried to confess to a major in his outfit, who questioned his version of the events and brushed off the notion that he had been at fault. Several weeks later, Kovic was on patrol when his unit came upon a hut they thought was occupied by a group of enemy soldiers armed with rifles. Someone gave the order to fire, and the soldiers emptied their guns into the hut. Afterwards, Kovic and another man went to count the number of dead and wounded. To their horror, their flashlights revealed that they had attacked not the enemy, but a group of children and an old man.

Struggling to reconcile his lifelong desire to be a hero with the appalling reality of what he had done and the cold indifference of his superior officers, Kovic became obsessed with the idea of going home. Concluding that his only way out was to be wounded, he began taking foolish chances, hoping to "get blown up enough to be sent home, but not enough to get killed." On January 20, 1968, his wish came true in a way he hadn't quite planned: while holding his position in a firefight during which nearly all the other men in his outfit retreated, a bullet tore through his right shoulder, passed through his lung, and smashed into his spinal cord, immediately paralyzing him from the mid-chest down.

Treated first in Vietnam, Kovic was later transferred stateside to a navy hospital in Queens, and from there to a veterans' hospital in the Bronx. Months of recuperation followed amid conditions so nightmarish—including dirty, rat-infested rooms and substandard medical care—that he began to have doubts about the war. After being discharged, Kovic fell into a deep and bitter depression, drank heavily, and brooded over the realization that his paralysis and disfigurement were "ugly and cold and final."

In the fall of 1969, determined to walk again with the help of leg braces, Kovic started a vigorous exercise program that came to a sudden end when he broke his thigh bone and ended up back in the veterans' hospital for six months. There he again endured treatment at the hands of doctors and aides who seemed indifferent, if not downright hostile, to his emotional and physical pain. Kovic's anger at his wound, at the hospital, and at the government officials he felt were responsible for it all slowly boiled up inside him, but he still found it hard "to think of speaking out against the war, to think of joining those I'd once called traitors."

The turning point for Kovic came in the spring of 1970, when National Guard troops fired on antiwar protesters at Ohio's Kent State University, killing four students and wounding several others. Later that same day, he attended his first campus demonstration, and within a few days he was on his way to Washington, D.C., to join thousands of protesters gathered there. Not long after, he teamed up with Bobby Muller, a fellow Vietnam veteran he had met in the hospital, and they began speaking at high schools, colleges, and universities about their experiences both during and after the war. Moving to Los Angeles in January, 1971, Kovic joined Vietnam Veterans Against the War (VVAW) and continued to give speeches and appear on television, believing "that if only I could speak out to enough people I could stop the war myself."

Despite this renewed sense of purpose, Kovic was still tormented by nightmares, so much so that he feared he was losing his mind. Compounding his emotional turmoil was the sense of betrayal he felt following an antiwar demonstration outside Richard Nixon's re-election campaign headquarters in Los Angeles, where he was arrested, beaten, and pushed from his wheelchair by police officers who had infiltrated the VVAW. Kovic withdrew from the movement for a while, battling loneliness, fear, depression, and hatred directed not only at himself but at what had been done to him and those he felt were responsible. Then he realized that by remaining silent he was doing exactly what his opponents wanted. So he vowed to "rise up out of this deep dark prison" and "make people remember."

In August, 1972, he headed for Miami to attend the Republican National Convention on the night President Nixon was scheduled to deliver his acceptance speech. Once there, Kovic bluffed his way into the hall and proceeded to shout his story to the crowd, creating such a stir that Roger Mudd of CBS News briefly interviewed him on live television. Kovic then joined a couple of other Vietnam veterans who had also managed to get into the hall and waved protest signs and chanted antiwar slogans in full view of network television cameras. Although he was eventually thrown out of the convention (after being spat upon and verbally harassed by some of the delegates), Kovic nevertheless considered the journey a triumph over "all the pain and the rage, all the trials and the death of the war and what had been done to me and a generation of Americans by all the men who had lied to us and tricked us."

Since that day, Kovic has remained active in various antiwar and veterans' rights causes, speaking out on behalf of better care for wounded soldiers and condemning U.S. nuclear policies, draft laws, and military intervention in Central America and the Persian Gulf. He has also continued to struggle with periodic bouts of depression, nightmares, and suicidal thoughts, especially during the early 1970s and again from 1978 until 1987. In both instances, working on his autobiography ended his despair.

Born on the Fourth of July took Kovic only two months to write, but when he was finished, he felt more at peace with himself than he had since coming back from Vietnam. Published in 1976, the book became a bestseller and scored well with critics, leading to talk of a movie deal and what Kovic hoped would be a chance to reach even more people with his message. But financing for the film collapsed just before shooting was to begin in the summer of 1978, leaving Kovic devastated. Nine years later, when director Oliver Stone told him that Hollywood was again interested in making a movie version of *Born on the Fourth of July*, Kovic told Robert Seidenberg of *American Film* that "it was like being given a second life. . . . Working on the script with Oliver was the first time that I began to understand that my sacrifice, my paralysis, the difficulties, the frustrations, the impossibilities of each and every day would now be for something very valuable, something that would help protect the young people of this country from having to go through what I went through." Released in December, 1989, *Born on the Fourth of July* was a hit with moviegoers as well as critics.

Kovic now feels that the worst days are behind him. "It was a terrible period of time. It was an impossible period of time. Sometimes I'm amazed I made it . . . ," he readily admits. "I know what it is like to have lived in a paralyzed body. . . . I know what it means to finally overcome the nightmares and sleep well at night. I know what it means to feel on top of it now—because for years it was on top of me."

Sources

➤ **Books**

Kovic, Ron, *Born on the Fourth of July*, McGraw, 1976.

➤ **Periodicals**

American Film, "To Hell and Back," January, 1990 (opening quote).

Harper's, "Missing in Action," September, 1976, pp. 80–82.

Newsweek, "Hell on Wheels," September 20, 1976, p. 88; "Kovic: Some of the Wounds Have Healed," May 9, 1983.

New York Times Book Review, "Growing Up the Hard Way," August 15, 1976, p. 1.

Premiere, February, 1990.

Maggie Kuhn

"There is a pervasive societal bias in the U.S., which contends that old age is a disaster and a disease. . . . On the contrary, it is a part of the continuum of life and ought to be a time when life can flower."

Born on August 3, 1905, in Buffalo, New York, Maggie Kuhn is the founder of the Gray Panthers.

Address: Gray Panthers, 3700 Chestnut St., Philadelphia, PA 19144.

Although Maggie Kuhn has been a lifelong crusader for social justice, it was not until she reached age sixty-five and was forced to retire from a job she enjoyed that she became truly militant. Since then, the self-proclaimed "wrinkled radical" has worked tirelessly to bring young and old together in a national movement known as the Gray Panthers. Dedicated to ensuring that elderly Americans can and do remain productive members of society, the Gray Panthers seek to bring about changes in health care, housing, and labor policies that will allow older people to "protect, care for, love and assist the young ones to provide continuity and hope."

Kuhn can quite literally trace her radicalism back to the day she was born. Her parents, Samuel and Minnie Kooman Kuhn, were living at the time in Memphis, Tennessee. Because Minnie found the South's tradition of racial segregation intolerable, she did not want to give birth in Memphis. Instead, she took up residence in her parents' home in Buffalo, New York, and it was there that her daughter Maggie was born. The Kuhns lived in Memphis until Samuel's job took him to Cleveland, Ohio, where Maggie completed high school and went on to attend Flora Stone Mather College of Case Western Reserve University as an English and sociology major. Strongly influenced by an aunt she admired who was a suffragist, the young woman helped organize a campus chapter of the League of Women Voters. She also wrote for the college magazine in her spare time.

After graduating in 1926, Maggie Kuhn went to work for the Cleveland YWCA, first as a volunteer and then as a full-time staff member. She stayed for eleven years, involved mostly in setting up programs for young women employed in clerical and commercial jobs. The experience radicalized Kuhn, who told Jan Fisher of *50 Plus* that "those young women in the 'Y' were victims of a very oppressed system. They worked long hours for low pay."

Kuhn left Cleveland for New York City in the mid-1930s, serving for a time as publications editor for the national office of the YWCA. She then worked briefly in Boston for the General Alliance of Unitarian Women before returning to New York City to accept a position with the United Presbyterian Church, an affiliation that lasted twenty-five years. Besides coordinating various social reform activities for the church, including programs on racism, women's rights, and the problems of the elderly, Kuhn edited and contributed to the church magazine *Social Progress* and was the

Presbyterians' alternate observer at the United Nations. It was a job she loved, and having to retire at age sixty-five left her angry and hurt. "There's nothing like arbitrary retirement being dumped on you all of a sudden to radicalize you," Kuhn remarked in an interview with J. Wandres of *Retirement Living*. "If you are not prepared, retirement at 65 makes you a non-person. It deprives you of the sense of 'community' that has previously defined your life." The woman who had spent much of her adult life fighting social injustice was now herself a victim of discrimination—age discrimination.

Looking back, Kuhn regards her forced retirement as a blessing in disguise, for it gave her the time and incentive to form the Gray Panthers in 1971. "It began with six of us," she told Fisher. "We decided we needed some kind of collective project just to keep us alive after we retired . . . and we chose the Vietnam war." All six soon discovered that retirement did indeed have its benefits; no longer caught up in the need to earn a living, they were totally free to support any cause they pleased in any way they saw fit, no matter how controversial. As Kuhn proclaimed in an article in *Aging*, "We who are old have nothing to lose! We have everything to gain by living dangerously! We can initiate change without jeopardizing jobs or family. We can be the risk-takers."

The group's opposition to the Vietnam war as well as its commitment to social action immediately created a common bond with many young people who felt the same, and within a year Kuhn and her fellow retirees merged with some of them to form the Consultation of Older and Younger Adults for Social Change. The presence of so many older radicals in the group—personified by Kuhn, the chief spokesperson and leader—soon prompted a local television reporter to dub them the "Gray Panthers," after a Black-American organization called the "Black Panthers." This name took hold nationwide as media coverage of their movement increased. Kuhn is quick to point out, however, that the Gray Panthers have always had young members (roughly one-third are under fifty years of age) and that they have never sought to advance "senior power" at the expense of everyone else. "Old people as 'elders of the tribe' should be seeking and safe-guarding the survival of the tribe—the larger public interest," she explained in *Aging*. "I believe the old people of America have the responsibility to . . . use our freedom to work for a just and humane society that puts people first."

To that end, the Gray Panthers have devoted their efforts to public-interest work of various kinds, merging with Ralph Nader's Retired Professional Action Group in 1973 to pursue common goals. At the state and local level, they have organized around such issues as nursing home reform, discrimination against the elderly on the job and in housing, public transportation for the handicapped, protection for the hearing-impaired against the fraudulent sales tactics used by some hearing-aid companies, and "living will" legislation. Nationally, they have lobbied Congress demanding changes in health care, the welfare system, social security, and the laws governing retirement. And they continue to speak out against American foreign policy, insisting that the money targeted for the military should instead be spent on social services.

The Gray Panthers have also taken their case to the private sector in an attempt to influence policy. For example, they have demonstrated at meetings of the American Medical Association to protest the profit-motivated approach to health care and call for socialized medicine and national health insurance. Dismayed by images of old people on television that make them look incompetent, the Gray Panthers have also formed a Media Watch Task Force to pressure the networks and persuade the National Association of Broadcasters to consider age along with race and sex as sensitive areas subject to the rules of the television code of ethics.

Kuhn believes that older people can be "recycled" to do many activities that benefit society as a whole. She would like to see senior citizens trained to act as patient advocates in hospitals and clinics, speaking on behalf of the patient when necessary and performing tasks currently handled by doctors and nurses that don't involve actual medical care. Kuhn also thinks that elderly people could serve as monitors—attending meetings of planning commissions, zoning boards, city councils, and so on, sitting in on court cases, and keeping an eye on the credit policies of banks and insurance companies. From time to time, she suggests, these groups could analyze their findings and hold a press conference to inform the public.

At the heart of Kuhn's continuing activism is her fervent wish to bridge the growing gap between young and old in the United States and foster an intergenerational approach to living and solving problems. "There's a very urgent need to do that," she told Francesca Lyman in a *Progressive* interview, "because there's a contrived effort to set the old against the young, to persuade the young people that old people are getting too much, that we're all rich and well-endowed and that they're getting robbed, which is not true." Kuhn sees a solid basis for cooperation, noting that "both the old and the young are marginalized. They're out of the mainstream, and they're not taken seriously. . . . The old and the young are both into the drug · scene. Different drugs and different pushers. . . . The old and the young are both in difficulty as far as jobs are concerned. . . . And they are both in conflict, or potential conflict, with the same people: the young with their parents, the old with their children."

As she looks toward the future, Kuhn has a more pressing goal—to make sure the Gray Panthers survive her as a strong and financially secure organization. "We've had enormous success," she told Lyman, "all out of proportion to our numbers. We have set a pace. We've been very outspoken in our positions, and we've caught the attention of the media." And yet to a much greater extent than she would like, the charismatic Kuhn *is* the Gray Panthers to many people. Some health problems have forced her to cut back on the thousands of miles she used to travel over the course of a year to give speeches and attend meetings, but she is still much in demand. Funds are always in short supply, a problem some attribute to the fact that the Gray Panthers champion too many different causes.

"Many things started by a person disappear when the person dies, but I'd consider my job a failure if that happened," Kuhn told Helen Benedict of *Working Woman* magazine. "[What] I dream of and yearn for is that the Gray Panthers will continue to be on the cutting edge of social change, and that the young and old together will continue to work for a just, humane and peaceful world." As for her own contributions to the fight for social justice, Kuhn has already come up with a simple epitaph that she feels is appropriate: "Here lies Maggie, under the only stone she ever left unturned."

Sources

➤ **Books**

Kuhn, Maggie, with Christine Long and Laura Quinn, *The Life and Times of Maggie Kuhn*, Ballantine, 1991.

➤ **Periodicals**

Aging, "Advocacy in This New Age," July, 1979, pp. 2–5.

Fifty Plus, "Whatever Happened to the Gray Panthers?," October,

1983; "Maggie Kuhn's Vision: Young and Old Together," July, 1986.

Ms., June, 1975, p. 91; "The Gray Pages: Shared Housing, Creative Work Plans, and Other Alternatives for a Sane and Secure Long Life," January, 1982, p. 83.

Progressive, "Maggie Kuhn: A Wrinkled Radical's Crusade," January, 1988, pp. 29–31.

Retirement Living, "Retirees Should Be Recycled for Public-Interest Work," December, 1975, pp. 40–44.

Saturday Evening Post, "Gray Power," March, 1979 (opening quote).

Working Woman, May, 1982, pp. 169–171.

Louis, Mary and Richard Leakey

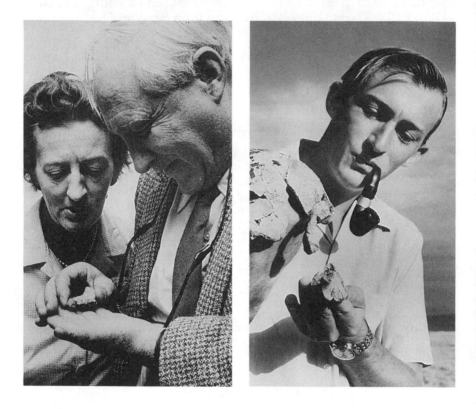

*"*I*n archaeology you almost never find what you set out to find."—Mary Leakey*

The Leakey's archaeological discoveries have revolutionized thought on the origins of man. Louis was born on August 7, 1903, in Kabete, Kenya, and died on October 1, 1972, in London, England; Mary was born on February 6, 1913, in London; and Richard was born on December 19, 1944, in Nairobi, Kenya.

I n the annals of paleoanthropology—the branch of anthropology that deals with the study of fossil man—there is no name better known to experts and the general public alike than "Leakey." From the early excavations completed by Louis and Mary at Kenya's Olduvai Gorge through the more recent ones undertaken by their middle son, Richard, at Lake Turkana along the border between Kenya and Ethiopia, the work of this pioneering family of scientists has enormously expanded our knowledge of the stages of human evolution and the conditions under which they occurred. Thanks to the Leakeys's dedication and perseverance over more than sixty years of research, the story of man's prehistory has revealed itself to be far more ancient and complex than ever before imagined.

Louis Seymour Bazett Leakey was the oldest of four children born to Anglican Church missionaries Harry and Mary Bazett Leakey, in a village outside Nairobi, Kenya. Louis spent his entire childhood and adolescence among members of the Kikuyu tribe and absorbed their traditions and language to the point that the chief once described him as "the black man with a white face." An early interest in bird-watching gave way to a fascination with archaeology after he came across some stone arrowheads and tools during one of his forays into the wild.

Leakey later pursued his formal education in archaeology and anthropology at England's Cambridge University, accompanying a British Museum archaeological expedition to Tanganyika (now Tanzania) when he was only twenty-one. From that moment on, he was sure there was much more to be uncovered in East Africa about the origins of man. His professors tried to discourage him, pointing out that it would be a waste of time for him to focus on Africa when everyone knew Asia was where man had originated. But throughout the late 1920s and early 1930s, Leakey alternated working on his doctorate at Cambridge with additional field research in East Africa, primarily Kenya.

In 1929, Leakey accidentally stumbled across a 200,000-year-old hand ax that convinced him he was indeed on the right track. During a 1931 expedition, his travels led him to remote Olduvai Gorge, an 800-foot-deep, 25-mile-long dry canyon that slices through what was once a shallow lake. (German scientists had first visited the site about twenty years before when a butterfly collector reported seeing some fossil bones, but World War I had interrupted their research, and they never returned.) On Leakey's very first day there, he uncovered some prehistoric stone tools and a few fossilized human remains—a hint of what he might encounter with more serious study. Thus Olduvai Gorge—which would turn out to be one of the richest troves of fossilized human and animal bones in the world—became the center of Louis Leakey's existence for virtually the rest of his days.

During one of his stays in England in 1933, Leakey met a young archaeologist and illustrator named Mary Douglas Nicol. A native of London, she was the only child of Cecilia Marion Frere Nicol and Edward Nicol, an artist. Mr. Nicol's profession kept him on the road a great deal, and as a result, Mary had a rather unconventional childhood; she didn't attend school, for example, until she was a teenager. Her father taught her to read, and he also instilled in her a love of ancient relics and monuments. On several occasions while the family was living in southwestern France, she was able to visit various prehistoric caves and excavation sites, seeing the magnificent cave paintings and even getting permission from some French archaeologists to sort through some of the objects they had unearthed. It was all Mary needed to persuade her to make archaeology her career.

From 1930 until 1934, Mary served as an assistant to archaeologist Dorothy Liddell at a major Neolithic site in southern Britain. Mary typically spent summers in the field and winters attending lectures in geology and archaeology at the University of London and the London Museum. Having inherited a considerable amount of artistic talent from her father, Mary also began to do some drawings of the stone tools uncovered at the excavation. When the drawings appeared in several scientific publications, they caught the eye of another archaeologist, Gertrude Caton-Thompson, who asked Mary to illustrate a book she was doing on some Egyptian stone tools she had uncovered. Caton-Thompson subsequently introduced Mary Nicol to Louis Leakey, who also asked for her help with some illustrations for his book *Adam's Ancestors*. Despite the ten-year age gap between them (as well as the fact that Louis was already married and the father of two children), they soon became constant companions. They made their first journey together to Olduvai in April, 1935, and on December 24, 1936, after Louis obtained a divorce, they married and left again for Africa a few weeks later.

Louis and Mary conducted excavations at various East African sites until World War II erupted in 1939 and Louis suspended his field work to serve with British military intelligence in Nairobi. Mary continued the excavations on her own throughout the war. During this time she gave birth to her sons Jonathan and Richard and daughter Deborah, who died in infancy. (A third son, Philip, was born in 1949.) Mary unearthed thousands of stone tools from various periods—including some that were the oldest known at that time—as well as samples of Iron Age pottery and the bones of numerous unusual, extinct animals, but she unearthed no human remains.

After the war, Louis was named the full-time director of Nairobi's Coryndon Museum, which only left him with a few weeks a year to devote to excavating Olduvai. (Funds were a problem, too, since research grants for such work were scarce.) Then, in 1948, while digging at a site on the island of Rusing in Lake Victoria, Mary discovered a fossilized skull and other bones that turned out to be those of an apelike creature about 25–40 million years old. Dubbed *Proconsul africanus,* it had manlike jaws and teeth and walked on its hind legs without using its arms. The first significant find to suggest that man may have originated in East Africa, the discovery focused world attention on the Leakeys and encouraged them to begin digging in earnest at Olduvai around 1952.

Seven years later, on July 17, 1959, a day when a feverish Louis was resting in his tent, Mary spotted some fossilized molars protruding from a small slope. Could they possibly belong to the human ancestor they had been looking for? Rushing back to camp, she awakened her husband and took him to see what she had found. Days of painstaking excavation with dental picks and brushes followed, uncovering a nearly complete, manlike skull some 1.75 million years old—nearly twice as old as scientists had previously estimated man's age to be. Because Louis initially believed it to be a distinct new form of hominid, he gave it the name *Zinjanthropus,* or "East Africa Man," and proclaimed it was the long-sought "missing link" between the more ape-like *Australopithecus* (discovered some years before in South Africa) and modern man. This was later shown to be incorrect—*Zinjanthropus* is now regarded as another form of *Australopithecus* and has been renamed accordingly—but because of its age, the *Zinjanthropus* was still a revolutionary find.

The publicity resulting from the *Zinjanthropus* discovery brought the Leakeys worldwide acclaim as well as much-needed funding from the National Geographic Society, which allowed them to live and work at Olduvai on a year-round basis. In 1960 and 1962 they unearthed fossil fragments, a skull, and some tools of a new species they named *Homo habilis,* or "Handy Man," in recognition of the fact that he made tools. More manlike than *Zinjanthropus* but of roughly the same age, *Homo habilis* was at that time considered the earliest known ancestor of the genus *Homo,* which includes the later *Homo erectus* and modern man, *Homo sapiens.* Also in 1962, at an excavation site forty miles east of Lake Victoria, Louis discovered a fourteen-million-year-old fragment of jaw and teeth belonging to an apelike creature similar to Mary's *Proconsul* find that he called *Kenyapithecus* (also known as *Ramapithecus*). By the mid-1960s, the Leakeys felt they had assembled enough evidence to prove that early man had existed in Africa at least two million years ago and perhaps as many as fourteen million years ago. Louis also created a controversy by stating that, contrary to the scientific opinion of the day, different strains of men and near-men had existed side by side in the same time frame.

Throughout the rest of the 1960s, Louis spent more and more of his time away from Olduvai on lecture tours, driving himself at such a furious pace that it affected his health. He also began making some grandiose claims that Mary, who was always the more careful scientist of the two, found difficult to support. And he was growing increasingly estranged from his middle son, Richard, the only one of his children to have shown an interest in carrying on the family's research. No longer physically able to work in the field after surgery for an arthritic hip in 1968, Louis remained active on the lecture circuit. In London for a speaking engagement in 1972, he suffered a fatal heart attack.

While Mary carried on the research at Olduvai, Richard Erskine Frere Leakey was starting to generate some headlines of his own. From the time he was an infant he had accompanied his parents on various excavations, and as a youngster he was able to identify fossils and rattle off the appropriate anthropological jargon. While the subject fascinated him, he was not about to try to make a name for himself in the same field as his strong-willed father; nor did he have any desire to go to college and study something else. So he dropped out of high school and hired himself out as a safari guide. (He already had many years of experience escorting visiting scientists around Olduvai.) Within just a few years he was making an excellent living but was thoroughly bored with the work. After quitting the safari business around 1963, on a lark he started doing some excavating in northeast Tanzania and unearthed the lower jaw of an *Australopithecus.*

Realizing that if he truly wanted to pursue anthropology he needed to broaden his scientific background, Richard went to London and packed two years of high school study into seven months. He then passed his university entrance exams but ran out of money before he could start classes. So he returned to Kenya and concentrated on gaining his education in the field.

In 1967, Richard signed on with an expedition his father had organized in southern Ethiopia, not far from the border with Kenya. While piloting his plane around the area, he spotted a desolate stretch of land along the shores of Lake Turkana that he thought looked like a promising place for some research. Accompanying his father to a business meeting with the National Geographic Society in 1968, the brash twenty-three-year-old Leakey asked for some funds of his own to check it out. The committee agreed, and before the end of the year Richard was established at Turkana in a camp named Koobi Fora, which has turned out to be what a *Time* reporter calls "an anthropological mother lode" even richer than Olduvai.

Almost immediately, the young and ambitious Leakey found a wealth of fossil evidence suggesting life had thrived in the area at least four million years ago. At first he and his team uncovered only animal bones, but then they located *Australopithecus* jaw fragments, then an *Australopithecus* skull, and finally some crude tools about 2.6 million years old that had to have been made not by the vegetarian *Australopithecus* but by a more manlike hunting hominid active in the area at the same time. In 1971, Richard discovered some remains of *Homo habilis*, which supported the theory that this manlike creature existed alongside the apelike *Australopithecus*. More proof of the theory surfaced in 1972 with the discovery of a *Homo habilis* skull dubbed "1470" (after its registration number) that was eventually determined to be 1.9 million years old, at that time the oldest known *Homo habilis* specimen and therefore an anthropological coup rivalling his mother's *Zinjanthropus* find. Based on what he had uncovered at Turkana, Richard concluded that at least three kinds of early men co-existed in East Africa approximately two to three million years ago: *Homo habilis* and two varieties of *Australopithecus*.

Richard's discoveries brought him instant acclaim and rocketed him to the forefront of those researching the origins of man. This led to some resentment on the part of academically-trained anthropologists, who looked on him as an untrained upstart. Richard's notoriety also strained relations with his father, who had dominated

African anthropology for so many years. Their feud ended just a few days before Louis's death in 1972, after he paid a visit to Turkana and expressed genuine excitement and pride at Richard's 1470 find and predicted even greater achievements for him in the future.

Since his big discovery, Richard has uncovered more evidence at Turkana that several varieties of early man co-existed there. In 1975, for example, in a layer of deposits that had already given up some *Australopithecus* remains, he found a *Homo erectus* skull approximately 1.5 million years old. *(Homo erectus* is the precursor of modern man, *Homo sapiens.)* Richard's hope is that anthropologists will one day be able to demonstrate a common origin for man and thus put superficial differences between humans (such as skin color) in the proper perspective.

Throughout the 1970s and into the early 1980s, Mary Leakey continued her work at Olduvai and gradually emerged from behind the shadow of her more flamboyant husband to become an effective and popular speaker and fund-raiser in her own right. She also made yet another exciting and significant discovery in 1978 when she came upon a beautifully-preserved stretch of hominid footprints—apparently of two adults and a child—at Laetoli on the Serengeti Plain in Tanzania, about thirty miles south of Olduvai. Nearby excavations from the same layer as the footprints unearthed human fossils dating back some 3.5 million years and similar to the well-known "Lucy" skeleton (properly known as *Australopithecus afarensis)* discovered in Ethiopia in 1974, also about 3.5 million years old. Anthropologists are still arguing over whether the bones at each site represent one or two species.

In 1982, Mary Leakey lost the vision in one of her eyes, prompting her to cut back on her research in the field. She eventually turned over the Olduvai Gorge camp to the Tanzanian Department of Antiquities and moved to Nairobi, where she still resides.

Richard, meanwhile, has turned over much of the research at Turkana to his wife, Maeve Epps, and is now focusing his efforts on another Leakey tradition: conservation work. Not long after his twenty-year tenure as director of the National Museums of Kenya ended in 1989, the lifelong environmental activist was named head of Kenya's Department of Wildlife Services. Since taking office, he has cracked down on the kind of corruption in the agency that allowed poaching to flourish and has thus taken the first major step toward preserving the endangered elephant population. He has also made it a goal to revitalize the country's many wildlife parks and do a better job of attracting and spending tourist dollars. Although his switch in careers puzzled some, Richard views his new job as a natural extension of his interest in the past. "People feel that we are here by predestination and that because we are humans we will be able to survive even if we make mistakes . . . ," he says. "[But] there have been thousands of living organisms, of which a very high percentage has become extinct. There is nothing, at the moment, to suggest that we are not part of that same pattern."

Much work is yet to be done in the field of anthropology to uncover the true origins of man, if indeed they can ever be identified with certainty. In January, 1991, for example, scientists working in Ethiopia reported finding older versions of a "Lucy" who walked upright dating back 4 million years, thus pushing the knowledge of human origins back at least another 500,000 years. A little over a year later, in February, 1992, another group of scientists revealed that a *Homo habilis* skull fragment originally discovered in Kenya in 1965 but only recently subjected to modern dating techniques is 2.4 million years old—half a million years older than Richard Leakey's 1470 skull from Turkana, the previous record-holder for *Homo habilis*. And in March, 1992, theories about East Africa being the center of evolution were turned upside down when anthropologists announced the unearthing of a 13-million-year-old jawbone belonging to an apelike creature in Namibia in southern Africa—an astonishing and unprecedented find that suggests evolution in apes and humans actually may have occurred over a much broader geographic area than previously believed.

This flurry of activity in anthropology owes much to the Leakeys. It is as a result of Louis and Mary's work, for instance, that research emphasis shifted from Asia to Africa and that experts came to accept that man's evolutionary descent took much longer than anyone had ever dreamed. Even though their *Zinjanthropus* find in 1959 led Louis to draw some conclusions that were later proved incorrect, the discovery is still considered the event that launched the modern scientific study of man because of the effect it had of stimulating scientists' imaginations and ambitions. And Richard's work at Turkana provided the first solid evidence to support his and his father's contention that evolution was not a linear progression but an overlapping process that saw several types of men and near-men living side by side. For these reasons, the name "Leakey" has become virtually synonymous with the search for and discovery of the fossilized remains of our earliest ancestors.

Sources

➤ Books

Leakey, Louis, *White African: An Early Autobiography*, Schenkman, 1966. Reprint of original 1937 edition, with a new preface.

Leakey, Louis, *By the Evidence: Memoirs, 1932–1951*, Harcourt, 1974.

Leakey, Mary, *Disclosing the Past*, Doubleday, 1984.

Leakey, Richard, *One Life: An Autobiography*, Salem House, 1984.

➤ Periodicals

Audubon, "An Interview with Kenya's Zookeeper," September, 1990, pp. 74–75.

Detroit News, "Skull Relic Found in Kenya Pushes Origin of Man Back 500,000 Years," February 20, 1992, p. 3A; "Fossil Opens Possibilities in Evolution," March 12, 1992, p. 3A.

Grand Rapids Press, "Scientists Report Find Predating Fossil 'Lucy,'" January 11, 1991, p. A8; "Ancient Skull Fragment Redefines Origins of Man," February 20, 1992, p. A7.

Humanist, "Interview with Richard Leakey," January/February, 1979, pp. 24–28.

National Geographic, "The Leakeys of Africa: Family in Search of Prehistoric Man," February, 1965, pp. 194–231; "The Leakey Tradition Lives On," January, 1973, pp. 142–144; "The Search for Our Ancestors," November, 1985, pp. 560–623 (opening quote).

Newsweek, "The Oldest Man?," November 20, 1972, p. 137; "The Leakeys' Telltale Skulls," July 15, 1974, pp. 72–77; "Bones and Prima Donnas," February 16, 1981, pp. 76–77.

New York Times, October 2, 1972, p. 40.

New York Times Magazine, "The Face of Evolution," March 3, 1974; "Can He Save the Elephants?," January 7, 1990.

People, "Anthropologist Richard Leakey Tracks the Grandfather of Man in an African Boneyard," January 8, 1979, pp. 30–35.

Psychology Today, "Stepping Up the Search for Early Man," July, 1978.

Saturday Review, "Louis S. B. Leakey, 1903–1972," October 28, 1972, pp. 70–72.

Time, "Puzzling Out Man's Ascent," November 7, 1977, pp. 64–78; "Leakey's Find," March 6, 1978, p. 75.

U.S. News and World Report, "'We Really Know Very Little about Man's Origins,'" December 24, 1984, p. 62; "Elephant Man," October 2, 1989, pp. 58–61.

Greg LeMond

"Anybody who wins the Tour de France is a champion. . . . It is the hardest race and you have to beat everyone to win it. No matter what year it is, no matter who wins, no matter who beats who, it's a great feat."*

Born in Los Angeles, California, on June 26, 1961, Greg LeMond is a three-time winner of the Tour de France.

Address: c/o ProServ, Inc., 1101 Wilson Blvd., Arlington, VA 22209.

On July 23, 1989, twenty-eight-year-old Greg LeMond amazed international cycling enthusiasts with a stunning come-from-behind win in the prestigious Tour de France, a more than 2,000-mile-long bicycle race widely regarded as the most grueling endurance test in the world of sports. They were astonished not because this upstart American was now a two-time winner of the race, but because they knew what he had overcome merely to *be* there, let alone triumph. For in the three years since his previous victory, LeMond had broken his wrist, nearly died in a hunting accident, survived an emergency appendectomy, and undergone surgery to repair an infected shin tendon. Few people—including LeMond himself at times—had ever expected him to be a serious competitor again.

LeMond first became interested in cycling during the summer of 1975, when his father bought a racing bike to get into shape and invited Greg to join him on his long rides around the hills near their Nevada home. Soon the teenager began entering races, quickly moving up the amateur ranks to win the 1977 junior national championship. In 1979, he picked up three medals at the junior world championships—the first rider ever to do so.

In 1980, his sights set on the Olympics, LeMond accompanied other hopefuls to Europe, where bicycle racing is second in popularity only to soccer. After the United States pulled out of the summer games to protest the Soviet Union's invasion of Afghanistan, LeMond accepted an invitation to join the Renault-Elf-Gitane professional cycling team, one of France's best. Having "ascended in his sport at a dizzying pace," to quote a *Sports Illustrated* reporter, LeMond now looked forward to "establishing himself among the European elite of cycling at a time when the U.S. was decidedly a Third World country in that sport."

LeMond stayed with the Renault team for three years, perfecting his racing techniques and trying to adjust to life in Europe. The latter assignment was almost the toughest; neither he nor his wife, Kathy, knew a word of French, and they missed their families and friends, not to mention Greg's favorite foods—hamburgers and french fries. In addition, the young American frequently found himself at odds with some of his French teammates, who criticized his diet and training habits, his unabashed enthusiasm, and his failure to observe the traditional "rules" discouraging contact with family members and fans while preparing for a race.

LeMond nevertheless continued to make impressive showings

throughout Europe, particularly at the 1983 world championship race in Switzerland, which he won by conquering an extremely hilly course marked by steep grades. His string of successes earned him the Prestige Pernod Trophy as the year's best cyclist, making him the first American and the youngest racer ever to win both the world championship and the Prestige Pernod Trophy.

The next year, LeMond was judged ready to enter the world's most famous—and most difficult—race of all, the Tour de France. Consisting of a rugged 2,000-mile-plus course completed over a three-week period, the Tour de France takes riders on a roughly circular route from Paris west to Normandy and Brittany, south to the Pyrenees Mountains, east to the Alps, and then north back to Paris. Although hampered by a severe case of bronchitis, LeMond managed to come in third, the highest finish ever for a non-European.

His chances looked even better in the 1985 Tour de France, which LeMond was gearing up to win with a new team, La Vie Claire. At race time, however, LeMond was asked to put aside his own desire for a win and instead help teammate Bernard Hinault achieve his fifth Tour de France victory. (In competitive bicycle racing, team members ride in a pack and focus on helping the teammate with the best chance of winning.) Hinault won the Tour with the support of LeMond, who finished second—still a historic accomplishment but not quite the ending he had expected.

By agreement with Hinault, the 1986 race was to be LeMond's. But once the race was under way, the Frenchman made it clear that he had no intention of helping LeMond; he was going after a sixth Tour de France win for himself. Astounded by Hinault's betrayal, LeMond was more determined than ever to go after the victory, even though it meant facing Hinault's hostility as well as that of most of his teammates and virtually all the French spectators. The psychological pressure was intense—so intense that LeMond seriously considered withdrawing from the race—but on July 27 he rode into Paris as the winner of the 1986 Tour de France.

LeMond was preparing for the 1987 Tour de France with the powerful Dutch team PDM when he broke his wrist during a race in Europe. Although this was a setback, it was nothing compared to what happened in April, 1987: while hunting in California, LeMond was accidentally shot by his brother-in-law. Approximately sixty shotgun pellets hit him in the back and side, striking his lung, kidney, liver, diaphragm, and intestine; two pellets lodged in his heart lining. Near death, he was rushed into surgery, where doctors were able to remove about half the pellets. Miraculously, none of his injuries did irreparable damage, and after a long and painful recovery, he slowly eased his way back into training.

Another setback came about four months after the shooting when LeMond underwent an emergency appendectomy, ending all hopes he might have had of racing during the 1987 season. In July, 1988, surgery for an infected shin tendon eliminated him from contention for that summer's Tour de France.

As the 1989 Tour approached, LeMond was probably at the lowest point in his professional career. Doubtful of his ability to perform, the PDM Team suggested a salary cut. "They had lost total confidence in me," LeMond recalled in a *Sports Illustrated* article. He left PDM and signed up with a less prestigious Belgian team, ADR, then continued preparing for the Tour de France. He performed well in some early races in Europe but came in a disappointing twenty-seventh in the first Tour de Trump, an American race held in May, 1989. Returning to Europe, LeMond struggled through the early stages of the Tour of Italy and considering quitting racing entirely until doctors discovered that he was severely anemic. He felt markedly stronger after receiving several iron injections and managed to eke out a morale-boosting second-place finish in the final stage. "It changed my entire outlook," LeMond declared. "Obviously, there was nothing wrong with me physically."

The Tour de France was next, and LeMond's performance made it very clear that he was still a competitor to be reckoned with. For the most part, the lead bounced back and forth between two riders: France's Laurent Fignon and—to everyone's amazement—Greg LeMond. Late in the race, when it appeared that Fignon's fifty-second lead would be impossible to beat, LeMond rebounded to set a speed record in the final Versailles-to-Paris leg. As he rode into the French capital, the American did not know whether he had managed to overcome his rival's edge. But after Fignon crossed the finish line and the numbers were tallied, a shocked LeMond was declared the winner. "I kept thinking about how I almost quit two months ago, and what a good thing it was that I never give up early," he later said about the moments following his victory. "That's what it taught me. Never give up early. The last two years have really reinforced that."

A few weeks after the Tour, LeMond put to rest any remaining doubts about his abilities by winning the world championship race in Chambery, France, making him one of only five riders to win both the Tour de France and the world championship in the same year. In recognition of his remarkable comeback, *Sports Illustrated* named LeMond its 1989 Sportsman of the Year.

In 1990, LeMond won his third Tour de France, this time as a member of the Z Team. According to *Bicycling* magazine's Geoff Drake, the victory put LeMond "on the threshold of becoming one of the greatest bike racers of all time." He is already credited with popularizing the sport among Americans and also with making it far more lucrative for participants, who have seen their compensation increase from a minimum of $7,000 in 1981 (the year LeMond turned pro) to the current level of $30,000. (The maximum team salary stands at $800,000, except for LeMond's $1.8 million.)

The 1991 Tour de France was a major disappointment for LeMond. He went into the race convinced he would win and did hold the lead as the pack left France and headed into the Pyrenees. But then illness and a series of mishaps left him far behind the eventual winner, Spain's Miguel Indurain. LeMond nevertheless pushed himself to finish and came in a humbling seventh. He was philosophical about the defeat, however, telling *Sports Illustrated* reporter Alexander Wolff that he actually felt relieved. "It would be too easy if I won every year," explained LeMond. "When you're bad, you appreciate when you're good, and this adds value to the victories I've had." He expects to go on competing in the Tour de France for another few years, then retire so that he can move back to America and spend more time with his family.

Although he enjoys the money and the life professional cycling has allowed him to lead—he and Kathy and their three children have homes in Belgium and France and one in suburban Minneapolis—money is not his prime motivation. "You never compete in the Tour just for money," he told *People* magazine reporter Cathy Nolan. "You don't suffer, kill yourself and take the risks I take just for money. I love bike racing."

Sources

➤ **Books**

Abt, Samuel, *LeMond: The Incredible Comeback of an American Hero*, Random House, 1990.

Porter, A.P., *Greg LeMond: Premier Cyclist*, Lerner Publications, 1990.

➤ **Periodicals**

Bicycling, "Europe's American Superstar, Greg LeMond," February, 1983; "Just Like in the Movies," January/February, 1984, pp. 72–78; "An American in Paris," November/December, 1984, pp. 113–115; "The Heir Apparent: Greg LeMond Takes on the Tour de France," July, 1985; "No More Mr. Nice Guy," April, 1988; "LeMond's Ultimate Challenge," May, 1989, pp. 60–68; "Fast Tracks," January/February, 1990, pp. 42–44; "LeMonster!," September/October, 1990, pp. 34–40; "Men of July," October, 1991.

New York Times Magazine, "Struggling Back," June 5, 1988.

People, December 22, 1986, p. 64; "An American in Paris Wins a Tour de Force Tour de France," August 6, 1990, pp. 77–78.

Sports Illustrated, "Climbing Clear up to the Heights," September 3, 1984, pp. 50–64; "A Good Turn at the Tour," July 29, 1985, pp. 16–21; "An American Takes Paris," August 4, 1986, pp. 12–17; "Le Grand LeMond," December 25, 1989, pp. 54–72; "Triumph," July 30, 1990, pp. 16–21; "Tour de Courage," August 5, 1991, pp. 26–31.

Maya Lin

"I *try not to editorialize on history but to document it. . . . I would never tell someone how or what to think. That's not what [my] pieces are about. They present facts."*

Born October 5, 1959, in Athens, Ohio, Maya Ying Lin is an architect and sculptor best known for designing the Vietnam Veterans Memorial ("The Wall") in Washington, D.C., and the Civil Rights Memorial in Montgomery, Alabama.

I n October, 1980, a Washington, D.C.-based group called the Vietnam Veterans Memorial Fund (VVMF) announced that it would pay $20,000 to the winner of a nationwide competition to design a monument honoring those who had served and died in the war. Nearly fifteen hundred people submitted proposals, and in May, 1981, a distinguished panel of judges representing the fields of landscape architecture, architecture, and sculpture revealed their unanimous choice: a simple V-shaped wall of polished black granite inscribed with the names of the approximately 58,000 men and women identified as killed or missing in action. To everyone's amazement, its designer turned out to be a twenty-one-year-old architecture student, Yale University senior Maya Ying Lin.

The daughter of Chinese emigres who fled their homeland in the late 1940s, Lin was born and grew up in Athens, Ohio, where both her father and mother were affiliated with Ohio University—Henry Lin as dean of fine arts and Julia Lin as a professor of Asian and English literature. Maya Lin's talent in mathematics and art led her to study architecture and sculpture at Yale, a rather unusual combination of fields that prompted some faculty members to suggest that she specialize in one or the other. "I would look at my professors, smile, and go about my business," Lin told Jill Kirschenbaum of *Ms.* magazine. "What they didn't realize, if they really looked at my work—it's always been an aesthetic that doesn't really get pocketed into one set career. I consider myself both an artist and an architect. I don't combine them, but each field informs the other."

Before she began working on her winning design, Lin had visited the proposed location, a two-acre parcel of land in the mall area between the Lincoln Memorial and the Washington Monument. The gradually sloping terrain and the strong vertical lines of the nearby buildings inspired her to opt for a low-walled structure set into the earth. Then Lin studied funerary art through the ages and contemplated the ways in which architecture helps people deal with death and grief. In addition, she read the journals of soldiers who served in World War I and analyzed some of the memorials from that era, especially those where the experience of merely walking into or through the memorial stimulates quiet reflection. "I wasn't as concerned by an artistic vision as by a people-motivated vision," Lin explained in a *McCall's* article. "I didn't want to make a political statement, either. The piece is about the people, not the politicians."

Lin's design for the monument had already been approved by the VVMF as well as the required government agencies when a small but vocal group expressed their displeasure. Their leader, Vietnam veteran Tom Carhart, characterized the wall as a "black gash of shame and sorrow," unquestionably "the most insulting and demeaning memorial to our experience that was possible." He also attacked the color of the granite Lin had chosen to use, declaring that "black is the universal color of shame, sorrow and degradation." Carhart and his supporters favored a white monument with a more traditional theme, something along the lines of the Iwo Jima Memorial of World War II.

The bitter debate raged for nearly a year, eventually involving not only veterans but also politicians of every persuasion, journalists, members of the art community, and private citizens. As more than one observer noted, including Elizabeth Hess of *Art in America*, "the battle went beyond the memorial's design to the Vietnam war itself," with hawks again squaring off against doves. At one point in the controversy, Lin was labeled a subversive for creating a monument whose shape reminded some people of the antiwar movement's peace salute; she also had to endure racist and sexist slurs from those who could not tolerate the thought of a Vietnam memorial designed by an Asian-American woman. Upset but determined to hold her ground, Lin tried to steer clear of the fray while defending her creation as apolitical. "It does not glorify the war or make an antiwar statement," she insisted in a *People* magazine article. "It is a place for private reckoning."

Finally, the opposing sides reached a compromise of sorts in which the VVMF agreed to add a flagpole and a second memorial sculpted by Frederick Hart, one of the entrants in the original competition. This second memorial—a veritable "tribute to John Wayne," in Hess's words—would depict three realistic but slightly larger-than-life-size soldiers standing near the wall and turned toward it. Lin was not consulted or informed about any of the changes and eventually heard about them on television, at which point she protested that incorporating a flag and the statue so near her memorial would be "like putting mustaches on other people's portraits." After more debate, it was decided that the statue and the flag would have to be positioned closer to the entrance to the site so as not to interfere with Lin's original design.

Construction of the memorial began in March, 1982, and was completed seven months later, just in time for its dedication on Veterans Day. Thoroughly disillusioned by her experience and weary of all the arguments and publicity, Lin had tried to distance herself from the entire project by returning to school, where she hoped she could once again be just another student and not a celebrity. In early 1983, however, she quit her graduate studies in architecture at Harvard University and dropped out of sight. She spent most of the rest of the year working quietly for a Boston architect, then resumed her studies at Yale, graduating in 1986 with a master's degree in architecture.

By this time, something unexpected but immensely gratifying had occurred that helped restore Lin's faith in herself and her abilities: the Vietnam Veterans Memorial, that so-called "black gash of shame," had become not only a highly respected work of public art but also the most visited monument in the entire country. In fact, from the moment it first opened to the public, "The Wall" has struck a special chord with surviving veterans, their families, and others who come to find—and touch—the names of loved ones and see themselves reflected in the highly polished black granite. Park Service officials routinely collect letters, clothes, photographs, dogtags, medals, and other personal mementos visitors leave behind. As Kirschenbaum notes, the Wall has clearly come to stand as "much more than a monument to the dead; it [is] an invitation to grieve." A downsized Plexiglass replica tours the United States for those who are not able to travel to Washington.

Although she had vowed never again to design a memorial—at least not a war memorial—Lin accepted a commission from the Southern Poverty Law Center in 1988 to create a monument honoring the civil rights movement. She prepared for the project in much the same way she had for the Vietnam Veterans Memorial; after familiarizing herself with the site, a large white granite plaza in front of the center's new headquarters in Montgomery, Alabama, Lin immersed herself in material on the subject (about which she knew very little), including books and videotapes provided by her contact at the center.

During the course of her research, Lin kept coming back to a line from Martin Luther King, Jr.'s, "I Have a Dream" speech, which incorporated one of his favorite biblical passages: "We will not be satisfied until 'justice rolls down like waters and righteousness like a mighty stream.'" Water, she reasoned, would offer a perfect contrast to the hot climate of Alabama, and the sight and sound of it gently flowing would create a calm and soothing atmosphere, ideal for contemplative thought.

After visiting Montgomery in May, 1988, Lin returned a few

weeks later with her proposal, a design as simple and serene as her earlier one. Again making use of black granite, she created a long, curved wall in front of which she placed a 12-foot-diameter disk that appeared to float a few feet above the plaza. Inscribed on the disk would be the names of more than fifty civil rights martyrs and key dates and events in the movement; inscribed on the wall would be the quotation from Martin Luther King, Jr., that inspired the design. A thin sheet of water would flow over both the wall and the disk, enticing visitors to study their own reflections in the polished stone and trace the words with their fingertips. "I'm trying to make people become involved with the piece on all levels," Lin explained, "with the touch and sound of the water, with the words, with the memories."

The proposed monument was approved and constructed without incident, and in a solemn and emotional ceremony held November 5, 1989, the new Civil Rights Memorial was dedicated amid much praise for the architect, who maintained it was her last such undertaking. Lin now devotes her time to many different projects—some personal, others commissioned, some involving architecture, others involving sculpture. She continues to shun fame, finding it necessary to withdraw from the public eye every now and then to focus on her own work. "You really can't function as a celebrity," she once told Jonathan Coleman of *Time* magazine. "Entertainers are celebrities. I'm an architect. I'm an artist. I make things. I just love the fact that I can make a work and put it out there and walk away from it and then look at it like everyone else."

Sources

> **Periodicals**

Architectural Record, "Touch Stone," February, 1990, pp. 186–187.

Art in America, "A Tale of Two Memorials," April, 1983, pp. 120–127.

Art News, January, 1983, p. 11.

House & Garden, "Maya Lin Is Young, Brilliant, Accomplished and Doesn't Like to Talk about It," March, 1990, p. 214 (opening quote).

McCall's, "The Wall: Monument to a Nation's Sacrifice," June, 1988.

Ms., "The Symmetry of Maya Ying Lin," September/October, 1990, pp. 20–22.

Newsweek, "Refighting the Vietnam War," October 25, 1982, p. 30; "Up against the Wall," January 20, 1986, p. 6.

New York Times Magazine, "Monument Maker," February 24, 1991.

People, "Maya Ying Lin's Memorial to the Vietnam War Dead Raises Hope—and Anger," March 8, 1982, pp. 38–39; "Maya Lin Lets Healing Waters Flow over Her Civil Rights Memorial," November 20, 1989, pp. 78–80.

Seventeen, "Doing the Rights Thing," June, 1990, p. 40.

Smithsonian, "'I Realized Her Tears Were Becoming Part of the Memorial,'" September, 1991, pp. 32–43.

Time, "First She Looks Inward," November 6, 1989, pp. 90–94.

Anne Sullivan Macy

*"*I *feel in every heartbeat that I belong to Helen, and it awes me when I think of it—this giving of one's life that another may live. . . . It is a privilege to love and minister to such a rare spirit."*

Dubbed the "miracle-worker" by writer Mark Twain, Anne Sullivan Macy was Helen Keller's beloved teacher and companion for nearly fifty years. She was born on April 14, 1866, in Feeding Hills, Massachusetts, and died on October 20, 1936, in Forest Hills, New York.

"**W**e walked down the path to the well-house. . . . Someone was drawing water and my teacher placed my hand under the spout. As the cool stream gushed over one hand she spelled into the other the word *water*, first slowly, then rapidly. . . . Suddenly I felt a misty consciousness as of something forgotten—a thrill of returning thought. . . . I knew then that "w-a-t-e-r" meant the wonderful cool something that was flowing over my hand. That living word awakened my soul." Thus did Helen Keller—robbed of her sight, hearing, and speaking ability at the age of nineteen months after a mysterious fever—recall her emergence from darkness and silence. The woman who brought about that amazing rebirth and guided her along the path to further knowledge was Anne Sullivan Macy.

Christened "Joanna" but more commonly known as "Annie" or "Anne," Sullivan was born near Springfield, Massachusetts, the daughter of Irish immigrants Thomas and Alice Chloesy Sullivan. Poverty and sorrow marked the first fourteen years of her life. Alice Sullivan developed tuberculosis when Annie was still a baby and died before her daughter's ninth birthday; Thomas Sullivan was an alcoholic who routinely beat Annie in an attempt to subdue her headstrong nature. Not long after his wife's death, Thomas abandoned his three children to the care of relatives and set off for Chicago to make his fortune, never to be heard from again.

Annie was by this time already partially blinded by an eye disease called trachoma; her younger brother, Jimmie, suffered from a tubercular tumor on his hip. Their baby sister, Mary, was taken in by one of Thomas's brothers and his wife, but no one wanted to assume permanent responsibility for a blind girl and a crippled boy. So, in February, 1876, Annie and Jimmie were sent to live at the notorious Tewksbury poorhouse, a squalid facility that served as a combination prison, asylum, and hospital. Jimmie died only a few months after their arrival, but Annie stayed for four years. Sympathetic doctors occasionally operated on her eyes or tried new medications, but nothing helped, and it seemed certain that she would remain at Tewksbury as a permanent ward of the state.

In 1880, Massachusetts government officials toured the poorhouse in response to widespread rumors about the appalling conditions there. Literally hurling herself at the investigators as they were about to leave, Annie begged for a chance to attend school. The head of the group, Frank Sanborn, was touched by her desperate plea and made arrangements for her to enter the Perkins Institution for the

Blind in Boston, where she underwent two operations on her eyes that finally enabled her to read printed words on a page.

Graduating from Perkins with honors in 1886, Sullivan now faced the prospect of having to make her own way in the world. Later that same summer, Arthur Keller of Tuscumbia, Alabama, wrote to the director of the Perkins Institution asking him to recommend a teacher for his six-year-old daughter, Helen, who was blind, deaf, and unable to speak. The director approached Sullivan, who, despite some serious doubts about her ability to take on such a monumental task, agreed to give it a try.

She arrived in Tuscumbia on March 3, 1887, about a month shy of her twenty-first birthday. Her plan was to win Helen's love slowly, then begin communicating the idea that everything has a name and that the name can be expressed by the use of a particular word. Sullivan intended to teach Helen the manual alphabet, a system originally developed for the deaf in which the letters are represented by finger positions. Helen, of course, would have to learn those finger positions by touch as Sullivan spelled words into her hand.

But the young teacher had a more pressing problem to solve first. Now almost seven years old, Helen was a strong-willed child who had always been allowed to have her own way. The Kellers could never bring themselves to punish their daughter and did not appreciate Sullivan's attempts to do so. Realizing that she needed to be alone with the little girl for a while, Sullivan moved into a small hunting cottage on the family property not far from the main house. There she worked to calm Helen's wildness and establish a bond of acceptance and trust. Two weeks later, a markedly more gentle child returned, one who seemed eager to learn and less inclined to fight.

It was on April 5—a mere month after Sullivan's arrival—that Helen first realized "w-a-t-e-r" was the name of the liquid flowing out of the pump in the well-house and that everything else had a name, too. Running out into the yard, she touched one object after another, demanding to know its name. Later that same exhilarating day, Helen pointed to Sullivan with an obvious question. "T-e-a-c-h-e-r," she spelled. And "Teacher" was what Helen—and many others—called her for the rest of her life.

Sullivan took advantage of her pupil's insatiable appetite for knowledge and worked with her virtually day and night. As Helen continued to excel, word spread about the deaf and blind "miracle child" in Alabama. On her first trip to Boston in May, 1888, Helen (accompanied by her mother and Sullivan) was treated like a celebrity.

The constant effort to observe, read, explain, and spell for Helen took its toll on Sullivan's health, and in 1889, she returned to Boston for eye treatments. Helen joined her later that same year and was once again the guest of honor at countless social gatherings. The invitations to these events often excluded Sullivan, however, for many people outside the academic community were unaware of her role in Helen's success and regarded her as little more than a servant. It was an image she was never able to shake completely, perhaps because she so willingly took a back seat to her pupil and downplayed her own accomplishments.

By the 1890s, the Kellers could no longer afford to pay Sullivan. Others offered her salaried teaching positions, but she had long before made her choice to stay with Helen. Helped by donations from friends and admirers and later by a small trust fund, the two settled near Boston to tackle Helen's next major goal: college. Sullivan was at her side through four years of preparatory school followed by four more years at Radcliffe, attending lectures and spelling them into Helen's hand, reading all of the required texts and interpreting them for her, and helping her prepare class assignments and papers. Once again, the strain threatened Sullivan's own vision; doctors warned her that she was in danger of going blind if she did not rest her eyes.

After graduating with honors from Radcliffe in 1904—the first time anyone with her handicaps had even entered college, let alone finished—Helen returned with her teacher to the home they had purchased the year before in Wrentham, Massachusetts. In 1905, Sullivan married John Macy, a Harvard instructor, author, and critic who had helped Helen edit her autobiography. He lived with the two women in Wrentham, but the marriage was not a happy one; he and Annie separated permanently around 1914. That same year, Polly Thomson became a companion to both Helen and Annie, whose deteriorating physical health and poor eyesight made it impossible for her to manage the household and tend to all of Helen's needs.

Despite her doctors' pleas, Macy continued to do all she could to further her pupil's blossoming career as a writer and lecturer. (Although Helen had begun taking speech lessons as early as 1890, she was never able to speak clearly. Consequently, Macy was usually on stage with her to interpret.) In a letter to a friend, Macy described her part in the process: "The genius is [Helen's], but much of the drudgery is mine. . . . The difficulties under which she works are so insurmountable. Someone must always be at her side to read to her, to keep her typewriter in order, to read over her manuscript, make corrections, and look up words for her, and to do the many things which she would do for herself if she had her sight." Helen's writings and speeches not only furnished some badly needed income, they also proved to be effective fund-raisers for charity.

Throughout the 1920s, Macy experienced increasing pain and infections in her eyes that left her able to read only for a few hours a day with the help of heavy, awkward, double-lensed telescopic glasses. More often than not, Polly Thomson took her place, particularly when Helen's work involved extensive preparation and travel. One of Macy's last projects was to help Helen update her autobiography. After that, cataracts claimed what little vision she still had left.

Anne Sullivan Macy died at home of a heart ailment on October 20, 1936. In a tribute to her that ran on the editorial page, the *New York Times* lauded Macy's "triumph over a dark and sordid environment and terrible poverty." Even more important, the writer went on to note, she had "brought light to one in a double prison of darkness and silence and liberated her spirit. She deserves a place among the world's greatest teachers."

Sources

➤ **Books**

Braddy, Nella, *Anne Sullivan Macy: The Story behind Helen Keller*, Doubleday, 1934 (opening quote).

Davidson, Margaret, *Helen Keller's Teacher*, Scholastic, 1972.

Keller, Helen, *The Story of My Life*, Doubleday, Page, 1903.

Keller, Helen, *Midstream: My Later Life*, Doubleday, Doran, 1929.

Keller, Helen, *Teacher: Anne Sullivan Macy*, Doubleday, 1955. Reprint. Greenwood Press, 1985.

Lash, Joseph P., *Helen and Teacher: The Story of Helen Keller and Annie Sullivan Macy*, Delacorte, 1980.

➤ **Periodicals**

New York Times, October 21, 1936, pp. 26–27.

➤ **Other**

"The Miracle Worker," William Gibson's account of Annie Sullivan's first few months with Helen Keller, has been produced as a television drama (once in 1957 on CBS and again in 1979 on NBC), a Broadway play (1959), and a movie (1962).

"Monday after the Miracle," also by Gibson, takes up the story twenty years later; it was produced as a Broadway play in 1982.

Malcolm X

*"**A** race of people is like an individual man; until it uses its own talent, takes pride in its own history, expresses its own culture, affirms its own selfhood, it can never fulfill itself."*

Malcolm X was a Black nationalist and Muslim leader whose militant advocacy of Black pride, separatism, and armed self-defense foreshadowed the Black Power movement of the late 1960s. He was born on May 19, 1925, in Omaha, Nebraska, and was assassinated on February 21, 1965, in New York City.

As even he himself stated in his autobiography, Malcolm X was a man of many different identities, a man who lived five or six lifetimes in one. Born Malcolm Little to Louise Norton Little and Earl Little, a Baptist minister, he had an especially turbulent and unhappy childhood. His father was an outspoken supporter of Black nationalist leader Marcus Garvey, and as a result the family incurred the wrath of various White vigilante groups. Driven from their home in Omaha, Nebraska, they moved to Milwaukee, Wisconsin, and from there to Lansing, Michigan, where they were harassed by a terrorist organization known as the Black Legion. Members of the Legion burned the Littles' house to the ground in 1929, and in 1931 Earl Little was found on some streetcar tracks with his skull crushed and his body nearly severed in half. The police called it an accident, but the family suspected that Legion members had actually beaten him to death and then thrown his body on the tracks to make it look as if he had been struck by a passing streetcar.

Left emotionally unstable by the years of turmoil and tragedy she had endured, Louise Little was committed to a state mental hospital in 1937. Little and his seven siblings were then divided among various foster homes and state institutions. Despite his unsettled family life, Little was an excellent student and class leader with dreams of becoming a lawyer. His dream was shattered when a White teacher he confided in cruelly advised him to be "realistic" about being Black and plan on becoming a carpenter instead.

Little dropped out of school not long after that and headed to Boston, where he worked at a series of menial jobs and drifted into petty crime, and then to Harlem around 1942. As a street hood nicknamed "Detroit Red" he ran a gambling operation, sold and used marijuana and cocaine, and hustled business for brothels. Returning to Boston, he organized a burglary ring, an activity that eventually led to his arrest and imprisonment in 1946.

Once in prison, Little—dubbed "Satan" by his fellow convicts because he was so full of hate and anger—set about transforming his life through a process of self-education. But the real turning point came when one of his younger brothers introduced him to the teachings of Elijah Muhammad, leader of the Lost-Found Nation of Islam, better known as the Black Muslims. The core of Muhammad's philosophy held that Whites were nothing but a "devil race" created to torment the Black race and that in order to flourish Blacks had to separate themselves culturally, economically, politically, and physically from Western, White civilization.

By the time Little was paroled in 1952, he had taken the Muslim surname "X" in place of the "slave name" Little and had wholeheartedly embraced the beliefs of the Black Muslims. Accepted into the movement after impressing Elijah Muhammad with his quick intelligence and forceful personality, Malcolm X was soon ordained a minister and given a position at a Detroit mosque. He followed that with a period of private study under Muhammad himself and was then sent to Philadelphia to establish a new congregation. From there he went on to serve as leader of the Harlem mosque, although he was frequently called upon to start new congregations across the country.

Throughout the 1950s and into the early 1960s, the charismatic Malcolm X took the Nation of Islam from an insignificant splinter group of about 400 people to an organization that boasted some 10,000 official members and an untold number of sympathizers. A talented and articulate speaker whose fiery, intense style bordered on demagoguery, he was by far the Nation of Islam's most effective and prominent preacher and was in almost constant demand on college campuses, at meetings of various associations, and on radio and television programs.

The message he shared with his audiences was the exact opposite of what people were accustomed to hearing from more "mainstream" civil rights activists such as Dr. Martin Luther King, who called for the integration of American society through nonviolent means. Malcolm X advocated Black separatism, and he advised Blacks to take up arms in self-defense against White hostility. As a result of his fiercely militant stance, he was hated and feared not only by most Whites but also by many Blacks, who worried that his tirades against "White devils" would provoke a catastrophic race war. The media enhanced this perception by consistently portraying him as a dangerous rabble-rouser and outlaw.

But the more famous Malcolm X became, the more tension and jealousy he provoked among the leaders of the Nation of Islam, who were also wary of his growing uneasiness with some of the more cultish aspects of the Black Muslim faith. If Elijah Muhammad were looking for an excuse to get rid of such a formidable threat to his own power, he found it in December, 1963, when Malcolm X publicly described the assassination of President John F. Kennedy as a case of "chickens coming home to roost" in a society that tolerated White violence against Blacks. Muhammad suspended his protege and forbid him from speaking on behalf of the Nation of Islam for ninety days. The estrangement became permanent in March, 1964, when Malcolm X announced that he was quitting the Nation of Islam to form two new groups of his own, the Harlem-based Muslim Mosque, Inc., and the multinational Organization of Afro-American Unity.

That same spring, Malcolm X made a pilgrimage to the holy city of Mecca and followed it with a prolonged period of study in the Middle East and Africa. Impressed by the sight of people of all races coming together as one in the name of Islam, he returned to the United States in late 1964 a changed man, proclaiming himself a convert to orthodox Islam and adopting a new name El-Hajj Malik El-Shabazz. His new philosophy combined elements of his religious faith with socialism, anticolonialism, and what eventually came to be known as "Black consciousness"—a sense of pride in being Black and a desire to foster links with other Blacks around the world based on a shared racial and cultural heritage. He softened his stance on a wide variety of issues and tried to downplay his menacing image. He admitted he had once been a racist but insisted that he no longer accepted Elijah Muhammad's belief that all White people were evil; economics, not color, was what kept Blacks from succeeding. He also condemned separatism as counterproductive and expressed a willingness to work within the system to secure political and civil rights for Blacks, and to that end he began making overtures to moderate Black leaders and progressive Whites.

Throughout the rest of 1964 and into early 1965, Malcolm X also became increasingly critical of Elijah Muhammad and the Nation of Islam, raising questions about financial irregularities and suspicious contacts with White supremacist groups and even denouncing his onetime mentor as a fake, a racist, and an immoral philanderer who had fathered at least eight children with several young Muslim secretaries. The conflict between the two men and their respective supporters escalated as both sides traded insults and accusations. The situation took an ominous turn after Malcolm X received a number of death threats and thwarted what he suspected were Black Muslim attempts on his life, including a firebombing incident at his home during the night of February 14, 1965.

Exactly one week later, on February 21, Malcolm X was preparing to address several hundred of his followers in Harlem's Audubon Ballroom when three Black men rushed up the center aisle toward him and opened fire with a shotgun and two pistols, striking him more than a dozen times. He died a short time later while undergoing surgery at a nearby hospital. The shotgun-toting man was quickly tackled and subdued by onlookers, and the other two suspects were apprehended some time later. All three men had ties to the Nation of Islam, but one of them later insisted that he had been paid by someone else to kill Malcolm X. A jury subsequently convicted them of murder, for which they were sentenced to life in prison.

The initial reaction to Malcolm X's death was mixed; the White press took the opportunity to moralize that those who live by the sword die by it, while Black leaders acknowledged his moderating views and termed the loss of his brilliance and passion a setback for the civil rights movement. It was not until the end of the year, after the publication of *The Autobiography of Malcolm X* (an as-told-to work he collaborated on with writer Alex Haley), that his message of Black unity, self-respect, and self-reliance truly began to strike a responsive chord. (The book has remained an enduring bestseller, posting a 300 percent gain in sales from 1988 to 1991 alone.) Later he was hailed as the first true Black revolutionary and the inspiration for the Black Power movement of the late 1960s.

The legacy of Malcolm X remains a powerful force in Black America, his affirmation of Black pride admired by people at opposite ends of the political spectrum, from conservative Supreme Court Justice Clarence Thomas to revolutionary playwright and poet Imamu Amiri Baraka. A great deal of the current interest in him can be attributed to filmmaker Spike Lee, who closed his movie *Do the Right Thing* with the famous "by any means necessary" quote from Malcolm X's "The Ballot or the Bullet" speech. Not long after that, the Black nationalist's likeness and slogans began showing up on T-shirts worn by Black and White teenagers in major U.S. cities. Then Lee began sporting a baseball cap featuring a large "X" on the front as a promotional gimmick for his film on the life of Malcolm X, which touched off a virtual explosion of interest in clothing and art bearing his image. Even the music world has taken notice; many rap artists, for instance, have incorporated Malcolm X's words and message into their songs.

The commercialization of Malcolm X bothers some people, who find it sad that so many young Blacks feel they have to look to the grave for leadership and ironic that a man who rejected mainstream culture has himself become a consumer good and pop icon. Yet his ongoing importance as a symbol of the Black struggle is undeniable. "Our generation said, 'Just topple the walls of segregation,'" explains Cornell University professor James Turner, the national chairman of the Malcolm X Commemoration Commission. "The walls are down but the barriers to social justice are still there. Young people are asking, 'Who are we, in this time?' Malcolm speaks to that." Howard Dodson of the Schomburg Center for Research in Black Culture agrees. "There's something in Malcolm that touches the core of younger people," he says. "He was willing to stand up, to talk straight. Malcolm was a man—a real man."

Sources

➤ **Books**

Breitman, George, editor, *Malcolm X Speaks: Selected Speeches and Statements*, Pathfinder Press, 1965.

Breitman, George, editor, *By Any Means Necessary: Speeches, Interviews and a Letter by Malcolm X*, Pathfinder Press, 1970.

Goldman, Peter, *The Death and Life of Malcolm X*, Harper, 1973, rev. ed., 1979.

Malcolm X (as told to Alex Haley), *The Autobiography of Malcolm X*, Grove, 1965.

O'Neill, William L., *Coming Apart: An Informal History of America in the 1960s*, Quadrangle, 1971.

Perry, Bruce, *Malcolm: The Life of a Man Who Changed Black America*, Station Hill Press, 1991.

Rummel, Jack, *Malcolm X: Militant Black Leader*, Chelsea House, 1989.

➤ **Periodicals**

Ebony, "Who Killed Malcolm X?," October, 1965, pp. 135–142; "Ten Greats of Black History," August, 1972, pp. 35–42; "The Legacy of Malcolm X," May, 1989, pp. 156–161.

Essence, February, 1992.

Grand Rapids Press, "Sister Guards the Memory of Malcolm X," November 17, 1991, pp. F1-F2; "Will 'X' Caps Spur Serious Interest in Malcolm X Among Youth?," November 17, 1991, p. F2.

Insight, "Young Blacks Thrust Malcolm X into the Air," September 4, 1989.

Mother Jones, "Malcolm, Let's Do Lunch," July/August, 1991.

Newsweek, "Death of a Desperado," March 8, 1965, pp. 24–25; "Satan in the Ghetto," November 15, 1965, pp. 130–132; "Rediscovering Malcolm X," February 26, 1990, pp. 68–69; "The Battle for Malcolm X," August 26, 1991, pp. 52–54.

New York Times, February 22, 1965.

Playboy, "The Playboy Interview: Malcolm X," January, 1989. Reprint of original 1963 interview.

Time, "Death and Transfiguration," March 5, 1965, pp. 23–25.

Wilma Mankiller

"*T here are people ... who don't realize our communities exist as they do today. ... Most people like to deal with us as though we were in a museum or a history book.*"

Born on November 18, 1945, in Stilwell, Oklahoma, Wilma Mankiller is the first woman to serve as head of a major North American Indian tribe.

Address: Cherokee Nation, P.O. Box 948, Tahlequah, OK 74465.

As leader of one of the largest Native American tribes in the United States—second in size only to the Navajo Nation—Wilma Mankiller is charged with helping the Cherokee people achieve economic independence and renewed pride in their culture. It is an enormous task, she admits, somewhat "like being chief executive officer of a large corporation, as well as being a social worker at the same time," as she once remarked to a reporter for *Southern Living.* Yet most observers believe Mankiller is uniquely qualified to do what must be done to achieve her ambitious goals.

She was born in rural Adair County, Oklahoma, one of eleven children of a full-blooded Cherokee and his wife, who was of Dutch-Irish ancestry. ("Mankiller" was originally a Cherokee military title one of her ancestors adopted as his own name.) The Mankillers barely eked out a living as farmers, and when a severe drought struck the area in the late 1950s, they were forced to turn to the government for help. As part of an assistance program designed to move Indians off the reservations and into the cities where jobs were more plentiful, the Mankillers were encouraged to relocate to Chicago, Oakland, or San Francisco. Since San Francisco was the home of Wilma's maternal grandmother, the family headed west to California.

Moving from rural Oklahoma to a big city ghetto was a profound cultural shock for Mankiller. "One day I was here [in Adair County], and the next day I was trying to deal with the mysteries of television, indoor plumbing, neon lights and elevators," she recalls in a *People* magazine article. Her father found work in a warehouse and became a union organizer, and the Mankillers eventually adjusted to urban life.

Throughout most of the 1960s, Mankiller pursued her studies in sociology and a career in social work. In 1963, she married a well-to-do Ecuadoran accountant; they had two daughters. Then something happened that "articulated my Indian feelings," to use Mankiller's words. In 1969, in an effort to call attention to the plight of Native Americans, a group of young Indians took over the former Alcatraz prison complex and held it for eighteen months. Raising funds to help the protesters propelled Mankiller into the American Native Rights movement and led her to reassess her life. By 1975, she had divorced her husband and moved back to Oklahoma with the idea of reclaiming her ancestral land and living a simple rural life with her daughters.

Over the next few years, Mankiller drew on her background in social work to develop and implement various self-help programs in the Cherokee community, first as economic stimulus coordinator for the Cherokee Nation and later as its program development specialist. (Her work was interrupted for a year beginning in late 1979 when a serious auto accident left her face crushed, ribs broken, and legs shattered.) In 1981, she founded the Community Development Department and served as its first director, focusing her efforts on rehabilitating substandard housing and providing water lines to rural areas. All of her plans stressed the building of self-esteem through community involvement, a concept she says is based on Indian traditions from an era when tribes "controlled their own destiny."

Mankiller's skill at obtaining funding for her programs as well as her ability to administer them successfully soon brought her to the attention of tribal leaders, including Ross Swimmer, who asked her to serve as his running mate in the 1983 election for principal chief and deputy chief. Despite the fact that they were political opposites—he was a conservative Republican and she was a liberal Democrat—they shared a common goal of wanting to see the Cherokee Nation become more self-reliant. Overcoming the objections of some male members of the tribe that a woman was not suited to be deputy chief, Swimmer and Mankiller won in a close contest, a victory that made Mankiller the first female deputy chief. Two years later, she became the first female principal chief when Swimmer resigned his post to accept a job with the Reagan administration.

In 1987, when she decided to run for principal chief in her own right, Mankiller faced an uphill battle. A bout with a rare form of muscular dystrophy left her weakened for a while (it is now in remission), and a serious kidney infection put her in the hospital for two weeks during the campaign. (In 1990, she was finally forced to undergo a kidney transplant.) And once again, some male members of the tribe expressed their doubts about electing a female chief. With the help of her second husband, Charlie Soap, a Cherokee who works on rural development projects for the nation, she was able to persuade the reluctant men that it was "safe" to vote for a woman.

Since that time, she says, opposition to her as a female chief has lessened considerably. "People are used to me. I don't get treated differently than anybody else. If I do a good job, people are happy; if I do something they don't like, they let me know they are unhappy." Besides, as she once explained to *Ms.* magazine's Michele Wallace, traditional Indian culture accords women a very strong role. "We adopted a lot of ugly things that were part of the non-Indian world and one of those things was sexism," notes Mankiller. "This whole system of tribal government was designed by men. So in 1687 women enjoyed a prominent role, but in 1987 we found people questioning whether women should be in leadership positions anywhere in the tribe. So my election was a step forward and a step backward at the same time." In June, 1991, Mankiller was elected to a second four-year term as principal chief, gaining eighty-three percent of the vote.

From her base in Tahlequah, the administrative center of the Cherokee Nation, Mankiller oversees social welfare programs and business activities involving the tribe's more than seventy thousand members, who live on some fifty-five thousand acres of land spread across fourteen northeastern Oklahoma counties. Like her predecessor, she continues to stress the importance of economic development; at present, the Cherokee Nation owns and operates a motel, a restaurant, two gift shops, an electronics manufacturing facility, a nursery, several industrial parks, and a cattle and poultry ranch. Future plans include building a hydroelectric plant and establishing numerous small farms that would supply major agricultural companies.

While her concerns mirror those of a typical governor (with unemployment, education, housing, and health care topping the list), Mankiller also faces the added challenge of bolstering the spirit of her people and bridging the gap between the old ways and the new. "In my generation, . . . we're trying to figure out a balance between the two worlds," she remarks in *Southern Living*. "There are the extremes on both sides. There are those who have turned their backs on being Cherokee. Then we have a few who refuse to speak much English and think children should only play stickball, not baseball or football. They are suspicious of the non-Indian world, thinking too much assimilation will cause one to stop thinking Cherokee."

Compounding the problem are the stereotypes about Indians that still exist in white society, Mankiller contends in a *U.S. News and World Report* interview. "Western movies always seemed to show Indian women washing clothes at the creek and men with a tomahawk or spear in their hands, adorned with lots of feathers," she says. "That image has stayed in some people's minds. Many think we're either visionaries, 'noble savages,' squaw drudges or tragic alcoholics. We're very rarely depicted as real people who have greater tenacity in terms of trying to hang on to our culture and values system than most people."

"For compassionate skills in building economic power and self-esteem as the first woman elected Principal Chief of the Cherokee Nation, and for enriching all Americans with a new style of leadership," Wilma Mankiller was named *Ms.* magazine's Woman of the Year for 1987. It is one of many honors she has received for her pioneering work. "I know what I'm doing and I like what I'm doing," she declared in a 1986 interview with *Ms.* "If I were rich, I would pay the Cherokee Nation to be able to do exactly what I'm doing right now."

Sources

➤ **Periodicals**

Ms., "Wilma Mankiller: Harnessing Traditional Cherokee Wisdom," August, 1986, p. 32; January, 1988, pp. 68–69.

People, "Activist Wilma Mankiller Is Set to Become the First Female Chief of the Cherokee Nation," December 2, 1985, pp. 91–92.

Southern Living, "Chief of the Cherokee," November, 1986, p. 190.

Time, "To Each Her Own: Combining Talent and Drive, Ten Tough-Minded Women Create Individual Rules for Success," Fall, 1990 (special issue).

U.S. News and World Report, "People Expect Me to Be More Warlike," February 17, 1986, p. 64.

Thurgood Marshall

*"*N*othing can shake my faith in my country. I still believe firmly that right will win out."*

A pioneering civil rights attorney, Thurgood Marshall later became the first Black American appointed to the United States Supreme Court. He was born on July 2, 1908, in Baltimore, Maryland.

On June 13, 1967, Thurgood Marshall, the great-grandson of a slave, became the first Black American to be nominated to the Supreme Court of the United States. While this in itself was a ground-breaking achievement, it was, in fact, the culmination of a long and distinguished legal career that had already secured for Marshall a place in history as one of the outstanding civil rights attorneys of the century. First in private practice and later as legal director of the National Association for the Advancement of Colored People (NAACP) for more than twenty years, he argued a series of cases that steadily chipped away at legally justified racial discrimination in such areas as education, voting, housing, jury service, and public accommodations. As a *Detroit News* editorial writer observed, the many victories of the man known as "Mr. Civil Rights" were directly responsible for "a largely bloodless revolution that extended liberty and dignity to a large segment of the American population."

A native of Baltimore who spent the first five years of his life in Harlem before returning to his hometown, Thurgood Marshall was the oldest of two sons born to Norma Williams, a teacher, and William Canfield Marshall, a waiter at a Whites-only club on Chesapeake Bay. He credits his father with instilling in him a rebellious spirit, recalling how he sternly admonished both his sons: "If anyone calls you a nigger, you not only got my permission to fight him, you got my orders to fight him." Marshall was a fun-loving and popular student in both high school and at Lincoln University, an all-Black college near Philadelphia. He graduated with honors in 1929, then went on to Howard University Law School after being denied admittance to the University of Maryland Law School on the basis of race. As a fledgling attorney, Marshall challenged that policy on behalf of another Black-American man whose application had been rejected and forced the school to admit its first Black student.

After graduating (again with honors) from Howard in 1933, Marshall went into private practice in Baltimore specializing in civil rights and criminal law, often representing clients who could not afford to pay. He also served as counsel to the Baltimore chapter of the NAACP, where his skills soon brought him to the attention of the organization's national president, Arthur Spingarn. In 1936, Spingarn persuaded Marshall to move to NAACP headquarters in New York City to become the assistant to the chief counsel. When the chief counsel resigned two years later, Marshall was promoted to the position, and in 1940 he was named director of the NAACP's newly formed Legal Defense and Educational Fund, a post he held until 1961.

As an *Ebony* magazine reporter once noted, "when Marshall came to the NAACP his life became the story of a man and an organization, both of which grew together." Their shared goal was to eliminate racial segregation by demonstrating in court on a case-by-case basis that the multitude of restrictive laws on the books—especially in the South—were unconstitutional. Throughout the 1940s and 1950s, Marshall masterminded the fight against discrimination, arguing thirty-two cases before the Supreme Court and winning twenty-nine of them. His ground-breaking victories covered a broad area; his efforts resulted in the striking down of laws making it difficult or impossible for Blacks to vote in so-called "White" primaries, to serve on juries or in the armed forces, to use sleeping and dining cars on trains, and to rent and buy real estate.

By far Marshall's most noteworthy battle came in 1954 with *Brown v. Board of Education*, a case that changed the entire nation. In appearances before the U.S. Supreme Court, Marshall successfully argued against school segregation, declaring that the "separate-but-equal" doctrine established in 1896 in *Plessy v. Ferguson* was unconstitutional because "separate educational facilities are inherently unequal." The ruling forced schools throughout the country to desegregate, a slow and sometimes violent process. Yet as Marshall himself later commented, the court's decision "probably did more than anything else to awaken the Negro from his apathy to demanding his right to equality."

In 1961, President John F. Kennedy proposed Marshall for a federal judgeship on the U.S. Court of Appeals for the Second Circuit (an area encompassing New York, Vermont, and Connecticut). Southern segregationists did everything they could to stall the process, and as a result his confirmation took nearly a year. There was much less opposition four years later when President Lyndon Johnson named Marshall solicitor general, a position in which he argued cases on behalf of the government before the Supreme Court. During his two years in the post, he won fourteen of the nineteen cases he presented. Many observers speculated that the next logical step in his career was an appointment to the high court itself, and in 1967 they were proved right when Johnson nominated Marshall to be the first Black-American associate justice. Again the confirmation process was delayed, this time by critics (led by South Carolina Senator Strom Thurmond) who attacked Marshall's liberal and "activist" legal bent. But as Senator Philip Hart of Michigan observed, never had there been a Supreme Court nominee "whose qualifications are so dramatically and compellingly established." Marshall was finally confirmed a little more than two months after he had been nominated.

Despite the claims of Thurmond and other conservatives, Marshall was a rather moderate voice among the five or six justices deemed liberal on most issues. But as presidents Nixon, Ford, Reagan, and Bush replaced retiring liberal justices with conservatives, Marshall often found himself standing almost alone as a champion of the liberal view and its insistence that the rights of the individual take precedence over the rights of the state. For example, he spoke out forcefully against the death penalty, characterizing it as an "excessive" punishment that unfairly discriminates against certain classes of people. Along with his liberal colleagues, Marshall upheld defendants' rights against questionable searches, surveillance, and interrogation practices and strongly supported the 1966 *Miranda v. Arizona* ruling and its provisions for obtaining and using confessions and guaranteeing a suspect's right to counsel. He also disagreed with government attempts to restrict First Amendment rights, particularly those dealing with freedom of speech and freedom of religion, and insisted that the right to privacy prohibits states from encroaching on a woman's right to an abortion.

Despite the changes that occurred on the Supreme Court during the 1980s, Marshall repeatedly declared that he expected to serve out his lifetime appointment and continued to voice his opposition to the conservative majority. Yet he grew increasingly dismayed by Reagan administration policies and new rulings that he felt eroded earlier civil rights gains. He was also frustrated by what he saw as a lack of understanding among his colleagues of racism's effects on American society.

In 1990, Justice William Brennan, a liberal appointee of former President Dwight Eisenhower, retired from the Supreme Court and left his good friend Marshall as the sole dissenting voice. In June of the following year, Marshall announced his own retirement from the bench, citing his "advancing age and medical condition." (The eighty-two-year-old jurist had suffered a heart attack in 1976 and since that time had experienced bouts of pneumonia and bronchitis, a dangerous blood clot in his foot, and deteriorating eyesight due to glaucoma.) But some attributed his resignation not so much to his health as to the fact that he felt ineffective against the solid conservative majority on the Court. Marshall himself declined to say much to reporters, noting only that "everything has to come to an end sometime, and I have given fifty years to it."

Indeed, few would argue that Thurgood Marshall had not done his part to advance the cause of the powerless during his long career as perhaps the century's most important lawyer and one of its most honorable jurists. "Marshall was the only black named to the high bench, so he merely needed to sit there to make history," noted longtime Supreme Court correspondent Lyle Denniston in a *Baltimore Sun* article that was reprinted in the *Detroit News*. "But he did his share of the work. . . . Without apology, [he and his fellow liberals] thought the law was supposed to be an engine of social reform and that they were the engineers." As Marshall himself once explained in an *Ebony* magazine profile, "I knew I couldn't finish the job, but I had to get the basic portion done."

Sources

➤ **Books**

Aldred, Lisa, *Thurgood Marshall*, Chelsea House, 1990.

➤ **Periodicals**

Detroit Free Press, "Marshall to Leave High Court," June 28, 1991.

Detroit News, "Liberals Lose Loudest Voice," June 28, 1991; "A Life of Service," June 28, 1991, p. 10A; "With Brennan, Marshall Shaped Court of '60s, '70s," June 30, 1991.

Ebony, "The Solicitor General," November, 1965, pp. 67–77; "Ten Greats of Black History," August, 1972, pp. 35–42; August, 1975, p. 6; "The Thurgood Marshall Nobody Knows," May, 1990, pp. 68–76; "Forty-Five Years in Law and Civil Rights," November, 1990, pp. 80–86; "Interview with Supreme Court Justice Thurgood Marshall," November, 1990, pp. 216–222 (opening quote).

Grand Rapids Press, "Marshall's Spot in History Won Before He Joined Court," June 30, 1991.

Newsweek, "A Great Original's Lives at the Law: Thurgood Marshall Made as Much History in Front of the Supreme Court as He Did Serving It," July 8, 1991.

New York Times Magazine, "Thurgood Marshall Takes a New 'Tush-

Tush' Job," August 22, 1965; "The Burger-Blackmun Court," December 6, 1970, pp. 60–80.

People, "Justices Marshall and Brennan Battle to Keep Liberalism Alive at the U.S. Supreme Court," July 7, 1986, pp. 53–54; "A Warrior Retires: The Son of a Black Steward in an All-White Club Rewrote the Rules about Race," July 15, 1991.

Time, "Negro Justice," June 23, 1967, pp. 18–19; "The First Negro Justice," September 8, 1967, p. 16; "A Lawyer Who Changed America," July 8, 1991.

U.S. News and World Report, "With Mr. Marshall on the Supreme Court," June 26, 1967, pp. 12–13; "With Another 'Liberal' on High Court," September 11, 1967, p. 21; "Embracing a Great Man's Gift to America," July 8, 1991.

Marlee Matlin

"We each have our own faults. Mine happens to be deafness."

The only hearing-impaired person ever to win an Academy Award for best actress, Marlee Matlin has gone on to achieve another first as the star of her own television series. She was born on August 24, 1965, in Morton Grove, Illinois.

I n 1986, movie audiences witnessed the debut of a gifted young actress in the person of Marlee Matlin, whose electrifying performance in *Children of a Lesser God* outshone that of her well-known co-star, William Hurt. Besides being an important first for Matlin, the film was also an important first for Hollywood: it was the first time a deaf actress had been cast in the role of a deaf person. At that year's Academy Awards ceremony, Matlin set another precedent when she became the first deaf person to be honored as best actress. Since then, she has kept busy with a variety of film and television roles and has dedicated herself to fighting for the needs and rights of other hearing-impaired people.

Matlin was born and grew up in suburban Chicago, the youngest of three children. For the first eighteen months of her life, she could hear normally. Then a severe bout of measles and a high fever led to a complete hearing loss in one ear and an eighty percent loss in the other. (She now wears a hearing aid in that ear and can pick up some sounds.) Her family had a difficult time accepting the diagnosis at first, but soon her parents and two older brothers learned sign language so that they could communicate with her. "I dealt with the outside world from the age of three," Matlin recalls. "I was not shut out."

Matlin nevertheless harbored a deep-seated anger about her hearing loss all through her childhood and readily admits that her parents "went through a lot with me." After attending several special schools, she was mainstreamed into a regular school with a program for hearing-impaired students. There she encountered classmates who often teased her, prompting the frustrated Matlin to respond with a temper tantrum. "I wanted to be perfect, and I couldn't accept my deafness," she now explains. "I was so angry and frightened."

Acting proved to be a refuge for the troubled child. For eight years she belonged to the Children's Theater for the Deaf, starring in such productions as *The Wizard of Oz, Mary Poppins,* and *Peter Pan.* (She signed along to recorded music whenever her character was supposed to sing.) Matlin gave up acting in high school to concentrate on other interests, and by the time she went off to junior college, she had decided to become a policewoman. But she dropped out of a criminal justice program after just a few semesters when she realized that her deafness would restrict her to office duty.

Around that same time, Matlin—at a friend's urging—auditioned for and won a supporting role in a Chicago revival of the 1980 Tony

Award-winning play *Children of a Lesser God,* the story of an idealistic teacher of deaf children and his stormy relationship with a young deaf woman who stubbornly refuses to lip-read because the hearing world won't learn sign language. A Hollywood casting director searching for an actress to play the female lead in the movie version of the play spotted Matlin on a tape of the Chicago production and asked her to come to New York for an audition with actor William Hurt, who had already been cast as the male lead. The chemistry between them was evident from the start, but two more auditions in Los Angeles followed before Matlin was hired for the role of the feisty and passionate Sarah Norman.

Filming ended in November, 1985, by which time Matlin and Hurt were romantically involved. (Their relationship, which has since ended, generated as much publicity as the movie did.) *Children of a Lesser God* was a hit with audiences following its 1986 release, and Matlin became one of the year's biggest entertainment stories. Her success reached its peak on Oscar night in 1987, when Hurt presented her with the Academy Award for best actress, making Matlin the first hearing-impaired performer to be so honored. But given the lack of parts for deaf actors, many in Hollywood wondered if she would ever be heard from again.

Matlin, however, was not quite ready to fade into obscurity. Since completing *Children of a Lesser God,* she has been featured in a couple of films, including the 1989 made-for-television movie *A Bridge to Silence,* the first speaking role of her career and one written with her in mind. Just a year earlier, she had spoken her first words in public when she presented the best actress Oscar to Cher at the Academy Awards ceremony. Matlin's failure to sign as she spoke offended some deaf people, who felt she was implying that sign language is an inferior means of communication. Although disappointed by their criticism, she was—and still is—not the least bit apologetic. "It was a great accomplishment for me," Matlin insists. "It's what I wanted to do, because a lot of people all over the world were able to see me for who I am."

Matlin's next big breakthrough came in the fall of 1991, when she teamed up with Mark Harmon to star in a new television series, *Reasonable Doubts*—another first for a hearing-impaired performer.

In her role as a deaf district attorney, Matlin speaks occasionally but primarily uses sign language to communicate; Harmon, who plays a police investigator, moves the story along by serving as an interpreter. The role is especially fulfilling for Matlin because her character's deafness is not the show's main focus, enabling her to play someone "who just lives life and happens not to hear."

Yet as more than a few people have noted, the feisty Sarah Norman character in *Children of a Lesser God* is perhaps a closer reflection of the real Marlee Matlin. Headstrong, volatile, and brimming with defiant self-confidence, she has become an outspoken advocate for deaf people, especially on matters related to the entertainment industry. Her own fight to make sure that no opportunity is denied her on account of her deafness has led her to demand that Hollywood not only acknowledge but accept hearing-impaired people. "There is no excuse not to use the deaf community," she has declared. "They used to be kept apart from the rest of the population, but that cannot continue."

She has also become active with the National Captioning Institute, a group working for closed-captioning on television shows and videocassettes. Her goal is to raise awareness of the obstacles encountered by hearing-impaired people who want to watch TV, including the lack of captioned programs and the expense of purchasing a decoder box. She has rallied many other celebrities to the cause and has even testified about the problem at a hearing on Capitol Hill. (Within just a few months after her appearance, Congress passed a law requiring that all TV sets bigger than thirteen inches sold after July 1, 1993, must be equipped with built-in decoder chips.) Matlin herself refuses to appear on programs that are not closed-captioned and says that her "dream is to have the access, through closed-captioning, to *everything* on TV and video."

In the meantime, she pursues her other interests (crusading for children with AIDS, the elderly, and the preservation of the rain forest) and, of course, continues to act on television and in some upcoming movie projects. And despite what other deaf people may think, Matlin has no intention of turning down roles in which she is expected to speak rather than sign; she is not about to let any hard-won opportunities slip through her fingers and resents the idea that anyone would want her to downplay her abilities. "Deafness is [just] a different viewpoint," she explains, "like being French or living in Mexico. I can be whatever I want to be."

Sources

➤ **Periodicals**

Detroit News, "Marlee Matlin's Future—All Signs Are Positive," September 13, 1991, p. 5F (opening quote).

Glamour, "Marlee Matlin: Is There Life After the Oscar? Yes!," January, 1988, pp. 150–151.

Harper's Bazaar, September, 1987, p. 296.

Ladies' Home Journal, "Marlee Matlin: Breaking the Silence," April, 1989, pp. 42–48.

New York, "Breaking the Sound Barrier," October 6, 1986, pp. 62–67.

People, "Deaf Actress Marlee Matlin Broke the Sound Barrier with New Love and *Lesser God* Co-Star Bill Hurt," October 20, 1986, pp. 122–127; "Actress Marlee Matlin Builds *A Bridge to Silence* to Star in Her First Speaking Role," April 10, 1989, pp. 158–160.

TV Guide, "Marlee Matlin Comes On . . . Loud and Clear," April 8, 1989, p. 18; "Breaking the Silence Barrier," November 24, 1990, pp. 12–13.

Chico Mendes

"If an angel came down from the sky and could guarantee that my death could strengthen this fight, it would be a fair exchange. But experience has taught us the opposite. And so I want to live. Because a lot of talk and many burials won't save the Amazon."*

Chico Mendes fought against the destruction of the Amazon rain forest in his native Brazil. He was born near Xapuri in December, 1944, and was murdered there on December 22, 1988, in retaliation for his activism.

Since the early 1970s, environmentalists estimate that Brazilian cattle ranchers, farmers, and land speculators have slashed and burned their way through more than 230,000 square miles of Amazon rain forest, an area larger than Florida and California combined. "Save the rain forest" has thus become a rallying cry for all those concerned about the impact of this devastation on the regional as well as the worldwide ecosystem. Beginning in the mid-1980s, one man in particular came to symbolize the conservationists' cause: Chico Mendes. Motivated at first by a desire to improve the lot of his fellow rubber tappers, whose livelihood was disappearing along with the fallen rubber trees, he soon realized that much more was at stake than strictly local labor issues. In short, as he later put it in an interview, "we became ecologists without even knowing that word."

Francisco Alves Mendes Filho was the oldest of eight children. He was born in Acre, a sparsely populated state in remote western Brazil that is home to mostly poor and illiterate peasants who have traditionally earned their living in the rain forest harvesting Brazil nuts or, like the Mendes family, working as rubber tappers. At the age of nine, "Chico" followed his parents into the rubber tree groves to learn how to cut the trunks so that the latex could be collected as it oozed out, a nondestructive process similar to extracting syrup from maple trees. He did not learn to read and write until he was eighteen, when he befriended a rather mysterious former army officer who claimed to be hiding in the jungle to escape persecution for his communist political beliefs. From him Mendes also gained a basic understanding of Marxism and an appreciation of the world that existed beyond the rain forest.

In 1971, Mendes moved to Xapuri, a village not far from where he had grown up. Over the next few years he dabbled in municipal politics and became involved in union-organizing activities on behalf of local agricultural workers (including his fellow rubber tappers), whose ability to earn a living was increasingly threatened by unchecked development. By this time, deforestation was already well under way in neighboring western states, where more and more land was being sacrificed for cattle and crops. At the same time, the Brazilian government launched ambitious road-building projects to support logging, mining, and hydroelectric operations and encouraged people from more crowded sections of the country to re-settle in the west. Indian tribes native to the rain forest were especially hard hit by this policy; many died in clashes with the newcomers or succumbed to newly introduced diseases like measles.

During the late 1970s, when a similar fate appeared to be in store for Acre, Mendes and his supporters began taking steps to halt the destruction. Using nonviolent tactics that prompted people to dub him "The Amazonian Gandhi," he led groups of rubber tappers and their families in a method of resistance known as *empate*. First, they tried to convince those who were actually doing the cutting and burning that their actions were only hurting fellow workers and that they, too, should join the fight against the landowners. If that was not enough to disrupt the day's work, everyone—even children—linked arms to form a human wall to protect trees from the bulldozers and chain saws. These techniques eventually saved about three million acres of rain forest.

Word of Mendes's movement quickly spread beyond Brazil to various ecology groups in the United States and Europe, whose members embraced him as a highly visible and articulate spokesman for the rain forest. In 1987, for example, he traveled to Miami, Florida, to address officials of the Inter-American Development Bank and persuaded them to suspend funding for a projected highway between Acre and the neighboring state of Rondonia. The following year, he coaxed the Brazilian government into reserving five million acres of land for the rubber tappers and nut collectors. In recognition of his efforts, Mendes received a Global 500 award from the United Nations, the National Conservation Achievement Award from the National Wildlife Federation, and the Environmental Award from the Better World Society, all for demonstrating that it is possible to exploit the rain forest economically without destroying it.

Back in Brazil, however, the situation continued to deteriorate. Landowners were outraged by attempts to interfere with what they considered to be their right to develop their property; some hired gunmen to terrorize or even kill anyone who dared challenge them. It is estimated that more than a thousand Brazilian workers, priests, lawyers, and others were murdered during the 1980s as a result of land disputes. Local law enforcement officials—often corrupted by bribes—usually refused to investigate or prosecute such crimes. The Brazilian government, equally resentful of what it felt was unjustified foreign meddling in its domestic affairs, ignored the violence on its frontier, denounced the environmentalists, and proceeded with its plans for the Amazon region.

While he was not the only target of the ranchers' wrath, Mendes was certainly the most hated and most feared. Landowners tried to buy him off, and although he was virtually penniless, he refused to take their money. He was arrested, beaten, and tortured on numerous occasions and escaped death in several ambushes. During the spring of 1988, however, Mendes clashed with a notoriously violent rancher, Darly Alves da Silva, over the purchase and clearing of three hundred acres of rain forest, which included the rubber plantation on which the activist had grown up. Shortly afterward Mendes received what Brazilians call an *anunciado*—an anonymous message formally notifying a person that he has been marked for execution. He contacted local and federal authorities about the threat and even named the Alves clan as likely suspects, but the police failed to act on the information and even denied him permission to carry a gun on account of his ties to "communizing" organizations. Family members and friends begged him to leave the country for his own safety, but Mendes refused, saying that he would stay and face whatever awaited him.

On the evening of December 22, 1988, Mendes stepped out the back door of his home and was shot and killed by gunmen who fled into the dark. Conservationists all over the world reacted with anger and directed harsh words at the Brazilian government, which was stunned by the fury and extent of the criticism. Coincidentally, Mendes's death occurred at about the same time as an outbreak of forest fires in the northern hemisphere and the release of new satellite photographs that graphically illustrated the horror of the burning season in the Amazon. As a result, he became the symbol—and the first real martyr—of the environmental movement, whose warnings about global warming and ecological devastation suddenly took on more urgency.

Local police launched an unprecedented manhunt for the assassins, and within just a few weeks, Darly Alves da Silva and his son, Darci Alves Pereira, surrendered to authorities. They finally went on trial in December, 1990, in what promised to be one of the biggest legal spectacles in Brazilian history. Thousands of rubber tappers and other interested observers from around the world flocked to Xapuri to attend the proceedings, determined to pressure the government not to let this particular murder go unpunished. Both father and son were quickly found guilty and sentenced to nineteen years in prison. It was the first time in Brazil that anyone responsible for a murder involving a land dispute had been tried, let alone convicted.

While Mendes's death delivered a severe blow to those working to halt the destruction of the rain forest, it may have sparked a few changes. In early 1990, for example, the Brazilian government officially created the first land reserve for rubber tappers and Indians; located near Xapuri, it was named after Mendes. (Three more regions were established later in the year.) Also, evidence suggests that the number of fires has decreased slightly since 1988, although the destruction is still considerable and incidents of violence against those who oppose ranchers have not declined.

At the very least, Brazil is now far more aware of how closely the world is scrutinizing its activities in the Amazon. The hope is that government officials will demonstrate an ability and willingness to reconcile the conflicts between landowners, Indians, and the rural poor and accept responsibility for preserving the rain forest. In that sense, "Chico Mendes taught the world an important lesson," declared Steve Schwartzman of the Washington, D.C.-based Environmental Defense Fund. "Environmental protection cannot be separated from social justice."

Sources

➤ **Books**

Cowell, Adrian, *The Decade of Destruction: The Crusade to Save the Amazon Rainforest*, Holt, 1990.

Dwyer, Augusta, *Into the Amazon: The Struggle for the Rain Forest*, Sierra Club Books, 1991.

Gross, Tony, *Fight for the Forest: Chico Mendes in His Own Words*, Monthly Review Press, 1989.

Hecht, Susanna, and Alexander Cockburn, *The Fate of the Forest: Developers, Destroyers and Defenders of the Amazon*, Verso, 1989.

Revkin, Andrew, *The Burning Season: The Murder of Chico Mendes and the Fight for the Amazon Rain Forest*, Houghton, 1990.

Shoumatoff, Alex, *The World Is Burning*, Little, Brown, 1990.

➤ **Periodicals**

Economist, "A Murder in the Forest," January 7, 1989, p. 36.

Maclean's, "Murder in the Amazon," January 9, 1989, p. 21.

Newsweek, "Chronicle of a Death Foretold," January 9, 1989, p. 62;

"A Life Under Fire in Brazil: Searching for the Real Chico Mendes," September 3, 1990, pp. 62–64.

New Yorker, February 20, 1989, pp. 27–28 (opening quote).

New York Review of Books, "The Mystery of Chico Mendes," March 28, 1991, pp. 39–48.

People, "A Martyr Who Died for the Amazon," January 15, 1990, pp. 28–35.

Time, "A Jungle Slaying," January 9, 1989, p. 38; "Playing with Fire," September 18, 1989, pp. 76–85; "Justice Comes to the Amazon," December 17, 1990, p. 76; "The Plot Thickens," December 24, 1990, p. 45.

U.S. News and World Report, "Amazon Parable," December 24, 1990, p. 18.

Karl Menninger

"*I*t is easier, more logical and more efficacious to help a child grow up with love and courage than it is to instill hope in a despondent soul. What a mother and father mean to them is more than any psychiatrist can ever mean.*"*

Widely regarded as the father of American psychiatry, Karl Menninger was born on July 22, 1893, in Topeka, Kansas, and died there on July 18, 1990.

Address: Menninger, Box 829, Topeka, KS 66601.

I n 1908, Dr. Charles Frederick Menninger, a general practitioner in Topeka, Kansas, visited the Mayo Clinic in Rochester, Minnesota, an innovative facility where doctors worked together to provide patients with the best diagnosis and treatment possible. Greatly impressed by the benefits of such a group practice, Menninger dreamed of one day opening a similar clinic in Topeka. In 1919, the dream at last began to take shape when Charles and his eldest son, Karl, a recent graduate of the Harvard Medical School, opened a small clinic. The Menninger Clinic has since then evolved from its humble beginnings to become a world-renowned center for psychiatric treatment, education, and research. Its guiding principle—"no patient is untreatable"—reflects the compassionate philosophy of Karl Menninger, who served as the facility's chief of staff for more than four decades and did more than perhaps any other individual to transform the way Americans regard mental illness.

A native and nearly lifelong resident of the capital city of Topeka, Kansas, Karl Augustus Menninger grew up in a deeply religious and nurturing atmosphere. Both Charles Menninger and his wife, Florence Knisely, stressed the importance of learning and instilled in their three sons a powerful drive to work hard and be of service to others. Two of the Menninger children—Karl and William—followed in their father's footsteps and studied medicine, while the middle son, Edwin, opted to go into journalism. Karl earned his bachelor's and master's degrees at the University of Wisconsin, then went off to Harvard Medical School, from which he graduated with honors in 1917. Internships and further study followed at Kansas City General Hospital and at Boston Psychopathic Hospital; he also taught briefly at Harvard Medical School and Tufts Medical School before returning to Topeka to go into partnership with his father.

A specialist in neurology and the relatively new field of psychiatry, Karl quickly convinced his father that their patients' mental health deserved as much consideration as their physical health. At first, Topeka residents balked at the idea of having a "maniac ward" in town, but the Menningers were very persuasive, and soon they had solicited enough support to establish a small hospital in a renovated farmhouse. By 1926, William had joined his father and brother in practice, and the Menninger facilities had expanded to include not only the clinic and the hospital but also a sanitarium and a pioneering residential treatment program for children that allowed them to live in a family-like atmosphere and attend school.

The Menninger complex continued to expand throughout the

1920s and 1930s, with Karl as its chief of staff and William as its administrative head and fund-raiser. In 1941, they formed the Menninger Foundation, a nonprofit umbrella corporation encompassing the many different psychiatric services offered by the Menningers and their associates. At the foundation's core were the hospital and the sanitarium; among the other major components were the Karl Menninger School of Psychiatry and the Topeka Institute for Psychoanalysis, both dedicated to training other professionals. The Menningers also wielded considerable influence in the affairs of the Topeka Veterans Administration Hospital and the Topeka State Hospital, where they challenged conventional "warehousing" methods for dealing with the mentally ill.

As chief of staff, Karl Menninger exercised a pivotal role in formulating and running programs in the key areas of treatment and education. Although he was trained in Freudian theory and accepted its basic principle that mental illness can be traced to a variety of subconscious causes rooted mostly in childhood, he did not ignore the importance of immediate, conscious causes in bringing on emotional distress. In fact, he attributed most mental illness to improperly handled feelings of aggression, hostility, and destructiveness brought on by external stress. Because he was not committed to any particular form of therapy, Menninger advocated constantly examining and re-examining successes and failures with an eye toward identifying what worked and what didn't so that treatment could be adjusted accordingly.

One especially innovative approach the Menningers developed went far beyond the usual basketweaving or leatherworking, which did little more for the patient than pass the time. Dubbed a "school in practice living," it re-taught patients how to channel their energies into healthy work, play, and learning activities that were tailored to individual needs and interests. Depending on the patient, these might have included such things as dancing lessons, language study, photography, or even scrubbing floors and walls. The Menningers found that such activities gave patients a feeling of accomplishment, restored a sense of order and discipline in their lives, and improved their relationships with others.

In Karl Menninger's view, a cold and unloving home environment was to blame for most instances of mental illness. With that in mind, his goal was to create at the clinic an atmosphere of caring and kindness in a family-type living situation. His philosophy emphasized that everyone who came in contact with patients—from the doctors to the groundskeepers—was part of the treatment team and had an obligation to offer understanding and support. Menninger also shied away from classifying patients along rigid diagnostic lines and even avoided using terms like *neurotic* or *psychotic,* which "only comfort the doctors and impress the relatives," as he once told Steven M. Spencer in a *Saturday Evening Post* article. "Pinning a label on a patient may actually impede his ultimate recovery. The word *schizophrenia* becomes a damning designation. To have it once applied to a young man can be to ruin a career, despite all evidence of subsequent healthiness."

Menninger shared his vision in a variety of ways. For example, his best-selling book *The Human Mind* (originally published in 1930 and revised several times since then) effectively explained psychiatry and psychiatric principles to a lay audience and brought its author national prominence. In subsequent years, he wrote about a dozen other books (some more technical in nature) and scores of articles, lectured extensively, and served as a consultant, "trying to show perceptive men and women in business, industry, medicine and the home that psychiatry is *their* business—not the esoteric specialty of a few doctors," as he put it.

But Menninger made his greatest impact as the foundation's director of education and head of its school of psychiatry, a post he assumed in 1946 and held for several decades. Under his supervision, the school trained more psychiatrists than any other facility in the world. Also central to its mission were seminars for other health-care professionals and people outside the medical field with an interest in human behavior, including ministers, lawyers, social workers, and business and industrial leaders.

In his later years, Menninger gave up teaching and seeing patients to devote more time to crusading on behalf of such causes as prison reform, neglected and abused children, the rights of Native Americans, and the environment. Having always believed that mental illness is linked to the problems that plague society on a national and even an international level, he decided that he could make a greater contribution to humanity by "preventing unnecessary suffering at the source, before individuals take or are forced to take the wrong road," as he put it.

Menninger was especially critical of the U.S. prison system, which he maintained does more harm to the inmates than the inmates have ever done to society. Noting that the crime rate has not decreased as the prison population increased, he proposed an alternative solution: rehabilitation programs offering a blend of job training and mental health counseling to help prisoners adjust to life. The counseling was especially important, he insisted, because crime is so often the way people seek revenge for physical or emotional abuse they suffered as children. While his views were at one time embraced by some prison reformers, they have increasingly fallen into disfavor amid cries for longer sentences and less "coddling" of criminals. Despite the backlash, Menninger held firm to his position. "I'm no ascetic saint, dedicated to trying to like unpleasant people," he told Daniel Goleman of *Psychology Today*. "But I do recognize that even they are people, not wild animals, and as suffering human beings they have my sympathy. . . . I've seen the jails and prisons where people are sent to receive their 'desserts.' I've seen them often, and my heart starts bleeding every time I enter them and aches when I leave."

Menninger remained actively involved in social reform efforts until shortly before his death in 1990 from abdominal cancer at the age of ninety-six. His legacy—and that of his father and brother as well—lives on in the Menninger Foundation and the services it offers through its network of clinics, hospitals, and other programs, including those established at satellite facilities in Kansas City, St. Louis, Phoenix, and Albuquerque. Now expanded to more than three dozen buildings on two separate campuses in Topeka and employing more than twelve hundred people, Menningers, as it is called, continues to pursue its goals of better mental health and mental health care for everyone through treatment, education, research, and prevention.

Sources

➤ **Books**

Menninger, Karl, *Sparks*, edited by Lucy Freeman, Crowell, 1973.

➤ **Periodicals**

Christian Century, "Karl A. Menninger: Psychiatrist as Moralist," August 22–29, 1990, pp. 758–759.

Newsweek, July 30, 1990, p. 57.

New York Times, "The Menninger Clinic, A Farmhouse in 1925, Now a World Center," November 13, 1975; "Experts Consider 'Caring

Society,'" November 13, 1975, p. 43 (opening quote); July 19, 1990, p. D19.

New York Times Magazine, "New Laurels for the Menningers," November 6, 1955.

Psychology Today, "Proud to Be a Bleeding Heart," June, 1978, pp. 80–91.

Saturday Evening Post, "The Menningers of Kansas," April 7, 1962, pp. 17–24; "The Hopeless Patient Is a Myth," April 14, 1962, pp. 34–38; "From Darkness into Daylight," April 21, 1962, pp. 52–57; "The Bridge of Hope," April 28, 1962, pp. 48–55.

Time, "The Kansas Moralist," August 6, 1973, pp. 60–61; July 30, 1990, p. 65.

U.S. News and World Report, July 30, 1990, p. 10.

Toni Morrison

"I *really think the range of emotions and percep-*
tions I have had access to as a black person and
as a female person are greater than those of people who
are neither. . . . So it seems to me that my world did not
shrink because I was a black female writer. It just got
bigger."

Considered one of the most prominent Black-American wom-
en writers in America, Pulitzer Prize-winning novelist Toni
Morrison was born on February 18, 1931, in Lorain, Ohio.

A gifted storyteller and stylist with a special sensitivity for small-town Black American life, Toni Morrison has won praise for a relatively small yet distinguished body of work that explores "some of the most complicated, interesting, mysterious people in the world," to use her words. She has focused in particular on "the evolution of self in Black women," creating in the process some of the most vividly imagined female characters in modern American literature at a time when Black male writers dominated the scene with books "that too often deified and dismissed, blamed, victimized or stereotyped black women," according to Marcia Ann Gillespie in *Ms*. Yet as Elizabeth B. House notes in the *Dictionary of Literary Biography Yearbook*, Morrison's work truly defies strict categorization, for "at the core of all her novels is a penetrating view of the unyielding, heartbreaking dilemmas which torment people of all races." She is especially drawn to the search for individual and cultural identity and what roles the family as well as the community play in that search.

Born Chloe Anthony Wofford to George and Ramah Willis Wofford, Toni Morrison grew up in the industrial town of Lorain, Ohio. Terrified by the prospect of facing unemployment during the Depression, George Wofford held down three different jobs more or less simultaneously for almost seventeen years while his four children were young—shipyard welder, road construction worker, and car washer; feisty Ramah Wofford, meanwhile, held landlords and social workers at bay during times when things were not going well financially. Morrison's maternal grandparents were also part of the family circle, and it was from this diverse group of people that she developed her own strong sense of self-worth and racial identity.

Morrison's father was a Georgia native who had been driven north by racial violence; as a result of his experiences, he was suspicious of all White people and avoided them as much as possible. Her maternal grandfather, having lost all of his Alabama farmland to some White people who then made him work it for a pittance, thought Black Americans were doomed. His wife disagreed, however, as did his daughter Ramah, Morrison's mother. Morrison's grandmother put her faith in religion and individual will as the key to improved relations between the races, while Ramah tried to regard each new encounter with a White person as a fresh start. Added to this swirl of conflicting opinions was Morrison's own experience growing up in an integrated, working-class community where Black children went to school with recently arrived immigrant children from all over Europe. As she told an interviewer for *Time:* "In becoming an American, from Europe, what one has in common with that other immigrant is contempt for *me*—it's nothing else but color. Wherever they were from, they would stand together. . . . Every immigrant knew he would not come as the very bottom. He had to come above at least one group—and that was us."

Within her family and community, young Morrison also received a thorough grounding in Black folklore (especially superstition) and in the art of storytelling, one of the most popular forms of entertainment in the Wofford household. Ghost stories were her favorite, and they were her father's specialty. "We were always begging him to repeat the stories that terrified us the most," she recalls.

Morrison was a voracious reader throughout her school years, graduating with honors from high school and then heading east to Howard University, in Washington, D.C., to study English. (It was at this point in her life that she changed her given name to "Toni" after meeting many people who seemed to have trouble pronouncing "Chloe.") However, she quickly grew bored and disgusted with the shallowness of many of her classmates and found the stimulation she craved only in the Howard University Players, a repertory company she accompanied on tour throughout the South. Seeing for herself what life was like for southern Blacks in the late 1940s and early 1950s brought the stories of her father and grandfather into sharper focus and gave her a greater appreciation of the pain and suffering they had endured on account of their race.

After obtaining her degree from Howard in 1953, Morrison enrolled in the Cornell University graduate program in English, receiving her master's degree in 1955. She then taught at Texas Southern University in Houston for two years before returning to Washington, D.C., and a post at Howard, where she joined the informal monthly get-togethers of a group of ten Black-American writers who shared their work with each other. She also married a young Jamaican architect, Harold Morrison, and had two sons, but the union was a rocky one. More and more, she found herself turning to writing to escape. "It was as though I had nothing left but my imagination . . . ," she later explained. "I wrote like someone with a dirty habit. Secretly. Compulsively. Slyly."

During the summer of 1964, Morrison and her family traveled to Europe. She returned with her two young sons but without her husband, whose expectations of wifely subservience she found stifling and ultimately intolerable. Jobless and without any definite prospects on the horizon, she stayed briefly with her parents back in Lorain before moving with her sons to Syracuse, New York, to accept a position as a textbook editor with a subsidiary of Random House publishers. She also took up writing in earnest, primarily as a way to cope with her isolation. "I had two small children in a strange place and I was very lonely," she later explained. "Writing was something for me to do in the evenings, after the children were asleep." Her first project was fleshing out a story she had hastily composed for one of the meetings of her Howard writer's group, a piece about a Black girl who wanted blue eyes that she had based on an incident from her own childhood. Once she had finished a novel-length work, she showed it to an editor at Holt, Rinehart & Winston, and in 1969 *The Bluest Eye*, a powerful examination of Black self-hatred in a White-dominated culture, was published to mixed reviews.

By then, Morrison had been transferred to New York City as a senior editor in Random House's trade division. She typically edited six or seven books a year, almost exclusively the works of Black-American writers such as Angela Davis, Toni Cade Bambara, Gayl Jones, and Muhammad Ali. Despite the fact that *The Bluest Eye* did not achieve widespread critical or commercial success, it did bring Morrison to the attention of the print media, and over the next few years she was kept busy writing articles and reviewing books, primarily for the *New York Times*. Morrison also devoted whatever time she could spare to working on her second novel, *Sula*, which appeared in 1973.

While *The Bluest Eye* had been told through the eyes of a child, *Sula* presented a more complex vision of life as experienced by two mature Black-American women—Sula Peace and Nel Wright—whose friendship dates back to childhood. Basically a study of good and evil that juxtaposes social conformist Nel with social rebel Sula, the novel was very well received. (It was, in fact, nominated for a National Book Award.) Critics especially admired Morrison's lean, yet poetic prose and vivid characterizations.

Morrison's next novel, *Song of Solomon*, represented a departure from her previous works in that the central character is a Black-American male, Malcolm "Milkman" Dead. The story focuses on a personal odyssey that takes Milkman from his middle-class home in the Midwest to the South in an attempt to understand his family heritage and, therefore, himself. With *Song of Solomon*, Morrison was acknowledged as a major Black-American woman writer who had successfully broadened her fictional world by tackling familiar themes of spiritual death and rebirth and the search for ethnic identity. Her most widely-acclaimed work to that point, it won a National Book Critics Circle Award and led to Morrison's appointment to the American Academy and Institute of Arts and Letters and the National Council of the Arts.

After the favorable reaction to *Song of Solomon*, Morrison decided to cut back a bit on her editorial duties at Random House and devote more of her time to writing. *Tar Baby*, published in 1981, was her first novel to deal not only with relationships between Black men and women but also between Blacks and Whites. Set on an exotic Caribbean island, it weaves elements of fantasy and reality together in its exploration of what Elizabeth B. House sees as its two major themes: "the difficulty of settling conflicting claims between one's past and present and the destruction which abuse of power can bring." A popular work that remained on best-seller lists for four months, *Tar Baby* received critical acclaim for its vivid characterization and poetic language.

While working on *The Black Book*, a 1974 Random House anthology of writings that illustrate the history of Black Americans, Morrison came across an account of the true story that became the basis of her most celebrated novel to date, *Beloved*, winner of the 1988 Pulitzer Prize for fiction. An exploration of the theme of "self-sabotage," or love of someone else that displaces the self (such as some forms of maternal love), *Beloved* tells the story of Sethe, a runaway Kentucky slave who, just moments before being recaptured, slashes her two-year-old daughter's throat rather than see her returned to a lifetime of bondage. The book is not about slavery as an institution, though, insists Morrison; it is, she says, "about these anonymous people called slaves. What they do to keep on, how they make a life, what they're willing to risk, however long it lasts, in order to relate to one another." In telling their often horrific stories, Morrison's goal was to rescue from oblivion the "sixty million and more" who died throughout the three-hundred-year history of slave trading in America. Critics were virtually unanimous in their praise for *Beloved*, with John Leonard declaring in the *New York Times Book Review* that it "belongs on the highest shelf of American literature, even if half a dozen canonized white boys have to be elbowed off."

As has been the case throughout her entire career, Morrison juggles her writing with a variety of other activities. She has held a number of academic positions, most recently at Princeton University as the Robert F. Goheen Professor of the Humanities. She also teaches writer's workshops and does occasional readings of her works, and she is still affiliated with Random House. Evenings, for the most part, are reserved for writing; her latest work, *Jazz,* was published in April, 1992.

Although some people are amazed at all she manages to accomplish, Morrison herself long ago learned to put it in perspective. "What compelled me in [the early] days was a very strong sense of some women and men in my family who had done some truly exceptional things," she says. "Because of them I felt, 'So, I can go to Cornell and get a master's degree or hold two jobs and raise my sons. What is that?' Because I remember the very real life-threatening obstacles people in my family faced, and whenever I would feel overwhelmed, that's all I had to think about." Besides, she adds, "If you surrender to the wind you can ride it."

Sources

➤ **Books**

Dictionary of Literary Biography Yearbook: 1981, Gale, 1982.

➤ **Periodicals**

Ebony, "The Magic of Toni Morrison," July, 1988, pp. 100–106.

Ms., "Toni Morrison," January, 1988, pp. 60–61.

Newsweek, "Toni Morrison's Black Magic," March 30, 1981, pp. 52–57.

New York Times, "Toni Morrison, in Her New Novel, Defends Women," August 26, 1987, p. 17 (opening quote).

New York Times Book Review, September 13, 1987.

New York Times Magazine, "The Song of Toni Morrison," May 20, 1979.

Time, "The Pain of Being Black," May 22, 1989, pp. 120–122.

Grandma Moses

"I *look back on my life like a good day's work. . . .
I was happy and contented. I knew nothing
better and made the best out of what life offered. And
life is what we make it, always has been, always will
be."*

Born on September 7, 1860, in Greenwich, New York, Anna
Mary Robertson Moses—better known as Grandma Moses—
took up painting at age seventy-six "to keep busy and to pass
the time away." Her landscapes of rural American life have
enchanted many. She died on December 13, 1961, in Hoosick
Falls, New York.

I n 1939, Louis Caldor, an engineer and art collector from Manhattan, was driving through upstate New York when he stopped at a drugstore in the village of Hoosick Falls. There he was captivated by four brightly-colored paintings on display in the window—"bustling scenes of country folk doing everyday chores," as a writer for *Time* magazine described them. Caldor bought all four and then asked about the artist. To his surprise, he learned she was a seventy-eight-year-old woman named Anna Mary Robertson Moses, better known to all in the area as Grandma. The next day, Caldor visited Grandma Moses at her nearby farm and bought about fifteen more of her landscapes, nearly everything she had painted since taking up the hobby about two years before.

Returning to New York City, Caldor exhibited three of the works at a Museum of Modern Art show in October, 1939. Throughout the next year, he also went back to Hoosick Falls several times, encouraging Grandma Moses to paint more of her landscapes and buying most of what she produced. In October, 1940, thirty-five of those paintings were featured in a one-woman show at a New York gallery, and, much to her astonishment, Grandma Moses found herself the toast of Manhattan art critics, who hailed her as an "authentic American primitive." Her detailed and sentimental depictions of nineteenth-century farm life had an almost universal appeal, as did her energetic cheerfulness and down-to-earth warmth and honesty. While not an artist of great stature, Grandma Moses came to be regarded as a beloved national treasure, a "felicitous combination of charm, spry antiquity, and talent for homespun storytelling in paint," to quote Katharine Kuh in the *Saturday Review*.

One of ten children of a farmer, Russell King Robertson, and his wife, Margaret Shannahan, Anna Mary Robertson Moses was born in the mountains of upstate New York just a few months before the election that put Abraham Lincoln in the White House. Like many children, she loved to draw. Working with blank sheets of newspaper her father brought home for her, "I did beautiful lambscapes. That's what I called them, lambscapes," she explained to Harold C. Schonberg of the *New York Times Magazine.* "I was six or seven at the time and my brother used to laugh at them. Mostly I used to paint red lambscapes because my only color was the red paint that Father used to mark sheep with. . . . To get other colors I had to squeeze out grape juice or lemon juice."

Such frivolity soon gave way to the harsh demands of farm life, however. After receiving only a few years' worth of formal education, Anna left home at the age of twelve to work as a hired girl. "It was a long, hard life," she remarked to Schonberg. "But I don't know as I could have bettered it." As she recalled on another occasion, the experience was "a grand education for me in cooking, housekeeping, in moralizing and mingling with the outside world."

In 1887, Anna married Thomas Solomon Moses, a farmer, and they lived for the next eighteen years near Staunton, Virginia. There she gave birth to ten children, only five of whom survived to adulthood. The family then returned to New York and settled on a farm in Eagle Bridge, not far from Anna's childhood home. After Tom Moses died in 1927, his wife continued to run the farm with the help of their youngest son. By the mid-1930s, however, arthritis made it difficult for Grandma Moses to do her chores, especially the heavy outdoor work. Yet after leading such an active life, the elderly woman found it impossible to remain idle. At first, she took up embroidery "to keep busy and out of mischief." When her crippled fingers could no longer hold a needle, she switched to painting instead, making use of some thresher cloth and old paint she found in the barn. Later, Grandma Moses ordered regular artists' paints and brushes from a Sears catalog and had her son cut pieces of masonite to serve as her "canvas." Perched on a battered swivel chair in front of an old table, she painted for five or six hours almost every morning, her masonite board lying flat so she could rest her elbows as she worked.

Grandma Moses's initial efforts were copies of various Currier & Ives prints or scenes she admired on illustrated postcards. But soon she was creating original works of art, turning to the ordinary events of farm life in days gone by for her subject matter: boiling maple sap to make syrup, picking apples, rounding up the Thanksgiving turkey. She painted strictly from her imagination, invoking memories from her youth during the 1870s and 1880s. As she once explained, "I'll get an inspiration and start painting; then I'll forget everything, everything except how things used to be and how to paint it so people will know how we used to live." She preferred to focus on what she called "pretty things," noting, "What's the use of painting a picture if it isn't nice? So I think real hard till I think of something pretty, and then I paint it. . . . Most of them are daydreams."

She gave away many of her early paintings as presents and sold a few for a couple of dollars each, mounting them in old mirror and picture frames culled from friends' attics. (She never liked to see people take her works without frames, saying it was "like sending my children out with ragged dresses on 'em. I like to see 'em dressed before they go.") Her first real "exhibition" was in 1936 at a local fair, when she submitted a few landscapes along with some of her canned fruits and jam. While the food won prizes from the judges and was a hit with fairgoers, no one seemed to notice the paintings.

Two years later, Louis Caldor's unexpected stop in Hoosick Falls lifted Grandma Moses from obscurity and put her at the center of the American folk art movement that was then gaining momentum. Within ten years, her paintings had been displayed in more than sixty-five exhibitions at galleries and museums throughout the United States. The public found her luminous colors, primitive draftsmanship, and childish perspective enormously appealing, a popularity many observers attributed to the unsettled times. "This charming talent of Grandma's could hardly have achieved such an enormous audience had it not coincided with the present need for escape into a serene and self-possessed world," noted a critic for *Art News*. "Our nostalgia for a rural past is heightened, no doubt, by our present insecurity." This view was shared by a writer for *Time*, who declared that she "seemed to recall something about America that America missed. She painted from memory, but her memory never told her of sickness, poverty or death. It sang of warmhearted, no-nonsense people had much too much to do to indulge in the luxury of despair. Her pictures were a tonic to the nation."

In July, 1961, after falling at her house in Eagle Bridge, Grandma Moses entered a nursing home. There she continued painting every day until her 101st birthday that September. Not long after, she grew too weak to hold a brush. She died on December 13, officially of hardening of the arteries, but in the words of her doctor, she "just wore out." During the last year of her life, she had produced more than two dozen pictures.

Grandma Moses won a devoted following with a combination of talent and personal charm and served as a delightful reminder that success can indeed still come at a time when it seems life should be winding down. As John Canaday and others noted, however, her real contribution was sharing the joy she felt in simply *living*. "[Grandma Moses's] reputation was all out of proportion to her achievement esthetically," wrote Canaday in the *New York Times*, "but the wonderful thing about her is that the last word she would have thought of using about what she had done would have been 'achievements,' and the last word she would have used concerning her painting would have been 'esthetics.' Her magic was that she knew how magical it was to be alive, and in her painted records of her life she managed to relay some of this magic to the rest of us."

Sources

➤ **Books**

Kallir, Otto, *Grandma Moses: American Primitive*, Doubleday, 1947.

Moses, Anna Mary Robertson, *My Life's History*, Harper, 1951.

Tompkins, Nancy, *Grandma Moses*, Chelsea House, 1989.

➤ **Periodicals**

Art News, "The Success of Mrs. Moses," May, 1951.

Coronet, "Why I Became a Painter," December, 1956, p. 53.

Newsweek, "Painting Daydreams," December 25, 1961, pp. 56–57 (opening quote).

New York Times, December 14, 1961.

New York Times Magazine, "An Afternoon with Grandma Moses," October 9, 1949; "Grandma Moses: Portrait of the Artist at 99," September 6, 1959.

Saturday Review, "Grandma Moses: Portrait of the Artist as a Centenarian," September 10, 1960.

Time, "Grandma Moses," October 21, 1940, p. 56; "Grandma's Imaginings," September 6, 1948, pp. 42–43; "The Old-Timey One," December 22, 1961, pp. 32–35.

J. Robert Oppenheimer

"**V**ery great evil is inherent in weaponry—
and where there is great evil is the opportunity for great good."

Often referred to as "the father of the atomic bomb" for his
work on the Manhattan Project during World War II, physicist
J. Robert Oppenheimer later became an advocate of nuclear-
arms control. He was born on April 22, 1904, in New York City
and died on February 18, 1967, in Princeton, New Jersey.

On July 16, 1945, in the desert near Alamogordo, New Mexico, the world entered the nuclear age with the successful test of the first atomic bomb. In a control room five miles away from the actual explosion, J. Robert Oppenheimer, the man who had directed and inspired the nearly four thousand scientists involved with the project, watched the billowing mushroom cloud rise in the morning sky. Contemplating the tremendous forces at work before his eyes, he thought of the words from a sacred Hindu poem: "I am become Death, the shatterer of worlds." While he did not assume personal responsibility for what he and his colleagues unleashed on the human race that day in New Mexico, Oppenheimer was nevertheless haunted by the event that "dramatized so mercilessly the inhumanity and evil of modern war." For the rest of his life, he wrestled with the moral dilemmas posed by a world in which science could no longer isolate itself from politics and everyday life.

Julius Robert Oppenheimer was the eldest of two sons born to Julius Oppenheimer, a wealthy textile importer who had immigrated to the United States from Germany as a teenager, and Ella Friedman, an artist and art teacher. Robert Oppenheimer displayed a keen intelligence and curiosity as a child, compiling an outstanding record as a student at New York City's Ethical Culture School. In 1922, he went off to Harvard University, completing four years of work in just three years and graduating with honors in 1925. Intrigued by the relatively new field of atomic physics, Oppenheimer then attended graduate school abroad at two institutions noted for their expertise in that area: Cambridge University in England and the University of Göettingen in Germany, from which he received his doctorate in 1927. Post-doctoral study followed at Harvard, the California Institute of Technology, the University of Leyden in the Netherlands, and the Technische Hochschule in Zurich, Switzerland.

After returning to the United States in 1929, Oppenheimer accepted concurrent appointments on the faculties of the University of California at Berkeley and the California Institute of Technology. Over the next eighteen years, he built the Berkeley theoretical physics program into one of the most highly regarded in the world. Although he made several significant discoveries in quantum mechanics, radiation, and high energy physics during this period, Oppenheimer exercised a more profound influence in the classroom, where he trained more of the era's brilliant young theoretical physicists than any of his peers.

Until the mid-1930s, Oppenheimer lived the life of a cloistered scholar, virtually oblivious to national and world events and the trappings of modern life. Then he fell in love with a woman whose leftist politics opened his eyes to life outside Berkeley and stimulated his social conscience. Disturbed by the Nazi persecution of Jews and the impact of the Depression on his students, many of whom were unable to get jobs, Oppenheimer "began to understand how deeply political and economic events could affect men's lives" and felt compelled "to participate more fully in the life of the community," as he later recalled. To that end, he donated his time and money to various communist, trade union, and leftist causes.

Oppenheimer's first contact with the fledgling nuclear program was in 1941, when he served on a special National Academy of Sciences committee investigating military uses of atomic energy. His own subsequent research on producing an atomic bomb convinced him that such a complex undertaking would require a team of specialists representing many different fields at work in a single location under a unified command. When the so-called Manhattan Project actually got under way in early 1943, Oppenheimer was named head of the Los Alamos laboratory where the United States intended to create the world's first synthetic nuclear explosion.

Oppenheimer supervised virtually every aspect of the laboratory. He oversaw its construction in the New Mexico desert, assembled all the necessary equipment, recruited a top-notch staff (including Enrico Fermi and Niels Bohr), coordinated their work, and solved the problems (professional as well as personal) that threatened to derail the project. He proved to be a superb administrator, and in two hectic years managed to fulfill his goal. As physicist Hans Bethe, one of his recruits, later recalled in *Science* magazine: "Los Alamos might have succeeded without him, but certainly only with much greater strain, less enthusiasm, and less speed. . . . He was a leader. It was clear to all of us, whenever he spoke, that he knew everything that was important to know about the technical problems of the laboratory, and he somehow had it well organized in his head. But he was not domineering, he never dictated what should be done. He brought out the best in all of us."

The postwar era brought many changes and considerable controversy to Oppenheimer's life. His work at Los Alamos had made him a public figure and a spokesman for the new age he had helped create, and he was actively involved in many governmental efforts to formulate an official policy regarding the use, control, and future development of nuclear weapons. At first, he supported an aggressive program of rapid development under military supervision in order to keep the United States ahead of the Soviet Union. But as the arms race quickly heated up, Oppenheimer began to view the control of atomic energy in a new light. By 1946, he had come out in favor of establishing an international civilian authority to head off a permanent arms race and possibly a nuclear war. He envisioned that such an authority would not only develop weapons (if necessary) but also encourage the peaceful use of atomic energy as a potential power source. His ideas met with resistance in some quarters, especially among members of the military, who argued that atomic weapons delivered the kind of massive retaliation conventional bombs could not. But the State Department endorsed Oppenheimer's proposal, and eventually it became official U.S. policy, only to be rejected by the Soviet Union when it was submitted to the United Nations for worldwide consideration.

A few years later, Oppenheimer was at the center of a far more angry debate when he was one of only a few scientists who spoke out against building a hydrogen "superbomb" shortly after the Soviets successfully exploded their first atomic bomb in 1949. As chairman of the general advisory committee of the Atomic Energy Commission (AEC), he wrote a strongly-worded statement condemning the hydrogen bomb, noting that it was not technically feasible at the time and that research should remain at the theoretical level. He also warned that the United States should not do anything to accelerate the arms race without first discussing with the Soviet Union an agreement not to develop hydrogen weapons. In 1950, President Truman overruled Oppenheimer's recommendations, and by 1952, a device invented by Dr. Edward Teller enabled the United States to explode a hydrogen bomb.

Oppenheimer's lack of support for the hydrogen bomb project, along with his earlier ties to leftist groups and causes, ultimately made him a target when anti-communist hysteria swept the United States during the 1950s. Despite having passed numerous security checks during the 1940s, he was barred from reviewing classified material in late 1953 after the former head of a congressional committee on atomic energy wrote a letter to FBI Director J. Edgar Hoover denouncing Oppenheimer as a Soviet agent. Several months later, he was suspended from his consultant's post with the AEC. Subsequent hearings conducted by the commission at Oppenheimer's request turned up nothing that cast doubts on his loyalty as a citizen, but he was nevertheless denied reinstatement of his security clearance on the grounds that he displayed "fundamental defects in his character" that made him a risk. The judgment outraged many of his fellow scientists and other Americans who felt he was actually being persecuted for criticizing the hydrogen bomb project and America's participation in the arms race.

In mid-1954, following an unsuccessful appeal of the AEC's decision, Oppenheimer returned to Princeton as director of the Institute for Advanced Study, a post he had held since leaving Berkeley in 1947. He remained there for the rest of his life, living quietly and devoting most of his time not to physics—for which he had lost much of his enthusiasm—but to philosophical and ethical concerns, especially the relationship between science and society and how scientific knowledge can best be put to use. Oppenheimer was also preoccupied with how humankind might achieve lasting world peace. He continued to speak out for disarmament, arguing that the countries *without* nuclear weapons would probably be less eager to acquire them if the countries *with* them would voluntarily give them up. Fostering such an atmosphere of cooperation requires communication, he told Thomas B. Morgan in a *Look* magazine interview. "I have been much concerned that in this world we have so largely lost the ability to talk to one another . . . ," explained Oppenheimer. "Two *countries* never understand each other. But many individuals in each country may, or may in part, understand one another, and this is good."

Although the AEC never restored Oppenheimer's security clearance, it extended an apology of sorts in 1963 by voting him its highest honor, the Enrico Fermi Award, given in recognition of outstanding contributions to the development of atomic energy. The last few years of his life were marred by increasingly poor health. He was forced him to retire from the directorship of the Institute for Advanced Study in early 1966, at which time he was appointed senior professor of theoretical physics (a position once held by Albert Einstein). He died of throat cancer on February 18, 1967, almost universally lauded as a scientific genius and a thoughtful critic of public policy who fell victim to cold war hysteria.

Sources

> **Books**

Michelmore, Peter, *The Swift Years: The Robert Oppenheimer Story,* Dodd, 1969.

Oppenheimer, J. Robert, *Science and the Common Understanding,* Simon & Schuster, 1954.

Oppenheimer, J. Robert, *The Open Mind,* Simon & Schuster, 1955.

Oppenheimer, J. Robert, *Robert Oppenheimer: Letters and Recollections,* edited by Alice Kimball Smith and Charles Weiner, Harvard University Press, 1980.

Rouze, Michel, *Robert Oppenheimer: The Man and His Theories,* translated by Patrick Evans, Eriksson, 1965.

➤ **Periodicals**

Look, "With Oppenheimer, on an Autumn Day," December 27, 1966, pp. 61–67 (opening quote).

Newsweek, "Honor to Oppenheimer," June 27, 1966, pp. 64–65.

New York Times, "J. Robert Oppenheimer, Atom Bomb Pioneer, Dies," February 19, 1967.

Physics Today, April, 1967, pp. 110–111; October, 1967, pp. 34–53.

Science, March 3, 1967, p. 1061 (editorial); "Oppenheimer: 'Where He Was There Was Always Life and Excitement,'" pp. 1080–1084.

Science News, "In Passing: Dr. Oppenheimer," March 4, 1967.

Time, February 24, 1967, p. 90.

Jesse Owens

*"*__A__*ny black who strives to achieve in this country should think in terms of not only himself but also how he can reach down and grab another black child and pull him to the top of the mountain where he is."*

At the 1936 Olympic games in Berlin, Germany, Jesse Owens won four gold medals and became a symbol of triumph over Nazism. He was born on September 12, 1913, in Oakville, Alabama, and died on March 31, 1980, in Phoenix, Arizona.

A lthough they are touted as friendly contests between some of the world's best athletes, the Olympics have on many occasions taken on strong political overtones. Never was this more true than in 1936, when the games were hosted by the government of Adolf Hitler in Berlin, Germany. Nazi propagandists tried to turn them into a demonstration of Germany's racial and ethnic superiority, but the amazing performances of one Black-American track and field athlete, twenty-two-year-old Jesse Owens, undermined that goal in especially dramatic and spectacular fashion. Over several days of competition, Owens set records in the broad jump, the 100-meter dash, the 200-meter dash, and the 400-meter relay, claiming four gold medals and the admiration of not only his fellow athletes but also the predominantly German crowd that witnessed his performances.

James Cleveland Owens was one of seven children of Alabama sharecroppers Henry and Emma Alexander Owens. In search of a better life, the Owens family headed north around 1922 and settled in Cleveland, Ohio, where nine-year-old J. C. (as he was then known) enrolled in school for the first time. When asked his name, the little boy answered, "J. C.," which the teacher misunderstood as "Jesse." Thus did J. C. become known as Jesse for the rest of his life.

Always a rather frail and sickly child, Owens nevertheless went out for track in fifth grade at the urging of his school's coach. He quickly developed into a strong and exceptionally graceful runner, and by the time he reached junior high he had set a new record for the 100-yard dash. He continued his winning ways throughout high school, coming out on top in an unprecedented three events (the 100-yard dash, the 200-yard dash, and the long jump) at the 1933 National Interscholastic Championships meet in Chicago.

Offered athletic scholarships to a number of colleges, Owens turned them down and opted instead to work his way through Ohio State University. He also managed to find time for track, earning the nickname the "Buckeye Bullet" in honor of his amazing speed. On May 25, 1935, at the National Intercollegiate Track and Field Championships meet in Ann Arbor, Michigan, Owens—despite being in intense pain from a back injury suffered just a week before—broke three world records (in the 220-yard dash, the 220-yard low hurdles, and the long jump) and equaled another (in the 100-yard dash) in a mere forty-five minutes of competition.

A little more than a year later, in August, 1936, the "Buckeye Bullet" found himself in Berlin as one of ten Black Americans on the sixty-six-member U.S. Olympic track and field team. The Nazis had scorned the participation of Blacks, repeatedly referring to them in public as sub-human "auxiliaries" to the U.S. team and boasting that they could surely be beaten by the unquestionably superior German contestants. Many people responded to these statements and other policies of the Hitler regime by calling for a boycott, but the games went on as scheduled in an atmosphere of hostility and extreme competitive pressure. German athletes scored victories in many of the early events, and for a time it appeared that they might indeed walk away with most of the medals.

But then came Owens. With seemingly little effort, he captured four gold medals, setting an Olympic record in the long jump, equaling the world record in the 100-meter dash, and setting new world records in the 200-meter dash and (along with his teammates Ralph Metcalfe, Foy Draper, and Frank Wykoff) the 400-meter relay. The German athletes he beat were exceedingly gracious and respectful in defeat, and even the predominantly German crowd regarded him with a mixture of curiosity and awe and cheered wildly for him as he accepted his medals.

As Olympic legend has it, Hitler was so furious that a Black athlete had trounced the Germans that he refused to congratulate Owens. In fact, after Hitler had made a point of conspicuously congratulating several medal winners (mostly Germans) on the very first day of the games, Olympic officials asked him to stop unless he intended to treat all of the athletes in a similar fashion; as a result, Hitler opted to forgo the public displays and instead met privately with victorious Germans. But the story of this apparent snub spread quickly and enhanced the symbolic importance of Owens's success as a triumph over Nazism.

Owens brushed off news of the snub, explaining many years later, "it was all right with me. I didn't go to Berlin to shake hands with Hitler, anyway." Of greater concern to Owens was what awaited him on his return to the United States. Although he was a top college athlete and an Olympic hero, he was still first and foremost a Black man in a racist society. "When I came back," he recalled, "after all those stories about Hitler and his snub, I came back to my native country, and I couldn't ride in the front of the bus. I had to go to the back door. I couldn't live where I wanted. Now what's the difference?"

Indeed, Owens's life for many years after the Olympics was a difficult one as he struggled to make ends meet and find meaningful employment. Unable to pay for his senior year at Ohio State, he dropped out for a while and worked briefly as a playground janitor, then agreed to participate in some publicity stunts in which he raced against cars, trucks, motorcycles, horses, and dogs. He also made a series of personal appearances, including tap dancing with Bill "Bojangles" Robinson and making speeches on behalf of Alf Landon, the Republican presidential candidate. With the money he earned from these exhibitions Owens was able to finish school, but because he had accepted payment for running, his career in amateur athletics was finished.

During the late 1930s, Owens pursued a variety of activities. He led a swing orchestra, had a bit part in a movie, served as an official with the Works Progress Administration (WPA) in Cleveland, worked as a salesman, and established a chain of dry-cleaning establishments. In 1939, however, the dry-cleaning business failed and Owens's partners disappeared, saddling him with heavy debts that forced him into personal bankruptcy. From 1940 to 1942 he was the Office of Civilian Defense's national director of physical education for Black Americans, and from 1942 to 1946 he served as director of Black personnel for the Ford Motor Company. He left that job to become a salesman for a sporting goods firm.

In 1949, Owens relocated to Chicago, his home for the next twenty-three years. There he again worked as a sporting goods salesman and became involved in a number of state and local programs devoted to keeping Black-American youths out of trouble by involving them in athletics. He took very seriously his status as a role model and an inspiration to all those facing the same obstacles and prejudices that had often held him back, noting that "regardless of his color, a man who becomes a recognized athlete has to learn to walk ten feet tall." Owens also downplayed the importance of material wealth and emphasized the other rewards that athletic competition has to offer. "We all have dreams," he once declared. "But in order to make dreams into reality, it takes an awful lot of determination, dedication, self-discipline and effort. These things apply to everyday life. You learn not only the sport but things like respect of others, ethics in life, how you are going to live, how you treat your fellow man, how you live with your fellow man."

Eventually, Owens's interests and skills led him into public relations, both as the head of his own firm and as a spokesman for various charities, the Olympics, and dozens of corporate clients. A powerful orator who approached his subject—usually a celebration of the virtues of fair play, clean living, and patriotism—with near-evangelical fervor, he was much in demand throughout the country, even after he moved to Phoenix and went into semi-retirement in 1972. In addition, Owens was also a longtime "ambassador of sports" for the U.S. State Department, a position that called on him to make periodic goodwill tours around the world. He continued these activities until just a few months before his death from lung cancer in 1980.

Despite the hardships he faced even after his success in the Olympics, Owens always looked back on the experience with pride and a pronounced lack of bitterness. "[The medals] have kept me alive over the years," he once explained. "Time has stood still for me. That golden moment dies hard." The brilliance of his athletic accomplishments has not dimmed, nor has his stature as one of the most famous and symbolic figures in recent Olympic history. With stunning victories that "made a mockery of the Fuehrer's words—and the Aryan 'master race' philosophy," wrote Pete Axthelm in *Newsweek*, Jesse Owens "seemed to embody the Olympic dream that sportsmen can reach across political and military lines in a noble quest for friendship and glory."

Sources

➤ **Books**

Gentry, Tony, *Jesse Owens*, Chelsea House, 1990.

Mandell, Richard, *The Nazi Olympics*, Macmillan, 1971.

Owens, Jesse, *Blackthink: My Life as Black Man and White Man*, Pocket Books, 1971.

Owens, Jesse, and Paul Neimark, *Jesse: The Man Who Outran Hitler*, Fawcett, 1985.

➤ **Periodicals**

Ebony, "A Farewell to Jesse Owens," June, 1980, pp. 66–72.

National Review, "Jesse Owens, RIP," April 18, 1980, pp. 456–457.

Newsweek, "The True Olympian," April 14, 1980, p. 60.

New York Times, "Owens Surpasses Three World Records," May 26, 1935; "110,000 See Owens Set World Record at Olympic Games," August 3, 1936; "Owens Captures Olympic Title, Equals World 100-Meter Record," August 4, 1936; "U.S. Captures Four Events;

Owens Sets Jump Record," August 5, 1936; "Owens Completes Triple as Five Olympic Marks Fall," August 6, 1936; "Jesse Owens First Among Track Aces," January 27, 1950; August 28, 1956; November 17, 1956, p. 25; "Jesse Owens Dies of Cancer at 66; Hero of the 1936 Berlin Olympics," April 1, 1980 (opening quote).

Sport, "The Man Who Put Hitler Down," August, 1980, pp. 69–70.

Time, "Man vs. Myth," April 14, 1980, p. 93.

Gordon Parks

*"*T*he first black this, the first black that. I don't appreciate that as much as people think I do. I have no doubt there were other blacks who could have done it just as well or a lot better."*

Gordon Parks paved the way for many Black-American photographers and filmmakers as the first Black-American photojournalist for *Life* magazine and the first Black American to become a leading filmmaker. He was born on November 30, 1912, in Fort Scott, Kansas.

Address: 860 United Nations Plaza, New York, NY 10017.

Gordon Roger Alexander Buchanan Parks was the youngest of fifteen children born to Sarah Ross Parks and Andrew Jackson Parks, who made a meager living as a farmer. Despite their poverty and the racism they encountered as one of the few Black-American families on the Kansas prairie, the Parkses were very close and loving and enjoyed a secure, happy home life. From his parents (especially his mother), Gordon learned to value the importance of honor, education, and equality. He was also left with a burning desire to make something of himself no matter what obstacles he might encounter. As his mother had told him countless times, "If a white boy can do it, so can you, so don't ever give me your color as a cause for failing."

At age fifteen, Parks lost his chief source of strength and guidance when his mother died. Sent to live with an older married sister in St. Paul, Minnesota, he suddenly found himself out on the streets in the middle of winter when he argued with his brother-in-law, who ordered him to leave. Young Parks rode the streetcars by night to keep warm and spent his days taking whatever jobs he could find (playing piano in a brothel, waiting tables, cleaning up in a flophouse) to earn money for food. He also tried to keep up with his high school studies but had to drop out in order to work. During whatever free time he had, however, he read at the public library, composed songs (he had been able to play the piano by ear since childhood), wrote essays, tried painting and sculpturing, and even played some semi-professional basketball. He later described those years of deprivation and despair as hellish. "I never thought about success," he recalls. "I thought about survival. Success was a big word. That I did survive was enough, because I had some brutal times."

While working as a hotel busboy in 1932, Parks caught the attention of a visiting bandleader who had heard him play a few of his own compositions on the ballroom piano. The visitor asked the young man if he would like to accompany the band on tour and Parks eagerly accepted. But in early 1933, he was stranded in Harlem after the band broke up. Unable to find work and unhappy in the city, Parks joined the Civilian Conservation Corps and cleared forest land for a year until marrying his first wife and settling in Minneapolis with her family.

For the next few years, Parks opted for security as a porter and dining-car waiter for the Northern Pacific Railroad on the St. Paul-Seattle run. One day he came across a magazine left behind by a passenger containing Farm Security Administration photographs of migrant workers. (The Farm Security Administration, or FSA, had been established by the U.S. government in 1935 to document the devastating effects of the Depression.) "Those pictures inspired me," he later said. "I felt, without really knowing how, that photography was the one way I could express myself about deprivation, about racial discrimination." A short time later, he sat in a Chicago movie theater and watched compelling newsreel footage of a Japanese attack on a U.S. gunboat in China, when he realized "all the things I could say through this medium. I sat through another show, and even before I left the theater I had made up my mind to become a professional photographer."

Parks bought his first camera for $12.50 at a Seattle pawnshop and immediately went out to take waterfront pictures at Puget Sound. Back in Minneapolis, Parks took the film to a downtown camera store to be developed. When he picked it up, the clerk complimented him on his pictures and told him he could have his own exhibition. Six weeks later, some of Parks's photographs were on display in the camera store window.

Within just a couple of years Parks had branched out into portraiture and fashion photography for an exclusive local women's store. In 1941, Marva Louis, wife of boxing champion Joe Louis, happened to see some of Parks's work and encouraged him to move to Chicago to take advantage of the opportunities the city offered. For a year or so he made his living taking pictures of society women (Black as well as White) while using his free time to record scenes of ghetto life. After he had accumulated a portfolio of documentary photographs, he applied for a Julius Rosenwald fellowship (a grant awarded to Black-American artists) and won the first ever given to a photographer. Temporarily free of the pressure to earn a living, Parks was at last able to pursue his interest and education in photography as he wished. He traveled to Washington, D.C., and went to work as a trainee under Roy Stryker, head of the FSA photography unit whose pictures Parks had admired during his days as a railroad porter.

On his very first day in the nation's capital, Parks was introduced to the segregation of the South when he was denied service at a drugstore lunch counter and a major department store. But he loved his job; the work was steady and interesting (mostly documenting the lives of everyday Americans) and the atmosphere was stimulating. His style was shaped by the FSA model, which stressed empathy, involvement, and factuality—qualities that he brought to his own depictions of the poor and dispossessed, emphasizing their vulnerability, suffering, and frustration. In short, says Parks, "I was an objective reporter with a subjective heart." He learned to think of his camera as a weapon that would fight the twin evils of poverty and racism.

In 1943, the Farm Security Administration disbanded, and Parks began searching for other work. He served briefly as a correspondent for the Office of War Information, quitting in disgust when he was denied the chance to go overseas to photograph the activities of an all-Black fighter pilot squadron, apparently because some influential whites in the capital had objected to the idea of giving so much publicity to Black-American soldiers. He then went to work again for Roy Stryker, who had signed on with Standard Oil of New Jersey to compile a photographic portrait of America. When that project ended in 1948, Parks secured some free-lance magazine assignments, including fashion photography for *Vogue* and *Glamour* and a memorable spread on Harlem gangs for *Life* that led to a permanent staff position with the magazine, a first for a Black-American photojournalist.

Over the next twenty years, Parks completed more than three hundred major assignments for *Life*, covering everything from junior high school science conventions to hurricanes, from urban crime to European royalty. He also contributed a number of significant pieces on events and figures associated with the civil rights and Black power movements, including segregation in the South, the March on Washington for Jobs and Freedom, Malcolm X and the Black Muslims, and the death of Martin Luther King, Jr. But among Parks's most moving photo essays were those he did on the poor, including a famous series on an asthmatic, malnourished boy named Flavio who lived in one of Brazil's worst slums. *Life* readers were so touched by the boy's plight that they flooded the magazine with donations, and a clinic in Colorado offered to treat him free of charge. Parks arranged for Flavio to travel to the United States, where he underwent successful asthma therapy. (Now married and the father of several children, Flavio still keeps in touch with Parks.) Flavio was not the only person the photographer helped, however; Parks saw to it that many of his subjects "who sacrificed their time and privacy were rewarded with new homes, medical care, new clothing, a chance for a better life."

Having become interested in filmmaking some years before while covering the shooting of several Hollywood productions, Parks left

Life in 1968 to try to break into the movie industry. All of his previous attempts to do so had met with failure; studios were not about to take a chance on a Black man. His first efforts, completed in the early 1960s, were documentaries for public television. Later on his actor-director friend John Cassavetes persuaded Warner Brothers-Seven Arts to sign Parks to a four-picture deal, making him the first Black American to direct a major Hollywood production.

Parks's first project was the film adaptation of his autobiographical novel *The Learning Tree*, a best-seller published in 1963. He not only directed the film but also wrote the screenplay and the score. (Regarded as a classic, it has been placed on the National Film Registry of the Library of Congress.) He followed it with the private-eye thriller *Shaft* and its sequel, *Shaft's Big Score*, and, finally, *The Super Cops*. Despite the commercial success of the "Shaft" movies in particular, Parks still could not secure the creative and financial freedom he needed to make the kind of sensitive dramas that would parallel what he had done as a still photographer. After one last attempt, *Leadbelly*, fell victim to a management change at Paramount Pictures in 1976, Parks left Hollywood to return to New York.

Since then, he has filmed several documentaries for both commercial and public television. He has also continued to write, composing several orchestral works and producing several works of poetry (accompanied by his photographs), two novels (including a historical one on eighteenth-century English painter J. M. W. Turner), and two volumes of memoirs: *To Smile in Autumn* (which takes up the story of his life at the point where his first volume of memoirs, the 1966 work *A Choice of Weapons*, left off) and *Voices in the Mirror*. He also wrote and scored a ballet, *Martin*, about Martin Luther King, Jr., and later filmed a production of the ballet for public television. Parks has received more than fifty awards and honors, including a Spingarn Medal in 1972, a National Medal of Arts in 1988, and the Paul Robeson Award from the Black Filmmakers Hall of Fame. Now in his eighth decade, Parks insists he has no plans to slow down. "I always feel there are other things to do out there," he explains. "That I must not stop and feel as though I've made it."

Sources

➤ **Books**

Berry, S. L., *Gordon Parks*, Chelsea House, 1991.

Parks, Gordon, *A Choice of Weapons*, Harper, 1966.

Parks, Gordon, *To Smile in Autumn: A Memoir*, Norton, 1979.

Parks, Gordon, *Voices in the Mirror: An Autobiography*, Doubleday, 1990.

➤ **Periodicals**

Detroit Free Press, "Parks Extends a Helping Hand," January 9, 1991, p. 3C (opening quote).

Detroit News, "The Life and Times of a Talented Role Model," December 19, 1990, p. 3G.

Modern Maturity, "A Passion for Living," June-July, 1989.

Newsweek, "Color-Blind Camera," April 29, 1968, pp. 84–87.

New York Times Book Review, "Prometheus in Motion," December 9, 1990, p. 19.

Smithsonian, "Shooting Straight: The Many Worlds of Gordon Parks," April, 1989, pp. 66–77.

Robert E. Peary

"I shall find a way or make one."

Explorer Robert E. Peary led seven expeditions in search of the North Pole before he and his longtime partner Matthew Henson finally met with success on their eighth attempt in 1909. He was born on May 6, 1856, in Cresson, Pennsylvania, and died on February 20, 1920, in Washington, D.C.

I n 1906, not long after he returned from his seventh expedition to the Arctic, Robert E. Peary stood before members of the National Geographic Society and accepted a medal for going farther north than anyone had ever gone before. But in his speech, he looked not at the accomplishments of the past but at the challenge of the future. "To me," he said, "the final and complete solution of the Polar mystery . . . is the thing which must be done for the honour and credit of this country, the thing which it is intended that I should do, and the thing that I must do." Indeed, Peary's goal—more precisely, his obsession—was to reach the ultimate "farthest north" destination: the North Pole. It was a dream that consumed nearly twenty-five years of his life.

Robert Edwin Peary was the only child of Charles and Mary Wiley Peary. He was only three when his father died, at which time he and his mother left Pennsylvania and settled in Portland, Maine, where he spent his boyhood. In 1877, after graduating with honors from the civil engineering program at Bowdoin College, Peary worked briefly as a surveyor and justice of the peace and ran a bird-mounting business on the side. But the quiet life of a country gentleman had little appeal for the ambitious young man. Around 1880 he headed to Washington, D.C., and took a job as a draftsman with the U.S. Coast and Geodetic Survey. This in turn led to a commission as a civil engineer in the U.S. Navy.

Peary's first big assignment was in Nicaragua as part of a survey team plotting the route for a proposed ship canal linking the Atlantic and Pacific oceans. While his work won praise from his superiors, it did not turn out to be the path to success that he had hoped it would be. Back in Washington, he read a book on Greenland, and from that moment on he knew that the glory he sought could be found in polar exploration. Obtaining a brief leave from the navy, he made his first trip to Greenland in 1886 and sledged a hundred or so miles out onto the ice cap.

In 1887, Peary returned to Nicaragua and the canal project, this time as the supervisor of a group of engineers. Accompanying him was a young Black man, Matthew Henson, whom he had originally hired as his personal servant. But over the course of the seven months they spent in Central America, Henson's skills as a guide and a surveyor greatly impressed Peary. During the return voyage to the United States, Peary told Henson of his dream to visit the North Pole—one of the last great frontiers left on earth and also one of the most challenging—and asked him if he would like to come along. Henson accepted, and for the next twenty years they were inseparable traveling companions.

Peary's first expedition was launched in June, 1891. Setting sail for Greenland from New York with his wife, Henson, and four others (including Frederick Cook, the ship's doctor and ethnologist), the thirty-five-year-old explorer knew that he was in a race against time; most of his competitors were younger and had already staked out their own territories, leaving Peary to conquer the more remote and dangerous areas. His first setback came while still at sea and the ship's rudder struck a chunk of ice, causing the heavy iron tiller to swing across the deck and smash into his lower leg, breaking both bones. Once in Greenland, Peary and Henson sledged twelve hundred miles across the ice cap into the extreme northeast, discovering new land and confirming Greenland's island status. But Peary had underestimated the amount of food they needed, and it was only Henson's hunting skill that saved them from starvation. Despite (or perhaps because of) the obstacles he had encountered, Peary was hailed as a hero upon his return to civilization and had no trouble financing another expedition.

But Peary's next trip north, which lasted from 1893 until 1895, was an even bigger disaster. The group battled severe weather, frostbite, and a disease that threatened to wipe out all of the sled dogs. Unable to face the prospect of going home without something to show for his efforts, Peary brought with him two of the three huge meteorites he had discovered early in the trip. The find intrigued the public, and scientists credited Peary with solving the mystery of where Eskimos had obtained iron before they had contact with European whalers in the early nineteenth century.

Subsequent expeditions in 1896 and 1897 were less eventful, although Peary continued to add to his growing expertise on the subject of arctic survival and travel. He also brought back what was then the largest-known meteorite in the world, a 34-ton chunk of iron that he sold to New York City's American Museum of Natural History. In between expeditions, he kept busy lecturing all over the country to help raise money for future trips.

Peary mounted his first serious assault on the pole during an expedition that ran from 1898 until 1902. Concerned that someone else might beat him to the prize, he ignored advice to wait until summer and instead set out with Henson and five others in December, 1898. Severe storms trapped them for weeks at a hut about 250 miles from their base camp, and Peary subsequently had to have eight of his toes amputated due to frostbite. He vowed to keep on pushing northward, however, and in May, 1900, he and Henson managed to make it farther north than anyone had ever gone before. They then tried to strike out across the Arctic Ocean but had to turn back. After another failed attempt in the spring of 1902, a despondent Peary wrote in his diary, "The game is off. My dream of sixteen years is ended."

At the urging of President Theodore Roosevelt, Peary tried again in 1905. But the expedition encountered severe weather and dangerous ice that cracked and shifted beneath the sledges. When it became obvious they would never reach the pole, Peary decided instead to go for a new "farthest north" record. Once that was accomplished he turned back, his ultimate goal less than 175 miles away.

In July, 1908, the fifty-two-year-old Peary set off one last time for the North Pole; he knew that physically and mentally he would not be up to making the journey again. For this final assault, he opted to use a plan that he had first tested on the 1905–1906 expedition. His 24 men (6 Americans and the rest Eskimos), 19 sledges, and 133 dogs were divided into seven self-sufficient teams. Only the main team—consisting of Peary, Henson, four Eskimos, and their dogs and equipment—was scheduled to make the complete 413-mile journey to the pole; the others were responsible for breaking trail and carrying supplies. One by one, at certain points along the way, the support teams were supposed to drop a load of supplies and turn back, thus reducing the number of mouths to feed as the group neared the pole.

The teams began heading out in early 1909, and by March 1, everyone was on the ice. On April 1, the last support party turned back, leaving only Peary and Henson's team to cover the remaining 133 miles. Over the next five days, the two men alternated breaking trail. On April 6, Henson, who was about forty-five minutes ahead of Peary on that particular leg of the journey, stopped when he thought he had reached the pole and waited for his companion. Peary showed up a bit later and, unknown to Henson, took some readings that indicated the pole was actually three miles farther north. While Henson slept, Peary set out with two Eskimos and crisscrossed the area making additional calculations. Still he was not able to determine beyond all doubt that they had reached the exact location, and the uncertainty ate away at him as he pondered whether he had once again failed to achieve his goal.

Later in the year, when Peary finally made his way to a wireless station to share the news of his journey with the world (he had finally convinced himself that he had indeed been successful), he was stunned to learn that his onetime friend Frederick Cook had announced just a few days earlier that he had reached the North Pole on April 21, 1908, a full year before Peary. A bitter controversy erupted, one that saw most scientists and other experts support Peary while the press backed Cook (and heaped abuse on Peary). Eventually Cook was revealed as a fraud, and Peary at last received the acclaim he deserved (including promotion to the rank of rear admiral in the U.S. Navy) as the leader of the first expedition to discover the North Pole.

Peary spent his remaining years living rather quietly on an island off the coast of Maine. He was very much interested in the development of aviation and actively campaigned for aerial military preparedness, making regular visits to Washington to lecture on the subject. Peary died in 1920 and was buried at Arlington National Cemetery, where a globe-shaped monument representing the earth marks his grave.

Although Cook's attempt to best Peary in the race to the North Pole was quickly exposed as a fake, a few skeptics have continued to question whether Peary and Henson actually made it; some insist that they never got any closer than fifty-five miles. In 1989, in an effort to put to rest such speculation, the National Geographic Society commissioned the Maryland-based Navigation Foundation to conduct a thorough review of all the available evidence. After a yearlong study, the foundation concluded that Peary and Henson had indeed made it to within about five miles of the pole, close enough to secure their status as co-discoverers.

But as arctic explorer and author Wally Herbert pointed out in a *National Geographic* article published before the results of the study were released, it really doesn't matter whether Peary ever stood precisely at the top of the world, because "from the higher ground of history [he] stands out as a pioneer who contributed to mankind. Impelled by the energy of his obsession, conquering with his exceptional courage man's fear of the unknown, he extended the bounds of human endeavor. Thus was his mission a success."

Sources

➤ **Books**

Weems, John Edward, *Race to the Pole*, Holt, 1960.

Weems, John Edward, *Peary: The Explorer and the Man*, Houghton, 1967.

➤ **Periodicals**

National Geographic, "Did Peary Reach the Pole?," September, 1988, pp. 386–413 (opening quote); "New Evidence Places Peary at the Pole," January, 1990, pp. 44–61.

Newsweek, "Peary Made It to the Pole After All," December 25, 1989, p. 71.

New York Times, February 21, 1921.

Scientific American, "Polar Heat," March, 1990, pp. 22–24; "Peary Redux: Are the Facts (If Any) Getting Lost?," June, 1990, pp. 25–26.

Time, "Peary on Top," December 25, 1989, p. 73.

U.S. News and World Report, "Pole Taker," December 25, 1989-January 1, 1990, p. 10.

Colin Powell

"What my color is is somebody else's problem, not mine. People will say, 'You're a terrific black general.' I'm trying to be the best general I can be."

Born on April 5, 1937, in New York City, four-star General Colin Powell is the first Black American to serve as chairman of the Joint Chiefs of Staff of the U.S. military forces.

Address: Office of the Chairman, The Joint Chiefs of Staff, Washington, D.C. 20318–0001.

Colin Powell made history on October 1, 1989, when he became the first Black-American chairman of the Joint Chiefs of Staff, the principal advisory body to the president, the secretary of defense, and the National Security Council (NSC) on military matters. A self-described "soldier's soldier" with a reputation for candor, efficiency, and level-headed practicality, Powell had long enjoyed the respect of Washington insiders. It was not until after the Iraqis invaded Kuwait in August, 1990, however, that the rest of the country came to know and admire him. Americans who followed the progress of operations Desert Shield and Desert Storm saw for themselves his strength, confidence, and occasional flashes of humor, and by the end of the Persian Gulf War, he was one of the nation's most popular public figures. While the adulation has died down a bit with the passage of time, Powell is still held in very high esteem as a role model for young people. According to political consultant Mari Maseng, he "is exactly what you want in a military man, the perfect antidote for what went wrong in Vietnam and the Iran-Contra affair."

The younger of Luther and Maud Ariel McKoy Powell's two children, Colin Luther Powell was born in Harlem but grew up in a multi-ethnic neighborhood in the South Bronx as part of a loving and close-knit family. Luther and Maud Powell had immigrated to the United States from Jamaica in search of a better life, and they found it in Manhattan's garment district, where Luther worked as a shipping clerk and Maud as a seamstress. Both parents instilled in their son and daughter a belief in the importance of education and a drive to achieve, and it was their high expectations that Colin Powell feels motivated him to make something of himself.

After graduating from high school, Powell went on to New York's City College, compiling an average scholastic record and obtaining a degree in geology in 1958. Outside the classroom, he was a standout in the college's ROTC unit, serving as commander of the precision drill team and graduating as a cadet colonel, the highest possible rank. He then joined the army, never dreaming that it would become his path to success. "My ambitions, such as they were, were much more modest at the time," he once told an *Ebony* reporter. "They were simply to get out of New York, get a job and go out and have some excitement. . . . My parents expected that, like most young men going in the Army, I would serve for two years . . . and then come home and get a *real* job."

Commissioned a second lieutenant, Powell initially was sent to

West Germany. In late 1962, he began the first of two one-year tours of duty in Vietnam as an advisor to a Vietnamese infantry battalion and earned a Purple Heart for injuries he received when he stepped on a Viet Cong booby trap that drove a stake through his foot. During his second tour, which ran from 1968 until 1969, Powell was an infantry officer at the battalion level and was awarded a Soldier's Medal for his daring rescue of several fellow soldiers from the fiery wreck of a downed helicopter.

Powell enrolled at George Washington University upon his return to the United States and was awarded his MBA in 1971. The following year, he received a prestigious White House fellowship in the Office of Management and Budget (OMB). There he met two men who were to figure prominently in his future: Caspar Weinberger, the OMB's director and later President Ronald Reagan's secretary of defense, and Frank Carlucci, the OMB's deputy director and later Reagan's national security advisor. As Carlucci's assistant, the competent and efficient Powell made an extremely favorable impression in what proved to be one of the pivotal positions of his career.

Over the next fifteen years, Powell alternated military duty with political appointments. He served at the battalion and division levels in a number of locations, including South Korea and Kentucky, and was periodically rotated back to Washington to take a staff job at the Pentagon. During one of his stays stateside he attended the National War College, graduating with distinction in 1976. As a member of the Carter administration he worked as a senior military assistant to the deputy secretary of defense followed by a brief stint in 1979 as executive assistant to the secretary of energy.

When Ronald Reagan took office in January, 1981, Powell stayed on for a few months in the Department of Defense and provided transitional support to the new staff. He then returned to military duty, first in Colorado and then in Kansas. In mid-1983, however, Secretary of Defense Weinberger summoned Powell back to Washington to serve as his senior military assistant, a position in which Powell made a name for himself as an organizer and a peacemaker who fostered cooperation between competing agencies and individuals.

Powell was also one of only five people in the Pentagon who knew about the NSC's secret efforts to secure the release of American hostages in the Middle East by selling arms to Iran, the profits from which were then channeled to the Nicaraguan *contra* forces to aid in their struggle against the Sandinistas. But he did not become involved in the so-called Iran-Contra affair until after the deal had won Reagan's approval, and Powell had made a point of sending a written memo to NSC director John Poindexter and his aide Oliver North reminding them of their legal obligation to inform Congress of the arms shipments to Iran and Nicaragua. Poindexter and North chose to disregard his memo, however, and as a result Powell's reputation for integrity and candor was enhanced rather than compromised when his role in the scandal came to light.

Powell left Washington in 1986 to assume command of the V Corps in Frankfurt, West Germany, a prestigious and much-coveted position that put him in charge of some 72,000 troops. A mere six months later, in January, 1987, he received a call from his onetime boss Frank Carlucci, the new head of the NSC, asking him to return to the capital as his assistant. A very reluctant Powell agreed only after his commander-in-chief—President Reagan—personally asked him to take the job.

Together with Carlucci, Powell then set about repairing the NSC's damaged credibility by reorganizing the staff and changing procedures to eliminate the risk of any future scandals. Later that same year, when Weinberger retired as secretary of defense and Carlucci was tapped to replace him, Powell was promoted to succeed Carlucci as head of the NSC. Unlike so many Washington appointments, this particular selection met with universal acclaim; Powell was held in high regard not only by the president and his cabinet but also by Congress and the top-level officials at the Department of Defense, the State Department, and the Central Intelligence Agency.

Powell served as national security advisor throughout the remainder of Reagan's term, playing a key role in the president's decision not to use military force to oust Panamanian dictator Manuel Noriega and not to press Congress for continued support of the Nicaraguan contras in their effort to overthrow the Sandinistas. In addition, Powell persuaded the administration to hold off investing in the technologically complex and very expensive Strategic Defense Initiative or "Star Wars" program. He was also the principal organizer of Reagan's last two summit meetings with Soviet leader Mikhail Gorbachev, which culminated in a major nuclear arms treaty.

After Reagan left office in January, 1989, Powell once again returned to military duty as head of U.S. Forces Command at Fort McPherson, Georgia. But no sooner had he settled into his new job (which put him in charge of one million troops) then President George Bush nominated him over dozens of more senior candidates to become chairman of the Joint Chiefs of Staff, one of the most powerful positions in the U.S. government. Quickly confirmed by Congress, Powell officially took over the reins in October, 1989, becoming the first black and the youngest man ever to serve as the president's chief advisor on military matters.

In peacetime, Powell's responsibilities revolve around setting budget priorities for investments in equipment and personnel, evaluating the military's welfare and readiness, and assuring a smooth flow of information between the various branches of the service and the White House. In wartime, however, his duties expand to include developing actual military strategies. His greatest challenge in that arena came after the Iraqis invaded Kuwait in August, 1990.

Although later reports have indicated that Powell favored waiting to see if economic sanctions would stop Iraq's Saddam Hussein before the United States resorted to force, once the decision had been made to engage Iraq militarily, Powell shaped the strategy of the allies' response and then sold his idea to the president and Congress. At his direction, the communications, operations, and authority of the multinational force were integrated under General H. Norman Schwarzkopf. Yet Powell was the man who planned all of the land, sea, and air campaigns and also advised the president on the many political decisions that had to be made, including setting a firm deadline for an Iraqi withdrawal. The goal of Operation Desert Shield was to mass troops and supplies in Saudi Arabia in the hope that their presence would deter any further Iraqi aggression; Operation Desert Storm then went on to demonstrate Powell's belief that "if you finally decide you have to commit military force, you've got to be as massive and decisive as possible," a lesson he had learned while serving in Vietnam.

The Persian Gulf War created many heroes, and in the eyes of more than a few people, Powell stands tallest. Balancing his country's political objectives against the realities of the military situation, he managed to handle both with exceptional skill and diplomacy and in the process restored public confidence in the armed forces. His unapologetic patriotism and humble background appeals to Americans in a way that transcends racial divisions, and as a result he has been urged to run for political office. He has also been showered with awards, including a Presidential Medal of Freedom and the 1991 Spingarn Medal from the National Association for the Advancement of Colored People (NAACP).

But Powell, an independent who has served both Democratic and Republican administrations with distinction, insists he harbors no political desires and prefers to be thought of as a role model rather than a hero. Reappointed to a second two-year term as chairman of the Joint Chiefs in October, 1991, he expects to retire from the military after his term expires and then become involved in another form of public service or perhaps work in the business sector. In the meantime, he struggles with post-Cold War budget cuts in defense spending and contemplates new ways of keeping the military effective as it downsizes. Powell also spends as much time as possible meeting with young people, sharing his life story with them and urging them to stay in school and be persistent. "There are no secrets to success," he says. "Don't waste time looking for them. Success is the result of perfection, hard work, [and] learning from failure."

Sources

➤ **Books**

Landau, Elaine, *Colin Powell: Four-Star General*, F. Watts, 1991.

Woodward, Bob, *The Commanders*, Simon & Schuster, 1991.

➤ **Periodicals**

Ebony, "Black General at the Summit of U.S. Power," July, 1988, pp. 136–146 (opening quote); "The World's Most Powerful Soldier," February, 1990, pp. 136–142.

Newsweek, "'The Ultimate No. 2' for NSC," November 16, 1987, p. 63; "Pragmatist at the Pentagon," August 21, 1989, p. 20; "Bush's General: Maximum Force," September 3, 1990, pp. 36–38; "The Reluctant Warrior," May 13, 1991, pp. 18–22.

People, "Colin Powell, America's Top Soldier, Has Taken His Influence from Harlem to the White House," September 10, 1990, pp. 52–55; "Colin Powell," December 31, 1990-January 7, 1991, pp. 60–61; "Colin Powell," spring/summer, 1991, pp. 38–39.

Time, "The General Takes Command," November 16, 1987, p. 22;

"A 'Complete Soldier' Makes It," August 21, 1989, p. 24; "Five Who Fit the Bill," May 20, 1991, pp. 18–20.

U.S. News and World Report, "'You Go in to Win Decisively,'" December 24, 1990, p. 26; "What's Next, General Powell?," March 18, 1991, pp. 50–53.

Paul Robeson

"I *shall take my voice wherever there are those who want to hear the melody of freedom or the words that might inspire hope and courage in the face of despair and fear."*

Born on April 9, 1898, in Princeton, New Jersey, Paul Robeson was a singer and actor who was blacklisted during the 1950s for supporting various causes deemed radical at the time. He died on January 23, 1976, in Philadelphia, Pennsylvania.

One of the most prominent victims of the anti-communist hysteria that swept the United States during the late 1940s and 1950s was Paul Robeson, a singer and actor. His magnificent bass-baritone voice and commanding physical presence had made him one of the best-known and best-loved Black Americans in the world. Yet his outspoken advocacy of such causes as international peace, racial justice, and workers' rights, as well as his harsh criticism of U.S. policy toward the Soviet Union and his own unabashed admiration of that country made him a dangerous man to some people. Harassed by the government and eventually blacklisted by the entertainment industry (which prevented him from earning a living), Robeson continued to insist on his right to freedom of speech. It was a position that ultimately cost him his career and, as Coretta Scott King observed just a few years before his death, left him "buried alive."

Paul Leroy Bustill Robeson was the youngest of eight children of Maria Louisa Bustill, a schoolteacher of Quaker heritage whose family had been active in the underground railroad during the Civil War, and William Drew Robeson, a former slave who escaped to the north as a teenager and fought for the Union Army before studying for the ministry. Growing up in several different New Jersey towns as a member of a well-respected family, Robeson did not have to contend with the effects of extreme racial prejudice until he tried out for the football team at Rutgers University, which he entered in 1915 on an academic scholarship. Opposed to the idea of playing alongside a Black American, some of Robeson's teammates deliberately tried to injure him during practice. He refused to be intimidated, however, and eventually won them over with his determination and athletic skill. By the time he graduated as class valedictorian in 1919, he had compiled an outstanding record not only in the classroom but also in athletics.

Robeson continued his education at Columbia University Law School. Encouraged by the woman who would become his wife and later his manager, Eslanda Cardozo Goode, Robeson also acted in a few community theater plays. Soon after their marriage in 1921, Eslanda Robeson persuaded her husband to take a break from his law studies and give acting a serious try. His first major appearance was in a play that ran briefly on Broadway and then toured England. Upon his return to the United States, Robeson returned to law school, earned his degree, and accepted a position with a New York firm. But it wasn't long before he became frustrated by a lack of opportunities and the resentment of his White co-workers (includ-

ing a secretary who refused to take dictation from him) and abruptly quit his job.

Once again, he found himself drawn to the stage. Signing on with
playwright Eugene O'Neill's Provincetown Players, Robeson won
acclaim in New York in 1924 with starring roles in *The Emperor Jones*,
the story of a Black dictator of a West Indian island, and *All God's
Chillun Got Wings*, a controversial domestic drama revolving around
an interracial couple. He soon went on to do other stage roles and
even a silent film, earning praise for performances that critics found
impressive despite his lack of formal training.

Robeson's singing career also began to blossom during this same
period. At the urging of friends and colleagues who had long
admired his voice, he put together a concert of Black-American folk
music. His triumphant New York debut in the spring of 1925 was
followed by an extended tour of the United States, Great Britain,
and Europe, where he quickly achieved celebrity status and made
the most of his stay by studying various languages (he eventually
mastered more than twenty) and adding folk songs from all over the
world to his repertoire. But it was the atmosphere of racial tolerance
in Europe that he and his wife found most inviting, and in 1928—
not long after the birth of their son, Paul, Jr.—the Robesons decided
to make their home in London.

Throughout the late 1920s, 1930s, and well into the 1940s, whenever he was not booked for a concert tour, Robeson enhanced his
reputation as an actor by appearing in a number of plays, including
the musical *Show Boat*, featuring what was to become his signature
song, "Ol' Man River." His masterful performance in the title role of
Shakespeare's *Othello* earned him accolades from London audiences upon his debut in 1930, but more than a decade passed before
American audiences were ready to accept a Black-American actor
in the same role with a White supporting cast. When *Othello* finally
opened in New York in 1943, Robeson again was hailed for his
moving and insightful interpretation. After a Broadway run of
nearly three hundred performances (more than any previous Shake-
spearean work), the play toured the country with Robeson still in
the lead. During this same period, he also made his mark in nearly a
dozen films, two of which—*The Emperor Jones* and *Show Boat*—
featured him in roles he had made famous on the stage.

At the same time that his critical and popular appeal was reaching
new heights, Robeson was becoming increasingly preoccupied with

political and social issues, especially those involving economics and racism. This coincided with a renewed sense of pride in his racial heritage and a stronger determination to promote African culture through his music. Following his first visit to the Soviet Union in December, 1934, Robeson—who chose to ignore the more unpleasant aspects of the Stalinist regime—wholeheartedly embraced the Soviet's brand of socialism, their belief in international fellowship, and their call for an end to colonialism in Africa and Asia. He subsequently became more active politically, performing at benefit concerts on behalf of anti-fascist groups, African national liberation movements, and various workers' rights organizations.

In 1939, with Europe on the verge of war, the Robesons decided to move back to the United States. Despite some rumblings about his "unpatriotic" Soviet sympathies, Robeson reached the peak of his career over the next few years. His concerts attracted huge crowds, he triumphed on stage as Othello, and he received numerous honorary degrees and awards, including the NAACP's Spingarn Medal. But once World War II ended, his ties with the Soviet Union again cast doubt on his loyalty. His increasingly vehement condemnation of American racism and economic policy coupled with his lavish praise for the Soviets only made the situation worse, and by the end of the 1940s, many of his former fans had turned against him. An especially damaging incident occurred in 1949, when Robeson declared it "unthinkable" that Black Americans could go to war against the Soviet Union on behalf of a country that had oppressed them for so many generations. His statement created an uproar in the United States and led to violence at two of his concerts, where some of those attending were stoned and beaten by angry onlookers. Dozens of subsequent concerts were canceled as the movement to boycott him gained momentum. Unable to tour in his own country, Robeson instead went to England, where his popularity remained intact.

In 1950, however, Robeson's U.S. passport was revoked and the State Department denied him a new one until he agreed to sign an oath stating that he was not a communist and that he would stop giving political speeches overseas. He repeatedly refused to do so and fought to regain his passport for eight long years, during which time he saw his income as well as his appeal dwindle to almost nothing. He continued to speak out, however; in fact, it seemed that the more Robeson was persecuted, the more radical he became. When he called for "Negro power"—the complete political, cultural, and economic independence of Black Americans—even prominent Black leaders began to shun him. To many, the final blow came in 1952, when he accepted the Soviet Union's Stalin Peace Prize.

In June, 1956, Robeson was questioned by the House Un-American Activities Committee (HUAC) about his ties to the Communist party. Appearing before members of the committee, he declined to answer their questions and instead angrily and eloquently denounced the hearings. The chairman of the committee eventually called for an adjournment when it became clear that Robeson could not be trapped into admitting anything about his political affiliations or activities.

As cold war fears died down, some people called for the government to ease the restrictions on Robeson in recognition of his pioneering work on behalf of the civil rights movement. Thanks to a court ruling on a related case, he regained his passport in 1958 and started performing again, giving a farewell concert in New York City's Carnegie Hall, touring the western United States, and recording an album before leaving the country on an extended tour of Europe, England, the Soviet Union, Australia, and New Zealand. It was while he was in Moscow in 1959 that he fell ill and had to be hospitalized. Increasingly poor health soon forced him to retire from the stage, and he spent much of the next few years in and out of hospitals and nursing homes battling exhaustion and circulatory problems.

In 1963, Paul and Eslanda Robeson returned to New York to live. Following his wife's death in 1965, Robeson completely withdrew from the public eye. By the time he died on January 23, 1976, from a stroke suffered some five weeks earlier, he was virtually unknown to younger Americans. Yet more than five thousand of their elders attended his funeral in Harlem, most of them men and women who had admired his integrity and firm commitment to his beliefs as much as his richly emotional singing voice. As *Newsweek* magazine's Hubert Saal noted, "Paul Robeson went early, if naively, into the battle for black freedom. He could have sat back on the 50-yard line, rich and famous. But he chose to stand up and be counted—risking everything. Robeson was a genuine tragic hero—'one that loved not wisely, but too well.'"

Sources

➤ **Books**

Ehrlich, Scott, *Paul Robeson*, Chelsea House, 1988 (opening quote).

Gilliam, Dorothy Butler, *Paul Robeson: All-American*, New Republic Books, 1976.

Hamilton, Virginia, *Paul Robeson: The Life and Times of a Free Black Man*, Harper, 1974.

Hoyt, Edwin P., *Paul Robeson: The American Othello*, World Publishing, 1967.

Robeson, Paul, *Here I Stand*, Othello Associates, 1958. Reprint. Beacon Press, 1971.

➤ **Periodicals**

American Heritage, "A Rough Sunday at Peekskill," April, 1976, pp. 72–79.

Black Scholar, "Paul Robeson: Beleaguered Leader," December, 1973, pp. 25–32.

Crisis, March, 1976, pp. 77–80, "Paul Robeson: A Remembrance," pp. 81–83.

Ebony, "Ten Greats of Black History," August, 1972, p. 38; "Paul Robeson: Farewell to a Fighter," April, 1976, pp. 33–42.

Freedomways, Vol. XVI, no. 1 (1976), pp. 8–24.

Nation, "Paul Robeson," February 7, 1976, pp. 132–133.

Negro History Bulletin, May, 1970, pp. 128–129.

Newsweek, "Tragic Hero," February 2, 1976, p. 73.

New York Times, January 24, 1976.

Time, February 2, 1976, p. 55.

Franklin Delano Roosevelt

"T he only thing we have to fear is fear itself— nameless, unreasoning, unjustified terror which paralyzes needed efforts to convert retreat into advance."

Ranked as one of the greatest presidents in the history of the United States, Franklin Delano Roosevelt was born on January 30, 1882, in Hyde Park, New York, and died on April 12, 1945, in Warm Springs, Georgia.

Few presidents in U.S. history have provoked such extremes of opinion as Franklin Delano Roosevelt during the twelve years and three months that he led his country through some of the darkest days of its existence. On the one hand was the anger and even hatred he inspired among many businesspeople and most of the wealthier members of society. On the other was the genuine affection millions of ordinary citizens felt for the man who had appeared on the national scene with an infectious grin and seemingly boundless energy at a time when everyone and everything was mired in despair and lethargy. Scholars still debate some of the major policies of his administration, but on one point they agree: Roosevelt definitely ranks among the top half-dozen men ever to serve as president of the United States.

He was born into a life of wealth and privilege at Springwood, his family's 600-acre estate along the Hudson River, about halfway between New York City and Albany. His father, James Roosevelt, was a country gentleman and sometime businessman. His mother, Sara Delano, came from an equally well-to-do background. Franklin was their only child and as such grew up happy and secure with the loving attention of both his parents, especially his strong-willed mother.

Until he was fourteen, Roosevelt was tutored privately at home. Traveling occupied much of his free time; he usually accompanied his parents on their frequent trips abroad, for example, and he spent summers at the family's vacation home in Maine. His formal education began at Groton prep school, where he was a good, but not brilliant, student. Upon entering Harvard University in 1900, Roosevelt plunged into a wide range of activities that made him well known on campus. He went out for sports teams and served as editor of the undergraduate newspaper. Charming, handsome, and very wealthy, he enjoyed an active social life that left him little time for his studies.

Shortly after graduating in 1904, he became engaged to his distant cousin, Anna Eleanor Roosevelt. To many people, it was a complete mismatch; the shy and awkward Eleanor seemed to have little in common with the good-looking and popular Franklin. Nevertheless, the two were married on March 17, 1905. Their partnership was an important influence on their later lives. From her husband, Eleanor learned to become more assertive; from his wife, Franklin gained an appreciation for the problems of the poor and the underprivileged.

From Harvard, Roosevelt went on to Columbia University Law School. After passing the New York State bar exam in 1907, he left school and went to work for a New York City law firm. In 1910, he answered the call from some local Democrats and entered the race for state senator from his home district, Hyde Park, normally a Republican stronghold. To nearly everyone's surprise, Roosevelt won by a substantial margin and immediately began making a name for himself in state politics. He easily won re-election in 1912 and at the same time attracted the attention of the new president, Woodrow Wilson, on whose behalf Roosevelt had campaigned vigorously. Shortly after the election came a job offer from Washington, and in 1913 the young and enthusiastic New Yorker resigned from the state senate to become assistant secretary of the navy, a position he held throughout World War I. The lessons he learned about preparedness during that national crisis served him well in later years.

In 1920, Roosevelt was nominated for the vice-presidency on a ticket that featured Ohio governor James Cox for president. Promising to continue Wilson's policies, including his rather unpopular belief that the United States should increase its involvement in world affairs, the Democrats lost in a landslide to Republicans Warren Harding and Calvin Coolidge. Stunned by this overwhelming rejection, Roosevelt decided to leave politics for a while and concentrate instead on managing his family's financial affairs and dabbling in business. But in August, 1921, all of his plans were put on hold when he contracted polio. The illness left his legs completely paralyzed and brought on a deep depression. Eleanor and his longtime friend Louis Howe encouraged the thirty-nine-year-old Roosevelt to stay active in politics. Their unwavering support helped restore his fighting spirit, and although he never gave up hope that some day he would be cured, he made up his mind never to appear dependent or defeated.

He spent most of the 1920s building up his strength and trying to walk again at a mineral-water health spa in Warm Springs, Georgia. The intensive physical therapy he received there enabled Roosevelt to move himself from his wheelchair into another chair and stand with the help of heavy steel leg braces and support from a podium or table; later he used crutches or canes to walk a few steps. He also learned to ride a horse and drive a specially-equipped car. But it was still a tremendous adjustment for a man as energetic and dynamic as Roosevelt to suddenly find himself so dependent on others for his basic needs. He rarely spoke of the difficulties he faced, but he was extremely conscious of his image and always made an effort to smile and display a positive attitude.

Except for the triumphant moment in 1924 when he attended the Democratic National Convention and walked slowly and painfully to the stage to deliver the speech nominating Alfred E. Smith for president, Roosevelt stayed out of politics while he fought to regain the use of his legs. But in 1928, he reluctantly agreed to run for governor of New York. He won the election and, as head of a populous, high-profile state, became a national political figure. He threw himself into the job with enthusiasm, obtaining valuable administrative experience and developing many social improvement programs. Well liked and well respected, he was easily reelected to a second term in 1930.

Meanwhile, the 1929 stock market crash and subsequent economic depression were beginning to ravage the country, and Republican president Herbert Hoover was saddled with much of the blame. On the eve of the 1932 national elections, the economy was in a state of near-total collapse, with bank failures, massive unemployment, homelessness, and starvation dominating the news. Pessimistic and discouraged voters were ripe for a change, and the buoyantly confident Franklin Delano Roosevelt—the Democratic party's choice for president—seemed full of hope for the future and promised reforms that stressed "a new deal for the American people." Support for him was enormous, and on election day, he won in a landslide.

Roosevelt went to work immediately after his inauguration on bringing his "New Deal" to life. Advised by a group of economists, educators, and other experts dubbed the "Brain Trust," he set about revamping the economy without destroying capitalism. Flexible and open minded, he was willing to try anything that seemed reasonable and did not hesitate to toss out what wasn't working and take a risk on a new approach.

For example, only two days after he took office, Roosevelt closed all of the banks and set up a committee to determine the soundness of each one before allowing it to reopen. The Federal Deposit Insurance Corporation (FDIC) was established to guarantee bank deposits and put an end to panic-induced failures. To address the urgent problems of starvation and unemployment, he created a veritable "alphabet soup" of programs and agencies, among them the Federal Emergency Relief Administration (FERA), the Civilian Works Administration (CWA), the Public Works Administration

(PWA), the Works Progress Administration (WPA), the Civilian Conservation Corps (CCC), and the National Recovery Administration (NRA). He proposed the Agricultural Adjustment Act, which paid farmers to cut back on production and thus force up prices. More significant legislation was passed during his first term (much of it during the first one hundred days) than in any other four-year period in U.S. history.

While these quick and decisive measures gave Americans a reason to hope and boosted Roosevelt's popularity, they alarmed some observers who feared that too much power was ending up in the hands of the federal government—especially the president. Critics also accused him of undermining capitalism with his "socialist" programs. Their objections grew louder as the reforms continued. In 1935, for instance, the Social Security Act marked the beginning of the government's commitment to furnish pensions to the sick and elderly. That same year, the Wagner Act guaranteed collective bargaining and prohibited employer interference with union activities, prompting a tremendous growth in unions and touching off violent confrontations between employees and management.

Roosevelt made a point of explaining all these programs to the American public via informal radio broadcasts, "fireside chats" as they were called. They added immeasurably to his popularity and gave him the opportunity to appeal directly to the people in a manner that conveyed warmth and sincere concern for their well-being.

By the time the 1936 election was held, Roosevelt's standing among voters was at an all-time high, and again he won in a landslide. However, much of his second term was spent fighting to preserve the reforms he had instituted during his first term. His biggest and most damaging battle was with the Supreme Court, which had begun to rule some of the New Deal legislation unconstitutional. Roosevelt proposed that he be allowed to appoint additional justices for every member age seventy or older who chose not to retire. (At the time, six justices qualified, four of whom were conservatives.) The plan met with almost universal rejection; angry opponents condemned it as an attempt to "pack" the Court and accused Roosevelt of being a dictator. He even failed to win the support of his fellow Democrats, some of whom were concerned that the New Deal was adding too many government regulations and turning the country into a massive welfare state. The defeat was an embarrassment to the administration, and even though seven justices eventually retired (allowing Roosevelt to replace them with liberals), the days of the New Deal reforms were numbered as Congress began questioning their long-term impact.

During the late 1930s, Roosevelt grew increasingly preoccupied with the disturbing news from Europe that Germany once again appeared to be preparing for war. With the painful experience of World War I still fresh in many minds, Americans were fiercely isolationist and opposed any attempt by Roosevelt to become openly involved. Even after war broke out in September, 1939, and early German victories threatened France and Great Britain, the prevailing sentiment continued to favor neutrality while supporting the notion that perhaps "something" should be done to help.

Roosevelt devised a cash-and-carry program that enabled the United States to sell arms to its friends—provided they paid cash and took away the goods on their own ships. Later, after France fell and left Britain to stand alone against the Nazis, Roosevelt's Lend-Lease Act made it even easier for England and China (which was fighting Japan) to obtain supplies from the United States. This led to charges that the president had all but officially entered the country into war. Such fears escalated after he instituted a draft, increased the defense budget, and declared a national emergency. Meanwhile, he enjoyed immense prestige overseas for his strong stand against Hitler and willingness to do whatever he could to help those he counted among the friends of the United States.

As the 1940 election drew near, Roosevelt decided to run for an unprecedented third term believing he had an obligation to remain in office at such a critical time. The third term became the main campaign issue for his opponent, Wendell Willkie, but it was not an issue for most voters, who returned Roosevelt to the White House.

The threat of war that had loomed for so long became a reality when Japanese bombers attacked Pearl Harbor on December 7, 1941, "a date which will live in infamy," as Roosevelt proclaimed the next day in an appearance before Congress. By December 11, the United States was at war not only with Japan but also with Germany and Italy. From that moment on, the president devoted nearly all of his attention to the war effort. He took steps to speed up industrial production (which effectively eliminated any lingering unemployment) and facilitate the movement of supplies, build up the armed forces, and assemble various boards whose members were charged with overseeing different aspects of the mobilization. He also consulted with American and British military leaders on strategy and met regularly with Allied partners Winston Churchill and Josef Stalin to discuss the progress of the war and plans for the postwar world.

All of this activity, coupled with the strain of the war itself (which went very badly for the Allies until late 1942), proved physically exhausting for Roosevelt. As the conflict dragged on, he looked increasingly haggard and seemed less and less his energetic, confident self. In 1944, his deteriorating health was the major campaign issue in the presidential race against Thomas Dewey, governor of New York, but again Roosevelt won easily.

In February, 1945, with Germany just months from certain defeat, Roosevelt met for the last time with Churchill and Stalin at Yalta to discuss postwar borders in Europe, the Soviet role in the war with Japan, and other outstanding issues, including the establishment of the United Nations. Shocked observers noted the president's tired and gaunt appearance and wondered if he was up to the task of confronting Stalin about Soviet ambitions in Eastern Europe and Asia. Ever mistrustful of the Russian leader, Churchill advised taking a hard-line approach and insisted that the time was right to take drastic action against Soviet expansionism. Roosevelt, on the other hand, opposed doing anything that could create a rift among the Allies and thus endanger the peace that was at last within reach. As a result, he gave in to most of Stalin's demands while Churchill steered clear of their discussions and carefully avoided giving any impression that he supported the outcome. In the decades since that historic meeting, critics have hotly debated Roosevelt's wisdom in virtually handing Eastern Europe to the Soviet Union, speculating that his physical condition led him to appease Stalin rather than argue with him.

Roosevelt's health continued to decline in the weeks following the Yalta Conference. That arduous trip had drained much of his energy, but he was not able to get away to Warm Springs for a rest until March 30. Although his stay in Georgia seemed to revive him somewhat, it was clear to those closest to him that he was slipping away. During the afternoon of April 12, 1945, while reviewing some paperwork, he suffered a massive stroke and died less than three hours later. He was succeeded by vice-president Harry S. Truman.

Roosevelt's death triggered among many Americans a deep sense of personal loss. For many, he was the only president they had ever known, a benevolent father figure who, remarked Bruce Bliven in the *New Republic,* "never seemed overwhelmed by his burdens. . . . He was a rock of security and confidence in a world of chaos." He was also a hero who never allowed himself to be defeated by self-pity just because polio had taken away the use his legs. Others judged him with somewhat less emotion, criticizing policies and errors in judgment that had brought the United States into war and then lost the peace to the Soviets. And there were those who never reconciled themselves to the economic changes of the 1930s that seemed to come too fast and with too little regard for what they would mean to the future of the country. But to most observers, Franklin Delano Roosevelt was a skilled leader and politician who orchestrated major victories over both a shattered economy and a group of nations intent on conquering much of the world. As Bliven noted, "he was the pivotal figure in one of the crucial moments of all history, and . . . with his help, the scales were balanced at last in the right direction. By that test alone, he can fairly be called one of the greatest leaders who ever lived."

Sources

➤ **Books**

Burns, James MacGregor, *Roosevelt: The Lion and the Fox,* Harcourt, 1958.

Burns, James MacGregor, *Roosevelt: The Soldier of Freedom,* Harcourt, 1970.

Freidel, Frank, *Franklin D. Roosevelt,* Little, Brown, 1953–73.

Israel, Fred L., *Franklin Delano Roosevelt,* Chelsea House, 1985.

Lash, Joseph, *Eleanor and Franklin,* Norton, 1971.

Leuchtenburg, William E., *Franklin D. Roosevelt and the New Deal,* Harper, 1963.

Miller, Nathan, *F.D.R.: An Intimate History,* Doubleday, 1983.

Schlesinger, Arthur M., *The Age of Roosevelt,* three volumes, Houghton, 1957–60.

➤ **Periodicals**

Commonweal, "Mr. Roosevelt," April 27, 1945, pp. 37–40.

Nation, "End of an Era," April 21, 1945, pp. 429–430; "Farewell to F.D.R.," April 21, 1945, pp. 436–437.

New Republic, "Franklin D. Roosevelt," April 23, 1945, pp. 546–549.

New York Times, April 13, 1945 (opening quote); April 14, 1945; April 15, 1945; April 16, 1945.

Time, April 23, 1945.

Wilma Rudolph

*"**W**inning is great, sure, but if you are really going to do something in life, the secret is learning how to lose. . . . If you can pick up after a crushing defeat, and go on to win again, you are going to be a champion someday."*

Born on June 23, 1940, in St. Bethlehem, Tennessee, Wilma Rudolph overcame a childhood bout with polio to become the first American woman to win three gold medals in Olympic competition.

I t was September 7, 1960, and the summer Olympic games were winding down in Rome. The U.S. women's track team—which had not been expected to do well against competitors from Europe and Russia—had already astounded the world by claiming the gold in the 100-meter dash and the 200-meter dash, the latter in record-setting time. Now the winner of those two races, twenty-year-old Wilma Rudolph, was set to run with three of her Tennessee State University teammates in the last major track-and-field event, the 400-meter relay. An unprecedented third gold medal awaited her if the U.S. team could beat its heavily favored rivals.

Once the race began, it was clear that Rudolph and her teammates were much better than the experts had predicted. By the time the second runner passed off the baton to the third runner, the United States had pulled nearly even with the leaders, a West German and a Russian. Winning the relay would fall to Rudolph, the team's fastest sprinter, who would be responsible for the fourth and final leg of the race. Despite fumbling the baton handoff (which would have caused the United States to be disqualified), she regained her footing just in time, only to see that the others had by now pulled far ahead of her. In an incredible burst of speed, the young woman pushed herself to the limit in the final ninety meters of the race and won it by three-tenths of a second, claiming the gold medal for the United States and establishing a new record in the process. Rudolph's victories were made even sweeter by the knowledge of what she had overcome to become "the world's fastest woman."

The twentieth of Ed and Blanche Rudolph's twenty-two children, Wilma Glodean Rudolph was born two months earlier than expected and weighed less than five pounds. During childhood, she fought off one illness after another; she was only four years old and recovering from a near-fatal bout of double pneumonia and scarlet fever when she apparently contracted a mild case of polio that resulted in the partial paralysis of her left leg and foot. Refusing to believe that her little girl would never regain full use of her leg, Mrs. Rudolph faithfully massaged it for several hours every evening and took Wilma to physical therapy sessions in Nashville, riding fifty miles on the bus twice a week for two years. Forced at first to wear a cumbersome leg brace and then a special orthopedic shoe, Rudolph could not attend school or play outside with other children. As the months dragged on and she showed little sign of improvement, "I remembered I started getting mad about it all. . . . I think I started acquiring a competitive spirit right then and there. . . . I was mad, and I was going to beat these illnesses no matter what."

When she was finally able to begin school at the age of seven, Rudolph had to endure the taunts of her classmates, who made fun of her shoe and awkward limp. Their cruel comments left her more determined than ever to conquer her handicap. She learned to play basketball with her brothers and sisters and their friends, ignoring her heavy orthopedic shoe as she pivoted and jumped with the rest of the players. Rudolph managed to take a few steps on her own for the first time at the age of ten, and two years later she discarded her special shoe for good.

Free at last to run, jump, and play as others did, Rudolph threw herself into athletics. During her sophomore year in high school, the graceful six-footer became a starter on the girls' basketball team and quickly emerged as a favorite with spectators. At that year's state tournament, she caught the eye of one of the referees, Ed Temple, who was scouting for his Tennessee State University women's track team, the Tigerbelles. Recognizing in Rudolph a potential champion sprinter, he invited the fifteen-year-old to train at the university with several other promising high school athletes over the summer of 1956.

At Tennessee State, Coach Temple worked with Rudolph to develop her physical skills—proper breathing, starts, endurance, muscle conditioning—as well as her mental attitude. A shy, quiet young woman, she found it difficult to allow herself to beat any of the Tigerbelles, whom she regarded with awe. But after she tried out for the 1956 Olympics with the Tennessee runners and made the cut, Rudolph no longer held back. "From that moment on," she later noted, "it seemed as if I wasn't afraid to challenge anybody anywhere. Whatever fears I had, fears of offending somebody else by beating them, fears of being rejected by my teammates if I did too well, all of those fears vanished." Despite this change in attitude, Rudolph did not perform well enough to qualify for either the 100- or 200-meter races at that year's summer games in Australia. Disappointed by her lackluster showing, she returned to the United States determined to win a gold medal in the 1960 Olympics.

Under Coach Temple's direction, Rudolph continued her training throughout her junior year of high school and again at Tennessee State during the summer of 1957. She entered her senior year full of hope for the future, which she was certain would include a college scholarship and another try at the Olympics. Then Rudolph received some news during a routine physical that left her stunned: she was pregnant. With the help and support of her family and coach, Rudolph finished high school and kept up with her track training as much as possible. She gave birth to a daughter one month after graduation, then entered Tennessee State on a full athletic scholarship in the fall of 1958. In the meantime, Mr. and Mrs. Rudolph agreed to care for the baby until Wilma could do so herself.

Once she arrived at Tennessee State, Rudolph made her studies and track training her top priorities. She easily made the team during her freshman year, but at the beginning of her sophomore year, Rudolph found herself losing races for no apparent reason. Then doctors discovered that a chronic tonsil infection was draining her of energy. Once she had her tonsils removed, Rudolph soon returned to form as the fastest Tigerbelle—a standing that secured her a spot on the 1960 Olympic team later that season.

Rudolph's amazing performance in the summer games that year was the best an American woman had done in track since 1932, when Babe Didrikson won two gold medals. More important to her personally was that she had duplicated the victories of her idol, Jesse Owens, who won his three gold medals at the infamous 1936 Olympics in Nazi Germany. Rudolph's unprecedented success, along with her naturally warm and friendly personality, made her an instant hit with the media, whose members dubbed her "the Black Gazelle" in honor of her exceptionally graceful and seemingly effortless stride. Reporters and photographers mobbed Rudolph in Rome and throughout Europe as the Tigerbelles traveled around to participate in other track events before flying back to the United States.

Rudolph's arrival in Nashville was marked by a huge victory celebration, as was her return to Clarksville. She spent much of the next year traveling across the country accepting some of the most prestigious awards given in the field of athletics. The Associated Press named her the Woman Athlete of the Year, and a group of European sportswriters chose her as Sportsman of the Year (making her the first woman to be so honored). In 1961, she received the James E. Sullivan Award as the year's outstanding amateur athlete; in 1962, she accepted the Babe Didrikson Zaharias Award as the most outstanding female athlete in the world. Reflecting on her accomplishments some years later, Jesse Owens wrote: "Wilma Rudolph's courage and her triumph over her physical handicaps are among the most inspiring jewels in the crown of Olympic sports. . . . She was speed and motion incarnate, the most beautiful image ever seen on the track."

Rudolph continued to compete in track events until 1962, when she decided to retire while she was still at the top of her form. She finished her studies at Tennessee State, earning a degree in elementary education in 1963. Throughout the 1960s and 1970s, she worked in a variety of teaching and coaching positions in schools and for community programs, and in the 1980s she served as a special consultant on minority affairs at Indiana's DePauw University. Today, she is involved in promoting women's health and fitness programs for Baptist Hospital in Nashville, Tennessee.

In 1981, she established the Wilma Rudolph Foundation, a non-profit organization dedicated to training young athletes for national and international competition while helping them plan for a life and a career after they give up sports. The latter goal is of particular interest to Rudolph, who stresses how important it is for youngsters to realize that being a "superstar" is not enough, especially for those involved in sports—like running—that have little or no potential as a profession. "You become world famous and you sit with kings and queens, and then your first job is just a job," she explained to a reporter for *Ebony*. "You can't go back to living the way you did before because you've been taken out of one setting and shown the other. That becomes a struggle and makes *you* struggle."

While her success in athletics may not have brought her financial riches, Rudolph is quick to point out that it gave her something much more valuable. "The Olympics were a positive aspect of my life," she says. "It sort of sent my way all the other positive things and feelings that I've had. That one accomplishment—what happened in 1960—nobody can take from me. It was something I worked for. It wasn't something somebody handed to me."

Sources

➤ **Books**

Biracree, Tom, *Wilma Rudolph*, Chelsea House, 1988 (opening quote).

Rudolph, Wilma, with Martin Ralbovsky, *Wilma*, New American Library, 1977.

➤ **Periodicals**

Ebony, "Whatever Happened to Wilma Rudolph?," February, 1984, pp. 84–88; "Great Olympic Moments," January, 1992, p. 68.

Reader's Digest, "The Girl Who Wouldn't Give Up," May, 1961, pp. 140–148.

Saturday Evening Post, "Wilma Rudolph: Gazelle of the Track," October, 1976, pp. 44–45.

Sports Illustrated, January 9, 1961, p. 34.

Women's Sports, "Yesterday's Heroes," September, 1984; "Wilma Rudolph," October, 1984.

Margaret Sanger

"**N**o woman can call herself free until she can consciously choose whether she will or will not be a mother."

Born on September 14, 1879, in Corning, New York, Margaret Sanger was a pioneer advocate of birth control. She died on September 6, 1966, in Tucson, Arizona.

One day in 1912, a maternity nurse named Margaret Sanger was called to a New York City tenement to help care for Sadie Sachs, a twenty-eight-year old mother of three who was near death from blood poisoning caused by a self-induced abortion. Weeks later, after she was well on the road to recovery, Mrs. Sachs begged her doctor for some information on how to prevent future pregnancies. His flippant words of advice—"tell your husband to sleep on the roof"—appalled Sanger, and the look of tragic desperation on the woman's face nearly drove her to tears. A few months later, Sanger found herself in the same tenement, but this time it was too late: an already comatose Sadie Sachs died within ten minutes, the victim of a back-street abortionist. "It was the dawn of a new day in my life . . . ," Sanger later wrote. "I knew I could not go back merely to keeping people alive." The revolution that was launched out of a single nurse's anger and disgust eventually overcame age-old taboos regarding birth control and made it acceptable not only to the medical profession but to the public at large.

Margaret Higgins Sanger was well acquainted with the potentially deadly results of unwanted pregnancies long before she ever met Sadie Sachs. One of eleven children of a stonecutter, Michael Hennessy Higgins, and his wife, Anne Purcell, she grew up watching her mother become steadily weaker and sicker from the combined onslaught of tuberculosis and eighteen pregnancies. Anne Higgins was only forty-eight when she died, and her suffering inspired her daughter to pursue a career as a doctor. With medical school out of the question financially, though, Margaret switched to nursing. She obtained her degree around 1900, but shortly afterward put aside thoughts of a career to marry architect William Sanger.

The newlyweds at first took an apartment in New York City but soon opted for life in the country when Margaret showed signs of developing tuberculosis. By around 1910, however, she was tired of small-town living. So the Sanger family—which now included three children—headed back to the more intellectually stimulating atmosphere of New York City. There both William and Margaret became involved in radical politics, primarily socialism.

Sanger then took a job as a public health nurse on the Lower East Side, a crowded neighborhood of mostly working-class and poor families. Her duties brought her into contact with thousands of women who were old and tired at thirty or thirty-five and who plunged into panic and despair at the thought of a fifth or sixth pregnancy. Many resorted to self-induced abortions, which often led to their deaths; others chose suicide. Still others died in childbirth, their bodies weakened by too many previous pregnancies. Observing the poverty, misery, and hopelessness of her clients, Sanger came to the conclusion that most of it was the result of unchecked childbirth. Since no one—not the socialists, not even the feminists—seemed interested in addressing this particular problem, she decided to take action on her own.

Several major obstacles confronted Sanger in her fight to make birth control information available. One was ignorance; she knew as much about contraception as most doctors did. Another was public opinion; many people considered family planning immoral and perverted, and discussing it was absolutely unthinkable. But by far the main obstacle was the Comstock law, a federal statute that classified all contraceptive information as pornography and expressly forbid its distribution through the mail. A number of states had enacted even more restrictive regulations, and violators—including doctors—faced hefty fines and lengthy prison sentences. In Sanger's home state, Anthony Comstock himself was the self-appointed judge of what constituted "pornography."

During the summer of 1914, Sanger's search for up-to-date, reliable information took her to France, where family planning was widely practiced and openly discussed. Returning to New York, she established a newspaper, *The Woman Rebel*, in which she published some of what she had learned and for the first time used the term *birth control*. Despite the fact that the newspaper contained no specific how-to information, Comstock deemed it unmailable, and at his urging Sanger was charged with violating federal law and faced a sentence of up to forty-five years in prison upon conviction.

While not afraid of going to prison, Sanger wanted the case against her to rest on something more fundamental than the generalized offenses of which she was accused. So she fled to England to avoid prosecution—but not before she hurriedly put together and began distributing a pamphlet entitled *Family Limitation*, which included the forbidden contraceptive information she had left out of *The Woman Rebel*. Once in England, she spent her time reading about birth control and meeting with medical experts on the subject. She then went on to the Netherlands, where she visited the world's first birth control clinics. A year later, she returned to the United States as a celebrity. Now fully prepared to face the charges against her,

Sanger was disappointed when the government backed down, reluctant to grant her a public forum and eager to avoid a test case that might lead to changes in the law.

It now became clear to Sanger that mounting a more direct challenge to Comstockian censorship was the only way to force the courts to reconsider laws governing the distribution of contraceptive information. She made her move in October, 1916; teaming up with her sister, Ethyl Byrne, she opened America's first birth control clinic in a poor Brooklyn neighborhood. Ten days later, Sanger and Byrne were arrested, and the clinic was declared a "public nuisance" and closed. The case attracted worldwide attention as the defiant sisters were quickly convicted in separate trials and sentenced to jail for thirty days. Their convictions were upheld on appeal, but they nevertheless won a partial victory in 1918 when the state law was reinterpreted to allow doctors to give contraceptive advice to married women whose health would be in danger if they were to become pregnant.

Despite continuing legal harassment and strident opposition from many anti-vice and religious groups, Sanger pressed on, passionately taking her case first to the medical profession and then to the public at large in an attempt to educate, garner support for the movement, and lobby for legislative change. (She was backed financially in large part by her second husband, millionaire oil company executive J. Noah Slee, whom she had married in 1922 following her divorce from William Sanger.) In 1923 she opened another New York clinic, this time staffed by a physician, Dr. Hannah Stone. It offered contraceptive counseling and instruction not only to neighborhood women but also to doctors who came from all over the country to learn the Sanger methods. In a scene reminiscent of the Brooklyn raid more than a dozen years earlier, police stormed the clinic in 1929, confiscated Dr. Stone's files, and harassed patients. This time, however, physicians immediately sprang to Sanger's defense, claiming that the police violated the privacy of the doctor-patient relationship by taking the files. The charges were soon dismissed, and the New York City police commissioner apologized for his department's actions.

Sanger kept up the battle for legalization of birth control throughout the 1920s and 1930s. In 1921 she formed the American Birth Control League (forerunner of the Planned Parenthood Federation of America), a national lobbying group that not only spearheaded action on the legislative front but also served as a clearinghouse for information on birth control research, education, services, population problems, food supplies, and world peace. While the league was defeated at almost every turn in its efforts to gain support for legislative change, it gradually chipped away at various restrictions in court. In 1936 the final Comstockian barrier crumbled when a judge affirmed the right of doctors to send and receive through the mail anything they felt was designed for the well-being of their patients, including contraceptive information and devices.

Also during the 1920s and 1930s, Sanger tried to expand the scope of her movement, setting up and presiding at a number of national and international conferences on birth control and population control that brought together economists, biologists, sociologists, and other experts from throughout the world. The success of these conferences brought Sanger worldwide recognition and acclaim, as did her lectures in Europe and in the Far East, where she took her message to audiences in Japan, China, and India and helped launch population control programs.

By the 1940s the birth control movement had won the acceptance of the medical profession and increasing numbers of the American public. Retiring from active leadership due to her frail health—she had never fully recovered from her bout with tuberculosis—Sanger turned her attention to lecturing and lobbying for more contraceptive research and government-sponsored programs to make birth control instruction and services available through the public health service. For many years she also served as head of the International Planned Parenthood Federation, which she co-founded in 1946. She died of hardening of the arteries on September 6, 1966, in a nursing home in Tucson, Arizona.

As the instigator of what was in the beginning almost a one-woman crusade, Margaret Sanger challenged the federal and state governments, churches, the medical profession, the press, public opinion, and even her fellow social activists to convince the world that family planning is a basic human right. Before she came along, birth control—if it was mentioned at all—was almost entirely a male prerogative. She turned that emphasis completely around, and in the process made it acceptable to discuss family planning and respectable to practice it. Enduring years of legal harassment and the proclamations of religious leaders who denounced her from their pulpits as a "murderer" and a "lascivious monster," Sanger persevered in her efforts to bring about a veritable revolution that is in many ways still being fought today.

Sources

➤ **Books**

Douglas, Emily Taft, *Margaret Sanger: Pioneer of the Future*, Holt, 1970.

Sanger, Margaret, *Margaret Sanger: An Autobiography*, Norton, 1938.

➤ **Periodicals**

American Heritage, "Faces from the Past—XXIV," June, 1970, pp. 52–53.

American Journal of Public Health, "Margaret Sanger: Birth Control's Successful Revolutionary," July, 1980, pp. 736–742.

Newsweek, "Sanger at 66," February 6, 1950, pp. 48–49; "Rebel with a Cause," September 19, 1966, pp. 34–37.

New York Times, "Margaret Sanger Is Dead at 82; Led Campaign for Birth Control," September 7, 1966.

Reader's Digest, "Margaret Sanger: Mother of Planned Parenthood," July, 1951, pp. 27–31.

Saturday Evening Post, "Margaret Sanger: Pioneer of the Future," May/June, 1977.

Time, "Every Child a Wanted Child," September 16, 1966, pp. 96–98.

Today's Health, "A Woman Who Changed Our History," January, 1969.

Wilson Library Bulletin, "Hughes, Twain, Child, and Sanger: Four Who Locked Horns with the Censors," November, 1969, pp. 278–286 (opening quote).

H. Norman
Schwarzkopf

"*A*ny soldier worth his salt should be antiwar. And still there are things worth fighting for."

General H. Norman Schwarzkopf rose to fame as the commander-in-chief of allied forces during the Persian Gulf War. He was born on August 22, 1934, in Trenton, New Jersey.

Address: c/o International Creative Management, 40 West 57th St., New York, NY 10019.

Described by a *Newsweek* reporter as "a warrior with a soul," General H. Norman Schwarzkopf captured the admiration and affection of his countrymen as commander-in-chief of operations Desert Shield and Desert Storm, the biggest deployment of U.S. forces and equipment since the Vietnam War. "Stormin' Norman" was virtually unknown outside military circles prior to the Iraqi invasion of Kuwait on August 2, 1990, but his no-nonsense demeanor and intimidating physical presence—"a cross between Willard Scott, Jonathan Winters and Attila the Hun," in the words of NBC-TV Pentagon correspondent Fred Francis—quickly became a familiar sight to Americans, who enthusiastically embraced him as a military man of whom they could be proud, "a leader who was blunt, not glib; passionate, not packaged, with the carriage of a man of courage and principle," as a reporter for *Time* observed.

H. Norman Schwarzkopf is the youngest of three children born to Herbert Norman Schwarzkopf and Ruth Bowman Schwarzkopf. (The elder Schwarzkopf detested his first name so much he gave his son only the initial.) A West Point graduate and veteran of World War I, H. Norman, Sr., distinguished himself in civilian life as founder and head of the New Jersey State Police, gaining national attention as the chief investigator in the 1932 Lindbergh baby kidnapping and later as host of the popular "Gangbusters" radio program.

Young Norman idolized his father and knew from the time he was a small child that he, too, wanted to go to West Point someday. He obtained his elementary education at a private military academy near his family's New Jersey home, then at the age of twelve moved with his mother and two sisters to Iran, where his father (who had re-entered the Army in 1942) had been assigned to help organize the national police force. Norman remained overseas for the next five years, living in Teheran for a year and then attending boarding schools in Germany, Switzerland, and Italy before returning to the United States to complete his secondary education at Valley Forge Military Academy in Pennsylvania. Then it was on to engineering studies at West Point, from which he graduated in 1956 as a captain, the highest cadet rank possible.

Commissioned a second lieutenant in the U.S. Army, Schwarzkopf trained at Fort Benning, Georgia, and then served with the 101st Airborne Division at Fort Campbell, Kentucky. His climb up the ladder continued with a two-year assignment in West Berlin followed by a stint in the United States in the career-officer course at

Fort Benning. In 1964, Schwarzkopf obtained his master's degree from the University of Southern California and then taught for a year at West Point before serving a one-year tour of duty in Vietnam as an advisor to a South Vietnamese airborne battalion. He later characterized that period as one of the most rewarding in his life because he was serving a cause in which he believed.

After teaching at West Point again for two years and attending Command and General Staff College at Fort Leavenworth, Kansas, Schwarzkopf went back to Vietnam in 1969 for a second tour of duty and found things had degenerated into a "cesspool" due to a lack of leadership. On a more personal level, too, it was a very difficult time. In 1970, the parents of a soldier killed by a misdirected U.S. artillery shell wrongfully blamed battalion commander Schwarzkopf for their son's death and relentlessly pursued an investigation into the affair. Their struggle to uncover the truth inspired the book (and later a television movie) *Friendly Fire* by C. D. B. Bryan, in which the author reveals Schwarzkopf as a concerned and honorable officer who was not at fault in the tragedy. Just three months after the friendly fire incident, Schwarzkopf emerged as the hero in a dangerous rescue that saw him go to the aid of a wounded and panicky young GI stranded in a minefield with a few of his equally frightened fellow soldiers.

Perhaps the toughest ordeal Schwarzkopf had to face in connection with his second tour in Vietnam—which he regards as the low point in his career—was returning home to face the antiwar movement. Schwarzkopf was spit upon and called a "baby burner," and this hostility prompted an intense period of self-evaluation. He finally concluded that "you've got to have faith in your government, in the decision makers of the country. The defense of the nation can't be left in the hands of someone who has an option to say, 'Well, I've evaluated [it], and I've decided today I will not defend the nation.'" Yet he realized that "if it ever came to a choice between compromising my moral principles and the performance of my duties, I know I'd go with my moral principles." Above all, Schwarzkopf vowed never again to fight in a war with no clear objectives or a war that did not have the support of the American public. His battlefield experiences also convinced him that the only way to win a war is to fight hard and end it quickly.

Throughout the 1970s, Schwarzkopf served in a series of two-year assignments at the brigade and division level in Alaska, Washington, Hawaii, and West Germany. In 1982, he became director of military personnel management in the office of the deputy chief of staff for personnel in Washington, D.C. Never one to like sitting at a desk, he eagerly took command of a mechanized division at Fort Stewart, Georgia, following his promotion to general in 1983. Later that year, he was tapped to head the U.S. ground forces during the invasion of Grenada and so impressed the Navy admiral in charge of the operation that he made Schwarzkopf the deputy task force commander. More Pentagon-based assignments followed in 1985 and 1987, with a command position as head of I Corps at Fort Lewis, Washington, squeezed in between.

In 1988, Schwarzkopf was promoted to four-star general and assumed the commander-in-chief post at U.S. Central Command at MacDill Air Force Base in Tampa, Florida. There he set himself the task of figuring out the most likely war scenario involving U.S troops. With the Soviet threat on the decline, he zeroed in on the Middle East and concluded that a regional dispute spilling over into countries where U.S. interests were at stake seemed very possible. So in consultation with his superiors at the Pentagon, he drew up a plan to deal with such a conflict and tested it in late July, 1990, with an exercise based on an Iraqi invasion of Kuwait. A mere five days later, on August 2, the invasion became a reality, and Schwarzkopf suddenly had the chance to put his plan into action as the basis for Operation Desert Shield.

By August 10, the first U.S. troops had left for Saudi Arabia to defend that oil-rich country from a potential invasion by Saddam Hussein's Iraqi forces. Over the next several months, more than a half-million soldiers were deployed to Saudi Arabia; another quarter-million troops soon arrived from the thirty or so other countries that along with the United States formed the coalition army assembled to intimidate Saddam. With them came more than one hundred ships and twelve hundred aircraft.

Overseeing everything was Schwarzkopf, whose skills as a planner, administrator, and commander of all land, naval, and air activities were put to the test. His considerable diplomatic and language expertise (he speaks French and German in addition to English) also received a workout in the multinational and multicultural environment of the coalition army. Although his fellow commanders were initially taken aback by what Briton called "his gung-ho appearance," they quickly came to appreciate him as "a highly intelligent soldier." Schwarzkopf also impressed the Saudis with his sensitivity when he banned U.S. troops from bringing pornographic magazines and alcohol into the country so as not to offend their Islamic hosts. And he proved to be an ace morale-booster on his frequent trips into the field.

On January 16, 1991, less than seventeen hours after a United Nations-approved withdrawal deadline passed and Saddam had made it clear that he had no intention of leaving Kuwait, Operation Desert Shield became Operation Desert Storm. The operation's goal was to eject the Iraqis by force through a well-coordinated plan of air strikes that would sever their supply lines, disrupt their command and control network, damage weapons facilities, and weaken Saddam's elite fighting unit, the Republican Guard. The air war was extremely successful, but both Schwarzkopf and his boss, Chairman of the Joint Chiefs of Staff Colin Powell, knew that a ground campaign would also be necessary to finish the job.

Launched on February 23 after last-minute peace negotiations fell apart, the ground war stunned the Iraqis. Powell and Schwarzkopf had worked out a clever plan that called for a faked amphibious assault on the Kuwaiti coast to distract Saddam's troops from their western flank, which allied forces then easily penetrated with some 200,000 troops and hundreds of tanks. Within days the Iraqi army was effectively surrounded in Kuwait, cut off from its supply sources and thoroughly overwhelmed. Demoralized Iraqi soldiers soon began surrendering by the thousands, and by February 28, it was all over.

The swiftness and thoroughness of the allied victory surprised almost everyone, even Schwarzkopf, who attributed it to a combination of well-trained troops and superb equipment plus poor Iraqi morale. As for the unexpectedly low allied casualty rate—147 killed and 357 wounded (they had prepared for up to 20,000 U.S. casualties alone)—Schwarzkopf termed it nothing short of "miraculous."

Throughout the brief but intense campaign, the sight of Schwarzkopf in his desert fatigues became a familiar one to all viewers glued to their television sets for the daily press briefings from Riyadh, Saudi Arabia. Juggling toughness with a certain self-mocking humor as he expertly went over maps and charts, he didn't gloat and he didn't speak "militarese," just plain English. His strict control of the flow of information on the war exasperated reporters, but his forthright displays of anger at Saddam, compassion for the families of the dead and wounded as well as for Iraqi soldiers, and irritation at some of the questions he was asked won the trust and hearts of viewers more accustomed to dour and colorless military men.

Schwarzkopf returned to the United States on April 21, 1991, to a thunderous reception at MacDill Air Force Base, followed by several victory parades, a flood of awards and honors (including the Presidential Medal of Freedom, a knighthood from England's Queen Elizabeth, and an appearance before a joint session of Congress), hundreds of speaking invitations, and, because he had announced that he planned to retire later that summer, countless job offers.

Since his official retirement from the service on August 31, 1991, Schwarzkopf has spent most of his time giving lectures around the country and working with a writer on his autobiography, which is due out in the fall of 1992. He has also taken time out to relax with his wife and three children and contemplate those causes—mostly having to do with education or the environment—that he might be able to serve in some capacity. Many have suggested that he run for political office, perhaps for the Senate or even for vice-president or president. Schwarzkopf, however, says any political plans he might have are far more modest than that; "being mayor of a small town" is closer to what he has in mind. "I'll find action," he assured a *People* magazine reporter. "There's always plenty if you're willing to step into the fray."

Sources

➤ **Books**

Anderson, Jack, and Dale Van Atta, *Stormin' Norman: An American Hero*, Kensington Publishing, 1991.

Cohen, Roger, and Claudio Gatti, *In the Eye of the Storm: The Life of General H. Norman Schwarzkopf*, Farrar, Straus & Giroux, 1991.

➤ **Periodicals**

New Republic, "Operation Desert Norm," March 11, 1991, pp. 20–27.

Newsweek, "'Stormin' Norman' Takes Command," September 10, 1990, p. 25; "'You Must Be the Thunder and Lightning,'" January 28, 1991, pp. 30–31; "A Soldier of Conscience," March 11, 1991, pp. 32–34; "Schwarzkopf: 'I Got a Lot of Guff,'" March 11, 1991, p. 34; "A Textbook Victory," March 11, 1991, pp. 38–42.

Parade, "What Makes an American Soldier?," July 7, 1991, pp. 16–20.

People, "As Washington and Baghdad Gird for Battle, America's

Desert Leader Is a General Who Is Known as the Bear," September 3, 1990, pp. 66–69; "Stormin' Norman: Born to Win," March 11, 1991, pp. 34–39; "Home Is the Hero," May 13, 1991, pp. 42–47.

Time, "Stormin' Norman on Top," February 4, 1991, pp. 28–30; "Sayings of Stormin' Norman," March 11, 1991, p. 27; "Welcome the Unknown Soldier," May 6, 1991, pp. 25–26.

TV Guide, "Norman Schwarzkopf: The Gutsy General Who Has Taken TV—and America—by Storm," June 29, 1991, pp. 2–7.

U.S. News and World Report, October 1, 1990, pp. 34–36; "The Bear," February 11, 1991, pp. 32–42 (opening quote); "A Mud Soldier's General Reflects on the Risks of War," February 11, 1991, pp. 36–37.

Albert Schweitzer

*"**W**hen one can do good, one never gives up anything. There is no sacrifice. I am one of the greatly privileged."*

Albert Schweitzer was an accomplished theologian, philosopher, educator, minister, organist, and musicologist who turned his back on a comfortable life in Europe at the age of thirty-eight to serve as a doctor in Africa. He was born on January 14, 1875, in Kaysersberg, France, and died on September 4, 1965, in Lambarene, Gabon.

B y the age of thirty, Albert Schweitzer had already made a name for himself in several fields. A promising and potentially brilliant career seemed well within his reach, yet he knew that it was not enough. Disturbed by the contrast between his own happiness and the suffering of others, he felt a strong urge to reach out to those who seemed to need help the most. It was this concern, coupled with his deep religious faith, that led him to give up a comfortable and secure future and instead practice medicine for more than forty years in one of the most inhospitable corners of Africa.

One of five children of Adele Schillinger Schweitzer and Louis Schweitzer, a minister, Albert Schweitzer was born and grew up in Alsace, a region that for many years had shifted back and forth between French and German control. Aside from demonstrating a gift for playing the organ, young Albert was an unremarkable boy who failed miserably in school. But even then his compassion and sensitivity were evident. When he saw that his poorer classmates could not afford warm coats, gloves, or leather shoes, Albert refused to wear them, too, so as not to appear privileged. His love for animals and other living things made it impossible for him to enjoy sports like fishing because he could not bear to bait a hook or watch a fish thrash around to break free of a line.

Through sheer determination, Schweitzer slowly improved his grades enough to gain acceptance to the University of Strasbourg. There he plunged wholeheartedly into courses in music, theology, and philosophy and continued his organ lessons, very much aware that others were not as happy or as fortunate as he was. Concluding that "whosoever is spared personal pain must feel himself called to help in diminishing the pain of others," the twenty-one-year-old Schweitzer vowed to pursue his own interests only until he reached the age of thirty, at which time he would devote himself "to the direct service of humanity."

Schweitzer then tackled a variety of activities that "would have done credit to an ordinary man's lifetime," as a *Time* reporter noted. Granted a Ph.D. in philosophy and a licentiate in theology by the time he was twenty-six, he served as curate at the Church of St. Nicholas in Strasbourg and a faculty member at the University of Strasbourg, where he soon advanced to become head of the theological school. He completed his first book, *The Philosophy of Kant*, began work on *The Quest of the Historical Jesus* (which created an international stir upon its publication in 1910 for its unorthodox views on the divinity of Christ), and wrote a biography of his idol, Johann Sebastian Bach. In addition, he kept up with his music studies and earned recognition not only as a concert performer but also as an expert on building organs.

Always in the back of Schweitzer's mind, however, was the commitment he had made to himself. Thus, in January, 1906, he enrolled in medical school to prepare himself for a career as a missionary doctor in Africa. He received his degree in 1913, and on Good Friday of that year, left Europe accompanied by his wife, Helene Bresslau, who had studied nursing so that she could work alongside her husband.

The Schweitzers' destination was Lambarene, a tiny French Protestant mission on the Ogowe River in what was then French Equatorial Africa (now Gabon). There they found conditions even more primitive and difficult than they could have ever imagined. The region was suffocatingly hot and humid, with countless varieties of dangerous animals. The insect life and vegetation were so dense it was difficult to keep land cleared. At first, Schweitzer set up his clinic in an old chicken house, working with the few medical supplies he and his wife had been able to carry with them. A bigger shipment arrived a few weeks later, but it was the end of the year before Lambarene boasted a bona fide four-room "hospital." (In addition to supervising its construction, Schweitzer also did a great deal of the actual physical labor himself.) Other buildings soon followed, including a waiting room and a ward for recovering patients.

World War I interrupted Schweitzer's work at Lambarene in 1914. As a native of German-held Alsace, he was considered an enemy alien, so local authorities put him under house arrest and prohibited him from working at the hospital until friends intervened on his behalf. Finally, in September, 1917, he and his wife were ordered to pack up and return to France as prisoners of war. They were held in various camps until August, 1918, when they were sent home to Alsace. By that time Albert was severely weakened by dysentery, and a pregnant Helene was still suffering from the lingering effects of her stay in the tropics.

The end of the war that November saw Alsace return to French control and marked the beginning of several very happy years in the Schweitzers' lives. Their only child, a daughter named Rhena, was born in January, 1919, and Albert found work as a doctor at the hospital in Strasbourg and served in his old position as curate at St.

Nicholas. He also resumed writing, lecturing, and playing the organ, activities that helped him pay off his debts and reinvigorate himself physically and spiritually. It was during this stay in Europe that he published his masterwork in ethics, the two-volume *Philosophy of Civilization*. In it he traced the development of ethical thought from its beginnings to his very own original contribution, which he called "Reverence for Life." This philosophy held that all life—no matter how insignificant it seems—is sacred and that once it is taken cannot be restored. To achieve a truly civilized world, Schweitzer concluded, man must devote himself to maintaining and furthering life rather than doing anything to damage or destroy it.

In February, 1924, Schweitzer left his wife and daughter in Europe and headed back to Lambarene, where he discovered that during his absence the hospital and his house had been reclaimed by the jungle. As a result, he spent the next four years as both a physician and a builder. (Late in the evening, he set aside time to write and play a specially modified piano given to him by the Paris Bach Society.) The arrival of two nurses and two more doctors by the end of 1925 eased his burden somewhat, but the growing patient load was straining the medical facilities to the limit. Lacking nearby space in which to expand, Schweitzer found a suitable building site about two miles away where he erected a new hospital and houses for the staff and planted gardens so that they would be more self-sufficient during food shortages.

Over the next decade, Schweitzer alternated fund-raising trips to Europe with more building projects at Lambarene. By the early 1930s, the work of "Le Grand Docteur" had earned widespread acclaim, and Schweitzer was showered with honors and attention wherever he went. Although such idolatry made him uncomfortable, he was grateful for the donations it attracted, which he used to purchase supplies and improve the hospital's facilities.

As World War II approached, Schweitzer turned his attention to stockpiling supplies and equipment at Lambarene. Despite his preparations, the war years were still very difficult. To conserve precious medicines and bandages, people whose conditions were not life-threatening were turned away. In addition, most of the European staff was called back home to serve in the armed forces, leaving Schweitzer—by then in his mid-sixties—responsible for more of the specialized medical care and routine daily chores.

After the war, life at Lambarene slowly returned to normal, and in 1948 Schweitzer went home to Alsace for his first long rest in twelve years. Now more famous than ever, he was received with a multitude of awards and affection by those who hailed him as the world's greatest living Christian, a virtual saint of a man who had truly put his faith into practice by serving others. The Nobel Committee acknowledged his humanitarianism in 1952 by naming him the winner of the year's Peace Prize.

Later in the decade, however, Schweitzer came increasingly under fire for what some viewed as his old-fashioned, paternalistic "do-goodism" that ignored the radical political and social changes then under way in Africa. His critics also blasted the unsanitary conditions in and around his hospital and scorned his medical techniques as primitive. At the other end of the spectrum were those who scoffed at his warning that civilization was doomed unless mankind abandoned nuclear weapons and destructive wars and revolutions.

In the wake of Schweitzer's death in Lambarene at the age of ninety, tributes from all over the world recalled not only his humanitarianism but also his brilliance as an organist, as a student and interpreter of Bach, and as a philosopher and theologian. Yet as a writer for *Christian Century* declared, "Nothing honors him more than the testimony of his detractors. . . . Doctors, going to Africa to see a saint, returned with supercilious complaints about Lambarene's antiquated equipment and Schweitzer's apparent indifference to Western codes of sanitation. But while the doctors who insisted on the latest and best methods and instruments came and went, Schweitzer stayed. The critics said—and they were correct—that Schweitzer was paternalistic in his treatment of the natives. But he healed sixty thousand of them and for good measure gave them hope." In short, concluded a *Time* magazine reporter, "the world weighed these extremes, consulted its feelings, and struck its balance on his humanity: he died admired by mankind."

Sources

➤ **Books**

Cousins, Norman, *Dr. Schweitzer of Lambarene,* Harper, 1960.

Merrett, John, *The True Story of Albert Schweitzer,* Children's Press, 1964.

Schweitzer, Albert, *On the Edge of the Primeval Forest,* translated from French by C. T. Campion, A. & C. Black, 1922, Macmillan, 1931.

Schweitzer, Albert, *Memoirs of Childhood and Youth*, translated from French by C. T. Campion, Allen & Unwin, 1924, Macmillan, 1925.

Schweitzer, Albert, *Out of My Life and Thought*, translated from French by C. T. Campion, Holt, 1933. New translation by A. B. Lemke, published as *Out of My Life and Thought: An Autobiography*, Holt, 1991.

Schweitzer, Albert, *More from the Primeval Forest*, translated from French by C. T. Campion, A. & C. Black, 1931, published as *The Forest Hospital at Lambarene*, Holt, 1931.

Schweitzer, Albert, *On the Edge of the Primeval Forest* [and] *More from the Primeval Forest: Experiences and Observations of a Doctor in Equatorial Africa*, AMS Press, 1976. Reprint of 1948 edition.

➤ **Periodicals**

Christian Century, "Schweitzer: Spiritual Adventurer," January 12, 1955, pp. 42–43; "To Schweitzer on His Ninetieth," January 13, 1965, p. 38; September 15, 1965, pp. 1116–1117.

Economist, "Lambarene's Lesson," September 11, 1965, pp. 963–964.

National Review, "Albert Schweitzer, RIP," September 21, 1965, pp. 807–808.

Newsweek, "'The Greatest Christian,'" July 11, 1949, pp. 58–60 (opening quote); "Schweitzer: Reverence for Life," September 13, 1965, p. 62.

New York Times, "Albert Schweitzer, 90, Dies at His Hospital," September 6, 1965.

Reader's Digest, "A Visit to Albert Schweitzer," August, 1954, pp. 43–49.

Time, "Reverence for Life," July 11, 1949, pp. 68–74; "Living with a Verity," September 17, 1965, p. 108.

Pete Seeger

"I know I'm just one more grain of sand in this world. But I'd rather throw my weight, however small, on the side of what I think is right."

Born on May 3, 1919, in New York City, Pete Seeger is a folk singer, songwriter, and musician who has used his talents to crusade on behalf of various political and social causes.

E ver since he left college at the age of nineteen to travel across the United States, Pete Seeger has made it one of his missions to reacquaint his fellow citizens with the rich tradition of American folk music, what he likes to call "homemade music." In the process he has become well known as a social activist—an advocate of working men and women, of the oppressed, and of the environment. This role has often brought Seeger into conflict with the government and with various conservative groups, but now, more than fifty years after he first took to the road, he is "still fighting the good fight," according to Scott Isler in *Rolling Stone.* Singing songs composed by others as well as those he himself has written or collaborated on—among them such memorable titles as "Turn, Turn, Turn," "Where Have All the Flowers Gone?," "If I Had a Hammer," and "We Shall Overcome"—the man Isler describes as "something approaching a musical saint" continues to take his message of fellowship and cooperation to audiences across the nation.

Music has a been a part of Pete Seeger's life virtually from the very beginning. The son of Charles Louis Seeger, an ethnomusicologist and university professor, and Constance de Clyver Edson, a violinist and teacher, Pete grew up listening to the classical pieces his parents favored. In 1935, however, he accompanied his father to a square dance festival in Asheville, North Carolina, where he fell in love with the sound of the old-fashioned five-string banjo and the mountaineers' simple songs of outlaws, heroes, and other characters encountered in everyday life.

Dreaming of a career in journalism or art, Seeger enrolled at Harvard in the fall of 1936. Two years later, he abruptly dropped out of school and hit the road, hopping trains or thumbing rides all over the United States. As he traveled, he supported himself by painting watercolors of the countryside and then trading them for food and shelter. He also sang wherever he could—migrant camps, saloons, churches, and even on street corners—and in the process greatly expanded his knowledge of folk music, picking up new songs and new banjo-playing techniques from people he met along the way, including singer, composer, and guitarist Woody Guthrie and blues performer Huddie "Leadbelly" Ledbetter. The year 1939 found Seeger in Washington, D.C., where he briefly worked at the Archive of American Folk Song, a section of the Library of Congress headed by a friend of his father's, John A. Lomax. There the young musician was able to listen to the many folk recordings already in the archive and accompany Lomax and his son, Alan Lomax, out into the field to record additional songs from all over the country.

In 1940, Seeger joined with Woody Guthrie and several other prominent folksingers of the day to form the Almanac Singers, a loosely knit group that toured the United States singing at labor meetings and migrant camps. Although their repertoire consisted mostly of folk tunes, it also included pro-union and anti-fascist songs, many composed by the group members themselves. America's entry into World War II eventually forced the Almanac Singers to go their separate ways, however. Seeger was drafted in 1942 and spent more than three years in the army entertaining troops stateside as well as throughout the South Pacific. Returning home after the war, he co-founded People's Songs, Inc., a combination songwriters' union, research center, and clearinghouse for topical songs and folk music from around the world. Seeger briefly served as national director of the organization, but drifted away as other projects began to capture his attention.

One of those projects was the Weavers, a now-legendary singing group he formed in 1948 with three other folk musicians, Lee Hays, Fred Hellerman, and Ronnie Gilbert. At first the Weavers had a hard time lining up jobs and were on the verge of breaking up when they were signed to perform at a shabby nightclub in New York City known as the Village Vanguard. Within six months of their debut there in late 1949, the Weavers were a national sensation, appearing on radio and television programs and singing in major concert halls, theaters, and clubs across the country. Their success led to a recording contract, and during the early 1950s the Weavers produced one hit after another with folk songs like "Goodnight, Irene," "On Top of Old Smokey," and "Kisses Sweeter Than Wine."

At the same time the Weavers were enjoying such acclaim, however, Seeger was increasingly the target of harassment from the FBI and U.S. Senator Joseph McCarthy, who was then garnering considerable public support for unmasking the allegedly "subversive" activities of prominent Americans from all walks of life. As far back as his days with the Almanac Singers, Seeger had made no secret of his sympathy for leftist causes; he and Woody Guthrie had even joined the Communist party around 1941 in the belief that it was helping the unemployed find jobs. The Weavers's fame once again put Seeger in the limelight and made him the target of protests and investigations that forced the group to disband in 1952.

Blacklisted on network television and the regular concert circuit,

Seeger defiantly pursued a solo career for the next few years, touring outside the United States and building on his already substantial popularity among young people by playing and singing on college and university campuses. His problems with McCarthy and the U.S. government came to a head in 1955, when he was called to testify before the House Un-American Activities Committee. Citing his First Amendment right to free speech and free association, Seeger refused to answer any questions regarding his political beliefs and affiliations and was subsequently indicted on ten counts of contempt of Congress. It was more than five years before the case came to trial, at which time Seeger was found guilty on some of the charges and sentenced to a year in prison. He appealed the verdict and in May, 1962, the charges were at last dismissed. Being cleared did nothing to make him more acceptable to television executives, however; the blacklist remained in effect, shutting Seeger off from the kind of nationwide exposure enjoyed by other artists.

Despite the shadow that clouded his life throughout the late 1950s and well into the 1960s, Seeger remained active in folk music in a variety of capacities. He performed with the Weavers again from 1955 to 1957, then left the group to pursue other projects, including organizing a revival of the Newport (Rhode Island) Folk Festival, writing numerous books on music and a regular column for *Sing Out!* magazine, composing, and recording. During this same period, folk music enjoyed an unprecedented surge in popularity, and many of Seeger's works were turned into hits not only by his fellow folksingers but also by musicians in fields ranging from country to rock. Television audiences did not see him perform any of them himself until 1967, however, when the Smothers Brothers successfully fought to overturn the decade-old ban barring Seeger from network appearances. His re-emergence was not without controversy—CBS censors cut one of his numbers, which led to a national outcry—but he nevertheless returned to the show several times as a featured guest and later appeared on other television programs, primarily on public broadcasting stations.

Although his return to network television generated widespread publicity, Seeger was already in the headlines for his outspoken opposition to the Vietnam War. Along with other folksingers like Joan Baez and Phil Ochs, he participated in many concerts protesting U.S. involvement in Southeast Asia. These enhanced his reputation among young people but once again angered politically conservative groups like the American Legion.

The 1960s also saw Seeger embrace the ecology movement, a subject that had interested him ever since he first read Rachel Carson's *Silent Spring* and realized that achieving peace and equality would mean little if the earth succumbed to the effects of pollution. As he sees it, the environmental problem is all part of "one huge crisis" in the world, a crisis that involves the very same issues that have concerned him for a lifetime. "It's many-faceted," he remarked to Leslie Ware of *Sierra*. "There's a side of it with a question of force and violence, war and peace; it's a crisis of discrimination, whether it's racism or sexism or ageism or whatever; it's a crisis of poverty amidst plenty."

Seeger has been particularly active in efforts to reduce pollution in the Hudson River near his home in Beacon, New York. Using a sailboat named the *Clearwater*, a replica of the nineteenth-century sloops that used to carry goods up and down the Hudson, Seeger and his neighbors have succeeded in drawing attention to their cause. Through education and fund-raising, the Clearwater group has initiated numerous clean-up efforts that have given new life to areas thought to be beyond help. Their achievements have convinced Seeger that such work must begin on a small scale before it can take root on a larger scale. "Our homes are going to be saved by people who fight for the world," he declared in a *Mother Earth News* interview. "But the world is going to be saved by people who fight for their homes."

Never interested in material gain, Seeger performs enough commercial concerts in a year to help pay the bills, leaving him free to perform at numerous benefits. (He frequently teams up with Arlo Guthrie, son of his old friend Woody Guthrie who died in 1967.) He and his wife of nearly fifty years, Toshi Ohta, live very simply in a small, rustic cabin they built themselves on a mountain overlooking the Hudson. From there he surveys the river and reflects on the odds that the kinds of changes he has lobbied for through his songs will occur in time to save humankind. "I still believe the only chance for the human race to survive is to give up such pleasures as war, racism and private profit," he told Isler. "Obviously, various attempts to solve these problems haven't met with the success I thought they might. But you never can tell. I've never been overoptimistic. . . . But I'm not that pessimistic either. I've seen people's heads turn 180 degrees in a few minutes. . . . All you have to do is listen."

Sources

➤ **Periodicals**

American History Illustrated, October, 1982, pp. 16–19 (opening quote).

Horizon, "Keeping the Faith," October, 1981, pp. 42–47.

Mother Earth News, "Pete Seeger: Singing to Save Our Earth," November/December, 1982, pp. 16–22.

Progressive, "Pete Seeger's Homemade Music," April, 1986, pp. 35–37.

Rolling Stone, "Pete Seeger: Still Fighting the Good Fight," October 18, 1979, p. 20.

Sierra, "Pete Seeger: Keeping the Dream," March/April, 1989, pp. 82–90.

Aung San Suu Kyi

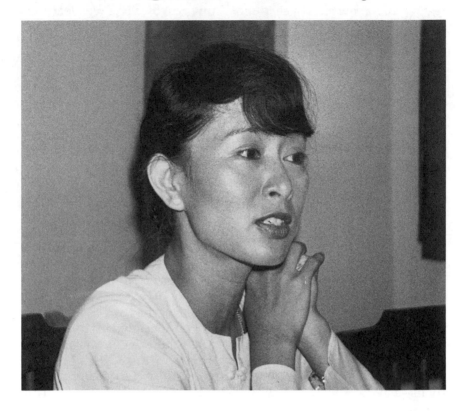

*"*C*oncepts such as truth, justice and compassion cannot be dismissed as trite when these are often the only bulwarks which stand against ruthless power."*

Winner of the 1991 Nobel Peace Prize, Aung San Suu Kyi has been described as the foremost prisoner of conscience in the world. She was born on June 19, 1945, in Rangoon, Burma, now known as Yangon, Myanmar.

Only a few short years ago, Aung San Suu Kyi was leading a quiet life in England as the wife of an Oxford University professor and the mother of two teenage boys. A native of Burma, where a brutal military dictatorship had ruled with an iron hand since 1962, she did not realize to what extent conditions had deteriorated in her homeland until she returned for a visit during the spring of 1988. Back in England, she had always steered clear of anti-government protests staged by Burmese exiles, but as she saw how much the people were suffering, she gradually found herself becoming involved in politics. "I obviously had to think about it," she later remarked. "But my instinct was, 'This is not a time when anyone who cares can stay out.'" Today, as the imprisoned leader of Burma's pro-democracy movement, she is regarded by her fellow citizens as a courageously defiant symbol of hope for a better future.

Aung San Suu Kyi is the daughter of an especially revered figure in Burmese history, U Aung San. Considered the founder of modern Burma, Aung San rose to prominence during World War II, when he founded and led the Burma Independence Army and later organized the resistance against the Japanese. After the war, he negotiated Burma's freedom from Great Britain and headed a transitional government that was supposed to rule until the country officially achieved independence in January, 1948. In July, 1947, however, thirty-year-old Aung San was assassinated by right-wing political rivals, leaving behind his wife, Khin Kyi, a son, and two-year-old Suu Kyi.

For the next fifteen years, Burma thrived under the leadership of Aung San's chief deputy, U Nu, becoming the richest nation in Southeast Asia. But in 1962, the government was toppled in a coup staged by U Ne Win, a brutal military strongman who advocated a curious blend of Buddhism, socialism, and isolationism, which left the country in financial ruin and its people in fear for their lives. Although General Ne Win stepped down in July, 1988, following a series of massive anti-government demonstrations, he is still believed to be very much in control of Burma by virtue of his close relationship with the current leader, General Saw Maung.

Because she had been away from Burma since 1960, Suu Kyi had witnessed none of the turmoil of Ne Win's authoritarian regime. As a seventeen-year-old, she had moved to India when her mother was appointed Burma's ambassador to that country. Later, she went to England, where she studied politics, philosophy, and economics at Oxford University. It was there that she met her husband,

Michael Aris, whom she married in 1972. The couple settled in Oxford in 1974 after Aris became a professor at the university, and Suu Kyi spent the next fourteen years tending to their two children. Despite the distance that separated her from Burma and its problems, Suu Kyi nevertheless felt that one day she would return to fulfill an obligation to her father. In fact, the more she learned about modern Burmese politics, the more she came to realize how much the memory of her father had kept alive "the spirit of truth and justice during all these years under a corrupt regime." As she later explained, "It is perhaps because of this strong bond that I came to feel such a deep sense of responsibility for the welfare of my country."

In April, 1988, Suu Kyi returned to Burma, her thoughts preoccupied not with politics but with nursing her dying mother. Late that summer, however, violent anti-government protests rocked Rangoon, resulting in the deaths of at least three thousand demonstrators at the hands of General Ne Win's troops. Horrified to see the military responsible for such death and terror—she had been brought up to regard the army as a friendly force allied with the people—Suu Kyi felt compelled to speak out. At first, curious crowds were drawn to her out of respect for her famous father. But soon they were coming by the thousands to hear her impassioned call for democracy and freedom from fear, which she maintained could be achieved through nonviolent civil disobedience. That fall, she and others with similar aims formed the National League for Democracy (NLD), the first organized, broad-based political party dedicated to reform since the 1962 coup that had put Ne Win in power.

Suu Kyi and the NLD kept up the pressure on the regime throughout the rest of 1988, defying government rules prohibiting gatherings of more than five people and public criticism of the armed forces. Suu Kyi in particular earned the admiration of her fellow Burmese for her determination and unflinching courage, even as she faced troops who had been ordered to shoot her. She was also forced to endure vicious personal attacks that criticized her longtime residency outside of Burma, her marriage to an Englishman, and her "tainted," mixed-race children. Suu Kyi persevered despite such attempts to discredit her, and the unrest continued. Finally, General Saw Maung, Burma's third head of state in just a few months, promised that his government would step down after democratic elections were held in May, 1990. In a move he said was intended to recognize the ethnic minorities in Burma, Saw Maung also announced that the country would thereafter go by the name *Myanmar*.

Very few Myanmarese believed that elections were ever likely to occur, especially if the protests stopped. So Suu Kyi persisted in speaking out against the government throughout the first half of 1989. In June, her speeches took on an even bolder tone when she called on troops to overthrow Ne Win, whom she accused of being personally responsible for Myanmar's many years of suffering. The government responded by increasing its harassment of both Suu Kyi and other NLD leaders, resulting in many arrests and widespread reports of torture and intimidation. In July, 1989, their attempts to silence her having failed, military officials put Suu Kyi under house arrest at what had been her mother's home in Yangon (formerly Rangoon), effectively cutting her off from Myanmar and the rest of the world.

In May, 1990, government leaders surprised everyone by living up to their pledge to allow the long-awaited democratic elections to take place. (Suu Kyi was barred from taking part on the grounds that she was not a resident of Myanmar and had ties to subversive groups.) But to absolutely no one's surprise, Saw Maung completely ignored the results—which showed that the NLD had won in a landslide with about eighty percent of the vote—and refused to relinquish power. Instead, he ordered the arrest of scores of NLD members who had won the election and Buddhist monks who had openly supported them.

As of mid-1992, Suu Kyi remains under house arrest, forbidden to see or even speak with her family and friends. (She last saw her husband and sons during the 1989 Christmas season; government leaders announced in April, 1992, that they would soon be allowed to visit her again.) Yet she is more popular than ever among Myanmarese: her image appears everywhere, on illegal T-shirts, posters, and buttons, her style of dress (a mix of Western and traditional Burmese designs) is widely copied (especially among young people), and her story is told in songs and poems. Myanmar's leaders have offered to release Suu Kyi if she agrees to leave quietly, but so far she has refused to do so unless they release all political prisoners, honor the 1990 election results, and allow her to address the nation on television and radio.

Her cause received its biggest boost in October, 1991, when she was awarded the year's Nobel Peace Prize for setting "one of the most extraordinary examples of civil courage in Asia in recent decades." (Suu Kyi's husband and sons traveled to Norway and accepted the prize on her behalf.) Human rights activists hope such worldwide recognition will pressure Western and other Southeast Asian nations to take a harder line against Myanmar, perhaps through economic sanctions. Others believe the prize may help keep Suu Kyi safe from execution as a troublemaker.

In the meantime, her voice is still silent. It is believed she spends most of her time in meditation and that she has continued to protest her arrest and the posting of soldiers in her home. According to reports from an anonymous source, she was "delighted" to hear that she had won the Nobel Prize because of its potential to bring about positive changes in Myanmar. Until then, she and her supporters remain hopeful that they will one day know freedom and that no sacrifice may be too great to achieve it. In a letter she wrote to her husband shortly before her arrest, Suu Kyi reflected on what she had already endured to rally support for her cause. "In spite of all the difficulties," she concluded, "I feel that what I am doing is worthwhile—the people of Burma deserve better than this mess of inefficiency, corruption and misuse of power."

Sources

➤ **Books**

Aris, Michael, editor, *Freedom from Fear and Other Writings* (essays by and about Aung San Suu Kyi), Penguin, 1991.

➤ **Periodicals**

Detroit Free Press, "Nobel Winner's Book Details Fight Against Burmese Tyranny," February 12, 1992, p. 3C (opening quote).

Interview, "Aung San Suu Kyi: Imprisoned by the State, Wanted by the People," July, 1991, p. 32.

Maclean's, "A Fight for Rights," October 28, 1991, p. 84.

New York Times, "Burmese Opposition Leader Wins the Nobel Prize," October 15, 1991, p. A10; "Burmese Whose Silenced Voice Echoes," October 15, 1991, p. A11; "The Power of the Peace Prize May Be Lost on Myanmar," October 20, 1991, p. 4E; "Book Frees Up the Voice of a Burmese Nobelist," November 24, 1991, p. 22; "Peace-Prize Winner: Free My Country," November 26, 1991, p. A21; "Son Picks Up Nobel Prize for an Unfree Burmese Dissenter," December 11, 1991, p. A16.

People, "The Wages of Courage," October 28, 1991, p. 129.

Time, "Locking the Gates," July 31, 1989, p. 30; "A Country Under the Boot," August 21, 1989, pp. 36–37; "Crossed Off the Ballot," January 29, 1990, p. 57; "Heroine in Chains," October 28, 1991, p. 73.

Corrie ten Boom

*"*I *believe that God delights to use His children in the fulfillment of His plans for the world. I am sure He loves to use small people to do great things."*

Born on April 15, 1892, in Amsterdam, Netherlands, Corrie ten Boom risked her life during World War II to shelter Jews from the Nazis, for which she was arrested and sent to a concentration camp. She died on April 15, 1983, in Placentia, California.

Address: Christians, Inc., P.O. Box 2040, Orange, CA 92669.

I n 1940, Corrie ten Boom was nearing the fiftieth year of a life that had long ago settled into a pleasant routine. Employed as a watchmaker in her father's shop—the first woman in the Netherlands to be licensed in that field—she had for many years devoted her spare time to religious activities. She and her older sister, Betsie, lived with their widowed father in the rooms above the watch shop, and there the three of them fully expected to end their days. Then Germany, already at war with most of Europe, invaded neutral Holland and conquered the entire country in only five days. Within months, the "Nazification" of the Dutch people began, and the quiet lives of the ten Booms were changed forever.

Cornelia Arnolda Johanna ten Boom was born in Amsterdam but grew up in Haarlem, the daughter of Casper ten Boom, a jeweler and watchmaker, and Cor Luitingh ten Boom. The ten Booms were strict Calvinists and quite poor, yet by all accounts the household was a happy one. The family tradition of offering shelter, food, and money to anyone in need insured that there were always visitors in the rooms above Casper's shop that served as the ten Boom home. (Several of Mrs. ten Boom's sisters were among the permanent guests.) Casper himself was highly regarded in the community as a kind and generous man who, like his father before him, had a deep love and respect for Jewish people, regarding them as "God's ancient people" and therefore worthy of special consideration from all Christians. Casper in turn passed the same lesson along to his own children.

During and after high school, Corrie supplemented the religious instruction she received at home from her parents with additional studies at a local Bible school. After being disappointed in a romance that she had hoped would lead to marriage, she decided to learn the watchmaker's trade so that she could join her father in the family business. She apprenticed briefly in a Swiss watch factory and then returned to Haarlem, working by day with her father to perfect her skills and devoting her evenings to helping her sister Betsie care for their ailing mother and aunts. Throughout the 1920s and 1930s, the ten Booms also opened their home to German war refugees and the children of missionaries who could not take them into the field. Affectionately dubbed the "Beje" (short for *Barteljorisstraat*, the name of the street it was on), the house was usually overflowing with "guests," some of whom stayed for years and grew to adulthood under the guidance of Casper, Betsie, and Corrie.

In addition to working in the watch shop and caring for the

children in the Beje, Corrie conducted Bible classes in the public schools and taught Sunday school, making a special effort to reach out to the mentally retarded. With the financial backing of several wealthy citizens of Haarlem, she also started youth clubs for teenage girls that provided religious instruction as well as lessons in music, singing, folk dancing, gymnastics, sewing, and handicrafts.

At first, the German occupation of Holland had little impact on the day-to-day routine of most Dutch people. By the end of 1940, however, the Nazis began imposing curfews and food rationing, confiscating property, and harassing Jews. When rules went into effect requiring Jews to wear yellow armbands, it was all Corrie and Betsie could do to convince their father that it would not be safe for him to wear one in protest.

As the situation grew more dangerous, the ten Booms started taking in resistance fighters hiding from the Gestapo and "underdivers" (Dutch Jews and young men wanted by the police). Dozens of them over a period of about four years used the Beje as a stopover on their way to other places, and about six to eight people stayed permanently. Under the bottom shelf of Corrie's closet was a door leading to a secret room, a cramped but essential hiding place in case the Gestapo came. To help those they could not shelter in Haarlem, the ten Booms also established a network of "safe houses" in the country. Corrie was the overseer of all these operations.

On February 28, 1944, the Beje was raided by the Gestapo. Everyone inside the house was arrested, as was anyone who came to the shop that day. In all, thirty-five people were taken into custody, including Corrie, Betsie, their brother Willem and his family, their sister Nollie and her family, and eighty-four-year-old Casper. Six people who had hidden in the secret room stayed there for nearly three days before managing to escape.

The ten Booms were split up and subjected to endless questioning by the Gestapo. Casper quickly grew weak and confused and died only ten days after his arrest; all of the other people arrested in the Beje—with the exception of Corrie and Betsie—were eventually released. Corrie, extremely ill with bronchitis, was shipped to a prison at Scheveningen. When she was strong enough to attend a hearing on the charges that had been brought against her, the judge assigned to her case was deeply moved by her strength, courage, and—most of all—her unwavering devotion to her faith. He later did what he could to help the ten Booms, even destroying incriminating papers that the Gestapo had found in the Beje.

Shortly after D-Day in June, 1944, Corrie was reunited with Betsie, and the two sisters were moved to the Vught concentration camp. To bolster morale and counter boredom and fear among their fellow prisoners, the women formed prayer groups and held discussion sessions, making use of a Bible Corrie had hidden in her clothes and smuggled into camp. As the allied armies drew closer, rumors of an impending release swept through the barracks. But it soon became clear exactly how the Nazis planned to empty Vught. First the men and boys were shot, then the women were shipped to Germany to perform hard physical labor at the Ravensbruck concentration camp.

Corrie continued her Bible studies as best she could, but conditions at Ravensbruck were considerably harsher than they had been at Vught and there was little time, energy, or opportunity to do much more than pray with and for other prisoners. Betsie, who had never been physically strong, died on December 16, 1944. Before her death, however, she told Corrie of a dream she had had about establishing a home for people who had suffered during the war and needed a safe and quiet place to recover before moving on with their lives. Betsie wanted Corrie to be the one to make the dream come true as well as spread the word about "the joy and pain of their suffering for Christ."

Two weeks later, on New Year's Day, 1945, Corrie was handed her release papers and abruptly told to leave the camp. She later learned that a clerical error was responsible for her freedom; while some Dutch prisoners were indeed released at that time, Corrie was not supposed to be among them. Within days after she left, all of the remaining women in Ravensbruck went to the gas chambers.

Corrie made her way back to Holland and, after a brief convalescence, she began speaking to small groups about her experiences at Ravensbruck and about Betsie's dream. Once the war ended, Corrie stepped up her efforts to fulfill her promise to her sister, soliciting donations and banding together with friends to establish a rehabilitation center that housed displaced persons and former prisoners and served as a training center for evangelical workers. Corrie took her story to a wider audience in 1947, when she made her first trip to the United States to spread her personal message of hope and faith. Over the next thirty years, until age and illness began to take their toll, she was on the move almost constantly, visiting nearly seventy other countries as a self-described "tramp for the Lord."

In 1977, at the age of eighty-five, Corrie settled in Placentia,

California, her first real home since she had been taken from the Beje in 1944. She wrote a few books and started a neighborhood Bible-study group, remaining active until August, 1978, when she suffered a severe stroke that left her unable to move or speak. A succession of strokes over the next few years left her weaker still, and she died on April 15, 1983—her ninety-first birthday. "Somewhere between beautiful humility and an almost unbelievable strength and indomitable spirit was the real Corrie," notes her biographer, Carole C. Carlson. "Not just a 'sweet little grandmother,' but a two-fisted old Dutch soldier for Christ."

Sources

➤ **Books**

Brown, Joan Winmill, *Corrie: The Lives She's Touched,* Revell, 1979.

Carlson, Carole C., *Corrie ten Boom: Her Life, Her Faith,* Revell, 1983 (opening quote).

ten Boom, Corrie, and John and Elizabeth Sherrill, *The Hiding Place,* Revell, 1971.

ten Boom, Corrie, and Jamie Buckingham, *Tramp for the Lord,* Christian Literature Crusade, 1974.

ten Boom, Corrie, and Carole C. Carlson, *In My Father's House: The Years before 'The Hiding Place,'* Revell, 1976.

➤ **Periodicals**

Christianity Today, May 20, 1983, pp. 52–53.

➤ **Other**

The Hiding Place, a movie based on Corrie ten Boom's autobiography, was released by Wide World Pictures in 1975.

Jim Thorpe

*"*H*e was the greatest athlete who ever lived. . . . What he had was natural ability. There wasn't anything he couldn't do. All he had to see is someone doin' something and he tried it . . . and he'd do it better."—1912 Olympic silver medalist Abel Kiviat*

A standout performer in football, baseball, track, and more than a half-dozen other sports, Jim Thorpe is ranked as one of the greatest athletes of all time. He was born on May 28, 1888, near Prague, Oklahoma, and died on March 28, 1953, in Lomita, California.

In 1912, a strapping young college football player named Jim Thorpe made Olympic history by picking up gold medals in two of the most grueling competitions in the games, the pentathlon and the decathlon, immediately earning for himself the title of the world's greatest athlete. Less than six months later, however, the International Olympic Committee (IOC) stripped him of his championships in a move that some say was fueled, at least in part, by prejudice. It was a blow from which Thorpe never fully recovered, and despite the tireless efforts of his family and friends, some seventy years passed before the IOC agreed to reverse its decision and restore his medals and his honor.

James Francis Thorpe was born and grew up in a one-room log cabin on an Oklahoma farm. A twin brother, Charles, died in childhood, but two other brothers and two sisters shared that modest home with Jim and his parents, Hiram and Charlotte View Thorpe. The Thorpes were of mixed Native American and European ancestry but identified primarily with their Indian heritage; in addition to his legal name, for example, Jim was also given a Sac-Fox tribal name, Wa-Tho-Huck or Bright Path.

After completing his elementary education at a nearby reservation school, Thorpe briefly attended a vocational school in Kansas before being sent in 1904 to a similar institution in Pennsylvania, the Carlisle Indian School. At Carlisle, a small school of about 250 students, he took classes in tailoring and went out for the football team, joining the reserve team as a backup guard. It was not until 1908, the year after he had made the varsity squad, that Thorpe truly began to flourish as an athlete. Under the direction of legendary coach Glenn "Pop" Warner, the husky Oklahoman came off the bench to become the best drop-kicker and punter on the team, as well as an exciting ball carrier. (His sudden fame also captured national attention; at the end of the season, he was named to the All-American third team.)

That same year, Thorpe astounded onlookers when he casually accepted a challenge to try high jumping; on his very first jump, he easily bettered the marks of everyone on the Carlisle team. Encouraged by Pop Warner (who was also the track coach) to see what he could do in some of the other events, Thorpe outran the sprinters and hurdlers and also won in the javelin throw, even though he had never picked one up until that day. Almost from the moment he officially joined the track team he was its dominant force, leading

Carlisle to victory over stronger rivals from much bigger schools, including Harvard University.

Thorpe left Carlisle in 1909 and headed south to the Carolinas, where he earned money for school by doing some farm work and playing for a few minor-league baseball clubs during the summers of 1909 and 1910, for which he received about two dollars a day to cover his expenses. Eager to have his star athlete back on the football field and perhaps earn a spot on the 1912 Olympic track team, Pop Warner convinced Thorpe to return to Carlisle in 1911. Two big seasons followed, during which time the twenty-three-year-old delivered outstanding performances not only on defense but also as a kicker and runner in games against Eastern powerhouse teams such as Harvard, Penn State, Princeton, Army, Georgetown, Pitt, and Syracuse. His gridiron exploits won him All-American first team honors in both 1911 and 1912 and easily made him the most famous college athlete in the country. When he was not playing football, Thorpe also managed to excel in other sports, including basketball, hockey, tennis, boxing, swimming, skating, baseball, lacrosse, and various track events.

At the 1912 Olympics in Stockholm, Sweden, Thorpe earned accolades as the world's most famous athlete. As part of the U.S. track team, he was a virtual one-man show at the games, becoming the first person ever to win gold medals in both the pentathlon (a five-event contest that includes running broad jump, javelin throw, discus throw, a 200-meter race, and a 1500-meter race) and the decathlon (a ten-event contest that includes running broad jump, running high jump, javelin throw, discus throw, shot put, pole vault, a 100-meter dash, a 110-meter high hurdles, a 400-meter race, and a 1500-meter race). In the pentathlon, Thorpe took first place in four of the five events, and in the decathlon, he took first place in seven of the ten events, amassing a record-breaking total of 8,412 points out of a possible 10,000. Amazingly, he had barely trained for any of the contests, devoting a little time to the jumps, hurdles, and shot put during the spring of 1912 and then practicing the pole vault, javelin, and discus just before the U.S. team tryouts. After the Olympics, Thorpe demonstrated that his marks in the races, high jumps, pole vaults, and throws were not flukes when he bettered them in other track meets.

Thorpe returned to the United States as a hero and played the 1912 football season at Carlisle. But shortly after the season ended, reports surfaced about the two summers he had spent playing minor-league baseball. The Amateur Athletic Union (AAU) reacted to this evidence of "professionalism" by revoking his amateur status and erasing his name from the record books. (In those days, college athletes often picked up a little money playing summer baseball but kept it under wraps by using aliases.) When questioned, Thorpe freely admitted that he had played a few baseball games in the minors—under his own name, because he didn't think there was any reason to keep it secret—but could not understand why it had any bearing on his amateur status in football and track.

Despite the fact that it was clear Thorpe had not understood the rules, the officials refused to back down, and by the end of January, 1913, the AAU and the U.S. Olympic Committee had pressured the IOC to erase Thorpe's name from its record books and demand that he return his gold medals so that they could be awarded to the second-place finishers. In retrospect, some believe that racism may have played a part in the affair; in their recommendation to the IOC, the AAU and the U.S. Olympic Committee acknowledged Thorpe's ignorance of the rules but suggested it might have occurred because he was "an Indian of limited experience and education in the ways of other than his own people."

In any case, with no future in amateur athletics, Thorpe officially made the switch to the professional ranks by signing on with baseball's New York Giants. He played on and off for various major- and minor-league teams until 1919, never becoming a big star but performing very well as an outfielder and somewhat less spectacularly as a hitter.

In 1920, Thorpe left baseball to help organize the American Professional Football Association, which two years later changed its name to the National Football League (NFL). He served as its first president and also played the game for seven years, initially as the star attraction of the Canton (Ohio) Bulldogs and then for several other teams, including ones in Cleveland and New York. The forty-one-year-old athlete's football career ended in 1929 when he retired from the game to seek his fortune elsewhere.

But Thorpe never again matched the glory of his youth, and the good times soon gave way to hard times. He had always had trouble managing his finances, and the Depression of the 1930s only made matters worse. To help make ends meet, Thorpe tried other sports, including golf and bowling, and even landed a few minor movie roles, but it was not enough. Within two years after his retirement from football, he was working in California as a day laborer on a construction project; he later held such jobs as night watchman and bouncer.

By the end of the decade, Thorpe's life had begun to turn around a bit. Returning to Oklahoma, he became involved in Sac-Fox tribal affairs. In 1940 he launched a career as a lecturer, traveling across the country to discuss his life story, sports in general, and Native American culture. Too old to serve in the regular armed forces during World War II, he instead signed up for a brief stint with the merchant marines in 1945. After the war ended, he moved back to California, where he spent his last years in relative obscurity and virtually penniless. Repeated efforts by his family and friends, elected officials, and various sports organizations to have his Olympic records reinstated and his gold medals returned were unsuccessful, leaving Thorpe increasingly bitter and discouraged. One of the last great moments in his life came in 1950, when the Associated Press named him the greatest football player and the greatest all-around male athlete of the first half of the century. Three years later, he died of a heart attack at the age of sixty-four.

The story of Jim Thorpe did not end with his death, however. Convinced that he had been wronged by the AAU and the U.S. Olympic Committee, his family and other supporters kept up the fight to restore the honors they felt were rightfully his. Blocking them at every turn was Avery Brundage, longtime chairman of the IOC and a former athlete who had competed against Thorpe—and lost—during the 1912 games. A partial victory came in October, 1982, when the IOC finally agreed to return Thorpe's medals to his children and change the record books to indicate that he "shared" his pentathlon and decathlon championships with the second-place finishers. But to fans like writer, producer, and director Bud Greenspan, who feels the IOC did not "go the full distance" in exonerating Thorpe, justice still eludes the man whose accomplishments "were larger and grander than those of any other male athlete in history."

Sources

➤ **Books**

Lincoln Library of Sports Champions, Volume 12, Sports Resources, 1974.

Richards, Gregory, *Jim Thorpe: World's Greatest Athlete*, Children's Press, 1984.

Wheeler, Robert W., *Jim Thorpe: World's Greatest Athlete*, University of Oklahoma Press, 1981.

➤ Periodicals

New York Times, January 25, 1950, p. 31; March 29, 1953; "Jim Thorpe's Olympic Medals Are Restored," October 14, 1982; "His Medals Returned, Has the Thorpe Story Ended?," October 17, 1982, section 5, p. 2 (opening quote).

Sports Illustrated, "The Regilding of a Legend," October 25, 1982.

Time, "'The Greatest Athlete,'" April 6, 1953, pp. 58–60.

➤ Other

Jim Thorpe's life story was dramatized in the 1951 film *Jim Thorpe: All American.*

Harry S. Truman

"I *don't give a damn what history thinks of me. I know what I did and that's enough for me."*

Harry S. Truman was thrust into the presidency of the United States on April 12, 1945, following the sudden death of Franklin Delano Roosevelt. While not especially popular or respected while in office, he is now ranked among the country's "near-great" chief executives. He was born on May 8, 1884, in Lamar, Missouri, and died on December 26, 1972, in Kansas City, Missouri.

On April 12, 1945, Harry S. Truman had been vice-president for a mere eighty-three days when he received word that President Franklin Delano Roosevelt had died. "I felt there must be a million men better qualified than I," Truman later said of that moment. Indeed, few men before him had been as unprepared as he was to step into the role. The Roosevelt presidency had been a virtual one-man operation; Truman was never let in on any of the details concerning the progress of World War II (then entering its final stages) or of the Allies' plans for restructuring the postwar world. Nor did he know anything about the atomic bomb, a weapon he would very soon be asked to approve for use against the Japanese. Yet as Richard Boeth of *Newsweek* observed, the new president "got the hang of things extraordinarily fast."

Faced with some of the most difficult and important challenges ever to confront an American chief executive—including bringing the war to an end, setting the stage for a lasting peace, rebuilding Europe, and stopping Soviet expansionism—Truman acted quickly and decisively to formulate and enact policies that influenced national and world events for decades. In the meantime, he endured the insults and patronizing attitudes of those who criticized his lack of education, his nondescript physical appearance, and his unpolished, shoot-from-the-hip style. Underestimated and unappreciated while in office and for many years afterward, Truman is now regarded by historians and others as a "near-great" president along with men such as Andrew Jackson and Theodore Roosevelt.

Harry S. Truman was the eldest of three children of Martha Ellen Young and John Anderson Truman. (His middle name was simply "S" because his parents couldn't agree whether to name him after his maternal grandfather Shippe or his paternal grandfather Solomon.) John Truman held a variety of jobs during his life, most of them related in some way to farming; Martha Truman was the college-educated daughter of a prosperous local farmer. Growing up primarily in or near Independence, Missouri (the town he always considered home), Harry was a rather sickly child with poor eyesight that forced him to wear thick glasses from the time he was six years old. As a result, he didn't play any sports or games and turned instead to more solitary pursuits such as reading and playing the piano.

As a youngster, Truman devised an ambitious plan to achieve "greatness." He concluded through reading about the lives of great men that a person needed experience in farming, finance, or the military. At first, he set his sights on attending West Point, but after failing the eye exam, he enrolled at a local business college. When his father suffered some financial setbacks that made going to school out of the question, Truman went to work, first as a time-keeper for a railroad construction company and then as a bank clerk in Kansas City, where he also joined the National Guard in an attempt to get some military experience. In 1906, however, he left Kansas City to join his family on a farm near Grandview that had belonged to his maternal grandfather.

Truman tackled farming with enthusiasm, reading extensively on the subject and experimenting with different crops and techniques. His success made him a standout in the community, and soon he was tapped for some local political offices, including postmaster, county road overseer, and school board member. But by 1917, Truman had grown weary of trying to earn a living as a farmer while paying off his father's old debts. Eager to make more money so that he could afford to marry his childhood sweetheart, Bess Wallace, he dabbled in a few speculative business ventures but did not do well at any of them.

America's entry into World War I put all of Truman's plans on hold. Somehow managing to get around the vision requirement, he enlisted in the army and quickly organized an artillery unit staffed by many of the men he had served with in the National Guard. He shipped out to France soon after and was put in charge of an artillery company.

Returning to Kansas City in May, 1919, Truman married Bess and, in partnership with a friend, opened a men's clothing store. Business was excellent at first, but a recession in 1922 forced the store to close, leaving Truman nearly $30,000 in debt (a considerable sum in those days). Although his partner declared bankruptcy, Truman insisted on paying off each one of his creditors in full, a process that took some fifteen years.

At the suggestion of an army buddy with family connections to Thomas J. Pendergast, a major Democratic "boss" in Missouri politics, Truman decided to run for Jackson County judge, a non-judicial administrative position responsible for county finances and such activities as road construction and other public works projects. He managed to win the election without the help of the Pendergast machine but was defeated in a 1924 bid for re-election. Realizing his minimal chances of winning any future elections in Missouri without Pendergast's backing, Truman turned to him for help and in

1926 won a seat as presiding judge, the chief administrative position in the county. He served for eight years and gained a reputation as an honest, efficient manager who was friendly with Pendergast but not one of his lackeys. While no evidence has ever surfaced that suggests Truman profited personally from the corrupt practices of the Pendergast machine, his association with it raised more than a few eyebrows in later years.

In 1934, Truman won a U.S. Senate seat in a tough contest marked by accusations that he was a puppet of the Pendergasts. He represented Missouri in Washington for the next ten years, a period he later described as the happiest time of his life. Making it clear that he was not working for the Pendergasts, Truman took a leadership position in the movement to monitor financial waste and mismanagement, particularly in the railroad and airline industries and later in the awarding of government contracts to the defense industry. He also consistently backed Roosevelt's New Deal programs and supported other legislation to help farmers and labor unions, earning a reputation as a populist—someone who favors the rights of "the common people" over those of big business. And although he was undeniably racially prejudiced in private life, he wholeheartedly lobbied for an end to legalized racial discrimination on the grounds that it violated the basic principles and ideals for which America stood.

Seeking a new term in 1940, Truman faced an uphill struggle. The Pendergasts had been forced out of power by the Missouri governor, who decided to run for Truman's senate seat. Although he failed to win endorsements from Roosevelt (who was leery of Truman's alleged ties to the Pendergasts) and the major Missouri newspapers, Truman did have the solid backing of his fellow senators as well as many railroad workers, labor unions, veterans and National Guardsmen, Black Americans, and other New Deal advocates. He narrowly triumphed in the Democratic primary, but easily defeated his Republican opponent to return to Washington, where he continued to enhance his reputation for loyalty, fairness, and efficiency.

As Roosevelt prepared to run again for president in 1944, Truman's name surfaced as a possible vice-presidential candidate. The choice was especially important in this election; the country was still at war (although Germany was near collapse) and the president's health was a major worry. Truman was not at all interested, however, citing his age (he was then sixty) and his feeling that he could be more effective if he stayed in the Senate. But Roosevelt finally persuaded him that his presence on the ticket would unite the Democrats and ensure a victory at a critical time in U.S. history. The appeal to Truman's sense of loyalty worked, and the two were easily elected.

A mere eleven weeks later, the man who had not even wanted to be vice-president was president. Truman had only met twice with Roosevelt since the election and had never been informed of the war's progress or strategy, including the atomic bomb project. Compounding his difficulties was the fact that he and Roosevelt's advisors did not get along; they resented the Missouri "hick," and he in turn bristled at their patronizing attitude toward him and was suspicious of their privileged backgrounds. Truman immediately announced his intention to continue Roosevelt's policies, but with a staff made up mostly of fellow Missourians who shared his no-nonsense approach. Unlike his predecessor, Truman believed in delegating authority to those who were better suited for certain jobs, but he never lost sight of the fact that the ultimate responsibility for running the government was his—a philosophy epitomized by a plaque on his desk that read "The Buck Stops Here."

The first crisis he faced as president involved ending the war. Peace came to Europe less than a month after Truman took office, but Japan was still a formidable foe. Informed of a new, presumably powerful, but yet untested atomic weapon, Truman recognized its potential to bring about a quick end to the war in the Pacific as well as keep the Soviets in line in the future. Military experts had estimated that invading the Japanese home islands might result in the deaths of at least 250,000 American soldiers. Truman felt strongly that Japan's earlier conduct in the war—including the surprise attack on Pearl Harbor and brutal treatment of prisoners of war—negated any claim it might have had to military honor and that bringing the war to an end by any means available was justified.

With few people to turn to for advice, Truman made the difficult decision after long and careful thought: on July 24, 1945, he authorized the military to use its atomic bomb and drop a second one if necessary. Of all the decisions ever made by American presidents, this one remains by far the most controversial. At the time, however, the implications of its use were not publicly debated or even widely understood. "I did not like the weapon," Truman later commented, "but I had no qualms, if in the long run millions of lives could be saved." On August 6, Hiroshima became the first target. Although approximately seventy thousand people died and another seventy thousand were injured, Japan refused to surrender. Another bomb was dropped on Nagasaki on August 9, killing forty thousand and injuring sixty thousand. Still the Japanese military leaders would not back down. Finally, Emperor Hirohito ordered the government to accept defeat, and a formal surrender followed on September 2 aboard the battleship *Missouri*.

After the war, Truman's attention turned toward building a lasting peace as leader of a country that was now *the* major world power. Under his leadership, the United States abandoned the isolationism of the past and assumed a much more active role in foreign affairs. His official policy—known as the Truman Doctrine—pledged U.S. help to those countries threatened by Soviet expansionism in Eastern Europe and elsewhere. (This doctrine set the tone for American foreign politics until well into the 1980s, serving as the basis for military intervention in places such as Vietnam.) Tensions between the former allies increased throughout the late 1940s as each side challenged the other in what soon came to be known as the cold war.

In 1947, for example, the battle lines were drawn in Greece and Turkey, where Soviet-backed rebels fought government troops financed by the United States; in 1948, the Soviets cut off West Berlin from the rest of the world, and Truman promptly responded with an airlift of food and other supplies that eventually broke the blockade. Another U.S. strategy during the cold war was the Marshall Plan (named after its chief architect, Secretary of State George C. Marshall), a massive aid program designed to restore prosperity to Western Europe and rebuild its shattered cities, thus lessening the chances of communism gaining a foothold while at the same time creating a market for American-made goods. A tremendously successful undertaking, it earned Marshall a 1953 Nobel Peace Prize. But it drove an even bigger wedge between the Soviets and the West and led to the formation of mutual defense agreements such as the North Atlantic Treaty Organization (NATO) and the Warsaw Pact.

On the domestic front, Truman faced the daunting task of transforming a wartime economy to a peacetime one. The mid- to late 1940s were marked by high inflation, shortages of food and other consumer goods, and labor unrest that resulted in several crippling strikes. Truman took a strong-arm approach to solving the latter problem in particular, ordering the government to seize control of certain key industries and transportation systems and threatening to draft striking workers into the army if they did not settle with management and return to their jobs.

But Truman's tactics and defensive attitude were extremely unpopular, and by 1948—a presidential election year—he was in big trouble politically. The public had grown increasingly disenchanted with his performance; some even suggested that he was not capable of running the country. The support he once enjoyed in the Senate and in his own party had eroded considerably, too. Truman only added fuel to the fire by issuing an executive order ending segregation in the military and the civil service and proposing sweeping civil rights legislation, moves that outraged Southerners.

The Democrats unenthusiastically nominated Truman, but many felt he had little chance to defeat his Republican challenger, Thomas Dewey. After a spirited campaign, Truman termed his subsequent upset win over Dewey the most satisfying of his entire political career.

Truman's second term got off to a rocky start from which it never really recovered. The nuclear arms race officially got under way in 1949 when the Soviet Union exploded its first atomic bomb. That same year, Truman was severely criticized for being "soft on communism" after the "fall" of China, which many attributed to his unwillingness to give unconditional support to the corrupt and brutal Nationalist Chinese in their fight against Mao Zedong and his communist revolutionaries. This same accusation spilled over to domestic politics when Senator Joseph McCarthy claimed that his investigations revealed communists had infiltrated the U.S. government, especially the State Department. The fear of communism even had an effect on Truman's ability to push his economic and social reforms (called the "Fair Deal") through Congress.

Perhaps the most frustrating and disappointing event of Truman's second term was the Korean War. Technically not a war but a "police action" sanctioned by the United Nations, the conflict erupted in June, 1950, when North Korean communist forces (backed at first by the Soviets and later by the Chinese) invaded western-backed South Korea. Viewing the invasion as a Soviet test of the West's resolve to halt communist expansion and still smarting from accusations that he was "soft on communism," Truman acted quickly and received U.N. approval to send in American troops led by General Douglas MacArthur, commander of allied forces in the Pacific during World War II. A series of decisions that lengthened the war and increased its toll in American lives, as well as a very public conflict with MacArthur, proved to be a great strain over the next two years.

In 1952, burdened with a variety of domestic and foreign crises, Truman opted not to seek another term as president. After ushering in his Republican successor, former general Dwight Eisenhower, he returned to a relatively quiet but busy life in Independence, writing his memoirs and supervising the establishment of the Truman Library.

Out of office, Truman enjoyed much more respect and affection than he had ever known while in office. This was especially true after his death in 1972, a time when many Americans were thoroughly disgusted with government and politicians in the wake of the Watergate affair and other scandals of the Nixon administration. To these people, Truman's honesty, decisiveness, and strong moral convictions were the very qualities in such desperately short supply.

This sentiment coincided with a movement among historians to re-evaluate Truman's presidency and cast it in a more favorable light. He is now praised for his forceful and courageous leadership during a critical period in history, not only in the United States but all over the world. Truman himself would have scoffed at the idea of being "redeemed" by a generation hungry for his plainness and forthright style. "I don't give a damn what history thinks of me," he once declared. "I know what I did and that's enough for me."

Sources

➤ **Books**

Donovan, Robert J., *Conflict and Crisis*, Norton, 1977.

Donovan, Robert J., *Tumultuous Years*, Norton, 1982.

Leavell, J. Perry, Jr., *Harry S. Truman*, Chelsea House, 1988.

Miller, Merle, *Plain Speaking: An Oral Biography of Harry S. Truman*, Berkeley, 1974.

Truman, Harry S., *Memoirs*, Vol. 1, *Year of Decisions*, 1955, Vol. 2, *Years of Trial and Hope*, Doubleday, 1956.

Truman, Margaret, *Harry S. Truman*, Morrow, 1972.

➤ **Periodicals**

America, January 13, 1973, p. 8 (opening quote).

National Review, "Harry S. Truman, RIP," January 19, 1973, pp. 79–80.

New Republic, "Harry S. Truman," January 6, 1973, pp. 10–11; "Memories of Competence in the White House: Truman Nostalgia," May 31, 1975, pp. 17–19.

Newsweek, "Farewell to Mr. Citizen," January 8, 1973, pp. 12–20.

New York Times, "Harry S. Truman: Decisive President," December 27, 1972.

Time, "The World of Harry Truman," January 8, 1973, pp. 15–18.

U.S. News and World Report, "Truman on His Presidency: 'I Tried to Give It Everything,'" January 8, 1973, pp. 25–28; "Harry Truman: New Folk Hero?," September 29, 1975, pp. 42–43.

Terry Waite

"**I** really do believe that we all have elements of good and bad in us. What I do is appeal to their better side, and they usually respond.''

Anglican church envoy Terry Waite worked behind the scenes during the 1980s to win the release of Westerners held hostage in the Middle East by fundamentalist Moslems until he, too, was kidnapped on January 20, 1987, in Beirut, Lebanon. He was born on May 31, 1939, in Styal, England.

Cameras clicked and whirred on January 20, 1987, as Anglican Church envoy Terry Waite left his Beirut hotel on yet another mission to win freedom for hostages held by Islamic Jihad, a pro-Iranian extremist group. Having requested a face-to-face meeting with the kidnappers, he headed for the home of his contact, a doctor from the American University Hospital. There he dismissed his Lebanese Christian bodyguards and awaited the arrival of the man who would actually take him to the meeting. The doctor later claimed that he was then called back to the hospital, only to return home and find that Waite was gone. Once lauded by a former hostage as "a man of hope in our darkest hour," the skilled negotiator had apparently become the latest casualty in the long-simmering conflict between fundamentalist Moslems and the West.

Terence Hardy Waite was born in a small village in northwestern England, the son of Lena Hardy and Thomas William Waite, a policeman. Eager to travel but not sure what he wanted to do with his life, he left school at sixteen and joined the British Army's Grenadier Guards. An allergy to the dye used in their uniforms soon forced him out of the service, at which time he decided to sign on with the Church Army, a religious organization similar to the Salvation Army.

In 1964, after completing studies at the Church Army College in London and at schools in Italy, Belgium, and the United States, Waite began working as a lay training advisor to the Anglican bishop of Bristol. His position required him to travel frequently to the United States and Africa, where he helped run a relief program in the Sudan for victims of a civil war. The challenges of performing church work in the Third World led him to accept a post as advisor to the first African archbishop of Uganda, Rwanda, and Burundi in 1968. He then went to work for the Vatican during the 1970s as a consultant on African missionaries before returning to England in 1980 to become the first layman to serve as personal assistant to the Archbishop of Canterbury, Robert Runcie. As Secretary for Communion Affairs, he was to function as liaison between the Church of England and its overseas affiliates.

No sooner had the archbishop's assistant settled into his new job than he found himself volunteering for a somewhat different assignment. After Iranian revolutionaries accused three Anglican missionaries of spying, Waite flew to Teheran on December 25, 1980, carrying a personal message to the Ayatollah Khomeini from Dr. Runcie. At an imposing 6'7" and approximately 250 pounds,

Waite wore the robes of a lay cleric to emphasize that his mission was on behalf of the Anglican Church, not the British government. Although no details were ever made public, he and Swedish embassy personnel worked together to secure the missionaries' freedom in early 1981. Hailed as a hero for his role in the affair, Waite was named a Member of the Order of the British Empire in June, 1982.

In late 1984, his expertise was again called upon to help resolve a hostage crisis, this time in Libya. It had begun earlier that year when a London policewoman was shot and killed by someone firing from inside the Libyan embassy at people demonstrating outside against the government of Colonel Muammar Gaddafi. Britain subsequently broke off diplomatic relations with Libya, expelling its embassy personnel and jailing several suspected militants. Gaddafi's response was to arrest four British citizens working in Libya.

The families of the prisoners appealed directly to Waite, who set off in November with hopes of meeting the Libyan leader. After weeks of behind-the-scenes negotiating, Gaddafi finally agreed to see Waite on Christmas Day. The Englishman spent most of their two-hour discussion trying to establish a personal rapport with his host, who seemed more inclined to want to talk about Greek philosophy and the relationship between Christianity and Islam in modern Africa than he did about the hostage situation. When at last the conversation turned to the problems between their countries, Gaddafi expressed concern about reports of Libyans being tortured in British prisons and harassed on the streets of London. Waite assured him that Libyans were not being tortured and suggested that the Anglican Church could set up a "hot line" for them to use to complain about harassment. The idea appealed to Gaddafi, and in February, 1985, he released the four hostages in exchange for Waite's promise that Libyans in Britain would get their hot line.

The envoy's popularity zoomed to even greater heights after his successful handling of the Libyan crisis. Later that same year, he played a key role in winning the freedom of three more prisoners: two Scottish engineers who had received unusually harsh sentences in Nigeria for conspiracy and the theft of a small plane, and the Reverend Benjamin Weir, a Presbyterian minister from the United States who had been kidnapped in Iran by Islamic Jihad and held for sixteen months.

News of these triumphs brought Waite even more acclaim. While he enjoyed the media attention he received for his efforts, he downplayed his image as some sort of diplomatic superman. "In any of these situations, there is no one single factor alone that achieves the release of anybody," he told a *People* magazine reporter. "There are complex patterns." His goal, he told another reporter from *People*, was "to behave responsibly and justly to all parties involved, captives and captors alike," never forgetting the need "to be perceptive and sensitive, to recognize that behind the stereotypes are people who are pushed into an extreme position, who are desperate or made to feel desperate."

In mid-November, 1985, Waite was asked to take on the most challenging and dangerous assignment of his career: negotiating the freedom of four American hostages kidnapped in Lebanon by Islamic Jihad. The four—the Reverend Lawrence Jenco, Terry Anderson, David Jacobsen, and Thomas Sutherland—had written a letter earlier that month to Dr. Runcie and President Ronald Reagan calling for new initiatives aimed at securing the release of all hostages held in Lebanon. Waite headed almost immediately for Beirut, leaving instructions that no ransom should be paid if he himself were kidnapped.

The confusing and ever-volatile political situation in Lebanon complicated the negotiation process, as did Islamic Jihad's insistence on linking the fate of the American hostages to that of seventeen Arab extremists jailed in Kuwait for the 1983 bombings of the French and American embassies. The governments of the United States and Kuwait refused to bargain on those terms, and even though talks continued sporadically throughout the rest of 1985 and into 1986, it appeared that Waite would never be able to bring about an agreement.

A breakthrough occurred in August, 1986, however, when Reverend Jenco was suddenly released, ostensibly for health reasons. Waite was in Beirut at the time but declined to comment on the details of his visit, noting only that his presence there was "not coincidental." Another victory came in November with the release of Jacobsen. Once again, virtually nothing was mentioned publicly about the extent of Waite's involvement other than the fact that his contributions had been crucial. "I'm not just a mailman," he told a *Maclean's* reporter. "It is very much a question of creative mediation."

The secrecy surrounding his missions soon prompted members of the press to speculate that Waite had made some sort of deal, perhaps one in which the United States government agreed to end its arms embargo against Iran—then at war with Iraq—in exchange for the hostages' freedom in what came to be known as the Iran-Contra affair. Such accusations infuriated the Anglican envoy, who declared that they threatened to destroy the trust he had cultivated for months among his Middle East contacts, thereby endangering his life and greatly reducing the chances that other hostages would be released.

Waite's worst fears came true in January, 1987. Convinced of the need to restore his damaged credibility, he decided to make his fifth trip to Beirut against the advice of British government officials and others concerned for his safety in the wake of the arms-for-hostages story. He quickly arranged a meeting with Islamic Jihad, whose members had promised to take him to see two of the Americans, Terry Anderson and Thomas Sutherland. Acknowledging that he was "walking on a minefield," Waite left his hotel on January 20 for what he hoped would prove to be another successful mission. Instead, he disappeared, and it was not until kidnapped British journalist John McCarthy was freed by his Islamic captors in August, 1991, that the world learned Waite had also been kidnapped and was still alive.

Throughout the fall of 1991, efforts to free all of the remaining Western hostages in Lebanon picked up steam. Finally, on November 18, after spending 1,763 days in captivity, Waite was released by Islamic Jihad, as was Sutherland. Most of that time, Waite later reported, he was kept chained to a wall in complete isolation and darkness and was periodically beaten and subjected to mock executions; later he shared a cell with Sutherland and Anderson.

But the joy over Waite's homecoming was quickly overshadowed by intense speculation that he had been used as a cover—perhaps unwittingly—by former White House aide Oliver North in the arms-for-hostages deal and that his involvement was the reason behind his kidnapping. Waite does not deny that he had contacts with North, but he insists he did not know that the United States was shipping arms to Iran in return for the release of American hostages. He also scoffs at reports that at the time of his kidnapping he was wearing a hidden transmitter given to him by North to make it possible for special-operations forces to track and rescue him. "People are playing games and governments are playing games all the time," he told reporters. "You just are walking through a minefield and one day you may tread on a mine. I treaded on a mine. That's about it."

Sources

➤ **Periodicals**

Detroit News, December 23, 1991, p. 3A.

Maclean's, "Waite's New Diplomacy," November 17, 1986, p. 44 (opening quote); "Hostages in Danger," February 16, 1987, pp. 18–19; "Hostages to Terror: The Ordeals of Anderson and Waite," April 30, 1990, pp. 40–41; "Clouds of Doubt," December 2, 1991.

Newsweek, "Terry Waite: A Decoy in Beirut?," December 2, 1991, p. 39.

People, "Hostage-Rescuer Terry Waite Flies in as a Missionary Impossible," August 18, 1986, pp. 59–60; December 22–29, 1986, pp. 54–56; "Terry Waite, a Symbol of Hope for Hostages in the Mideast, Vanishes on a Mercy Mission," February 23, 1987, p. 109; "Three Years after Terry Waite's Kidnapping in Beirut, His Mother Clings to Faith in His Return," January 22, 1990, pp. 85–88; "At Long Last, Freedom!," December 2, 1991, pp. 64–67.

Time, "Waite's Secret Mission," December 2, 1985, pp. 48–49; "An Extraordinary Envoy," November 10, 1986, p. 40; "The Sweet Taste of Freedom," December 2, 1991, p. 23; "Have Cloak, Will Travel," December 9, 1991, p. 44.

U.S. News & World Report, "Hostage Negotiator Who Stands Tall," November 25, 1985, p. 13.

Raoul Wallenberg

"*When there is suffering without limits, there can be no limits to the methods one should use to alleviate it.*"

Born on August 4, 1912, in Stockholm, Sweden, Raoul Wallenberg saved thousands of Hungarian Jews from extermination at the hands of the Nazis during World War II. He disappeared on January 17, 1945, while in the custody of the Soviet Army.

Address: Raoul Wallenberg Association, Riddargatan 10, S-114, 35 Stockholm, Sweden.

In July, 1944, Raoul Wallenberg arrived at the Swedish embassy in Budapest on a special mission: save as many Hungarian Jews as possible using whatever means he felt necessary. At first glance, the soft-spoken thirty-two year old did not fit the profile of a man who would be likely to undertake an assignment as dangerous as the one he faced in Budapest. A member of a distinguished Protestant family sometimes referred to as the "Rockefellers of Sweden," Wallenberg grew up in an atmosphere of wealth, prestige, and extensive foreign study and travel.

After graduating from the University of Michigan in 1935, Wallenberg went to work for a variety of banking and commercial concerns and ended up in Haifa, which was then part of Palestine. While there, he met many German-Jewish refugees and talked at length with them about the escalating persecution of Jews under the Nazi regime. He then joined an export firm whose Hungarian-Jewish owner could no longer risk visiting the central European countries under Hitler's control. Over the next two years, Wallenberg made several trips to Budapest and soon became aware of the growing discrimination against Hungarian Jews.

In the spring of 1944, Adolf Eichmann—the mastermind behind the deportations and concentration camps of the Holocaust—arrived in Hungary with orders to dispose of the country's Jews and other "undesirables." Determined to mount a rescue effort, representatives of the World Jewish Congress and the U.S. government's War Refugee Board approached neutral Sweden with a plan to send someone to Budapest to work under diplomatic cover in the Swedish embassy. Supplied with unlimited funds from the United States, this person would be responsible for cutting swiftly through bureaucratic red tape to help Jews escape. Raoul Wallenberg's name soon surfaced as the ideal candidate: intelligent, resourceful, and energetic, he had the necessary background and desire to pull off such a delicate mission.

Wallenberg jumped at the opportunity to rescue Hungarian Jews, despite the personal risks involved. "If I can help, if I can save a single person, I will go," he told the representative of the War Refugee Board. But the eager young man drove a hard bargain. He demanded free rein to do whatever he deemed necessary to save lives, including offering bribes and payoffs to the enemy. The Swedish government balked at this violation of protocol but finally relented in the face of Wallenberg's insistence.

The new "diplomat" arrived in Budapest on July 9, 1944. He

immediately made contacts with the other neutral embassies in Budapest—the Vatican, Switzerland, Spain, and Portugal—and with those Hungarians who were sympathetic to his cause. He recruited spies within the Hungarian fascist party and the Budapest police and even cultivated relationships with key Nazis, including Adolf Eichmann. Wallenberg's preferred tactic when dealing with his enemies was to threaten them with prosecution for war crimes. As Kati Marton observed in the *Atlantic*, "Wallenberg was capable of beating the Nazis at their own game. He bribed, flattered, forged, and smuggled; he learned to survive in a state of total anarchy and terror."

Against the advice of his fellow diplomats, Wallenberg issued hundreds of protective passports to the city's Jews. To speed up the process, he set up a special branch of the embassy in the Jewish quarter and hired some four hundred people (mostly Jews) to staff it, a move that automatically granted them diplomatic immunity. He also established thirty-two "safe houses" in Budapest, buildings rented by the embassy that were considered extensions of Swedish territory and therefore entitled to diplomatic protection. These safe houses eventually sheltered about twelve thousand people.

Events soon forced Wallenberg to adopt even bolder measures. Witnesses recall him chasing after a group of Jews on a forced death march to the Austrian border and pulling hundreds out of line, then persuading the German officers in charge to release them because they were carrying Swedish passports or other protective documents. On another occasion, he won freedom for hundreds more Jews who were already on board trains bound for Auschwitz by standing on top of one of the cars and handing out passports to anyone who could reach them. When he ran out of passports, he distributed food and medical supplies. Recalling the impact of such visits, a survivor remarked, "He gave us the sense that we were still human beings. . . . He talked to us and showed us that one human being cared about what was happening to us."

The pressures on Wallenberg intensified in October, 1944, when the relatively moderate Hungarian government was overthrown by a fascist regime more brutal than the Nazis. As the Germans withdrew, these Hungarian fascists set out to finish what the Nazis had begun. Wallenberg was now a man on the run, moving from one safe house to another to keep a step ahead of his enemies.

By January, 1945, the Russians occupied Budapest, and Wallenberg's mission was officially over. But he had formulated a master plan for rebuilding the city and helping resettle refugees, and he wanted to discuss it with the Soviets before heading back to Sweden. The Soviets were equally eager to talk to him. Suspicious of his contacts with the Hungarians, the Nazis, and the Americans, and well aware that he was a member of one of Europe's wealthiest families, they asked him to report to their army headquarters for questioning. No doubt believing that his diplomatic immunity would continue to protect him, Wallenberg agreed. He disappeared for two days, then returned to Budapest in the company of several Soviet soldiers. Remarking to a colleague that he wasn't sure if he was the Russians' guest or their prisoner, Wallenberg set out again on January 17 for what he believed to be another meeting at Soviet army headquarters. No one affiliated with the Swedish embassy ever saw him again.

Eager to establish good postwar relations with the Kremlin, Swedish government officials were reluctant to press the Soviets for information about Wallenberg's whereabouts. The Russians maintained that he was not in their custody and speculated that he had been kidnapped by Hungarian Nazis before leaving Budapest. Yet more than a dozen former Soviet prisoners who made their way back to the West shortly after the war reported seeing Wallenberg in various Moscow prisons. Throughout the rest of the 1940s and the 1950s, Swedish diplomats continued to make half-hearted inquiries about the missing man, usually in response to requests from the Wallenberg family. The Soviets either ignored the inquiries or denied any knowledge of Wallenberg.

Finally, on February 6, 1957, the Soviets issued a brief memo stating that Wallenberg had been imprisoned in Moscow until his death from a heart attack on July 17, 1947. This explanation did not satisfy Wallenberg's family or the Swedish government, which demanded some hard evidence of the diplomat's fate. Kremlin officials stood by the contents of the memo, insisting that Wallenberg was dead and their files contained no additional material. Meanwhile, reports of Wallenberg sightings at prisons throughout the Soviet Union surfaced sporadically during the 1960s, 1970s, and 1980s, most recently in 1987.

In the years since a series of articles published in the late 1970s brought his story to the attention of a worldwide audience, Raoul Wallenberg has become an international symbol of courage and Soviet heartlessness. Several investigative committees have sprung up in Great Britain, the United States, and Israel in an effort to free the diplomat or at least learn the truth about his disappearance.

Human rights activists and the Wallenberg family—especially Raoul's half-brother, Guy von Dardel, and half-sister, Nina Lagergren—remain convinced that the Russians have yet to tell the truth about what really happened to Raoul Wallenberg once he vanished from Budapest. The recent opening up of Soviet society has sparked hope that new information will be forthcoming. In December, 1991, for example, documents made public for the first time show that the KGB concealed evidence about the Wallenberg case from the rest of the Soviet government until 1956. The same documents also support the claim that Wallenberg died in prison of a heart attack in 1947, although they furnish no conclusive proof and offer no clues as to why he was held in the first place.

Few observers believe Wallenberg is still alive, but von Dardel and Lagergren cling to the hope that he might have survived somewhere in the Soviet prison system. "People often say I am indulging in wishful thinking, imagining my brother is still alive," remarks Lagergren. "They are wrong. It is wishful thinking to imagine him dead. To believe he has been spared these years of being buried alive. That is wishful thinking."

Sources

➤ **Books**

Anger, Per, *With Raoul Wallenberg in Budapest: Memories of the War Years in Hungary*, translated from Swedish, Schocken Books, 1981.

Bierman, John, *Righteous Gentile: The Story of Raoul Wallenberg, Missing Hero of the Holocaust*, Viking, 1981.

Lester, Elenore, *Wallenberg: The Man in the Iron Web*, Prentice-Hall, 1982.

Marton, Kati, *Wallenberg*, Random House, 1982.

Rosenfeld, Harvey, *Raoul Wallenberg, Angel of Rescue: Heroism and Torment in the Gulag*, Prometheus Books, 1982.

Smith, Danny, *Wallenberg: Lost Hero*, Templegate, 1986.

Werbell, Frederick E., and Thurston Clarke, *Lost Hero: The Mystery of Raoul Wallenberg*, McGraw-Hill, 1982.

➤ Periodicals

Atlantic, "The Wallenberg Mystery," November, 1980, pp. 33–60.

Detroit Free Press, "Soviets Allow File Search for Swedish Hero," August 28, 1990.

Encyclopedia of World Biography: Twentieth Century Supplement, McGraw-Hill, 1987, pp. 512–513 (opening quote).

Maclean's, "Where Is Raoul Wallenberg?," November 26, 1979, p. 12; "On the 35-Year-Old Trail of a Missing War Hero," March 2, 1981, p. 16; "A Pain-Filled Mystery," October 30, 1989, p. 47.

National Review, "The Last of the Pimpernels," August 17, 1979, p. 1019.

New Statesman, "What Happened to Wallenberg?," May 18, 1979, p. 715; "Is Wallenberg Alive?," February 27, 1981, p. 3.

New York Times, "Soviet Files Show K.G.B. Cover-Up in the Disappearance of Wallenberg," December 28, 1991, p. 6.

New York Times Magazine, "The Lost Hero of the Holocaust: The Search for Sweden's Raoul Wallenberg," March 30, 1980.

Reader's Digest, "The Haunting Riddle of Raoul Wallenberg," January, 1991, pp. 114–118.

U.S. News and World Report, "A Lost Prisoner of the Gulag Still Holds Moscow Hostage," June 26, 1989, pp. 34–36.

➤ Other

A dramatization of Raoul Wallenberg's life entitled "Wallenberg: A Hero's Story," was broadcast as a television miniseries in 1985.

Booker T. Washington

"$\mathbf{N}$*o race that has anything to contribute to the markets of the world is long in any degree ostracized."*

Booker T. Washington, founder of Alabama's Tuskegee Institute, was the most prominent Black-American leader in the United States for twenty years around the turn of the century. He is believed to have been born on April 5, 1856, in Hale's Ford, Virginia, and died on November 14, 1915, in Tuskegee, Alabama.

On September 18, 1895, Black-American educator Booker T. Washington delivered one of the opening speeches at the Cotton States and International Exposition in Atlanta, Georgia. Addressing a racially-mixed audience, he declared that it was time for Black Americans to put aside their desire for civil and social equality and concentrate instead on making themselves a vital part of the nation's economy through education and productivity. Once they had demonstrated their ability to contribute and succeed, he maintained, Black Americans would most certainly be granted the rights that years of protests had not yet won.

As a result of that single, fifteen-minute speech—later dubbed the "Atlanta Compromise"—Washington gained the enthusiastic support of Whites and many Blacks across the country and reigned for the next twenty years as the preeminent spokesman for Black America. Although his conservative philosophy of "accommodation" was eventually discredited by more militant Black Americans who thought it was naive and potentially self-defeating to assume that Whites would ever willingly grant Blacks equality without a struggle, Washington still commands respect for his role in motivating Black Americans—especially southern Black Americans—to strive for self-improvement through education.

Born into slavery on a small Virginia plantation, Booker Taliaferro (he added the Washington later) was the son of an unknown White man and the plantation's cook, a woman named Jane. Not long after her son's birth, Jane married a fellow slave, Washington Ferguson, who fled to Malden, West Virginia, during the Civil War. The family was reunited there after the war, and at his stepfather's insistence, nine-year-old Booker went to work. He labored first in the salt and coal mines and later as a houseboy for a Mrs. Ruffner, whose husband owned the mines. Mrs. Ruffner was a very strict and proper New Englander, and she instilled in her young employee a lifelong appreciation for cleanliness, order, and sound work habits.

Booker attended school whenever he could but was largely self-taught. Despite his humble background, he dreamed of attending college, and at the age of sixteen he set out to fulfill that dream. Traveling mostly on foot and with virtually no money, he made his way to Hampton, Virginia, taking odd jobs along the way to finance his trip. Arriving bedraggled and dirty at the Hampton Institute, a well-known Black college that emphasized training in practical skills and adherence to high moral standards, he managed to secure admission to the school and was hired as a janitor to help defray the cost of his tuition and room and board.

Washington graduated from Hampton with honors in 1875 and went back to Malden, where he taught school for several years. He then moved to Washington, D.C., and briefly attended the Wayland Seminary, but its classical academic curriculum and lack of work-study opportunities only served to convince him that Hampton's approach was more in tune with the needs of Black Americans and the realities of the life they faced, particularly in the South. In 1879 he returned there to teach, renewing his friendship with the man he considered to be his mentor, Samuel Chapman Armstrong, the White principal of the institute. Washington had been a member of the faculty for only two years when Armstrong recommended him for the principal's job at a proposed vocational school for Black Americans in Tuskegee, Alabama. Despite the fact that Alabama officials had been looking for a White man, they hired Washington.

The youthful (he was only twenty-five) educator's eagerness to assume his new position quickly turned to dismay when he discovered upon reaching Tuskegee that the Alabama legislature had not purchased any land or buildings or hired any staff other than himself. Furthermore, the state had appropriated only $2,000 toward the establishment of the school, and that sum was earmarked just for salaries. So Washington launched a one-man campaign to bring the Tuskegee Institute to life, recruiting students and teachers, developing a curriculum in keeping with his belief in practical education, and raising funds for land, buildings, and supplies. His most generous supporters were northern industrialists like Andrew Carnegie, who admired Washington's climb from slavery to success, his moderate politics, and his emphasis on the virtues of hard work, frugality, and self-reliance. At the same time, he had to reassure angry and suspicious southern Whites that the school would improve, not ruin, the Black labor force.

The first classes were held in 1881 in an old, rundown shack donated by a local church, but within just a few years, several new buildings—constructed with brick from the institute's own kilns and a considerable amount of student labor—rose on the site of an abandoned plantation just outside town that became Tuskegee's permanent home. By the end of the decade, the institute offered training in a variety of skilled trades, including carpentry, blacksmithing, printing, and shoemaking. Male students also studied agriculture, and female students took courses in sewing, cooking, and other subjects related to homemaking; all received instruction in manners and personal hygiene, and all were required to attend religious services and observe a strict daily schedule of work and study. Agricultural extension programs and special farm conferences run by one of the institute's most distinguished faculty members, George Washington Carver, earned national praise and were credited with improving the lot of Black-American sharecroppers throughout the South.

Washington dominated life at Tuskegee throughout the thirty-four years he served as its president, shaping it into one of the most prestigious Black institutions in the United States as well as the best funded, thanks to his ability to attract the support of White philanthropists. As significant and enduring as this achievement was, he wielded even greater influence as a nationally-recognized spokesman for Black Americans. From the late 1890s until shortly before his death in 1915, Washington was unquestionably the most powerful Black man in the country. Dozens of business leaders and politicians (including presidents Theodore Roosevelt and William Howard Taft) regularly sought his advice on race relations, southern politics, appointing Black Americans to federal jobs, and granting funds to Black institutions. As a result, he built up an extensive network of loyal supporters (Black and White) who came to be known as the "Tuskegee Machine." These people helped publicize and promote Washington's beliefs, advance the careers of those who agreed with him, and stifle the voices of those who did not.

Younger, more liberal Black-American intellectuals such as W. E. B. Du Bois took issue with Washington's accommodationist philosophies and attempts by the Tuskegee Machine to squelch all dissent. They denounced his tolerance of segregation and restrictive voting laws and accused him of perpetuating racial stereotypes. They also criticized him for focusing only on vocational training and ignoring (and even scorning) higher education, a policy they felt would create a permanent underclass of Black-American laborers and a shortage of Black-American leaders. The Tuskegee Machine responded by defending Washington and trying to discredit the liberals, especially Du Bois, whom Washington regarded as his chief rival. This in turn further antagonized the liberals and ultimately prompted them to form groups of their own, including the National Association for the Advancement of Colored People (NAACP).

Among White Americans, however, Washington continued to enjoy immense personal prestige and influence, for the conservative and conciliatory views he publicly championed on economics, politics, society, and race did not differ substantially from those of most White Americans. Yet behind the scenes, he quietly and subtly pursued a somewhat more "radical" agenda of which none of his White contemporaries and few of his Black ones were aware. In the South, for example, he secretly backed efforts to block passage of restrictive voting and segregation laws and financed attempts to challenge such laws in the courtroom. He agreed with those who advocated that all citizens must meet certain educational and taxpaying requirements before being allowed to vote but repeatedly urged that the requirements be applied equally to Blacks *and* Whites. And he spoke out against educational inequities and racially-biased residential zoning laws. By the early 1900s, however, race relations in the United States had markedly deteriorated. Facing more restrictions than they had in decades, some Black Americans felt Washington and his accommodationist policies were at least partly to blame.

The beginning of the end for Washington came in March, 1911. While in a New York City apartment building searching for the home of a friend, he was beaten by a man named Ulrich, a White resident of the same building who mistook the renowned educator for a burglar and also accused him of peeking through the keyhole of an apartment occupied by a White woman. Washington filed assault charges but gave such vague and evasive answers in court that Ulrich was acquitted.

His personal reputation tarnished by the highly-publicized incident and subsequent trial, Washington saw his influence start to decline. Another blow came in 1912, when Democrat Woodrow Wilson was elected to the presidency, marking the first time in more than fifteen years that the Republicans—ardent supporters of Washington's views—were not in charge of the government. The post-election fallout also affected members of the Tuskegee Machine, who suddenly found themselves stripped of political power.

By the time Washington succumbed to hardening of the arteries and exhaustion in 1915, he had lost many of his followers to the NAACP and its more militant approach to achieving racial justice and equality. Yet in his heyday, he had managed to achieve some rather ambitious goals—not the least of which was establishing the Tuskegee Institute—by winning over a very diverse group of progressive southern Whites, northern Whites with an interest in the South, and most of his fellow Black Americans.

Sources

➤ **Books**

Adair, Gene, *George Washington Carver*, Chelsea House, 1989.

Harlan, Louis R., *Booker T. Washington: The Making of a Black Leader, 1856–1901*, Oxford University Press, 1972.

Harlan, Louis R., and others, editors, *The Booker T. Washington Papers*, fourteen volumes, University of Illinois Press, 1972–1989.

Meier, August, *Negro Thought in America, 1880–1915: Racial Ideologies in the Age of Booker T. Washington*, University of Michigan Press, 1963.

Schroeder, Alan, *Booker T. Washington*, Chelsea House, 1992.

Stafford, Mark, *W. E. B. Du Bois*, Chelsea House, 1989.

Thornbrough, Emma Lou, editor, *Booker T. Washington*, Prentice-Hall, 1969.

Washington, Booker T., *The Story of My Life and Work*, J. L. Nichols, 1900. Reprint. Greenwood Press, 1970.

Washington, Booker T., *Up from Slavery*, A. L. Burt, 1901. Reprint. Viking Penguin, 1986.

Washington, Booker T., *My Larger Education*, Doubleday, Page, 1911. Reprint. Mnemosyne Publishing, 1969.

➤ **Periodicals**

Ebony, "Ten Greats of Black History," August, 1972, pp. 35–42.

New York Times, November 15, 1915.

Ryan White

*"R*yan and his family always believed there would be a miracle. But that didn't happen. I believe God gave us that miracle in Ryan. He healed a wounded spirit in the world and made it whole."— Reverend Raymond Probasco at Ryan White's funeral.

Born December 6, 1971, in Kokomo, Indiana, Ryan White became a national symbol of courage and optimism as he fought to gain acceptance for AIDS patients. He died from complications of the disease on April 8, 1990.

R yan White was only three days old when doctors told his mother, Jeanne, that hemophilia was the cause of her son's unusually severe bleeding following a routine circumcision. An inherited disease marked by a lack of sufficient clotting factor in the blood, hemophilia was a life-threatening condition until researchers discovered that infusions of a blood-clotting compound known as Factor VIII could help hemophiliacs control the profuse bleeding that often followed a minor cut or bruise.

At first, Ryan was hospitalized two or three times a month to receive his infusions, which were obtained from the concentrated blood of many donors. Eventually, Jeanne White learned how to infuse her son at home. (Ryan's father, who was divorced from Jeanne, had little contact with Ryan and his younger sister, Andrea.) Despite the treatments, Ryan still had to avoid most physical activities because of the danger of injury.

In December, 1984, Ryan came down with a bad cold that wouldn't go away. He began to lose weight and soon became too ill to attend school. Finally, doctors concluded that the cause of Ryan's mysterious decline was AIDS—acquired immune deficiency syndrome. They speculated that he had contracted the fatal virus from a contaminated batch of Factor VIII, which at that time was not being screened for AIDS.

Ryan hovered near death for a while from a type of pneumonia common in AIDS patients, then gradually responded to treatment and improved enough to leave the hospital by the spring of 1985. An honor student, he kept up with his schoolwork at home by means of a telephone hook-up with his classroom. But his real wish was to go back to school as soon as possible. "I can't play sports; school is all I have," Jeanne White remembers him saying. "I want to be with my friends, like everybody else."

When Ryan was strong enough to return to class, he encountered strong opposition from some parents in Kokomo who feared that he might infect their children with the AIDS virus. Even though all medical evidence indicated that there was virtually no chance Ryan's classmates could catch AIDS from him, district officials invoked an old state law barring students with communicable diseases. An outraged Jeanne decided to fight the ban in court.

Six tension-filled months later, victory for the Whites appeared certain when a county public health official declared that routine contact with Ryan did not endanger the lives of his fellow students.

Ryan attended classes for only one day in the spring of 1986 before worried parents were again successful in their efforts to have him barred. Jeanne White appealed until July, when her opponents ran out of funds. In August, 1986, a judge ruled that Ryan could attend high school *if* he used a separate bathroom and disposable utensils in the cafeteria and did not sign up for gym class.

Although the judge's ruling ended the legal battle, the war was far from over for the Whites. Hostile townspeople slashed the tires on their car and bombarded it with eggs, left piles of garbage on their lawn, sent hateful anonymous letters, and even fired a bullet through their living room window. At the grocery store, clerks threw Jeanne's change on the counter to avoid touching her hands. In school, Ryan was often subjected to cruel jokes and name calling. Through it all, the quiet teenager—who was also dealing with a steady onslaught of AIDS-related health problems—remained firm in his resolve to live as normal a life as possible.

Ryan's nationally publicized fight to return to school made that dream difficult, however. When his health permitted, the unwilling celebrity appeared on television and radio programs and gave talks on AIDS, especially to other teenagers. He felt it was important to share with as many people as possible what he knew about AIDS and what he had experienced as an AIDS patient.

Ryan also inspired others to take up his cause against fear and prejudice. Singer Elton John was one of the first to come forward, offering his support during the Kokomo ordeal and eventually becoming very close to the Whites. Fellow Indiana native Michael Jackson was also a special friend, as were several other prominent entertainers, sports figures, and politicians.

Despite such encouragement, the Whites soon could no longer bear the strain of living in Kokomo. In mid-1987, the proceeds from a television movie on Ryan's plight enabled the family to move to Cicero, a much smaller town nearby. The residents of Cicero extended an unexpectedly warm welcome, and Ryan flourished. Healthier than he had been in years due to the experimental drug AZT, he gained weight, strength, and confidence. He lined up a summer job in a skateboard shop, earned his driver's license, and made the rounds of the local fast-food restaurants with friends. He still found his celebrity status embarrassing (he often declared that he wouldn't hesitate an instant to trade his fame for good health), but understood his value as a teacher and role model. "I'm helping people, I think, and I don't want people treated like me," Ryan told a reporter for *People* magazine. "But now I just want to be like everyone else, 'cause that's what counts in high school."

Ryan spent most of the next two years living the normal life he craved. Halfway through his senior year, however, he began to suffer from an increasing number of AIDS-related health problems. In March, 1990, while in Los Angeles to attend the Academy Awards ceremony and present an award to former President Ronald Reagan, Ryan developed an unusually sore throat and severe coughing spells. The Whites left immediately for Indiana, arriving early in the morning of March 29 and driving directly to the hospital. Ryan's condition deteriorated rapidly over the next few days, and as news of his latest crisis spread, the hospital was flooded with calls, letters, telegrams, and presents from thousands of well-wishers.

A week later, on April 8, 1990, Ryan succumbed to complications from the disease he had struggled against for more than five years. Over fifteen hundred people—friends as well as strangers—attended his funeral in Indianapolis, and flags flew at half-mast throughout Indiana on orders from the governor. Elton John led the congregation in singing a hymn and then performed a song he wrote in honor of the young man whose compassion, courage, and optimism had set an example for an entire nation. Observed Reverend Raymond Probasco in his eulogy: "It was Ryan who first humanized the disease called AIDS. He allowed us to see the boy who just wanted, more than anything else, to be like other children."

Sources

➤ **Books**

Cunningham, Ann Marie, and Ryan White, *Ryan White: My Own Story*, Dial, 1991.

➤ **Periodicals**

Ladies' Home Journal, "'I Don't Want My Son to Be Forgotten,'" August, 1990.

New York Times, April 9, 1990, p. D10; April 12, 1990, p. B12.

Newsweek, "AIDS in the Classroom," March 3, 1986, p. 6; "Remembering Ryan White," April 23, 1990, p. 24.

People, "AIDS: A Diary of the Plague in America," August 3, 1987; "The Quiet Victories of Ryan White," May 30, 1988, pp. 88–96; "Candle in the Wind," April 23, 1990, pp. 86–97; "A Year After Ryan White's Death, His Mother, Jeanne, Picks Up the Pieces and Carries on His Fight," April 8, 1991, pp. 118–119.

Saturday Evening Post, "The Happier Days for Ryan White," March, 1988.

Scholastic Update, "The Battle against Disease: Three Stories," April 20, 1987, p. 4.

Time, "The 'Miracle' of Ryan White," April 23, 1990, p. 39.

U.S. News and World Report, "The Little Hostage to a Killer in the Blood," September 8, 1986, p. 10; "To a Poster Child, Dying Young," April 16, 1990, p. 8.

Simon Wiesenthal

"I think I am one of the last witnesses. And a last *witness, before he leaves this world, has an obligation to speak out. . . . My work is a warning for the murderers of tomorrow."*

Born on December 31, 1908, in what is now Ukraine, Simon Wiesenthal narrowly escaped death as a concentration camp inmate during World War II. He has devoted his life since then to the hunt for Nazi war criminals.

Address: Jewish Historical Documentation Center, Salztorgasse 6/IV/5, 1010 Vienna, Austria.

On May 5, 1945, an armored unit of the U.S. Army rolled into Austria's notorious Mauthausen concentration camp. Thirty-six-year-old Simon Wiesenthal—one of the few inmates still alive—staggered into the courtyard and touched the white star on the first tank to enter the camp, then collapsed into the arms of an American officer. Six feet tall and weighing only ninety pounds, Wiesenthal was barely more than a walking skeleton. But after having spent almost four years as a Nazi prisoner, he had resolved to greet his liberators on his feet, not amid the dead and dying in the bunkhouse.

Wiesenthal's long journey to Mauthausen began in Buczacz, Galicia, part of the Austro-Hungarian Empire at the time of his birth in 1908, but later annexed by the Soviet Union. Poles, Austrians, and Ukrainians routinely fought over the region, and much of their hostility was taken out on the local Jewish community. In 1925, the Wiesenthals finally left Buczacz when Mrs. Wiesenthal, who was widowed during World War I, remarried and moved her family to a town in the Carpathian Mountains not far from Lvov.

After a brief but pleasant stay in his new home, Wiesenthal went off to college, graduating from the architectural engineering program at the Czech Technical Institute in Prague and then returning to Lvov to set up a private practice. In 1936, he married his childhood sweetheart, Cyla Muller, and they quickly settled into what they both believed would be a happy and prosperous life together.

With the outbreak of World War II in September, 1939, however, the Soviets occupied Lvov and began arresting Jews, confiscating their bank accounts, and forcing them out of certain jobs; Wiesenthal had to close his architectural firm and go to work as a factory mechanic. The persecution entered a new and more terrifying phase after the Nazis invaded the Soviet Union in June, 1941. Wiesenthal and his wife were taken first to a concentration camp and then to a special forced-labor camp, from which Cyla escaped in late 1942 with the help of the Polish Underground. Supplied with false papers, she passed herself off for the rest of the war as a Polish gentile named Irena Kowalska.

Wiesenthal spent the next three years in several different concentration camps, facing certain death on several occasions but always winning last-minute reprieves from execution. He even managed to escape and hide for several months early in 1944 but was captured and sent back to camp, where he made two unsuccessful suicide attempts. In January, 1945, as the Soviet Army began heading west into Poland, Wiesenthal and thirty-three of his fellow prisoners were forced to march to Germany and then were taken by truck to the Mauthausen concentration camp, where he remained until the U.S. Army arrived in early spring.

As he regained his strength, Wiesenthal was at first consumed by an overwhelming desire for violent revenge. But soon he realized that if he killed his former enemies, the world might never learn the extent of their crimes. Making sure that the millions who had died were not forgotten thus became more important than punishing those responsible. As he explained to *New York Times Magazine* reporter Clyde A. Farnsworth, "To go on living was a burden, but someone had to live on and tell what it was really like."

Just a few weeks after his liberation, Wiesenthal volunteered his services to a U.S. Army war crimes unit, taking statements from witnesses and gathering evidence for use in the upcoming trials of suspected war criminals. After the unit moved to Linz, Austria, Wiesenthal talked with hundreds more survivors as head of the Jewish Central Committee, a relief and welfare organization that helped refugees track down members of their families. He recorded not only their names but also their stories for later use in identifying and prosecuting war criminals.

In late 1945, Simon and Cyla Wiesenthal—both of whom had believed the other was dead—were at last reunited. Their joy was tinged with sadness, however; of ninety-one family members, only the two of them had escaped death. Lvov was in ruins, its Jewish community virtually wiped out. More than ever, Wiesenthal felt it was his responsibility as a survivor to make sure justice was done.

He continued his investigative work for the U.S. Army until 1947, when he and some thirty volunteers established the Jewish Historical Documentation Center in Linz, an association dedicated to assembling evidence for future trials. But prosecutions of war criminals declined as relations cooled between the United States and the Soviet Union, and in 1954 a frustrated Wiesenthal closed the documentation center and went into refugee work. But one dossier in particular still haunted him: that of Adolf Eichmann, the Gestapo chief who had implemented Hitler's "Final Solution" and then disappeared after the end of the war. Knowing that numerous top Nazis had carefully planned their escapes in the event of a German defeat, Wiesenthal speculated that Eichmann was among those who had found a safe haven somewhere.

Throughout the rest of the 1950s, Wiesenthal sifted through the various clues his many informants passed along to him. When Eichmann's wife tried to have him declared legally dead, Wiesenthal was able to block her petition by exposing the fact that her key witness was her own brother-in-law; he also produced sworn statements from an SS officer and other witnesses testifying that they had seen Eichmann alive after the war. In 1952, Mrs. Eichmann and her children vanished, and Wiesenthal soon learned that she had been issued a passport under her maiden name. He interpreted her disappearance to mean that Eichmann now felt safe enough to have his family join him in exile.

The turning point in the case came about eighteen months later. Wiesenthal, who had taken up stamp collecting as a hobby, was looking over some unusual stamps with a fellow collector. The man then brought out an especially beautiful one he had just received on a letter from a friend in Argentina, a former German officer. Reading aloud to Wiesenthal from the officer's letter, the man noted that his friend had met many fellow Germans in Argentina, including that "awful swine Eichmann who ordered the Jews about. He lives near Buenos Aires. . . . "

Wiesenthal immediately shared this and other information with the World Jewish Congress and the Israeli government. By late 1959, it appeared that Eichmann was indeed living with his family in Argentina under an assumed name. Israeli agents subsequently confirmed his identity and kidnapped him in Buenos Aires. Tried and convicted in Israel thanks in large part to evidence collected and handed over by Wiesenthal, Eichmann was hanged for his crimes on May 31, 1962.

Encouraged by the renewed interest in Nazi war criminals following Eichmann's capture and trial, Wiesenthal reopened the Jewish Historical Documentation Center in 1961—this time in Vienna—and vowed to devote full time to the pursuit of justice. Funded by donations and the proceeds from Wiesenthal's speeches and writings, the center has continued to assemble dossiers on more than six thousand suspected war criminals, about eleven hundred of whom have been tried. Among the most notable have been Karl Silberbauer, the Gestapo officer who arrested Anne Frank; Franz Murer, the so-called "Butcher of Wilno" who was responsible for the deaths of 80,000 Lithuanian Jews; Erich Rajakowitsch, who was in charge of deporting and exterminating Dutch Jews; and Franz Stangl, commandant of the Treblinka and Sobibor concentration camps, where hundreds of thousands of people died.

Although much work remains to be done—the German government's files on war criminals list 160,000 names—Wiesenthal has resigned himself to the fact that most of the guilty will never be brought to justice; the ones located and tried in recent years are quite elderly, and many are in poor health. As a result, he is spending more of his time nowadays educating young people about the Holocaust and speaking out against neo-Nazi movements, because, as he says, "the new generation has to hear what the older generation refuses to tell it."

Yet Wiesenthal has not given up entirely; with the help of a few young assistants, he continues his work at the documentation center. "I simply have a moral obligation to keep after these men," he explained in a *Reader's Digest* article. "They must know that they are still held accountable, and none of them at this moment knows whether or not justice is just a step behind him."

Sources

➤ **Books**

Noble, Iris, *Nazi Hunter: Simon Wiesenthal*, Messner, 1979.

Wiesenthal, Simon, *Justice Not Vengeance*, translated from German by Ewald Osers, Grove Weidenfeld, 1989.

Wiesenthal, Simon, *The Murderers Among Us: The Simon Wiesenthal Memoirs*, edited, with a profile of the author, by Joseph Wechsberg, McGraw-Hill, 1967.

➤ **Periodicals**

Maclean's, "Stalking the Nazis," December 9, 1985, pp. 6–7; "A Career of Nazi Hunting," May 25, 1987, p. 40.

New York Times Magazine, "Sleuth with Six Million Clients," February 2, 1964.

People, "On Location in Budapest, Nazi Hunter Simon Wiesenthal Relives the Horrors of His Past," August 1, 1988, pp. 48–49.

Reader's Digest, "The Man Who Will Not Forget," February, 1973, pp. 154–164.

Time, "Wiesenthal's Last Hunt," September 26, 1977, pp. 36–38.

William Griffith Wilson

*"***S***uddenly the room lit up with a great white light. . . . It seemed to me, in the mind's eye, that I was on a mountain and that a wind not of air but of spirit was blowing. And then it burst upon me that I was a free man."*

Known simply as "Bill W." to all but those closest to him, William Griffith Wilson co-founded Alcoholics Anonymous. He was born in East Dorset, Vermont, on November 26, 1895, and died in Miami Beach, Florida, on January 24, 1971.

Williⁱⁱⁱam Griffith Wilson was a twenty-two-year-old army officer facing the prospect of combat in World War I when he had his first taste of alcohol. He had grown up in rural Vermont, a shy, gawky boy whose parents divorced when he was ten and left him in the care of his maternal grandparents. Made fun of by other children and plagued by feelings of loneliness and inadequacy, Wilson "developed a fierce resolve to win—to be a No. 1 man." He pushed himself to excel at everything he tried just to prove that he could do it, whether it was playing the violin in the school orchestra or serving as captain of the baseball team.

Wilson went on to attend Vermont's Norwich University, where he majored in engineering. He then enrolled in Officers Training School when the United States entered World War I and ended up stationed near New Bedford, Massachusetts. At a party one night, Wilson accepted a cocktail, hoping it would help him overcome the self-consciousness he always experienced at social gatherings. "That barrier that had always stood between me and other people came down," he later recalled. "I felt I belonged, that I was part of life. What magic there was in those drinks! I could talk and be clever."

But alcohol had a frighteningly powerful physical and emotional effect on the young man; instead of developing a gradual dependency, he became hooked from the very beginning and was never able to stop after just one drink. More often than not, he drank until he passed out. Wilson nevertheless managed to hide his growing problem from his fiancée, Lois Burnham, and the two were married just before he shipped out to France.

After the war, Wilson and his wife settled in New York City, where he went to work as a fraud investigator for an insurance firm and attended Brooklyn Law School at night. But he soon succumbed to the lure of the stock market, and during the 1920s he became one of the most successful and respected analysts on Wall Street. He and Lois enjoyed all the comforts of an upper-middle-class lifestyle, including a luxurious apartment and country club memberships. But his drinking was now out of control, and his behavior had grown increasingly violent and abusive. Particularly shameful incidents led Wilson to vow afterward that he would quit drinking, but that promise was usually forgotten by the end of the day. "Men of genius conceive their best projects when drunk," he told Lois.

The stock market crash in 1929 accelerated his mental and physical deterioration. He and Lois lost everything, and they were forced to move in with her parents. Lois went to work as a sales clerk at Macy's, while her husband stayed home and drank, reduced to downing bathtub gin and bootleg whisky once Prohibition made it impossible to obtain alcohol legally. His sporadic attempts to recover financially were invariably derailed by drinking, and by 1934 he had hit rock bottom, consumed by fear and self-hatred.

That summer, Wilson checked into Manhattan's Charles B. Towns Hospital, a special facility for the treatment of alcoholics. His doctor, William Silkworth, did not adhere to the prevailing view that alcoholism was the result of a lack of willpower, character, and moral discipline; instead, he preferred to regard alcoholism as a disease. Under Dr. Silkworth's care, Wilson did manage to stay sober until November, when he slipped back into his old habits.

At about this same time, an old friend named Ebby Thatcher stopped by for a visit. Wilson offered him a drink, but Thatcher refused, explaining that he had given up alcohol with the help of a friend named Rowland. According to Thatcher, Rowland had gone to Swiss psychoanalyst Carl Jung to conquer his addiction once and for all. When his patient resumed drinking after a period of sobriety, Jung refused to continue treatment, noting that the only way some alcoholics are able change their behavior is to undergo a profound spiritual experience. Jung had tried—and failed—to bring about such an experience in Rowland, who subsequently found emotional salvation in an evangelistic organization known as the Oxford Group. Rowland passed the word along to Thatcher, who also overcame his drinking problem with the help of Oxford Group principles. And now Thatcher wanted to share the message with Wilson.

Wilson was not quite ready to hear it, however. While he could not get Thatcher's story out of his mind, he rejected the notion that some "higher power" could make a difference in his life. He continued drinking and soon found himself back in the hospital. Once again, Thatcher paid him visit, and once again, Wilson listened to his story. "Ebby told me he had to admit he was licked," explained Wilson. "He had to openly admit his sins, make restitution to people he had harmed, and give love without a price tag. He had to pray to whatever God he believed in—and if he didn't believe in a God, to act as if he did."

It took another drinking binge and another stay in the hospital before Wilson felt desperate enough to try anything. One sleepless night, he called out, "If there is a God, let him show himself!" Then came the bright white light and the sudden feeling of peace. At first, he thought he might have been hallucinating, but Dr. Silkworth convinced him to accept the episode as a genuine "psychic occurrence." Brimming with enthusiasm, Wilson checked out of the hospital on December 18, 1934, determined to help other alcoholics experience a similar spiritual awakening.

For six months he pursued his goal with zeal, pulling drunks out of bars and taking them to Oxford Group meetings. These initial efforts were disastrous—no one stayed sober except Wilson—until Dr. Silkworth pointed out that he was *preaching* rather than *talking*, and that he might do better if he emphasized medical facts over religion. Wilson did not know quite what to do with this advice. How could he, a businessman, ever hope to speak authoritatively on medical matters, especially to an uncooperative audience?

The solution to his problem came from an unexpected source. While on a business trip to Akron, Ohio, in the spring of 1935, Wilson found himself tempted to drink at the end of an especially frustrating day. Realizing he needed to talk to another alcoholic to overcome the urge, he picked up a directory of local churches and called one at random. He explained his situation to the clergyman who answered and asked if there was anyone in town who would be willing to meet with him. The call led him to Dr. Robert H. Smith ("Dr. Bob"), a surgeon who had recently admitted to an Oxford Group member that he was an alcoholic. The two men talked for hours, and Wilson's desire for a drink vanished as he listened to Smith tell his story of a life and career in ruins. Wilson stayed with the Smith family throughout the rest of his trip. One month later, on June 10, 1935, "Dr. Bob" took his last drink and immediately began teaming up with "Bill W." to share their "experience, strength and hope" with others in need.

Although several years passed before the organization really got off the ground, that day in June is regarded as the official beginning of Alcoholics Anonymous (AA). The fledgling self-help movement grew slowly but steadily thanks to the efforts of both men. According to a *Saturday Evening Post* article, Smith "was unsurpassed at working personally with alcoholics," treating thousands without charge as he worked to rebuild his surgical practice. Wilson's forte, on the other hand, was organizing and promoting; in 1938, he wrote a 164-page book entitled "Alcoholics Anonymous" that gave the group its name and documented its philosophy and methods. National publicity came in the form of articles appearing first in

Liberty magazine and then in the March 1, 1941, issue of the *Saturday Evening Post,* sparking orders for Wilson's book and boosting membership from two thousand to eight thousand in just a year.

Finances were always a problem for AA, especially in the early years when its founders were often broke from their efforts to keep the organization going and re-establish their own careers. In 1937, Wilson approached John D. Rockefeller, Jr., with a grandiose plan for promoting AA on a major scale. Rockefeller listened carefully but said, "I think money will spoil this," and refused to bankroll the plan. Instead, he urged Wilson to practice "corporate poverty," the idea being that the less money and property there was to argue over, the less likely it was that they would be distracted from their real mission. To this day AA subsists solely on small donations from members. Wilson never drew a salary from the organization; he supported himself on the royalties from the four books he wrote for AA and on the pay he received from working part-time on Wall Street.

Wilson remained active in AA even after his retirement from a leadership role in 1962, speaking regularly at banquets and conventions. Heralded as "the greatest social architect of the century," to quote writer Aldous Huxley, he was justifiably proud of the movement he had watched grow from meetings in his apartment to a worldwide organization consisting of thousands of chapters. His wife, Lois, also contributed to AA by co-founding Al-Anon and Alateen, support groups for spouses and children of problem drinkers.

Because AA members identify themselves only by their first name and last initial—a policy intended to emphasize the importance of putting "principles before personalities"—few knew of Wilson's accomplishments until after his death from emphysema and pneumonia in 1971. With his permission (granted in a signed statement dating back to 1966), obituaries revealed the identity of "Bill W." in their profiles of a man who shunned personal gain and prestige to save the lives of those who, like him, were slaves to alcohol.

With nearly two million members worldwide who meet in over eighty-five thousand local chapters, Alcoholics Anonymous is unquestionably the largest organization of its kind in existence today. It has also inspired numerous similar programs for compulsive drug users, gamblers, overeaters, and other troubled people determined to conquer their addictions—thanks in large part to the work of a man who once described himself as "just another guy named Bill who can't handle booze."

Sources

➤ **Books**

Kurtz, Ernest, *Not-God: A History of Alcoholics Anonymous*, Hazelden Foundation, 1979.

➤ **Periodicals**

New York Times, January 26, 1971.

Newsweek, February 8, 1971, p. 102.

Reader's Digest, "Unforgettable Bill W.," April, 1986, pp. 65–71.

Saturday Evening Post, "Alcoholics Anonymous: Freed Slaves of Drink, Now They Free Others," March 1, 1941; "Alcoholics Anonymous Celebrates Its 50th Year," July/August, 1985 (opening quote).

Time, "Anonymous Ally," February 8, 1971, p. 52.

U.S. Catholic, "The Drunk Who Helped Millions Get Sober," February, 1989, pp. 10–12.

➤ **Other**

"My Name Is Bill W." was a 1989 made-for-television movie.

Oprah Winfrey

"I *don't think of myself as a poor deprived ghetto girl who made good. I think of myself as somebody who from an early age knew I was responsible for myself, and I had to make good.''*

Born on January 29, 1954, in Kosciusko, Mississippi, Oprah Winfrey hosts television's highest-rated syndicated talk show. She is also an actress and businesswoman.

Address: Harpo Productions, 110 North Carpenter St., Chicago, IL 60607.

In January, 1984, Oprah Winfrey left her job as co-host of a popular Baltimore talk show and signed on with Chicago's faltering morning program, "A.M. Chicago." A long-time loser in its time slot, "A.M. Chicago" experienced a swift change under the direction of its new host, who scrapped the tired old format with its cooking and make-up tips and replaced it with a dynamic new approach that highlighted more topical and controversial subject matter. Then there was Winfrey herself; as Joan Barthel noted in *Ms.*, "Oprah did not so much host the show as immerse herself in it, with a style that blended earthiness, humor, spontaneity, and candor, with a unique personal touch."

Only one month after the debut of the new "A.M. Chicago," Winfrey pulled even in the ratings with fellow Chicagoan Phil Donahue and his nationally syndicated talk show, a perennial ratings powerhouse. After three months, she surpassed "Donahue." A year and a half later, "A.M. Chicago" was no more; expanded to an hour, it became "The Oprah Winfrey Show." In September, 1986, the program went into syndication in more than 130 cities across the country (making it the first talk show hosted by a Black-American woman to do so) and quickly dominated the airwaves. Since then, Winfrey has become one of the richest and most powerful women in the entertainment industry, a veritable one-person "media mini-empire"—a truly remarkable achievement for a former teenage runaway who was nearly sent to a juvenile detention center for her rebellious behavior.

Born on a farm in Mississippi, Oprah Gail Winfrey is the daughter of Vernita Lee and Vernon Winfrey. Her unmarried parents drifted apart and moved elsewhere not long after she was born, leaving her in the care of her maternal grandmother, whom Winfrey credits with fostering her outgoing personality and precociousness. She was reading by the age of two and a half and giving little speeches in church by the age of three, a favorite activity throughout her childhood. "I was a champion speaker," she once recalled. "I spoke for every women's group, banquet, church function—I did the circuit. Anybody needed anybody to speak anything, they'd call me."

At the age of six, Winfrey went to Milwaukee to live with her mother, who was working as a maid. Adjusting to an urban ghetto after enjoying the quiet peace of a Mississippi farm proved extremely difficult for the little girl. Making matters worse was the fact that her mother, preoccupied with her own problems, paid scant attention to her. This lack of supervision enabled several different men—among them a cousin and her mother's boyfriend—to abuse her sexually. (Years later, during a show she was doing on incest, Winfrey burst into tears and shared with her audience the story of her own ordeal.) Confused, ashamed, guilt-ridden, and afraid to tell anyone what was being done to her, Winfrey began to "act out, looking for love in all the wrong places," as she later explained. Her increasing belligerence and delinquency, which included running away from home, slowly drove her mother to distraction, and at last Vernita Lee gave her daughter a choice: she could either go live with her father and stepmother or be sent to a juvenile detention center. Winfrey opted to move in with her father, a barber and city councilman in Nashville, Tennessee.

As Marcia Ann Gillespie observed in *Ms.*, "living with her father . . . gave the vulnerable child protection and security, the wild child structure and discipline, and both a father who reaffirmed her grandmother's early teachings and belief in excellence and pride." Vernon Winfrey "turned my life around by insisting that I be more than I was and by believing I could be more," his daughter declared in a *Good Housekeeping* interview with Alan Ebert. "His love of learning showed me the way." In Nashville, Winfrey became an honor student and rediscovered her flair for public speaking, emerging as a standout performer in oratory and debate. (She was even hired to do radio newscasts for a local station during the last few months of her senior year in high school.) Her skills earned her a scholarship to Tennessee State University, where she majored in speech and drama and won "Miss Black Nashville" and "Miss Black Tennessee" pageants by virtue of what she says was her poise and talent rather than her looks. "I was raised to believe that the lighter your skin, the better you were," Winfrey told Barthel. "I wasn't light-skinned, so I decided to be the best and the smartest."

At nineteen, while she was still in college, Winfrey accepted a position as Nashville's first Black-American woman anchor on the evening news. She remained there until she graduated in 1976. She then took a job as a reporter and evening news co-anchor for a Baltimore television station, where her boss, critical of her looks, urged her to get a complete makeover. A too-strong permanent solution at one beauty salon she visited left her temporarily bald and shattered her self-esteem, resulting in a deep depression. Winfrey says she turned to food to help ease this depression. Although this eventually created the much-publicized weight problem that still plagues her today, the experience also convinced her of the need to "live my own life, to always be myself."

Winfrey stayed with the Baltimore station for eight years, relinquishing her evening anchor duties in 1977 to co-host the "Baltimore Is Talking" morning show. There she found her niche, displaying her uncommon ability to connect intellectually and emotionally with a wide variety of people and topics. She held that position until 1984, when her producer sent an audition tape to Chicago's WLS-TV. Impressed by Winfrey's talent and the ratings she generated, the station manager hired her away from Baltimore and brought her to Chicago, where she began a meteoric rise to the top of her profession.

Throughout its run, "The Oprah Winfrey Show" has touched on a wide variety of subjects, including divorce, child rearing, sexual abuse, homosexuality, racism, breast cancer, agoraphobia, and suicide, to name only a few. What sets the program apart from others of its kind is Winfrey herself. Explained Gillespie: "In Oprah, America got a talk-show host who laughed and cried right along with her guests, shared her troubles and tragedies, made people feel comfortable talking to millions of viewers about the most intimate stuff. Yet what she said was never predictably 'make nice' talk. . . . Nor is it empty-headed spout. What looks to some people like top-of-the-head questioning and commentary is, in fact, the result of carefully done homework." To Winfrey, the show has an almost religious purpose. "In a profound yet subtle way," she once observed, "it is a ministry, and it does what a ministry should do: uplift people, encourage them and give them a sense of hope about themselves."

While her television program remains the focus of her life, Winfrey is also involved in many other activities. In 1985, for example, she made her debut as a dramatic actress in the film adaptation of Alice Walker's *The Color Purple* and received an Academy Award nomination for her performance. She followed that up a year later with a starring role in *Native Son*, the movie version of Richard Wright's novel. In 1989, she acted in the television mini-series "The Women of Brewster Place" and reprised her role in 1990 during its brief run as a regular series. One of her dreams is to one day play Sethe, the leading character in Toni Morrison's novel *Beloved*.

Winfrey is also involved in the business end of film and television production through her own company, Harpo Productions. Established in 1986, its original purpose was to handle the fan mail and publicity for "The Oprah Winfrey Show." Its scope broadened in 1988, however, when Harpo took over the ownership and production of "The Oprah Winfrey Show." Since then, Winfrey has expanded her company's goals to include bringing high-quality projects to film and television. ("The Women of Brewster Place" was produced by Harpo, and the company is scheduled to do all of ABC-TV's "Afterschool Specials" for the 1992–1993 season.) With that in mind, she purchased a huge production facility in Chicago, becoming the first Black-American woman and only the third woman in history (after Mary Pickford and Lucille Ball) to own and run such a complex.

Despite her busy schedule—she typically puts in fourteen-hour days at the office—Winfrey is very generous with her time and money for many charitable causes. She makes time to meet regularly with a group of teenage girls from Chicago's notorious Cabrini-Green housing project, taking them to movies or to dinner or perhaps on a shopping spree. As the creator and sponsor of the club, she set the simple but strictly enforced rules: stay in school and don't get pregnant. Winfrey has also established scholarships at her alma mater, Tennessee State University, and at Atlanta's Morehouse College, and she keeps in touch with the recipients to monitor their grades and progress in school. In addition, she recently lobbied Congress on behalf of a bill she helped draft that proposes creating a national registry of people convicted of child abuse so that child-care providers can better evaluate potential employees.

When asked why she thinks she "made it" despite experiencing things that would have defeated many other women, Winfrey told Ebert, "I honestly don't know. Someone has to show you the light in order to survive, the light of love, and I truly don't know who showed me mine. Except, perhaps God. I always felt He was there." Because of her strong religious faith, she gives little thought to what the future might hold for her. As she remarked to Mary-Ann Bendel in a *Ladies' Home Journal* article, she believes that every decision she makes is guided by "a spirit—call it holy, call it good, call it God—that works for my highest good always." This confidence has brought her a deep spiritual comfort and the sense that she has nothing to fear, not even failure. "I just do what I do," says Winfrey, "and I know that it will keep me in the best place."

Sources

➤ **Periodicals**

Essence, "An Intimate Talk with Oprah," August, 1987; "Walking in the Light," June, 1991.

Good Housekeeping, "Oprah Winfrey Talks Openly about Oprah," September, 1991, pp. 62–66.

Ladies' Home Journal, "TV's Superwomen," March, 1988; "Oprah's Wonder Year," May, 1990; "Next on Oprah . . . ," August, 1991.

Ms., "Here Comes Oprah!," August, 1986 (opening quote); "Winfrey Takes All," November, 1988, pp. 50–54.

People, "Oprah's Crusade," December 2, 1991.

Reader's Digest, "Oprah Winfrey: How Truth Changed Her Life," February, 1989, pp. 101–105.

Saturday Evening Post, "TV's New Daytime Darling," July/August, 1987, pp. 42–45.

Stevie Wonder

"The only people who are really blind are those whose eyes are so obscured by hatred and bigotry that they can't see the light of love and justice."*

Blind virtually since birth, Stevie Wonder is a musician, singer, and composer whose work has earned praise for its creativity and themes of love, humanity, and justice. He was born on May 13, 1950, in Saginaw, Michigan.

Address: Stevland Morris Music, 4616 Magnolia Blvd., Burbank, CA 91505.

One day in 1960, Stevland "Stevie" Morris, a blind ten year old whose musical talents were the talk of his Detroit neighborhood, auditioned for Berry Gordy of the local Hitsville USA recording company. Impressed by what he heard, Gordy signed the youngster on the spot. For the next few years, Stevie spent every free moment he had hanging around the Hitsville studios, learning to play a wide variety of instruments, sitting in on recording sessions, and even writing songs. Before long people were calling him "the little boy wonder," and in 1963, he was billed as "Little Stevie Wonder" on a Hitsville recording of an energetic dance tune entitled "Fingertips Part 2." It was a smash hit, claiming the number one spot for fifteen weeks and selling over a million copies. "Fingertips" not only helped Hitsville (later Motown Records) establish itself as a force in the music business, it also took a child prodigy and launched him on a career path to pop superstardom.

Stevie Wonder—who was born Stevland Judkins but later took the name Stevland Morris—was the third of his mother Lula Mae's six children. His premature arrival and fragile health required him to remain in an incubator for nearly two months after his birth. Doctors later concluded that the high concentration of oxygen he received was probably responsible for destroying sensitive nerve tissue behind his eyes, resulting in total blindness. Thanks to his two older brothers, however, Stevie enjoyed a fairly typical childhood. He ran, climbed trees, and even rode a bicycle (as long as someone else steered), learning to rely on sound to judge distance and identify the things he could not see.

Around 1957, Lula Mae divorced Stevie's father, Calvin Judkins, and moved to Detroit. Afraid for her son's safety in a strange new neighborhood, Lula Mae kept him inside for a while. There the youngster passed the time singing or beating spoons on pots, pans, and tabletops in rhythm with songs on the radio. As his love of music grew, so did his desire for some real instruments of his own. His mother, who was struggling to support the family, could not afford to buy the things Stevie wanted. But others soon came through. His barber, for example, bought him a harmonica. At a Lions Club Christmas party one year, he received his first set of real drums. (He had already worn out several toy sets.) And when he was seven, a neighbor who was moving gave him her piano.

By the time he was nine years old, Stevie had already made a name for himself as a musician and a singer who performed lead parts in his church choir and belted out rhythm-and-blues or rock-and-roll songs on his neighbors' porches. It was on one of those porches that a Motown singer first heard Stevie and brought him to Berry Gordy's attention.

After the success of "Fingertips," Stevie Wonder became a bona fide star. He began touring extensively with other Motown acts (a tutor accompanied him so that he could keep up with his studies at the Michigan School for the Blind). Stevie demonstrated with his joyfully exuberant performances that he was a born entertainer. Already a master of the keyboards, drums, and harmonica, he continued to work with other instruments, compose more songs (often in collaboration with fellow Motown writers and lyricists), and record a few singles, including the hits "Uptight" (1965) and "I Was Made to Love Her" (1967).

By the late 1960s, however, Wonder had begun to resent the strict control Motown exercised over his life and career. The company controlled his earnings and dictated what type of music he could sing and the image he was to project. Wonder was tired of the "Little Stevie" label and the glossy soul sound of all the Motown artists; he longed to express his feelings about the racial unrest sweeping the country. Although he experimented briefly with folk ballads such as "Blowin' in the Wind" and "Mr. Tambourine Man," from 1968–70 he released a string of hits that were still in the old Motown vein: "For Once in My Life," "My Cherie Amour," "Yester Me, Yester You, Yesterday," and "Signed, Sealed, Delivered, I'm Yours."

On May 13, 1971, Wonder turned twenty-one and immediately took charge of his finances and his career, breaking with Motown and eventually establishing his own studio, production company, and publishing house. It was a rather bitter split, but one that he felt he had to make in order to record and produce *his* kind of music. "I wasn't growing," he later explained. "I just kept repeating the Stevie Wonder sound, and it didn't express how I felt about what was happening out there. . . . I wanted to see what would happen if I changed."

Free of the pressures he had faced at Motown, Wonder entered a period of tremendous personal and professional growth. Already thoroughly skilled in the recording and producing process by virtue of his years at Motown, he set out to familiarize himself with the legal and financial aspects of the music business. He also enjoyed a renewed burst of creativity, fueled in part by his experiments with synthesizers, which allowed him to perform all parts of a song himself and control the effects. The first album to display these new ideas was *Music of My Mind*. By this time he had patched up his differences with Berry Gordy, and Motown agreed to promote and distribute the album for him. But even Motown's considerable clout couldn't top the exposure Wonder received during the summer of 1972, when he accompanied the Rolling Stones on tour and gained nationwide exposure for the new Stevie Wonder sound, which was a huge success.

Following the tour, Wonder quickly produced two more albums: *Talking Book*, which contained "Superstition," his first number-one hit since "Fingertips," and the Grammy Award-winning *Innervisions*, which included such memorable songs as "Living for the City," "Don't You Worry 'Bout a Thing," and "Higher Ground." Then, in August, 1973, Wonder was involved in a near-fatal automobile accident that prompted him to reassess his life and the direction his career was taking. "It became very clear to me that it wasn't enough *just* to be a rock and roll singer or anything of that nature," he later recalled. "I had to make *use* of whatever talent I have. . . . When an audience comes to hear me perform, they know I'm not going to put them to sleep with my moral indignation. . . . I entertain them— because I *am* an entertainer . . . but at the same time I can . . . *enlighten* them a little."

Since then, Wonder has committed himself to fostering greater understanding, love, and respect between people of different races and different social and economic classes. He was very active in efforts to have Martin Luther King, Jr.'s birthday established as a national holiday, and he has also lent his support to world hunger relief, AIDS research, the anti-apartheid movement, and drunk-driving education. On behalf of these causes, he has written (or helped write) and performed a number of songs, including "We Are the World," "That's What Friends Are For," "It's Wrong (Apartheid)," and "Don't Drive Drunk."

Wonder records albums less frequently than he did before his accident, partly because his causes often take him away from the studio, but also because he prefers to mull over a song for a very long time before he feels ready to record it. His legendary perfectionism has resulted in some carefully crafted albums that feature stirring social commentary as well as easy-going love songs. Among his most notable releases since the mid-1970s are *Fulfillingness' First Finale* (which contains "You Haven't Done Nothin'," an angry indictment of white liberals for not doing enough to fight racial injustice); *Songs in the Key of Life,* a three-record set that held the number one position for fifteen weeks; *In Square Circle;* and *Characters.* He has also done several movie soundtracks, including *Woman in Red* with its Academy Award-winning single, "I Just Called to Say I Love You," and Spike Lee's *Jungle Fever.* His efforts have netted him more than fifteen Grammy Awards, and he has been inducted into the Songwriters' Hall of Fame and the Rock and Roll Hall of Fame.

By and large, Wonder has refused to consider his blindness as a handicap. He strives to be as independent as possible, making use of high-tech electronics such as a reading machine that scans printed material and translates it into spoken words, a computer that enables him to produce braille printouts of information he has keyed in, and even a tennis ball that beeps so that he knows where to swing his racket. He is still hopeful that someday a technological or medical breakthrough will allow him to see. In the meantime, he continues to pursue his highly spiritual and utopian vision of international racial and cultural harmony. "Neither this country nor the world will be right until people begin to accept people as being people and not let their insecurities determine the future of this society, this country, this world," he told a reporter for *Jet* magazine. "Sometimes, I feel I am really blessed to be blind because I probably would not last a minute if I were able to see things. God knew what he was doing."

Sources
➤ **Books**

Haskins, James, *The Story of Stevie Wonder,* Lothrop, Lee & Shepard, 1976 (opening quote).

➤ **Periodicals**

Detroit Free Press, "Fever Pitch," June 9, 1991.

Ebony, "The Secret Life of Stevie Wonder," April, 1980; "The Secret Dreams of Stevie Wonder," December, 1986.

Essence, "Stevie Wonder: Still Reaching for Higher Ground," December, 1984.

Jet, "Stevie Wonder Says His Message Music May Shock but His Songs Talk about Social Wrongs," May 30, 1988, pp. 58–60.

New York Times, "Stevie Wonder's Message," October 7, 1985, p. C15.

New York Times Magazine, February 23, 1975.

People, "Airplay and Airports: For Stevie, It's a Wonderful Life," March 3, 1986, pp. 88–90.

Rolling Stone, "The Timeless World of Wonder," April 10, 1986; "Stevie Wonder," November 5-December 10, 1987; "Rock and Roll Hall of Fame," February 9, 1989.

Time, April 8, 1974.

Babe Didrikson Zaharias

*"***B***efore I was even out of grade school, I knew what I wanted to be when I grew up. My goal was to be the greatest athlete that ever lived."*

A champion in track and field, basketball, and golf, Babe Didrikson Zaharias broke more records than any other female athlete in history. She was born on June 26, 1911, in Port Arthur, Texas, and died on September 27, 1956, in Galveston, Texas.

Born Mildred Ella Didriksen in a gritty Texas oil town, Babe Didrikson Zaharias was the daughter of Hannah Marie Olson and Ole Didriksen, a carpenter and furniture refinisher who immigrated to the United States from Norway in 1905 and was joined three years later by his wife and three oldest children. Four other Didriksen offspring, including Babe, followed in quick succession. (Babe later changed the spelling of her surname from Didriksen to Didrikson.) Providing for such a large family was difficult, and all the Didriksen kids were expected to find jobs as soon as they were old enough. As a seventh grader, Babe spent her after-school hours working in a fig-packing plant. Later, she landed a better-paying job sewing potato sacks.

Despite their hardscrabble life, the Didriksens always made time for athletics. Hannah had been known as a fine skier and ice skater in her native Norway, and Ole placed a great value on exercise and physical fitness. While nearly all of their children showed a natural athleticism, it was Babe who very early on was "the best at everything." So powerful was her baseball swing that playmates in her hometown of Beaumont, Texas, shortened her childhood nickname "Baby" to "Babe" in honor of the great Babe Ruth.

She first went out for organized sports in high school, taking up basketball, baseball, golf, swimming, tennis, and volleyball. (She was barred from trying out for the football team.) Her highly competitive nature and determination to excel alienated many of the other students, and as a result Babe had few friends. But her talent on the basketball court quickly gained her statewide recognition, and in 1930, during her last semester in high school, she accepted an offer to join a team sponsored by the Dallas-based Employers Casualty Company. At that time, many large businesses throughout the South and Midwest financed sports teams made up of outstanding women athletes who spent part of their time doing office work—usually at a fairly good salary—and the rest of their time involved in a variety of professional sports. Babe played her first game with the Employers Casualty team the very night she arrived in Dallas and thrilled spectators by singlehandedly outscoring the entire opposing team.

In the off-season, Babe was a member of Employers Casualty teams in swimming, diving, and track. The latter sport in particular fascinated her; although she had never even *been* to a track meet before moving to Dallas, she practiced to the point of exhaustion in an effort to master the necessary skills, establishing a pattern she would follow for the rest of her life. Within just a few months she had set new national records in the javelin and baseball throws and regional records in the shot put, high jump, and long jump. At the Amateur Athletic Union (AAU) women's track and field championship in 1932, Babe competed as a one-woman team and took six of the eight events she entered, accumulating *by herself* nearly twice as many points as all twenty-two members of the second-place team and thus securing a spot in the upcoming Olympics. Awed by the lopsided victory of this swaggering, tough-kid athlete who seemed determined to show up everyone, the media showered Babe with attention and dubbed her "the wonder girl."

It was at the Olympics, however, that Babe Didrikson truly became a national sensation. Competing in three events, she set world records in the javelin throw and the 80-meter hurdles and was bumped from first to second place in the high jump only after judges objected to the fact that her head crossed the bar before her feet. (This style of jump was later legalized.) In recognition of her performance in the AAU championships and at the Olympics, the Associated Press (AP) named her 1932's Woman Athlete of the Year.

While she was still in Los Angeles after the Olympics, Babe picked up a golf club for the first time. Although her overall game was rough and uneven, she amazed the men she was with by outdriving them on virtually every hole. Convinced that she had found yet another sport at which she could excel, Babe decided then and there to become a golfer. Before she could afford to take the time to master the game, however, she had to put aside enough money to support herself and her elderly parents. To that end, she spent several years during the early to mid-1930s on the promotional circuit, making personal appearances, playing in exhibition games (she once suited up with the New York Rangers hockey team and also pitched for a few major league baseball teams during spring training), and even doing a vaudeville act. At one point, she briefly went back to work for Employers Casualty, then left to play on a traveling basketball team known as Babe Didrikson's All-Americans. Later, she joined the House of David baseball team, a traveling group of long-haired, bearded men who belonged to a cult-like Christian brotherhood. Since most of these activities were purely for show and had little to do with real competition, Babe was criticized by people who thought they reflected poorly on her achievements as an amateur athlete.

In 1934, Babe quit most of her touring and returned to Texas, where she once again took a job with Employers Casualty. The company paid for her golf lessons at a local country club, and by November of that year, she felt ready to enter her first tournament. Eliminated in first-round play, she buckled down and started working on her game six days a week and, six months later, won the Texas Women's Amateur Championship. Her success caused quite a stir in the world of ladies' golf, a genteel sport of wealthy women who resented the aggressive, rough-edged outsider. Because of Babe's past involvement in professional sports, they also complained about her amateur status and eventually persuaded the United States Golf Association (USGA) to disqualify her. Since there was only one professional ladies' golf tournament in existence at the time, Babe returned to promotional work—this time strictly as a golfer—and ended up sharpening her own game by playing in exhibition matches with some of the best male golfers in the world. At one such match in early 1938, she was teamed up with wrestler George Zaharias, nicknamed the "Crying Greek from Cripple Creek." The two immediately hit it off and were married on December 23 of that year. Zaharias subsequently quit wrestling (which had already made him a wealthy man) and from then on skillfully managed his wife's career.

Determined to compete again in the amateur ranks, Babe reapplied to the USGA in 1940 and was finally reinstated after a three-year waiting period during which she could not accept money for playing golf or for commercial endorsements. To pass the time, she continued to take golf lessons and also took up tennis, which she dropped when she was ruled ineligible to play in amateur matches. She then turned to bowling and quickly excelled at that, too.

In 1943, Babe re-entered golf as an amateur, thus launching what was to become the most spectacular winning streak in the history of the sport. By late 1947, she had won seventeen straight tournaments, including the Western Women's Open in 1944 and 1945 (an event she had also won in 1940 as a professional, making her the first three-time winner), the National Women's Amateur, and the British Women's Amateur, considered the premier women's match in the world. (A victory there had always eluded American players until Babe came along.) Acknowledging her total domination of the sport, AP named her Woman Athlete of the Year in 1945, 1946, and again in 1947. Her fame led to dozens of new promotional offers, so in late 1947 Babe decided to give up her amateur status.

Two years later, determined to make tournament play more

lucrative for professional women golfers, she co-founded the Ladies Professional Golf Association (LPGA). By lining up corporate sponsors, the LPGA was able to set up more tournaments and provide larger cash prizes. Babe herself became the star of the tour during its first few years of existence, winning more tournaments and taking home more prize money than anyone else. Her involvement lent credibility to the fledgling organization, to professional women's golf, and to women's athletics in general. In 1950, AP named her the Outstanding Woman Athlete of the Half Century.

Late in 1952, Babe began to feel exhausted all of the time and even lost several tournaments. She finally went to the doctor the following spring, was diagnosed with rectal cancer, and successfully underwent surgery. Returning to tournament play just a few months later, she did poorly at first but kept at it and started to win again in early 1954, taking top honors at five competitions. Her unexpected comeback earned her AP's Outstanding Woman Athlete of the Year award for the sixth time. Fulfilling a promise she had made to herself in the hospital, Babe also began doing promotional work for the American Cancer Society, making radio and television spots, appearing at local events in towns where she was playing golf, and establishing a fund for research.

Babe continued golfing into early 1955 but grew steadily weaker and eventually ruptured a disk in her back. She played in terrible pain through several tournaments before submitting to another operation, at which time doctors discovered that the cancer had invaded her spine. She retired from the tour in mid-year and died a little more than a year later, on September 27, 1956.

In a *Sports Illustrated* article published shortly after her death, longtime friend and admirer Paul Gallico paid tribute to the woman he called "a champion of champions" as much for her athletic prowess as for the bravery she displayed during her fight against cancer. "It may be another 50 or 75 years before such a performer as Mildred Didrikson Zaharias again enters the lists," he declared. "For even if some yet unborn games queen matches her talent, versatility, skill, patience and will to practice, along with her flaming competitive spirit, . . . there still remains the little matter of courage and character, and in these departments the Babe must be listed with the champions of all times."

Sources

➤ Books

Lynn, Elizabeth A., *Babe Didrikson Zaharias*, Chelsea House, 1989.

Zaharias, Mildred Didrikson, *This Life I've Led*, Barnes, 1955.

➤ Periodicals

New York Times, September 28, 1956; September 29, 1956, p. 19; September 30, 1956, p. 86.

Reader's Digest, "The Girl Who Lived Again," October, 1954, pp. 50–55.

Saturday Evening Post, "Babe Didrikson Takes Off Her Mask," September 20, 1947; "This Life I've Led" (excerpts from her autobiography of the same title), June 25 (opening quote), July 2, July 9, July 16, July 23, 1955.

Sports Illustrated, "Farewell to the Babe," October 8, 1956, pp. 66–68.

Time, October 8, 1956, p. 92.

Photo Credits

Permission to reproduce photographs appearing in *Contemporary Heroes and Heroines, Book II*, was received from the following sources:

V. J. Lovero, Courtesy of the California Angels: p. 1; AP/Wide World Photos: pp. 6, 18, 64, 76, 100, 105, 111, 121, 133, 138, 147, 153, 159, 171, 177, 205, 211, 223, 231, 243, 261, 267, 273, 279, 285, 303, 309, 320, 330, 336, 348, 360, 366, 371, 383, 406, 412, 452, 459, 465, 482, 515, 526, 538; Jane Addams Memorial Collection, Special Collections, The University Library, University of Illinois at Chicago: p. 12; Courtesy of Marian Anderson: p. 24; The Institute of Jazz Studies: pp. 30, 189; Jeanne Moutoussamy-Ashe: p. 36; Matthew Rolston, Courtesy of Joan Baez: p. 42; Woods Hole Oceanographic Institution: p. 47; Don McKenzie, Courtesy of Christiaan Barnard: p. 53; Courtesy of the American Red Cross: p. 59; U.S. Office of War Information, Prints and Photographs Division, Library of Congress: p. 70; Dick Swanson, Courtesy of Handgun Control, Inc.: p. 82; Courtesy of the Pearl S. Buck Foundation, Inc.: p. 94; The Pennsylvania Academy of the Fine Arts, Philadelphia: p. 127; Prints and Photographs Division, Library of Congress: pp. 165, 291, 400, 446; Courtesy of the Archives, Institute for Advanced Study: pp. 183, 394; Steve Turville, Orange, California, Courtesy of Jose Feliciano: p. 200; Judy Lawne, Courtesy of the Pediatric AIDS Foundation: p. 217; Manni Mason's Pictures: p. 249; Courtesy of Jim Henson Productions: p. 255; Bill Smith, Courtesy of the Chicago Bulls: p. 297; Julie Jensen: p. 314; Courtesy of the American Foundation for the Blind, New York: p. 342; Courtesy of Cherokee Nation Communications: p. 355; Courtesy of Menninger/Bern Ketchum: p. 377; National Portrait Gallery/Art Resource, New York: pp. 389, 509; Courtesy of the Department of Defense: p. 418; U.S. Department of Agriculture, Farm Security Administration, Prints and Photographs Division, Library of Congress: p. 425; Courtesy of the Franklin D. Roosevelt Library: p. 431; UPI/Bettmann Newsphotos: pp. 440, 503; Reuters/Bettmann: p. 471; Russ Busby: p. 477; U.S. Army, Courtesy of the Harry S. Truman Library: p. 488; Courtesy of the Archbishop of Canterbury's Office for Broadcasting, Press and Communications: p. 497; Courtesy of the Simon Wiesenthal Center: p. 520; Courtesy of Harpo, Inc.: p. 532; Courtesy of the Ladies Professional Golf Association: p. 544.

Index

Personal names, place names, events, institutions, awards, and other subject areas or key words contained in *Contemporary Heroes and Heroines, Book II,* entries are listed in this index with corresponding page numbers indicating text references. Inclusive page numbers are given in bold type for each of the volume's main entries. Also cited are the names of people with main entries in the original *Contemporary Heroes and Heroines,* as indicated by the abbreviation "CHH" in bold type after a name.